MULTILINGUAL MATTERS 52
Series Editor: Derrick Sharp

English in Wales: Diversity, Conflict and Change

Edited by

Nikolas Coupland

in association with

Alan R. Thomas

MULTILINGUAL MATTERS LTD
Clevedon · Philadelphia

For Ray M.

Library of Congress Cataloging in Publication Data

English in Wales: diversity, conflict, and change/edited by Nikolas Coupland in association with Alan R. Thomas
p. cm.—(Multilingual matters: 52)
Bibliography: p.
Includes index.
1. English language—Dialects–Wales. 2. English language—foreign elements—Welsh. 3. Welsh language—Influence on English. 4. Wales—Languages.
5. Languages in contact—Wales. I. Coupland, Nikolas, 1950-.
II. Thomas, Alan R. III. Series: Multilingual matters (Series): 52.
PE1771.E5 1989
427'9429—dc19   88–25856

British Library Cataloguing in Publication Data

English in Wales: Diversity, Conflict and Change (Multilingual matters; 52).
1. Wales. English language
I. Coupland, Nikolas II. Thomas, Alan R.
(Alan Richard), 1935–
420'.9429

ISBN 1-85359-032-0
ISBN 0-85359-031-2 Pbk

Multilingual Matters Ltd
Bank House, 8a Hill Road,   &   1900 Frost Road, Suite 101
Clevedon, Avon BS21 7HH   Bristol, PA 19007
England   U.S.A.

Index compiled by Meg Davies (Society of Indexers)
Typeset by Photo·graphics, Honiton, Devon
Printed and bound in Great Britain by WBC Print, Bristol

English in Wales:
Diversity, Conflict and Change

Multilingual Matters

Afrikaner Dissidents
JOHA LOUW-POTGIETER
Aspects of Bilingualism in Wales
COLIN BAKER
Australian Multiculturalism
LOIS FOSTER and DAVID STOCKLEY
Bilingualism and the Individual
A. HOLMEN, E. HANSEN, J. GIMBEL and J. JØRGENSEN (eds.)
Bilingualism in Society and School
J. JØRGENSEN, E. HANSEN, A. HOLMEN and J. GIMBEL (eds.)
Code-Mixing and Code Choice
JOHN GIBBONS
Communication and Cross-cultural Adaptation
YOUNG YUN KIM
Communication and Simulation
D. CROOKALL and D. SAUNDERS (eds.)
Conversation: An Interdisciplinary Perspective
D. ROGER and P. BULL (eds.)
Cultural Studies in Foreign Language Education
MICHAEL BYRAM
Evaluating Bilingual Education
MERRILL SWAIN and SHARON LAPKIN
The Interdisciplinary Study of Urban Bilingualism in Brussels
E. WITTE and H. BAETENS BEARDSMORE (eds.)
Key Issues in Bilingualism and Bilingual Education
COLIN BAKER
Language Acquisition of a Bilingual Child
ALVINO FANTINI
Language Attitudes Among Arabic–French Bilinguals in Morocco
ABDELALI BENTAHILA
Language and Ethnic Identity
WILLIAM GUDYKUNST (ed.)
Language and Ethnicity in Minority Sociolinguistic Perspective
JOSHUA FISHMAN
Language in Geographic Context
COLIN WILLIAMS (ed.)
Methods in Dialectology
ALAN R. THOMAS (ed.)
Minority Education: From Shame to Struggle
T. SKUTNABB-KANGAS and J. CUMMINS (eds.)
Minority Education and Ethnic Survival
MICHAEL BYRAM
Minority Language Conference: Celtic Papers
G. MacEOIN, A. AHLQVIST, D. O'hAODHA (eds.)
Minority Language Conference: General Papers
G. MacEOIN, A. AHLQVIST, D. O'hAODHA (eds.)
Neurotic and Psychotic Language Behaviour
R. WODAK and P. Van De CRAEN (eds.)
Perspectives on Marital Interaction
P. NOLLER and M. A. FITZPATRICK (eds.)
Talk and Social Organisation
G. BUTTON and J. R. E. LEE (eds.)
The Use of Welsh: A Contribution to Sociolinguistics
MARTIN J. BALL (ed.)

Please contact us for the latest book information:
Multilingual Matters, Bank House, 8a Hill Road,
Clevedon, Avon BS21 7HH, England.

Contents

Preface and Acknowledgements

August this year sees the Welsh National Eisteddfod, that symbolic corner-stone of Welsh ethnolinguistic identity, taking place in Gwent, just outside Newport and, by some accounts, dangerously close to the English border in south-east Wales. The press, radio and television are overflowing with reports and interviews, and not a single reporter or presenter seems as yet to have failed to raise some opening query about the place of a quintessentially Welsh cultural festival in the most English of Welsh counties. How can it be justified? Will south-east Welshness sully the ethnic purity of the event? Do the Newport locals feel threatened, or perhaps merely disaffected? Will people from north and west Wales come at all? If they do, what *lingua franca*, perhaps a 'Wenglish' pidgin, will be coined for communication, *if* there is any? . . .

The 1988 Eisteddfod (which, we should note, has not succumbed to any of these dire forecasts) provides a most appropriate backdrop to the later stages of this book's production. The event seems to have crystallised, in the popular consciousness and in the media, the social and linguistic issues in contemporary Wales which lie at the heart of the present volume. What is the relationship between Welsh and English, descriptively, historically, politically, ideologically? What might we project as to the future role of English in Wales? Are Welsh and English locked into an enduring conflict as bearers of mutually exclusive identities and affiliations, or is the language/ ethnicity relationship less direct than this, more tolerant of overlap and negotiation? Might there in fact be a Welsh English consciousness that can be reflected through varieties and uses of the majority language, English, in Wales? If so, how 'valid' might it be deemed to be?

In compiling the present collection, it has been most satisfying to discover, progressively, just how many shared interests and common questions of this sort centring on the distribution and diverse forms of English in Wales are currently emanating from quite distinct research traditions. The book has ultimately come to represent much of the best recent work in Wales in the fields of dialectology and phonetics, sociolinguistics and bilingualism, cultural and historical geography, and social psychology. It would be wrong to over-estimate the level of direct interchange there has been to date among these traditions, though the chapters of this book provide an ample basis for more concerted coverage in the future.

All chapters here, apart from Jack Windsor Lewis' transcribed 'Specimen of Cardiff English' — a historic document indeed, reprinted from *Le Maître Phonétique* of 1964 — are original contributions, a mixture of reports of new studies and syntheses of long-established research traditions. Amongst general thanks owed to contributors for their commitment to the volume and their patience during its production, special acknowledgement is owed to Beverley Collins and Inger Mees. These scholars generously undertook detailed reading of all descriptive dialectological sections of the book, offering expert and gratefully received editorial comments to their co-authors (and this despite the vagaries of international mail).

It is particularly pleasing to have been able to publish substantial descriptive reports from the influential (though in both cases well-guarded) work of Jack Windsor Lewis and David Parry. It is also very rarely that the opportunity is found to present, in a single volume, original work by scholars of such international standing as Howard Giles, W.T.R. Pryce, J.C. Wells and Colin Williams. It is a matter of regret that other commitments precluded Alan R. Thomas, whose role in the early stages of the book's development was crucial, from featuring far more prominently in the volume. The volume already owes a great deal to the range and insight of his seminal work on the sociolinguistics of Welsh and Welsh English.

Thanks are also due to several colleagues who do not appear as authors here: Justine Coupland, Penny Rowlands, Gwen Awbery, and particularly Glyn Williams, who have in various ways supported the preparation and conceptual development of the volume. Mike and Marjukka Grover and Ken Hall have overseen the production of the book with skill, judgement and patience. The intellectual and administrative horrors of an interdisciplinary edited book would not have been tolerable without the support of all these friends and colleagues.

Nikolas Coupland

Centre for Applied English Language Studies,
University of Wales College of Cardiff
August 1988

1 Introduction: Social and Linguistic Perspectives on English in Wales

NIKOLAS COUPLAND and ALAN R. THOMAS

English and Welsh in the Sociolinguistics of Wales

In Wales, the Welsh language and its role in a bilingual community have tended to occupy the foreground of linguistic and sociolinguistic research. This is an understandable and defensible emphasis, given the urgency of political and policy considerations attending Welsh as a threatened minority language (see, for example, Bellin, 1984; G. Williams, 1986), the complexities of assessing its geolinguistic distribution and historical decline (Stephens, 1973; Thomas, 1982; also, C. Williams; Pryce[1]), and the need for a better understanding of the social functioning of varieties of Welsh at a critical period in its history (Ball, 1988). None of the contributors to this volume would wish to challenge this pattern of priorities.

Quite conversely, this book has in part grown out of the realisation that our understanding of 'the language situation in Wales' requires attention to the dominant majority language as well as to the threatened minority language; that the nature, use and, of course, the very survival of Welsh in Wales are contingent upon the nature, use, institutional support and social significance of English, historically and in contemporary life. Given the past and present cross-referencing and interaction between Welsh and English in Wales, it in fact makes little sense to restrict our investigations absolutely (even *if* it were to be possible empirically) to either language in isolation. The book is therefore an attempt to explore the broad sociolinguistic character of Wales, through an *initial* focus on English language concerns. In all corners of this exploration — historical distributional accounts, dialect

1

descriptions, sociological and socio-psychological analyses — interpretations are continuously couched in relational terms: what do we learn about the conflictual, integrative or other stances of the two principal languages in use, and what can linguistic studies as a whole tell us about Wales?

English in Wales has not been examined in any integrated way, and the most general aim of the volume is to begin the synthesising of existing work, as a platform for future developments. As the following chapters attest, there is indeed sustained original research to report, overviewed and exemplified here in the historical and distributional accounts of English and Welsh in Wales (in Part One), in traditional and systemic descriptions of dialect varieties (Part Two), and in variationist sociolinguistic and social-psychological studies of Welsh English varieties (Part Three). But it is still the case that there has been virtually no formal interchange among these traditions. So it is intriguing to note how, in the following chapters, descriptive accounts regularly reflect on processes of diachronic change; how geolinguistic surveys appeal to socio-psychological constructs of 'motive', 'attitude' and 'identity'; how socio-psychological studies build on sociolinguistic categories; how variation studies presuppose detailed dialect descriptions, and so on. The essentially interdisciplinary nature of the book's theme is altogether apparent, and it must be the case that more unified approaches in years to come will reap rich benefits.

On the other hand, the language question in Wales is sufficiently highly charged that some might infer that even to pay analytic attention to English in Wales, or 'Welsh English' in the terminology of several contributors here, represents an ideological position, perhaps even a form of capitulation, or collusion with the forces threatening the Welsh language. Certainly, academic work is not often value-free either in intent or in effect, and the case for the defence needs arguing. G. Williams (in a personal communication) suggests that 'establishing "Welsh English" or even discussing its possible existence is a political act', one that invokes distinctions such as that between 'the state' (and its language — necessarily English) and 'the region' (and its 'subordinate' variety of the state language — Welsh English). These are not, in our view, challenging but inevitable inferences from the treatments of English in Wales offered in the contributions to the volume. Welsh English is variously defined in the following chapters, though always as a preliminary designation to be clarified through particular analyses. One goal of sociolinguistic inquiry in Wales and beyond must be to build considerations of political ideology as variables into its own analyses, to consider the radically diverse ways in which the presence of English in Wales is and has been construed and responded to.

Majority and Minority Languages in Conflict

It is clear that Wales has seen highly variable reactions to the presence of English. In surveying the political, commercial and educational forces which have introduced English into Wales over the centuries, C. Williams (Chapter 2) points to some extremes in this respect. Williams shows how anglicisation has been conceptualised variously as 'a barrier to the realization of the nation's full potential', and at the other pole as ' "liberation" from traditionalism and conservatism', with English being 'the language of progress, of equality, of prosperity, of mass entertainment and pleasure'. Both Williams and Pryce (Chapter 3) refer to the debate (triggered by Brinley Thomas) over whether industrialisation, often taken to embody the most radical threat to Welsh language and cultural integrity, was ultimately more of a friend or a foe to the Welsh language. While it is true that any consideration of English in Wales evokes themes of conflict, struggles over national identity and ethnic continuity, it is also demonstrably the case that minority ethnic groups can, among their own members, adopt quite polarised and often internally very complex ideological positions towards majority languages.

On the other hand, taking a broad perspective in a recent monograph, J.R. Edwards (1985) has articulated what he sees as a consistent pattern of minority groups' accommodation of majority languages. He contends (1985: 114) that social evolution, dictated by economic pressures, is inevitable and for the good (1985: 114), and that majority group culture is indeed *generally* desirable to and in fact *desired by* minorities, who thereby themselves typically sponsor language loss (1985: 113). Moreover, Edwards (1985: 97) argues that language itself is not a necessary component of ethnic identity, at least in its use for communicative exchange, though it may be retained 'as a symbol . . . in the absence of the communicative function' (1985: 111) alongside other symbolic markers such as national dress, ornamentation, dance and song (1985: 112). This general scenario of linguistic capitulation by minority groups is strikingly at odds with the general assumptions of much writing in the sociology of language and social psychology (e.g. Giles, 1977). Fishman (1977: 25), as a case in point, is widely quoted for asserting that language is a highly potent ethnic marker as 'the recorder of paternity, the expresser of patrimony and the carrier of phenomenology'. It is therefore interesting to set Edward's arguably overgeneralised view (see also Coupland, 1986) against the general tenor of the accounts of anglicisation given in this volume by Williams and Pryce.

Williams notes that, however warmly the populace may have welcomed the 'liberation' of anglicisation in the wake of the 1870 Education Act, it is nevertheless true that the 'modernisation' process 'saw the denigration of Welsh accompanied by a debased self-awareness on behalf of its speakers'. Pryce meticulously charts the surprisingly late anglicisation of Gwent, today the most anglicised of all Welsh counties. In doing so, he cites the views of Anglican clergy, magistrates, landowners and other dignitaries from the Education Report of 1847, to the effect that the advancing English language 'would make the people more deferential to their "superiors", bringing greater "respect for the law", [and] would make the lower orders "more peaceful and submissive"'. To suggest, then, that anglicisation in Wales has been *less than* a straightforward and open-armed welcoming of industrially-driven economic progress is seemingly not at all the romantic idealism of academic linguists that Edwards has contended. It is certain that the appeals of English have been historically underwritten by a good deal of unromantic hegemony and coercion.

The Shaping of Welsh English

But if English and the English state do deserve to be labelled the aggressors to Welsh language and ethnicity, we should not underestimate the power of communities to redefine the cultural essence of language varieties. J.R. Edwards's (1985) account arguably also plays down the potential of the dominant language, English, in Welsh throats, to continue to carry highly significant and multiple kinds of cultural content. In the present book's descriptive second section, English can often be seen to have become the property of Welsh people, and to reflect its ownership sometimes in very profound respects. These descriptions of English in various communities in Wales clearly show how the nature of English varieties in Wales renders them more or less naturally disposed to carrying symbolic, traditional 'Welshness' in the degree to which they preserve Welsh-language-derived or -influenced features — 'substratal' features as one of us has previously referred to them (Thomas, 1983; 1984; 1985). The concept is reminiscent of Windsor Lewis's designation in Chapter 6 of the present book of some varieties of Glamorgan English as 'Cymric'. And the Welsh language substratum has contemporary as well as historical significance. Through their English usage, Welsh people to greater and lesser degrees have the means of symbolically aligning themselves with (and, of course, of distancing themselves from) Welshness, Welsh institutions, traditions, values and concerns — processes which Giles (1987) models within his theory of interpersonal 'accommodation' (see also Chapter 16 in this volume). It is this general semiotic dimension of Welsh English usage that is traced in the analysis by Coupland of Welsh political figures' dialects in Chapter 15. Many of the socio-psychological studies reviewed in Giles's chapter here are also directly contingent. The whole domain of ethnic affiliation and disaffiliation in Wales is clearly negotiated in and through the use of English just as it is through Welsh (cf. also Chapman *et al.*, 1977).

The nature of Welsh English varieties is clearly related, at some general level, to the process of anglicisation itself — the periods and places at which English came to be widely used. Most obviously, we must expect that the Welsh substratum will be most visible in the dialects geographically most remote from the earliest incursions of English. A subset of the community 'sketches' in Part Two allows us to trace, although rather grossly, one of the principal 'corridors' of anglicisation, along the south Wales coast: from Cardiff (Collins & Mees, Chapter 4) and Glamorgan in general (Windsor Lewis, Chapter 7) via Port Talbot (Connolly, Chapter 8) and Abercrave (Tench, Chapter 9) to north Carmarthenshire (Parry, Chapter 10). It is generally the case, as Wells's (Chapter 12) postscript also notes, that attested Welsh-language influence increases from east to west along this continuum, from being negligible (Windsor Lewis claims absent) in Cardiff English, to accounting for 'just about all the *distinctive* characteristics of the English spoken in north Carmarthenshire' (Parry).

Future research should explore the more particular legacies of progressive anglicisation. Some of the potential here may be illustrated with an example of our own, relating to the semantics of the Welsh English aspect system in its use of auxiliaries *do* and *be*. Both *do* and *be* can occur as periphrastic forms of the present in its habitual meaning, alongside the standard use of the inflected present tense verb. Thus we find parallel occurrences such as the following:

he goes to the cinema every week (inflected present)
he do go to the cinema every week (*do* plus non-inflected verb)
he's going to the cinema every week (inflected *be* plus inflected verb)

In the non-standard second and third examples, the auxiliaries *do* and *be* are always unstressed, and *do* is always uninflected; *be* is always regularly inflected for person and number. (Past tense equivalents also exist, again with habitual meaning (*he did go* . . . ; *he was going* . . .). The precise distribution of the two non-standard types is interesting, though no formal study (to our knowledge) exists. Still, it is possible to tease out a general distributional pattern from Parry's (1977, 1979) data. In the industrial areas of Gwent and Glamorgan (cf. Windsor Lewis, Chapter 7) and the rural areas of Brecknock and east Radnor, the attested form is exclusively the one with *do*. It also occurs sporadically elsewhere, in Pembroke, Cardigan

6 ENGLISH IN WALES

and west Radnor, but there the more frequent form is that with *be*. This pattern reflects the distinction between areas of 'early' and 'late' bilingualism in Wales, and ultimate anglicisation (cf. Williams, Chapter 2; and Pryce, Chapter 3). The periphrastic construction with *be* can be directly correlated with an equivalent Welsh language form, in which the verb *bod* (*be*) is followed by a subject nominal, a predicator *yn* (semantically related to the English preposition *in*) and an uninflected verb-noun, as in:

mae ef yn mynd i'r sinema bob wythnos
(he goes to the cinema every week)
(lit. 'is he in go to the cinema every week').

The *do* pattern, on the other hand, is historically connected with English dialects of the West Midlands, and therefore fits into a long-established dialect subcontinuum reaching out from neighbouring English counties into Wales. The *be* pattern seems to be characteristic of the speech of those Welsh people who are subject to a dominant Welsh language influence, in being either bilingual or first-generation monolingual English speakers. The fact that the more 'conservative' western areas show instances of forms in *do* alongside those in *be* suggests a westward spreading of *do*. Future studies could consider the possible stylistic functioning of *do* and *be* forms in areas where they co-occur.

In general, of course, it is also important to recognise the contemporary functioning of such 'corridors', as contemporary influences on Wales and its English varieties alike continue to spread east to west along the principal arterial route (M4) into south Wales. But it is also true that patterns of social and geographical mobility *within* Wales are allowing the relatively 'English' urban centres, and particularly Cardiff, simultaneously to be centres of Welsh-language growth in recent years (Williams). Partly for this reason, future survey-based dialect research may well pick up a blurring of the predictable 'advanced-to-substratal' continuum along the original routes of English penetration and consolidation. Naturally enough, several other quite distinct influences have also conspired very significantly to shape varieties of English in Wales, as represented in the volume. Windsor Lewis (Chapter 7), for example, notes the impact of Flemish and Scandinavian influences on Glamorgan English lexis. Poor communications within Wales have doubtless been a further geolinguistic factor (cf. Williams), which must have inhibited the coalescence of more 'northern' and more 'southern' Welsh English varieties amongst themselves. There is also the important consideration of the precise nature of the contact and influence of English varieties. Windsor Lewis (Chapter 7) again notes the south-western (English) character of some south-east Wales features (cf. also Coupland, 1988). But Parry also finds very extensive similarities between the features he samples in south Pembrokeshire (in the south-western promontory) — the most distinctively 'non-Welsh' of Welsh English communities — and south-west England varieties.

Although no systematic investigations have as yet been disseminated,[2] future research needs (as Wells notes) to attend also to north-western English influence through the north Wales coastal 'corridor' into one of the principal traditional Welsh-language heartlands in Gwynedd and Clwyd. The current development of the north Wales coastal expressway (A55) is again to be looked to as a source of accelerated in-migration and tourism, and with these the penetration of Merseyside English into north-west Wales. The extent of the penetration of urban Midlands English varieties into Wales is also still quite uncharted. Another clear need is to document the nature and extent of the inroads being made by the type of rhoticity typical of western England and of related features into the Welsh Marches, at least as far as Newtown in Mid-Wales, and not far east of Newport in the south. (Our own notes on the long-anglicised former Welsh counties of Breconshire and Radnorshire show at least two features associated with neighbouring dialects in English counties — fronted [æ] realisation of short /a/, and [r]-colouring or retroflexion in *earth, car, burn*, etc.) In the absence of a wider range of detailed community surveys than we are at present able to assemble, and there is a most regrettable though unavoidable southern bias in the data available for the book's second section, a highly valuable overview is available in the pages of Wells's (1982: II, 377ff.) discussion of Welsh accents of English (cf. also our notes on some typical north Wales English features, below).

Despite their limited geographical coverage, the sketches presented here certainly offer some highly valuable directions for further research. Collins & Mees have distilled a decade or more of observational and empirical research into their description (hardly a 'sketch') of Cardiff phonetics and phonology, and the end-product will doubtless serve as a model both for future work in the capital itself and for contrastive analyses of other communities. Windsor Lewis's detailed overview of the distinctive lexical and syntactic characteristics of Glamorgan (Chapter 7) is richly evocative in its own right. But, cross-referenced with the observations by Connolly (Port Talbot, Chapter 8) and Parry (north Carmarthenshire and south Pembrokeshire, Chapters 10 and 11), these taxonomies open the door for future studies of lexical variation in the contemporary dialects of Welsh English — a plane of sociolinguistic variation that has been swamped in recent years by Labovian phonological emphases. Morris Jones (Chapter

14) shows the potential of quantitative, non-phonological studies in Wales, and there is clearly no shortage of raw data. Tench's survey of the pronunciation of English in Abercrave (Chapter 9) is most welcome, not least for its extended section on intonational characteristics — a rare detailed exploration of what is stereotypically held to be the most strikingly apparent feature of English in Wales. Parry's two sketches, culled from original materials of the *Survey of Anglo-Welsh Dialects* (Parry, 1977; 1979), exemplify a different tradition of dialect research from that of Collins & Mees, Connolly, Tench and Wells, but comparisons and contrasts with sketches of other communities are easily and profitably established. Between themselves, north Carmarthenshire and south Pembrokeshire are admirably contrasted, showing almost polarised varieties of English in south-west Wales.

Towards a Typology of Welsh English Varieties

The descriptive sketches in this volume as a whole reveal at least part of the extensive variability of Welsh English. Previously, the sociolinguistic literature has tended to describe and interpret Welsh English (to the extent that it has done this *at all*) as a unitary, undifferentiated variety, or at best recognising some north–south divide. (An Appendix to Chapter 15 by Coupland critiques some of the observations made in Trudgill & Hannah, 1982, on the descriptive nature of a supposedly standard variety of Welsh English.) Earlier work (e.g. Thomas, 1984) has described Welsh English as a heterogeneous system of varieties, and the particular community descriptions offered here both confirm and extend previous accounts. Of course, the common assumption of *homo*geneity, clearly at odds with the objective facts, is not uninteresting in its own right. As Giles suggests in this volume, future research could usefully explore the degree to which varieties of Welsh English are *in fact* discriminated (and discriminable) by people inside and outside of Wales. Thereafter, it might be possible and enlightening to explore the social functioning of a *stereotyped*, supposedly uniform 'Welsh English' — particularly, say, in advertising, humour and mimicry (see also note 3, below). Coupland's protestations against a simple describable 'standard' variety of Welsh English similarly do not deny the existence of some perceptual stereotype of 'the educated Welsh voice', a notion that may well influence teachers', parents' and employers' preferences and prejudices in Wales.

On the available evidence, and recognising many significant exceptions (including south Pembrokeshire, perhaps the Gower peninsula and the English dialect contact zones), it would seem plausible to posit two broad varietal types of English in south Wales and a third north Wales type. South-west Wales, with its still high proportion of bilingual speakers, shows considerable contemporary and substratal influence from Welsh in phonology, lexis and grammar in most social groups' vernacular usage. South-eastern varieties show far less substratal influence, and may (though we acknowledge the term might be contentious) be said to be more 'evolved', almost entirely free from significant contemporary influence from the Welsh language. In the urban south-east, dialects have developed which are 'Welsh' English only in the sense of being geographically distributed within Wales. They can be expected to develop independently of Welsh influence, and to consolidate their uniqueness in a British context. In their most formal pronunciation, speakers here are more likely than in the south-west to orient to the conventional prestige model of south-east England, Received Pronunciation, and they will find this model regularly in use in their midst. There are no good reasons to suppose that the dialects of the south-west will not come increasingly under the influence of the dialects of the south-east — still the industrially and commercially dominant region.

Throughout the whole of Wales, formal grammatical and lexical usage appears to be modelled very largely on Standard English English (or 'Southern British Standard'), and uniformly so in the south-east. Hence, we venture that variety choice in south-east Welsh English is quite distinct from that which has been said to function in the Welsh language in Wales. For Welsh itself, 'lifestyle' ('chapel or pub', as it is simplistically put) may be a covariate of stylistic choice; for Welsh English in the urban south-east, socio-economic class appears to be the dominant factor, given the override one expects from distinctive regional features. Future research could take up the hypothesis that some bilingual speakers may in consequence find a conflict if their social network allegiances differ between the two language contexts, requiring different social conditions for varietal choices.

As we have noted, the southern varieties of English in Wales are quite well represented in this volume. The third principal varietal category — the north Wales type — is, to our knowledge, the *most* dependent on Welsh for its distinguishing characteristics. We cannot offer a detailed characterisation here, but can at least point to some salient features of the type that can be taken up in future detailed work. North Wales has the monophthongal forms of *mate*, *great*, etc., vowels, but the orthographic diphthongs 'ei', 'ai', 'ey' also tend to have /e:/ — *weight* is often /we:t/, *tail* is /te:l/ and *prey* is /pre:/. Correspondingly, the sporadic south Wales *nose* versus *knows* contrast is characteristically levelled in favour of /o:/ in North Wales. Some varieties in the north-west also carry over a feature of the dialects of Welsh indigenous to the area. Welsh did not historically have a contrast between long and short close front vowels, having only a long form. A short *retracted* form did exist, however — the 'barred i' of north Welsh. English close front short vowels have tended to be assimilated to the north Welsh system, though only in stressed monosyllables (*tip* is [tɨp], *pit* is [pɨt]. Relatedly, north-west treatment of the orthographic 'oy' diphthong retains the length of the first element and assimilates the second element to the same 'barred i': *boy, toy* can thus be [bɔːɨ], [tɔːɨ]. This again derives from Welsh having only this long diphthong in the front-to-mid-close position, and it occurs only in open, stressed monosyllables.

A distinctive consonantal feature of north Wales English is dental realisation of the alveolars /t/, /d/ and /n/ (*two* is [t̪u], *do* is [d̪u], *now* is [n̪əu]). The common lengthening of word-medial intervocalic consonants we find in many Welsh English varieties is accompanied by strongly aspirated release of voiceless plosives in this position in northern varieties. At the same time, voiced plosives here tend to be devoiced in their release stage:

[ɪppʰər] *ripper*; [vɪkkʰər] *vicar*
[rəbb̥ɪʃ] *rubbish*; [ləg̊ɡ̊ɛtʃ] *luggage*

Perhaps the most distinctive consonantal feature of north Wales English derives from the fact that Welsh itself has no voiced sibilant /z/. Hence, for many speakers of English in north Wales the following pairs are homophonous:

seal, zeal /siːl/
sink, zinc /sɪŋk/
pence, pens /pɛns/
use (n.), *use* (v.) /ɪus/

The affricates are not indigenous to Welsh either, and the voiced affricate /dʒ/ is likewise interpreted in north Welsh English as a voiceless phoneme. Again, then, the following pairs are homophonous:

chin, gin /tʃɪn/
choke, joke /tʃoːk/
rich, ridge /rɪtʃ/

In their nature, the descriptive sketches risk overrepresenting the 'regional' or 'basilectal' quality of the community varieties in question. Since their aim is to convey the distinctiveness of particular communities' English usage, they have focused quite uniformly and deliberately on the 'least standard' manifestations of the dialects in question — often, though not necessarily, associated with male, working-class speakers. Yet it is clear (as, for instance the later chapters of the book demonstrate) that the high-prestige poles of dialect usage in Wales can be almost equally revealing. It in fact makes little sense to designate the varieties described in the sketches as uniformly 'non-standard', unless we can demonstrate the pattern of dialectal social stratification (Labov 1966) through which the terms 'standard' and 'non-standard' become meaningful. This seems to be a clear area of dialect research in Wales which demands further attention. We might hypothesise that the major urban centres in Wales will be largely modelled on the 'classic' Labovian lines, with 'standard English English' (including Received Pronunciation) featuring in most high-status groups' speech. Geographical mobility within British urban life makes its effects felt here, and a sizeable segment of 'Welsh English', if defined on purely distributional demographic grounds, of course *is* the English of non-Welsh indigenous speakers. Within the indigenous groups, we might then expect to find a demarcation between those Welsh people whose ethnic affiliation is uniformly, partially, fitfully, or not at all, to Wales, and who will predictably mark these differences in their styles of talk.

Meanings and Uses of Welsh English

The immediate appeal of some dimensions of Welsh English as repositories of cultural experience has been admirably captured in the series of popular booklets by J. Edwards (1985, for example) on 'Wenglish'. Although sociolinguists will rightly doubt the reliability of such collections as constituting 'evidence', it would be quite wrong and indeed naive to dismiss them as irrelevant or valueless. First, Edwards (and some others writing in similarly lighthearted ways about English in Wales) gives us sensitively observed catalogues of local usages, in some senses enviably free from the constraints of audio-recording, transcribing and reproducing documented instances. They can certainly provide pointers for more systematic research. But second, such popular accounts are in themselves a significant sociolinguistic phenomenon, undeniably highlighting sociolinguistic variation in the community, reflecting and perhaps contributing to the creation of popular linguistic ethnicities — in Wales and beyond.[3] Future research should profitably explore the impact of popular variationist accounts, which seem always to be slanted towards the most nostalgic and slightly self-denigratory dialect experiences, and the lore of childhood and rural life. A popular 'Wenglish consciousness' may well be denigrated as a 'bogus' or 'invalid' Welsh ethnicity, though it would be unwise to assume ethnic affiliation is always of 'pure' or 'historically validated' kind.

In a more traditional academic vein, the four chapters of Part Three of this volume focus on specific social and psychological processes at work in the use of Welsh English in specific contexts. There is an infinite range of questions open to sociolinguistic accounts of the functioning of varieties in Welsh communities, though the book's final section introduces and develops some key themes. All chapters here focus on the dynamic, variable role of Welsh English in society.

Mees (Chapter 13) reports selectively from two meticulously detailed, interview-based, quantitative investigations of phonetic variability in the speech of Cardiff schoolchildren. The report dwells on methodological matters of very general interest to sociolinguistic research, prior to an account of variation across six phonological variables, by 'class' and 'style', generally within the Labovian paradigm. Basing her interpretations on occurrence frequencies, Mees argues there is a ranking of stigmatisation across four of her variables in the Cardiff data, from variables associated with word-initial /h/, through the 'ng' feature, to intervocalic /r/ (most-to-least stigmatised). Interestingly, 'ng' appears to be less strongly disfavoured by Cardiff children than in the general adult population; also, glottalisation appears to be a relatively *high*-prestige feature being introduced to Cardiff speech by the higher socio-economic classes.

The real-time dimension that Mees is able to adopt, comparing the speech of the same children across a five-year span, is a relatively rare resource in sociolinguistic studies (though cf. Prince, 1988; Yaeger-Dror, 1988) and is highly suggestive. Mees tentatively suggests that her data support the picture of working-class Cardiff males moving away from the prestige norms during adolescence, with lower-middle-class females moving somewhat towards this. The study thereby captures developmental processes *both* as change in community pronunciation norms *and* as age-grading in speech. The enduring picture in Mees's research is of speakers in urban environments engaged in very local dialect practices which are always open to modification and redefinition. This process of continual flux contrasts sharply with the impression of stasis we derive from the descriptive snapshots of communities in the earlier sections, and points to the need for variationist data in all communities — rural as well as urban.

Morris Jones (Chapter 14) draws on an impressively large corpus, also of child-language data (children aged 5–7), to investigate patterns in the use of 'Welsh [language]-influenced English'. These data are a particularly important source, spanning several diverse Welsh communities, and gathered in naturalistic play environments. The immediate focus is on a specific subset of Welsh English features — syntactic and lexical variables which are very plausibly derived from Welsh-language usage. Through attending to the spontaneous occurrence of these features, Morris Jones is able to offer generalisations about the synchronic geographical and social distribution of Welsh influence, and (tentatively) about developmental processes (through a combination of, again, real-time and apparent-time observations). It emerges, for example, that Welsh-influenced forms are more strongly represented in less anglicised areas of Wales, endorsing our view that certain (e.g. south-eastern) varieties of English in Wales can plausibly be labelled more 'evolved', as independent of contemporary Welsh language influence.

Most intriguingly, Morris Jones offers us the scenario of at least one dimension of Welsh English usage following the pattern of decline of the Welsh language itself. He also posits a plausible developmental sequence: from Welsh language use, to Welsh-influenced English, to an admixture of Welsh influence plus non-Welsh influence, to altogether non-Welsh-influenced English. Several salient methodological points also emerge, not least that there are severe limitations to the supposedly normal covariation of educational and occupational criteria as predictors of language use in non-urban Wales. Future sociolinguistic studies in Wales would do well to explore the complexities of the multi-dimensional configurations of 'class' in Wales (cf. Coupland; also Williams, 1986).

The volume's last two chapters explore more obviously symbolic dimensions of the use of English in Wales. Coupland (Chapter 15) offers a series of brief case studies, exploring apparently high-prestige varieties of Welsh English. The source data are the dialects of some candidates for Welsh political office during the run-up to the general election of 1987. An attempt is made to unravel some of the complexities inherent in the notion of a 'standard variety' of English in Wales, and no altogether tenable definition of 'standard' emerges. It is argued that prestige can be available to almost the full range of varieties of English in Wales in specific contexts, given the way some varieties enshrine Welsh ethnic pride, some a valued lower-class affiliation (and others the converse), and still others pan-British power and influence, and so on.

Giles (Chapter 16), on the other hand, offers a major review of some 20 years of empirical research on attitudes to Welsh English. It is Giles's own assiduous, theoretically robust research over this period that has done most to give Welsh sociolinguistics its international profile over this period. His detailed conspexus shows how socio-psychological research has captured the diverse social meanings of the use of Welsh English, connoting not only ethnic loyalty and socio-economic class provenance, as hinted above, but also personality types and even affective states. Giles teases out the threads of these complex interrelations of social meanings with attention to detail and frank acknowledgement of some inconsistencies and omissions. Even so, here is an instance where interdisciplinary exchange must once again significantly colour future research directions. The social psychological paradigm can still find clarification if it recognises greater linguistic diversity in Wales, as Giles's own valuable research agenda for future studies acknowledges. It is certainly the case that our interpretations of geolinguistic distribution, of dialect change, and of dialect diversity can in turn be enriched through sensitivity to the complex relationships between attitude and use.

Overall, we would not want to underplay the developmental role of this collection. Let us re-emphasise some limitations. The geographical bias — towards analysis of issues and varieties in *south* Wales — is a major weakness, and a sad testament to the underinvestigation, as yet, of the *whole* of Wales's sociolinguistic nature. Such surveys of English in Wales as we have been able to draw on here are, of course, limited in various other ways, too — in attending exclusively to rural *or* urban dialects in their geographical zones, in some aspects of their methodologies, or simply in their scope. Still, there is unquestionably an ample fund of material here to launch more ambitious designs (perhaps profitably with a more dynamic thrust than is still conventional, attending to more varied contextual uses of Welsh English varieties and their stylistic variation). Though Williams and Pryce have both brought their own analyses of anglicisation processes pretty well up to date, there is again need for continual updating on the societal forces — through the media, education, government and economic life — operating to undermine or bolster varieties of Welsh and English in Wales. Mainstream sociolinguistic research, as Wells observes, has really only just begun on English varieties in Wales. It is to be hoped that this volume will have offered researchers and interested 'participant-observers' a range of data and theories, issues and ideas, facts and controversies, that will stimulate them to add to what we already know.

Notes to Chapter 1

1. Undated author citations in this Introduction refer to contributions to the present volume.
2. Penhallurick (1986) gives a valuable survey of English in Gwynedd and Clwyd.
3. Other relevant popular cultural phenomena of this sort in a Welsh context might include the Welsh English dialect performances of comedians, singers and popular radio and television broadcasters (cf. Coupland, 1985b; 1988), and stereotyped portrayals of Welsh characters in these media and in advertising. One might conclude that the public endorsement of idealised Welsh English forms in this

way constitutes a very particular form of 'institutional support' for Welsh English in contemporary Wales (cf. Giles).

References

BALL, M. 1988, *The Use of Welsh*. Clevedon: Multilingual Matters.
BELLIN, W. 1984, Welsh and English in Wales. In P. TRUDGILL (ed.), *Language in the British Isles*. Cambridge: Cambridge University Press, 449–79.
CHAPMAN, A.J., SMITH, J.R. and FOOT, H.C. 1977, Language, humour and intergroup relations. In H. GILES (1977: 137–70).
COUPLAND, N. 1985a, Sociolinguistic aspects of place-names: ethnic affiliation and the pronunciation of Welsh in the Welsh capital. In W. VIERECK (ed.), *Focus On: England and Wales. Varieties of English Around the World G5*. Amsterdam: Benjamins, 29–43.
———1985b, 'Hark, hark the lark': social motivations for phonological style-shifting. *Language and Communication*, 5, 3: 153–72.
———1986, Review of J.R. Edwards (1985) *Language, Society and Identity* (Oxford: Basil Blackwell). *Journal of Language and Social Psychology*, 5,1: 63–69.
———1988, *Dialect in Use: Sociolinguistic Variation in Cardiff English*. Cardiff: University of Wales Press.
EDWARDS, J. 1985, *Talk Tidy: The Art of Speaking Wenglish*. Cowbridge: Brown and Sons.
EDWARDS, J.R. 1985, *Language, Society and Identity*. Oxford: Basil Blackwell.
FISHMAN, J.A. 1977, Language and ethnicity. In H. GILES (1977: 15–57).
GILES, H. 1977, *Language, Ethnicity and Intergroup Relations*. London: Academic Press.
LABOV, W. 1966, *The Social Stratification of English in New York City*. Washington, DC: Center for Applied Linguistics.
PARRY, D. 1977, *The Survey of Anglo-Welsh Dialects, Vol.1: The South-East*. Swansea: University College.
———1979, *The Survey of Anglo-Welsh Dialects, Vol.2: The South-West*. Swansea: University College.
PENHALLURICK, R.V. 1986, A phonological, lexical, morphological and syntactic survey of the Anglo-Welsh dialects of Gwynedd and Clwyd. PhD thesis, University College of Swansea.
PRINCE, E. 1988, On choosing a model for dialect shift: a case-study from Yiddish. In N. COUPLAND and H. GILES (eds), *Communication Accommodation: Recent Developments*. Special double issue of *Language and Communication*, 8, 3–4.
STEPHENS, M. 1973, *The Welsh Language Today*. Llandysul: Gomer.
THOMAS, A.R. 1982, Change and decay in language. In D. CRYSTAL (ed.), *Linguistic Controversies*. London: Edward Arnold, 209–20.
———1983, The English language in Wales. In Y. MATSUMURA (ed.), *English Around the World*. Tokyo: Kenkyusha, 137–93 (in Japanese).
———1984, Welsh English. In P. TRUDGILL (ed.), *Language in the British Isles*. Cambridge: Cambridge University Press, 178–94.
———1985, Welsh English: A grammatical conspectus. In W. VIERECK (ed.), *Focus On: England and Wales. Varieties of English Around the World G4*. Amsterdam: Benjamins, pp. 213–22.

TRUDGILL, P. and HANNAH, J. 1982, *International English: A Guide to Varieties of Standard English*. London: Edward Arnold.

WELLS, J. 1982, *Accents of English* (3 vols). Cambridge: Cambridge University Press.

WILLIAMS, G. 1986, The Sociology of Welsh. *International Journal of the Sociology of Language*, 66.

YAEGER-DROR, M. 1988, Speech accommodation: an Israeli example. In N. COUPLAND and H. GILES (eds), *Communication Accommodation: Recent Developments*. Double special issue of *Language and Communication*, 8, 3–4.

Part 1
Perspectives on Anglicisation

2   The Anglicisation of Wales[1]

COLIN H. WILLIAMS

'Anglicisation' is one of those myriad terms in general use which everyone understands and hardly anyone defines. It concerns the process by which non-English people become assimilated or bound into an English-dominated cultural and ideological system. In this chapter, I will be using it as a shorthand term to describe the vast and complex process whereby the core values of a burgeoning English society penetrated Wales from the early modern period onwards, so as to transform large parts of Wales and the majority of its inhabitants, in time, into citizens whose only language was English, and whose principal loyalty was to the Crown and to the British state idea.

The anglicisation of Wales is a moderate, if historically significant, element in the development both of a homogenous British polity and a larger creation, the British Empire. On a world historical scale, Wales might be considered as the first colony of an expanding English state (cf. Coupland, this volume), from the early mediaeval period onward, when territorial annexation and partial political incorporation brought scattered local nobles and their bondsmen under the central authority of a feudal monarch. This was formalised by the Acts of Union (the Laws in Wales Acts, 1535 and 1542), which presaged a more rapid and thoroughgoing anglicisation, particularly of the gentry. Subsequent relations between the two peoples, the English and the Welsh, might be categorised as a classic illustration of both the tensions and the harmony generated when a dominant majority seeks to incorporate a subservient minority into its sphere of influence, though of course the precise explanation for such a relationship has as much to do with political interpretation as it has with the analysis of 'objective' historical facts.

Clearly anglicisation is an essential element in the development of British society. At various junctures in the past it has been an adjunct to more specific acts of exploitation, modernisation and incorporation. At other times it has been pursued as an end in itself, a precondition for the fulfilment of constitutional and strategic aims, such as the subjugation of Ireland or the promotion of Reformation Protestant ideology. However, anglicisation is not coterminous with the other major processes which have laid the foundation for a social and political transformation of Britain in the past four centuries: modernisation, the uneven development of capitalism, secularisation, the changing patterns of state activity, the enfranchisement of the masses, adult literacy through compulsory education, to name just a selection. To be sure, anglicisation incorporates many of these trends but it is not synonymous with them, for it has a differential impact because of the intervening role of culture. Worsley (1984) has argued that culture is an underemphasised variable in modern social science, and I would agree wholeheartedly. Because culture has normative and conative meanings, in addition to cognitive ones (Worsley, 1984: 43) it is capable of embracing patterns and processes of change from a holistic and contextual perspective. It is this perspective that I adopt here through an analysis of socio-demographic change within the wider domain of state integration.

Conceptions of anglicisation invite moral and political judgements on the effects of incorporating Wales into a British state. Three broad interpretations of this multi-faceted integration process may be cited here to serve as refractors on a larger reality, the development of the autonomous state within a world system. The Tory interpretation would highlight the necessity of incorporating the Celtic peoples into an English realm so as to secure an historically transcendent Protestant monarchy. The established Church, the Acts of Union of 1535 and 1542, the rule of law and the incorporation of the Welsh gentry were all necessary concomitants of the Welsh variant on this general theme, designed to secure the borders against Catholic incursions from abroad, and to promote the Tudor ascendancy at home. If pushed, the Tory view might even advance the position that the Tudor dynasty was, after all, a primarily Welsh house in its genesis, and could have been accused in its initial period of actively favouring Welsh developments, and promoting Welsh interests through the power of the central agencies of state. The Whig tradition would emphasise the necessity of state centralism so as to promote the Anglo-Saxon virtues of individual freedom and responsibility, tempered by a commitment to law and limited government. The Welsh were eventually to share in, and help develop, the rule of parliamentary government. A more modern nationalist historiography (C.H. Williams, 1988) would argue that the assimilation of the Welsh was not only unnatural, but also a barrier to the realisation of the nation's full potential, because Wales was animated by rhythms which emanated from London and kept her in a dependent position, determined by the structures of British statehood.

Two caveats need to be entered, however. We should be wary not to treat anglicisation as if it were a historically autonomous force. It is neither inevitable nor homogenous in its impact on specific peoples and places. Neither should we reify the process. There is a great danger in a mode of analysis which treats anglicisation only in terms of migration patterns, socio-economic change, and the like. This chapter will certainly focus upon aggregate-structural features but will emphasise the fact that these are mediated in local communities by individuals and their actions. It will also allude to the socio-psychological referents of the superordination/ subordination power relations inherent in the process.

The Context of Anglicisation in Pre-modern Wales

I will assume as given many of the major preconditioning factors prior to the nineteenth century. However, we may list several of the more pertinent triggering factors which facilitated anglicisation (Figure 2.1; Table 2.1): the initial demarcation of Welsh territory by the construction of Offa's Dyke between AD 778 and 796; the Edwardian conquest and settlement in 1282; the accession to the English throne of Henry VII after the defeat of the Yorkist cause on Bosworth Field in 1485; the Tudor Acts of Union of England and Wales of 1535 and 1542; the consequent diminution in Welsh customs, law and popular language; the political consolidation of the principality through legal ordinances and public administration reform, particularly the installation of local JPs, and the consolidation of local landowning families as commissioners of the peace. These latter changes demonstrate the degree to which patronage and office-holding were a central feature of the Henrician innovations in Welsh administration (Robinson, 1988: 15). With the dissolution of the monasteries, and the superimposition of a religious and socio-political order embodied in the Church of England came a new system by which the populace could be reached and socialised. This was particularly effective after the translation of the Bible into Welsh in 1588, a feature which scholars claim has done more to preserve the language and its related culture than any other single event in the nation's history. In the seventeenth century the penetration of new religious movements heralded the way for subsequent religious affiliations beyond those of the established Church. In the great age of nonconformist dissent from the mid-eighteenth century to the age of Liberal Radicalism either side of the turn of the twentieth century the values of modern Wales were formed. New codes of worship brought new ideas of change which were transmitted to a largely literate population through a mass media created

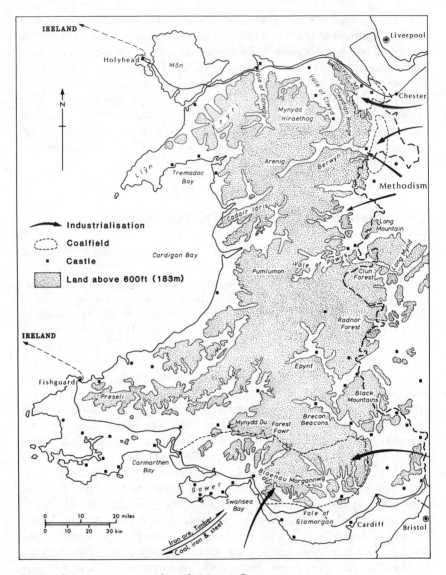

FIGURE 2.1 *A summary of anglicising influences.*
Source: Topographic base map after Morgan & Thomas (1984: 14).

by print capitalism. Finally, the primary products of Welsh agriculture, particularly the exportation of livestock, brought Wales into closer contact with her eastern neighbour and the wider world beyond. In sum, social capital, political power and economic wealth were, in general, dependent upon external agencies, and were mediated, by and large, through the English-orientated market system. They also served to widen the pre-existent internal differentiation of language communities and regions, as detailed below.

The Pre-Census Source Evidence

Accurate reconstruction of the cultural geographic effect of these factors is difficult in the extreme, owing to the paucity of national data before 1891, the date of the first official census in which Welsh language data were collected. Prior to this, one has to rely on individual surveys and surrogate measures, such as the language of church worship, as the data base for the reconstruction of language zones in Wales. Pryce and Williams (1988) have surveyed the pre-census evidence and suggested means by which historical data sources can be manipulated to yield interesting, if approximate, patterns of language change up to 1891. These sources include the detailed statistical evidence gathered for the Education Report of 1847 (dubbed Brâd y Llyfrau Gleision) which indicates the numbers of Welsh monoglots, English monoglots and bilinguals, and the national origin of individuals. Government inquiries, however, were rare occurrences; a more common source of data was the attempt by concerned individuals to plot the health of the Welsh language at specific periods and places. Ravenstein's 1871 survey of Scotland and Wales, derived from 1,200 questionnaires together with a 'voluminous correspondence', provides the basis for a series of language maps depicting areas where, it was estimated, Welsh was spoken by (a) the majority, (b) 25–50%, and (c) 10–15% of the population. As Pryce & Williams (1988: 209) argue,

> despite several printing errors in the statistical estimates, there is no doubt that, in every respect, Ravenstein's "statistical survey" constitutes a remarkable and pioneering piece of research. Even today it retains much interest.

Together with the dialectologist A.J. Ellis, and the educationalist Southall, who produced maps of language divides, strongholds and transitional zones for Welsh and Anglo-Welsh culture, this trio of late nineteenth-century enquirers laid the foundations for more informed census-based constructions of language areas in the twentieth century.

Today, by virtue of more informed scholarship, improved techniques for data handling and the methodological development of subdisciplines in

TABLE 2.1   *Factors Promoting the Anglicisation of Wales in the Modern Period*

	Polity	Economy	Culture/society
Macro	The Edwardian conquest.	Land transfer.	Alien nobility.
	State integration via the Acts of Union, 1535 and 1542.	Early urbanisation. Agricultural depression.	Outlawing of Welsh language. Estrangement of the gentry.
	Establishment of state Church.	Promotion of urban bourgeoisie.	Translation of Bible, 1588.
	Parliamentary Representation after the Reform Act 1867.	Urbanisation and industrialisation. Integration into the world	Educational reform and value reorientation.
	Expansion of suffrage.	economy.	Inter-generational language loss.
	Education Act 1870.	Welsh out-migration and regional change.	
	Warfare and conscription.	Non-Welsh immigration to selected areas.	
Meso	Local government reforms.	Developing bureaucracy and economic	Denominational religious diversity.
	Political radicalism, Chartism, party political electoral representation.	accountability. Trade unionism. Transport and communication infrastructural improvements. Print capitalism.	Popular mass entertainment. Social movements. Adult education.

history, geography and linguistics, we are able to reconstruct the territorial distribution of the Welsh and English languages in the pre-census period with far more confidence. Of the very many, often ingenious, reconstruction techniques, I want to concentrate on the most exhaustive and satisfying research efforts, that of Rees Pryce, whose application of the general

(TABLE 2.1 *continued*)

	Polity	*Economy*	*Culture/society*
Micro	Voter participation. Political party membership. British identification. State support in wartime. Dependence upon state agencies. Educational opportunities through the medium of English.	Entering wage economy. Residential mobility. Socio-economic and class consciousness. Individual material advances. Benefits of welfare state policies.	Inter-ethnic marriage patterns. Language switching and language loss, increased bilingualism. Secularisation and reorientation of value system. Passive receptive entertainment.

principles of historical linguistic geography is evident in his analysis of Gwent in Chapter 3 of this volume.

Drawing on the conceptual advances of scholars such as E.G. Bowen, H. Carter, G. Lewis and D. Meinig, Pryce sought evidence for a reconstruction of Welsh linguistic regions into a proposed tripartite division of core, domain, and periphery. The Welsh core, otherwise known as heartland, fortress, or Inner Wales, identified areas where the majority spoke Welsh as a daily language; the domain was the transitional bilingual zone where Welsh and English competed for dominance; and the periphery was the outer margin of Welsh speech, where anglicisation had all but engulfed a vestigial Welsh culture.

The only data suitable for such time-series analysis in the pre-census period were those on the language of public worship collected by the Anglican Church, and preserved in the Church in Wales archives at the National Library of Wales. This source includes returns from some 646 (out of a total of 1,022) parish churches from *c*.1750; 673 (of a total of 1,038) parishes from *c*.1800, 913 (out of 1,086) from *c*.1850 and 773 (from a total of 1,173) parishes from *c*.1900. In addition, a survey conducted in 1906 and published in the Report of the Royal Commission on the Church of England in Wales in 1910 provides verification in its returns from 1,143 (from a total of 1,200) parishes throughout Wales (Pryce & Williams, 1988: 214).

Having categorised the linguistic character of each parish according to the criteria summarised in Table 2.2, Pryce transferred the data on a master base map and recorded precise locational information for each period. Next, point symbols, representative of each of the six language statuses, were placed over the site of each parish church. These form the data base from which the areas shown in Figure 2.2 are interpolated to give three language zones: (1) overwhelmingly Welsh areas, (2) the bilingual zone, and (3) dominantly English-speaking areas.

It is evident that the consistently English zones over the period 1750–1900 reflect early zones of English penetration in the border country and along the southern coastal belt with enclaves based on Llantwit Major, Gower and south Pembrokeshire. Adjoining this zone is the wider belt of country which had become English during this period. For most of this region a standard pattern of language replacement obtained: Welsh, bilingual then English. An earlier work (Pryce, 1978) presents characteristic statements in the visitation returns from throughout this region e.g. 'from Boughrood (Co. Radnor) the bishop was informed, no Welsh is spoken in the county'. Other returns recorded provision of Welsh-medium church services but the local clergy soon abandoned these because 'too few came to encourage me to continue' (Pryce, 1978: 25). Parental demands that their children be taught the catechisms in English and the growing divide between an anglicised established Church and a predominantly Welsh nonconformist cause combine to present a picture of incipient consolidation of the English language in the churches of industrial south Wales and several of the border districts.

Active penetration by English settlers of Welsh districts, the means by which areas became anglicised, is best seen in the formation of the bilingual zone of Figure 2.2. Urbanisation and economic development were a spur to the penetration of English migrants, especially along the north Wales coast as far as Menai Strait, consolidating the linear resort towns and overspilling up the Vales of Clwyd and Conwy. Pryce (1978: 24) reports that in 1900,

> compared with their dominantly Welsh or their bilingual status half a century earlier, Rhuthun and Rhyl; Colwyn Bay; Llandudno and Conwy; Penmaenmawr, Llanfairfechan and Holyhead; Pwllheli, Port-madoc and Barmouth; Aberystwyth and Fishguard held only English [services]. And with the immediate hinterland of most of these growing centres, bilingual parishes rapidly graded into the dominantly Welsh-speaking communities of the countryside.

TABLE 2.2 *Language Classification of Sunday Services in Anglican Parish Churches*

Language status	Statements as to the language or languages used in parish churches
1. Welsh	1a. All services in Welsh 1b. Welsh but not more than one English service in three months 1c. Welsh but some English in summer months for visitors
2. Mainly Welsh	2a. Welsh but one English service each month 2b. Welsh always in the evenings but morning services alternately Welsh or bilingual 2c. Welsh always in the evenings but two morning services, one in Welsh and one in English 2d. Bilingual services but more Welsh than English
3. Bilingual	3a. Two services every Sunday, one in each language 3b. Alternating Welsh and English services
4. Mainly English	4a. English always in the evenings but morning services alternately in English and Welsh 4b. Bilingual services but more English than Welsh 4c. Main services in English but afternoon services alternately in English and Welsh 4d. English but one or two services in Welsh each month
5. English	5a. English with rare use of Welsh (at most four times in the year) 5b. All services in English

Source: Pryce (1978)

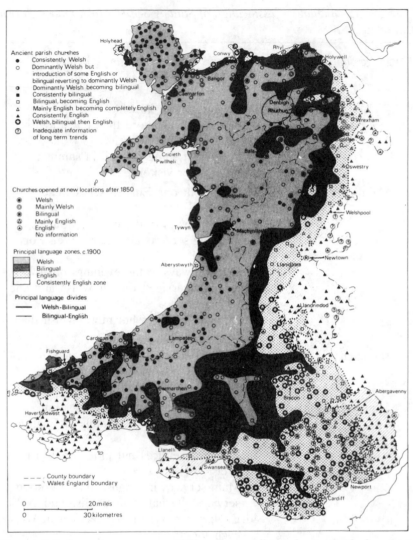

FIGURE 2.2 *Language zones, c.1900 and overall trends at specific locations, c.1750–1900.*
Source: Pryce (1978)

In the rest of Wales, vast areas of the central and southern fringes of the cultural core area were now also functionally bilingual, with occasional outliers of consistently Welsh speech being 'marooned' in the surging tide of anglicisation (N.B. There were inliers of Welsh near Tumble, on the

Carmarthen–Brecknock border, on the Flintshire plateau, as at Gwaunysgor and Ysgeifiog and on the Denbighshire–Flintshire boundary in the parishes of Eryrys and Treuddyn) (Pryce, 1978).

Girdled by the bilingual zone there remained the Welsh core, its population attenuated, but nevertheless still talking to its Master through the medium of Welsh in the majority of its ancient parish churches. Telltale signs of later collapse are evident in Figure 2.2 in the form of bilingual areas around most market towns and ports, and the outliers of anglicisation at Aberystwyth, Cricieth and Pwllheli, whose service-oriented economies and suburbanisation patterns would help diffuse English via the local social communication networks into their spheres of influence in the rural hinterland.

It should be remembered that these bilingual areas were zones of language coexistence where large numbers of Welsh monoglots and English monoglots formed micro-culture regions. At the meso scale we can now reconstruct the pattern of language shift within the borderland up to 1900 based upon the visitation returns of Pryce (1978), the Sunday School data investigated by Lewis (1979; 1980), and the regional studies for north-east Wales (Pryce, 1975) and Gwent. In industrial Wales, if we look beyond the demographic census-data evidence of mass migration, there is the whole contradiction of what effect modernisation was to have on attitudes and beliefs. Its social structure, settlement patterns, population composition and incipient radicalism all testified to the wholesale ravages wrought by the badgering of its coal-rich seams. The marginality of Wales's pre-industrial existence was swamped by a frenzy of commercial and social activity, the like of which had not been seen in contemporary Europe. Massive dislocation, an immigration rate second only to that of the United States of America, and the reconstruction of local issues and concerns as British issues and imperial concerns transformed the insular periphery into an active participant in Britain's quest for global hegemony. And yet, in one fundamental respect, south Wales remained marginal:

> The South Wales economy which enabled the country to sustain its phenomenal population increase and to retain it within its borders, was geared almost wholly to export. It worked to exactly the opposite, inverse rhythm to every other industrial region in Britain (G.A. Williams, 1981: 198).

'King Coal' became cold comfort barely a generation-and-a-half later, but for the moment it spawned a renaissance of Welsh 'national' institutions, and financed the multi-layered social and cultural developments of an

TABLE 2.3   *Classification of Long-term Language Trends, c.1750–1906*

Ecclesiastical parish	Ancient county	Language status (see Table 2)					Trend classification*
		c.1750	c.1800	c.1850	c.1900	1906	
Aberffraw	Anglesey	1	?	1	1	1	W
Garthbeibio	Montgomery	1	1	1	1	1	W
Llanfihangel-ar-arth	Carmarthen	1	1	1	1	2	W
Abergwili	Carmarthen	3	3	2	2	2	aW
Betws-yn-Rhos	Denbigh	1	1	1	2	2	aW
Llanasa	Flint	2	2	3	2	2	aW
Llanerfyl	Montgomery	2	1	1	2	2	aW
Morfil	Pembroke	?	1	2	1	1	aW
Beddgelert	Caernarfon	1	1	2	2	3	WB
Cadoxton-juxta-Neath	Glamorgan	1	?	3	?	3	WB
Llanerchaeron	Cardigan	1	2	3	3	3	WB
Treuddyn	Flint	1	1	1	3	3	WB
Halkyn	Flint	3	3	3	3	3	B
Kidwelly	Carmarthen	3	?	3	3	3	B
Llandeloy	Pembroke	?	3	2	3	3	B
Llandybie	Carmarthen	3	3	2	3	2	B
Meifod	Montgomery	3	3	3	2	2	B
Aberystwyth	Cardigan	?	3	3	3	4	BE
Castell Caereinion	Montgomery	3	4	3	5	5	BE
Chirk	Denbigh	3	5	5	5	5	BE
Conwy	Caernarfon	3	3	3	4	4	BE
Llanfoist	Monmouth	3	5	5	?	5	BE
Llangorse	Brecknock	?	3	1	5	5	BE
Beaumaris	Anglesey	4	3	4	?	4	bE
Cregina	Radnor	4	5	5	5	5	bE
Llangibby	Monmouth	4	5	?	?	5	bE
Cardiff	Glamorgan	5	?	5	?	4	E
Erbistock	Denbigh	5	5	5	5	5	E
Hay	Brecknock	?	5	5	?	5	E
Laugharne	Carmarthen	5	?	5	5	5	E
Aberysgir	Brecknock	?	1	1	5	5	WBE
Bonvilston	Glamorgan	1	4	5	?	5	WBE
Colwyn Bay	Denbigh	1	1	4	5	4	WBE
Cwm-iou	Monmouth	1	3	5	?	5	WBE

TABLE 2.3 *continued*

Ecclesiastical parish	Ancient county	Language status (see Table 2)					Trend classifi- cation*
		c.1750	c.1800	c.1850	c.1900	1906	
Denio	Caernarfon	1	1	3	4	4	WBE
Ferryside	Carmarthen	1	?	5	5	5	WBE
Llanfair Caereinion	Montgomery	2	3	3	3	4	WBE
St. Dogwells	Pembroke	?	2	3	5	4	WBE
St. Harmon	Radnor	1	2	3	5	5	WBE

*W: consistently Welsh;
aW: dominantly Welsh but introduction of some English; or bilingual, reverting to dominantly Welsh;
WB: dominantly Welsh, becoming bilingual;
B: consistently bilingual;
BE: bilingual, becoming English or dominantly English;
bE: mainly English, becoming completely English;
E: consistently English;
WBE: originally Welsh, then bilingual before becoming English or dominantly English.
Source: Pryce (1978)

industrial, Welsh, nonconformist proletariat (C.H. Williams, 1985: 29). For all the fears of anglicisation, there were still more people who could speak Welsh in 1901 than in 1801, comprising some 50% of the total population. However, the social life of urban, especially coastal, Wales was becoming far more English in its mores, values, orientation and behaviour. Professor Gwyn Williams would qualify this statement by adding that it was becoming far more transatlantic in tone than hitherto.

Having established the patterns of language shift in the nineteenth century, let us now focus on the anglicisation process by examining the pivotal role of industrialisation.

Modern Forces for Anglicisation

The most important period of 'popular anglicisation' was the second half of the nineteenth century, when south Wales in particular underwent a vast industrial expansion. There is little current agreement regarding the effects of industrialisation and urbanisation on Welsh language maintenance. Thomas (1959) contends that Welsh was saved in the nineteenth century by the redistribution of a growing population consequent to industrial expansion.

Williams (1971) supports this thesis, arguing that, as industrialisation generated internal migration, the Welsh, unlike the Scots and the Irish, did not have to abandon their language and homeland for employment abroad, particularly in the New World. The rural–urban shift was capable of sustaining a new set of Welsh institutions, which gave a fresh impetus to the language and culture, institutionalising them within a new, modernising industrial domain. Geographical variations in the migration patterns of incoming Welsh and English migrants further strengthened the threshold density of specific urban communities, making some valley communities particularly Welsh in speech and some coastal towns more anglicised than hitherto. I.G. Jones (1980: 50) argues that non-Welsh migrants showed 'a preference . . . for coastal towns rather than upland valleys [which] helped to preserve relatively undiluted the essential Welsh language basis of the new culture'.

Thomas's (1959) original thesis has been challenged on two grounds. The more general criticism concerns his underplaying of the residual effect on rural socio-cultural environments by mass out-migration. The pull of urban and industrial employment weakened the demographic base of rural Wales which was so vital to the reproduction of its economic and social order. The emasculation of heartland Wales is clearly an over-exaggerated metaphor in post-war literary and political criticism, but the effect of industrialisation on rural Wales does deserve far more research, particularly by political economists, so as to reconstruct the temporal and spatial variation in the reaction to modernisation during the period 1881–1914.

The conventional view is that rural Wales suffered acute decline as a result of the urban drift of its fecund, relatively well-educated, population. The reduction of 'ethno-linguistic vitality' (cf. Giles, this volume) in the core had long-term effects upon cultural reproduction. Others have argued that there was little that was unique to rural Wales in this process. Thus a specific criticism raised by Baines (1985) is that, contrary to his earlier assertions, Thomas's (1959) industrialisation thesis is incorrect in asserting a qualitative difference to Welsh emigration from that obtaining elsewhere in these isles:

> Emigration [abroad, including Scotland and Ireland] from rural Wales was at its peak in the decade [1880s] when the South Wales coalfield was at its maximum rate of expansion in the century . . . The pattern of emigration from rural Wales was no different from most of the English urban and rural counties. Consequently, the industrialization of Wales cannot have seriously affected either the rate or the timing of emigration from the Welsh rural counties (Baines, 1985: 270; quoted in Thomas, 1987: 419).

Thomas (1987) counters this objection with a reworking of Baines's own statistical evidence and concludes (1987: 421) that

> the volume of direct net emigration abroad from rural Wales in the 1880s is 23,500 not 40,600 (i.e. 2.4% of the native population, not the 4.2% which Baines observes). In the last twenty years of the nineteenth century the Welshness of the industrial transformation of the country could not be doubted. The main explanatory factors are the net migration of rural Welsh into industrial areas, and the natural increase of these in-migrants and of the indigenous Welsh in the industrial areas for those who left Wales.

Thomas's recent reformulation portrays the industrialisation of Wales as a drama in three acts. The first act, spanning the formative period of 1780–1800, witnessed Wales in the vanguard of the Industrial Revolution, and exhibiting the traits which would come to full fruition a century later — religious dissent, cultural renaissance and political radicalism. The second act, which spanned the period 1800–1846, saw the beginning of a specifically Welsh urban form and culture (Carter, 1965; Carter & Wheatley, 1978). Wales's prime urban focus, Merthyr Tydfil, boasted a population in 1846 of 33,000, 84% of whom were Welsh-born, overwhelmingly nonconformist in religion and experimenting with the construction of a working-class ideology bent on independent political action. Its engagement in the 1831 Merthyr rising has been dubbed the threshold of the working-class consciousness. Indeed G.A. Williams (1978: 230) concludes his study of this rising with the memorable epitaph: 'In Merthyr in 1831, the prehistory of the Welsh working class comes to an end. Its history begins.'

The third act of the industrial trilogy, set in the period 1846–1900, is the crucial testing ground for the assertion that, in the nineteenth century, industrialisation did not necessarily accelerate language decline. It was a time when the twin forces of free trade economics and mineral exploitation combined to transform the coalfield regions into the foundry of empire. The steam-coal export trade witnessed a sevenfold increase in annual output from 8.5 million tons between 1854 and 1913 (Thomas, 1986: 15). But in terms of the migration and language thesis under investigation, two further developments need to be cited. The first is that the growth in the 1901 Welsh-speaking industrial population was due not only to in-migration from the core area, but also to the natural increase of a burgeoning urban population.

> In the forty years, 1861–1901, the population of Glamorgan went up by more than half a million; less than a third of this (167,000) was

due to net inward migration, and over two-thirds (367,000) was due
to excess of births over deaths. The bountiful number of children
raised in the Welsh coal-mining valleys was a major factor (Thomas,
1987: 487).

The second feature worth considering is the differential geographical
concentration of migrants. P.N. Jones's (1969) research demonstrates that
Welsh migrants were far more likely to relocate in the coalfield than in the
coastal ports of Newport, Cardiff, Penarth, Barry and Swansea which
attracted large numbers of non-Welsh born workers (Table 2.4). These
centres were critical foci for the operation of a cultural division of labour
(Hechter, 1975) and exhibited in their morphology, development, and
institutional life the new-found confidence of an urban, industrial culture,
largely but not exclusively devoted to the formation of an Anglo-Welsh
identity. Timing is critical in this development. The decade 1901–1911 was
a watershed beyond which anglicisation cascaded inexorably:

> Table [2.5] shows clearly how this flood of non-Welsh migrants
> penetrated the largely Welsh coal mining valleys of Glamorgan; the
> number of non-Welsh lifetime immigrants enumerated in the coal-
> mining area of the county doubled between 1891–1911 (from 71,687
> to 141,464) whereas the number of Welsh immigrants enumerated
> there went up by only a third (from 95,569 to 126,169). Between 1891
> and 1911 the proportion of Welsh people in the stock of lifetime
> immigrants in the coal-mining districts fell from 56% to 47% and in
> the country as a whole from 49% to 42%. The watershed revealed in
> Table [2.5] must be regarded as significant in that it threatened the
> future of the Welsh language (Thomas, 1986: 16).

TABLE 2.4   *Lifetime In-migrants Enumerated in Glamorgan in 1891 and 1911,
by Nationality and District of Residence*

| | 1891 | | | 1911 | | |
Nationality	Coalfield	Non-coalfield	Total	Coalfield	Non-coalfield	Total
Welsh	98,569	24,396	122,965	126,169	24,963	151,132
Non-Welsh	71,687	57,597	129,284	141,464	68,033	209,497
Total	170,256	81,993	252,249	267,633	92,996	360,629

Source: Jones (1969: 87–9), cited in Thomas (1986: 15).

TABLE 2.5 *Decennial Natural Increase as a Percentage of the Population at the Beginning of Each Decade*

	1861–71	1871–81	1881–91	1891–1901
Glamorgan	18.6	20.3	18.8	19.2
England and Wales	13.6	15.1	14.0	12.4

Source: *Census of England and Wales* (1911), PP (1912–13), CXI, Cd. 6258, p. 11, cited in Thomas (1986: 18).

Rural Wales, the natural domain of the Welsh language, was also changing as a result of world economic forces. Morgan (1981: 81) suggests that for two decades either side of the turn of the century, nearly 90% of the land was occupied by small-scale tenant farmers; most holdings amounted to fewer than 50 acres in size, incapable of sustaining their tillers during the periodic depressions of the times. Added to the external grain competition from the American Midwest, Argentina and the Russian steppes, was the severe financial plight of most tenants. Land hunger, class-conflict and depopulation fuelled the radical dissent of upland farming communities, separated from their landlords by religion, language and political persuasion (Jones, 1981; C. H. Williams, 1985). It was here, rather than in the prosperous industrial counties, that the seeds of Cymru Fydd and anti-anglicisation were sown with vehemence by young Welsh Liberal spokesmen such as Tom Ellis and Lloyd George (Morgan, 1970). And it was here that the mythology of a rural communitarian 'Welsh way of life' would be given fresh impetus in the form of a twentieth-century struggle for Welsh cultural defence against the sweeping tide of anglicisation (G.A. Williams, 1982).

At the national scale the material base of economic transformation was accompanied by the closer social integration of Wales and England as the century wore on. Increasingly it was the state itself which came to be identified as the chief agent of anglicisation, particularly through its education policies. It is far too limiting to argue that the introduction of compulsory education subsequent to the Education Act 1870 was the turning point in this state-wide process of cultural readjustment. However, it is undeniable that this act, together with its associated educational legislation, the Welsh Intermediate Education Act 1889, enforced English as the sole medium of education and introduced, through the formal study of language, a new awareness of English values and culture, and gave a powerful institutional fillip to anglicisation.

The children of the Welsh masses, urban and rural alike, were exposed to overriding influences which sought to downgrade regional cultures and identification and exalted the culture of the dominant state core and its value system. How the masses welcomed this 'liberation' from traditionalism and conservatism is best evidenced by the wholesale generational language shift in the period 1914–45, as reported above. English was perceived as the language of progress, of equality, of prosperity, of mass entertainment and pleasure. The wider experience of Empire-building, understandably, made acquisition of English a most compelling and instrumental motivation, and the key to participation in the burgeoning British-influenced world economy.

Closer economic and administrative association with the rest of the UK followed the standardisation of education and local government (C.H. Williams, 1982; 1985). The whole modernisation process reinforced the dominance of English and saw the denigration of Welsh accompanied by a debased self-awareness on behalf of its speakers. Refusal to speak Welsh with one's children was a common enough reaction to the status differential which developed between the language groups. Added to this was the failure to utilise Welsh in a wide range of new speech domains. Whether by policy choice or the habit of neglect, Welsh became increasingly marginalised. It lost ground especially among those groups most exposed to the opportunities of an improved standard of living in the urban culture of the south and north-east.

A prime vehicle of modernisation was the rapidly expanding communication network of the late nineteenth century. Social communication theorists have long stressed the importance of both physical and social communication in the development of self-conscious nations and in the process of cultural reproduction and replacement. In Wales, geographic isolation had provided some basis for cultural differentiation. However, the development of an externally-derived communication system had served to reduce that isolation. Technology was to overcome the friction of distance. The critical factors influencing the development of the transport system were defence and commerce, in that it was designed to facilitate through-traffic from England to Ireland. The main routes ran east–west along the northern and southern coasts respectively, with branch lines penetrating the resource-rich hinterland, allowing the exportation of slate, coal and steel. This had the effect of integrating south Wales economically with the Bristol region and London, and north Wales with the Lancashire conurbations of Liverpool and Manchester. Wales's poorly developed internal road and rail system hardly contributed to the creation of a nationally shared space and territorial identification (Figure 2.1).

The Socio-demographic Profile of Change: Census Evidence, 1891–1981

Before we reconstruct the dominant changes identified by the census returns it is vital that we cite several source and methodological problems. A persistent problem in identifying long-term language trends for small areas is the fact that information is not presented on a systematic basis. As Pryce & Williams (1988) demonstrate, no single territorial unit has ever been adopted consistently from 1891 onwards. Apart from data collected at the national scale, no other scale-specific data are available for the whole census period. Important innovations were made in 1921 when statistics were recorded at the civil parish level, and again in 1961 when urban wards were treated as the equivalent in statistical terms to the existent civil parishes in rural areas. Thus, though voluminous, census data do not permit a comprehensive time-series analysis of change at the local scale, a major drawback in the analysis of such a finely-tuned and complex process as anglicisation.

The major socio-linguistic feature to note is that at the beginning of the period (1891) 54% of the Welsh population were recorded as Welsh-speaking, of whom 30.1% were monoglot Welsh in speech. By 1901 Wales had experienced a sharp decline in the monolingual Welsh reserve (a 50% reduction), a consequent increase in the bilingual category and an overall increase in the proportion able to speak English from 68.9% to 84.6%. These trends were associated with the increasing industrialisation of Wales, which internally required proficiency in spoken English, and externally induced migration into the coalfields, ports and market towns of the country. Thus the proportion of the settled Welsh population born in England rose at previous census counts from 11.3% in 1871, to 13.4% in 1881, 15.8% in 1891 and 16.1% in 1901.

These changes represented an actual population composition in 1901 of 928,222 monoglot English speakers, 280,905 monoglot Welsh speakers and 648,919 Welsh-English bilinguals. A total of 1,577,141 identified themselves as able to speak English, and 929,824 reported themselves as Welsh speakers. Interestingly, Welsh monoglots were concentrated in the heartland counties of Anglesey (48.0%), Caernarfon (47.6%), Merioneth (50.6%), Cardigan (50.4%) and Carmarthen (35.6%). They were able to communicate and live a fully Welsh daily life because these same core counties were overwhelmingly Welsh-speaking at this time, Merioneth (93.7% Welsh), Cardigan (93.0%), Anglesey (91.0%), Carmarthen (90.3%) and Caernarfon (89.5%) being clearly differentiated from the rest of Wales (Figure 2.2). The language data reveal a preponderance of middle-aged and elderly Welsh speakers, especially amongst monoglots, a characteristic early warning sign of the demise of the minority monoglot population. However, the overwhelming concentration of Welsh speakers within predominantly rural areas should not overshadow the fact that as late as 1901 there were still 50 urban districts, of a national total of 105, with over 50% of their population returned as Welsh-speaking. The proportion of the national total of Welsh speakers within urban environments would never reach that peak density again in the twentieth century.

In the early decades of the twentieth century English continued to displace Welsh as the dominant language. Between 1901 and 1911, the monoglot Welsh population shrank from 15.1% to 8.5% of the total population. After 1911, understandably, the bilingual category fell from a peak of 35.0% to 30.8% in 1921. Since 1891 there had been an average decline among all Welsh speakers of 5.63% per decade, but this general decline subsumed the specific decline of 23.8% among the monoglot Welsh category. By 1921 this represented a population composition of 155,990 monoglot Welsh, 766,103 bilinguals and 1,446,211 monoglot English.

During this period several counties effectively lost their constituent Welsh monoglot populations. For example, monoglot Welsh proportions fell by 20,000 in Glamorgan, while Carmarthenshire and Caernarfonshire suffered losses in excess of 10,000 in the period 1901–11, with the greatest loss being: 9,396 monoglots in Caernarfonshire, 6,179 monoglots in Glamorgan and just less than 5,000 in other counties.

The bilingual pattern fluctuates. Between 1901 and 1911 the number of bilinguals was increasing at a slightly higher rate than the general population. Glamorgan (1901–11), which contained 45.0% of all bilinguals, experienced an increase of 70,000 recorded bilinguals, only to display a decline of 18,616 in the next decade (1911–21). Of the remaining counties six show marginal increases in their bilingual population while the other six show an absolute decline. The largest increase was recorded for Carmarthenshire, at 11,893.

After 1918 anglicisation was quickened by the economic depression of the late 1920s and the structural effects of a second war. Both events were to have socially and geographically specific impacts on language choice by domain, on the economy, on patterns of interregional migration, employment levels and feelings of identification with a wider British population. Allowing for all the myriad fluctuations in group- and occupation-specific prosperity, in general the combined effect of the depression and of the war was to set in train the embryonic growth of the service sector, which gradually began to displace the once dominant extractive and secondary manufacturing industries (C.H. Williams, 1980). The short-term effect was an increased awareness that the structure of Welsh-industry was ill-suited to the demands of the post-war recovery which necessitated massive capital investment in the infrastructure of both commercial and public institutions and a redeployment of the labour force to the developing industrial areas.

The link between warfare and ethnic identification has been under-researched, and that between the state's war demands and anglicisation hardly broached in Wales. We need to know far more about the effects of conscription, of migration, of socialisation experiences, of identity re-evaluation, in short of the necessary intrusion of anglicising state institutions into all spheres of Welsh life, before we can identify the full impact of war on the minority 'Welsh way of life' (C.H. Williams, 1980: 220–21; J.E. Jones, 1970: 215–97). Our problems of measurement are compounded by the absence of the 1941 census poll. However, at the next census in 1951, 714,686 Welsh speakers were recorded, a decline of 194,575 (21.4%) from the 1931 figure of 909,261. Again, as might be expected, the sharpest decline was in the Welsh monoglot category, which fell by a staggering 58.0%, from 97,932 in 1931 to 41,155 in 1951. In contrast, the proportion of monoglot English speakers during the same period increased by 12.5% (see Figure 2.3). Successive inter-censal decline of 8.4% (1951–61) and 5.2% (1961–71) reduced the total Welsh speaking population to 542,425 by 1971, a loss of 113,577 persons in a decade. A further decline to 503,549 by 1981 brought the proportion of Welsh speakers down to its lowest ever level of 18.9% of the population. This represents a proportional loss of 24.6% in the period 1911–1981.

It is evident from Table 2.6 that the monolingual reservoir of Welsh speech has all but disappeared in the period 1921–81. Purists might argue that this spells the eventual demise of the language, for without an independent pool of monolinguals, no separate, autonomous Welsh culture exists. I do not accept this position, but the elimination of the monolingual element is a significant factor in its own right and should not be underplayed. To all intents and purposes the current Welsh-speaking population is functionally bilingual, though of course the census does not indicate which is the dominant language in this bilingual context.

Neither should we interpret Table 2.6 as indicating that in the counties of Gwynedd and Dyfed, Welsh is the predominant first language of 61% and 46% of the population respectively. The census records language ability and potential usage, *not* actual usage; we have to rely on detailed, local socio-cultural surveys to elicit the range and intensity of spoken Welsh, and then use these data to inform our interpretation of census results. However, we can suggest that, whereas Gwynedd and Dyfed are still the strongholds of a resurgent Welsh-speaking culture, industrial south Wales, as represented by Mid- and West Glamorgan, has lost its significant Welsh-speaking element

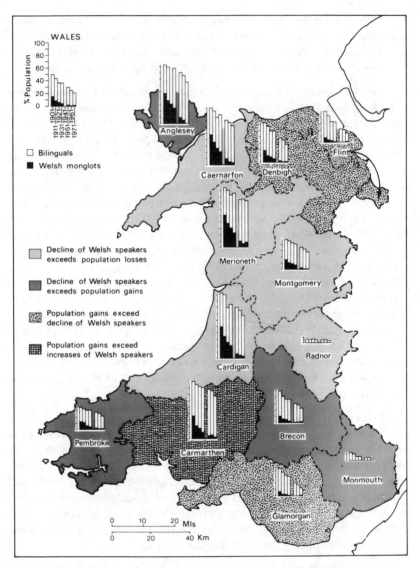

FIGURE 2.3 *Welsh monoglots, bilinguals and patterns of change in relation to population movements, 1901–71*
Source: Pryce (1978: 231)

(cf. Mid-Glamorgan — 38% in 1921 down to 8% in 1981 — and West Glamorgan — 41% in 1921 down to 16% in 1981). Indeed, the only signs of proportional growth in the last decade are in Gwent and South Glamorgan, a feature we will examine in relation to demographic change and education policies.

TABLE 2.6 *Proportion of Population Speaking Welsh, by county, 1921–81*

	Percentage of all persons speaking Welsh						Percentage of all persons speaking Welsh only					
	1921	1931	1951	1961	1971	1981	1921	1931	1951	1961	1971	1981
Wales	37.1	36.8	28.9	26.0	20.8	18.9	6.3	4.0	1.7	1.0	1.3	0.8
Counties												
Clwyd	41.7	41.3	30.2	27.3	21.4	18.7	5.8	3.4	1.3	0.8	1.4	0.8
Dyfed	67.8	69.1	63.3	60.1	52.5	46.3	15.3	9.6	4.1	2.4	2.4	1.6
Gwent	5.0	4.7	2.8	2.9	1.9	2.5	0.2	0.1	0.1	0.2	0.1	0.1
Gwynedd	78.7	82.5	74.2	71.4	64.7	61.2	28.1	22.1	9.1	5.2	4.9	2.6
Mid-Glamorgan	38.4	37.1	22.8	18.5	10.5	8.4	2.3	0.8	0.3	0.4	0.8	0.5
Powys	35.1	34.6	29.6	27.8	23.7	20.2	6.1	3.9	1.6	0.9	1.0	0.9
S. Glamorgan	6.3	6.1	4.7	5.2	5.0	5.8	0.2	0.1	0.1	0.1	0.4	0.2
W. Glamorgan	41.3	40.5	31.6	27.5	20.3	16.4	3.6	1.3	0.5	0.5	1.0	0.8

Source: Census 1981 Welsh Language in Wales, Table 4, p. 50.

Although Pryce (this volume) alludes to the inroads made by recent developments in Welsh-medium education as a spur to the age-specific growth in the numbers of Welsh-speakers in Gwent and, we may add, also South Glamorgan, it is still salutary to document that in 1986 28,167 (91.2%) of Gwent's secondary school pupils received no lessons in Welsh whatsoever. The figure for South Glamorgan is also very high (60.5%), in contrast with 22 students (0.1%) in Gwynedd. At the primary level Gwent's distinctiveness is even more evident, for in 233 schools (97.5%) no Welsh is taught at all, compared with South Glamorgan's better performance at the primary level of only 60 schools (38.7%) not teaching Welsh. In Gwynedd by contrast only one school (0.5%) did not teach Welsh.

These are disturbing statistics, for despite the opening of new primary and secondary schools in these two most anglicised counties, the overwhelming proportion of their children at secondary level will not have had the opportunity to study many subjects, let alone Welsh itself, through the medium of Welsh, and this must surely increase the trend toward anglicisation in these more prosperous and populous counties.

The contemporary scene is replete with new opportunities, old ironies and continuing paradoxes in Welsh–English language relations. Almost all Welsh-speakers are bilingual; thus bilingualism refers to a personal capacity as well as a societal norm which operates in many parts of the country. However, unlike the nineteenth century, bilingual Wales does not refer to a cultural zone of transition between a Welsh monoglot heartland and an anglicising periphery. The geographical parameters of language have changed markedly and these will have profound implications for the ability of Welsh to maintain itself in old domains, let alone penetrate new ones. The territorial dimension of language loss has become a central issue in the analysis of anglicisation (see Figure 2.4).

In the past decade attention has focused on the possibility of adopting a language districts policy, drawing in part on the Canadian and Finnish experiences (C.H. Williams, 1987: 24–27). However, whereas a monolingual Welsh-speaking territory may have been able to be rooted in a formal local government region in 1951, the geolinguistic fragmentation that has occurred since has rendered any such comprehensive language districting on a county level obsolete (C.H. Williams, 1987). Because Welsh-speakers are now scattered throughout the land, I argued that a locally sensitive and functional piecemeal organisation of territory would lead to greater inter-communal harmony and the respecting of both language groups' rights, than would a system based upon the formal principles of language planning. Without recourse to the establishment of a national language plan, a language ombudsman, a language commissioner or a new Welsh Language Act,

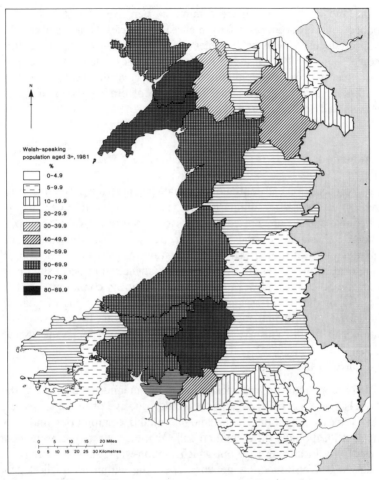

FIGURE 2.4 *The Welsh-speaking Population Aged 3+ in 1981.*
Source: Williams (1984: 118)

Gwynedd County Council has, through stealth and local political diplomacy, gone a long way to establishing a functional as well as a formal bilingual administrative regime, and this may be the most realistic way forward for language planning at the local level.

The land is not just a context for the recognition of language rights, it is also significant in other respects, such as a material base for specific socio-economic existence, a repository for cultural memories, and a sense of place. Land and language are intimately related in Welsh history and the concern with the defence of the Welsh heartland today is explicable in terms of the one resource which the community perceives that it owns, and has not been entirely appropriated by anglicising agencies. Defence of community naturally focuses on those variables which give distinction and identity to a people. Thus we do not argue that the language struggle is the essence of all conflict between a community and central government, but that through the discourse of language struggle, a range of other communal issues can be mediated and addressed (G. Williams, 1986).

Conclusion

Anglicisation will continue to animate passions and prejudices in Wales. The historic processes summarised in Table 2.1 have still not yet run their full course and we are poised at a delicate juncture in Welsh socio-political history. Resistance to the anglicising trend is evidence enough of the malintegration of the British state formation, at least in so far as it affects a minority within the minority. However, anglicisation bespeaks the wider political and cultural power not just of the majority community in the UK, but also of the world system itself, which shows no signs of abandoning English as its principal medium of communication. In consequence, any national attempt to conserve the Welsh language which denies the significance of an historically transcendant English-inspired culture and context is idealistic and naive in the extreme.

A more realistic and socially informed manner of promoting the use of Welsh within a bilingual context would conceive of its target population less in terms of national heartland–hinterland communities and more in terms of locationally differentiated collectivities, who may in some counties constitute a local majority, but which, nation-wide, should be regarded as nodes in a Welsh-medium network operating within an anglicised public sector environment. This does not automatically consign Welsh to being a functionally dependent language, for, as we have seen, since the 1950s considerable progress has been made in institutionalising Welsh as an equal language in several public domains. Local primacy can be effected through control over the local state apparatus, as has happened in Gwynedd County Council. And we now have a rudimentary foreshadowing of a desirable bilingual public service in such fields as education, public health, the law and the mass media. Welsh-medium education is particularly vital in cultural reproduction for it has become the main agency by which second language learners have been added to the critical mass of Welsh speakers, and through which both first and second language speakers become socialised into a relatively autonomous Welsh cultural system (C.H. Williams, 1985). However, as I have alerted elsewhere, there is also a real danger in underresourcing and overburdening the education system as 'the saviour of the Welsh language' (C.H. Williams, 1987).

Incremental change seems likely to improve the range of sociolinguistic domains within which the Welsh language may be used legally. The current debate on language planning has already signposted a number of pressing reforms in the infrastructure of the local state, and the Welsh Office is currently considering widespread structural support for the language at the national level. It is, of course, quite a different question as to whether or not such reforms will be paralleled in the world of industry and commerce, a vital domain for the institutionalisation of Welsh-language rights if they are to expand beyond public sector recognition. It is also worth speculating, having established the legal precedent for language usage in wider social domains, whether individual behaviour will accommodate to this new found freedom of expression in hitherto restricted domains.

Let me close by reiterating the duality of anglicisation. It is on the one hand a liberating force, permitting an entry into a British social order and the wider world beyond with all its positive advantages to the individual; simultaneously, it is a competitive set of instruments through which English hegemony was established over vast parts of Wales. The crisis of the modern Welsh character is that it is derived both from the original Welsh and the Anglo-Welsh cultures, but in a very real sense we must conclude that, as all Welsh speakers are bilingual, even their Welsh culture is heavily infused by the influence of anglicised values and behaviour patterns. In that respect it may be that we are currently witnessing the abandonment of a traditional autonomous Welsh culture and its reproduction as a small but significant variation on a more universal theme, the post-modern advanced industrial society.

Note to Chapter 2

1. I wish to thank Jane Williams and Paul Taylor for their cartographic assistance and Nik Coupland and W.T.R. Pryce for their comments on an earlier draft. I should also like to thank W.T.R. Pryce and David Thomas for their permission to reproduce material in the figures.

References

AITCHISON, J.W. and CARTER, H. 1987, The Welsh language in Cardiff: a quiet revolution. *Transactions of the Institute of British Geographers*, 12: 482–92.
AMBROSE, J.E. and WILLIAMS, C.H. 1981, On the spatial definition of minority. In

E. HAUGEN et al. (eds), Minority Languages Today. Edinburgh: Edinburgh University Press.

ATTRIDGE, D. et al. 1987, Post-Structuralism and the Question of History. Cambridge: Cambridge University Press.

BABER, C. and WILLIAMS, L.J. (eds) 1986, Modern South Wales. Cardiff: University of Wales Press.

BAINES, D. 1985, Migration in a Mature Economy: Emigration and Internal Migration in England and Wales, 1861–1900. Cambridge: Cambridge University Press.

BENDIX, R. 1978, Kings or People. Berkeley: University of California Press.

CARTER, H. 1965, The Towns of Wales. Cardiff: University of Wales Press.

CARTER, H. and WHEATLEY, S. 1978, Some aspects of the spatial structure of two Glamorgan towns in the nineteenth century. The Welsh History Review, 9: 32–56.

DEVINE, T.M. and DICKSON, D. (eds) 1983, Ireland and Scotland, 1600–1850. Edinburgh: John Donald.

DURKACZ, V.E. 1983, The Decline of the Celtic Languages. Edinburgh: John Donald.

HECHTER, M. 1975, Internal Colonialism: The Celtic Fringe in British National Development, 1536–1966. London: Routledge and Kegan Paul.

HOWELL, D.W. 1974, The impact of the railways on agricultural development in nineteenth-century Wales. The Welsh History Review, 7: 40–62.

HUME, I. and PRYCE, W.T.R. (eds) 1986, The Welsh and their Country. Llandysul: Gomer.

JONES, D.V. 1966, The Merthyr riots of 1831. The Welsh History Review 3: 173–205.

JONES, I.G. 1980, Language and community in nineteenth century Wales. In SMITH (1980).

JONES, J.E. 1970, Tros Gymru. Swansea: Tŷ John Penry.

JONES, P.N. 1969, Some aspects of the immigration into the Glamorgan coalfield between 1881 and 1911. Transactions of the Honourable Society of Cymmrodorion, 87–89.

LEWIS, G.J. 1979, The geography of cultural transition: the Welsh borderland 1750–1850. The National Library of Wales Journal, 21: 131–44.

——1980, The geography of religion on the middle borderlands of Wales in 1851. Transactions of the Honourable Society of Cymmrodorion, 123–42.

MORGAN, K.O. 1970, Wales in British Politics, 1868–1922. Cardiff: University of Wales Press.

——1981, Rebirth of a Nation: Wales 1880–1980. Cardiff: University of Wales Press.

PRYCE, W.T.R. 1975, Industrialism, urbanisation, and the maintenance of culture areas: north-east Wales in the mid-nineteenth century. The Welsh History Review, 7: 307–40.

——1978, Welsh and English in Wales, 1750–1971. Bulletin of the Board of Celtic Studies, 28: 1–36.

PRYCE, W.T.R. and WILLIAMS, C.H. 1988, Source and methods in the study of language areas: a case study of Wales. In C.H. WILLIAMS (ed.), Language in Geographic Context. Clevedon: Multilingual Matters, 167–237.

ROBINSON, W.R.B. 1988, The Tudor revolution in Welsh government 1536–1543: its effect on gentry participation. The English Historical Review, January, 1–20.

SMITH, D. (ed.) 1980, A People and a Proletariat. London: Pluto Press.

THOMAS, B. 1959, Wales and the Atlantic economy. Scottish Journal of Political Economy, 6: 169–92.

——(ed.) 1962, The Welsh Economy: Studies in Expansion. Cardiff: University of Wales Press.

——1986, The Industrial Revolution and the Welsh Language. In BABER and WILLIAMS (1986).

——1987, A cauldron of rebirth: population and the Welsh language in the nineteenth century. *The Welsh History Review*, 17: 418–37.

WALTERS, R. 1980, Capital formation in the south Wales coal industry, 1840–1914. *The Welsh History Review*, 10: 68–91.

WILLIAMS, C.H. 1980, Language contact and language change in Wales: a study in historical geolinguistics. *The Welsh History Review*, 10: 207–38.

——(ed.) 1982, *National Separatism*. Cardiff: University of Wales Press.

——1984, Ideology and the interpretation of minority cultures. *Political Geography Quarterly*, 3, 105–25.

——1985, When nationalists challenge: when nationalists rule. *Environment and Planning, C*, 3: 27–48.

——1987, The land in linguistic consciousness: evidence from the British Isles. *Sociolinguistica*, 1: 13–29.

——(ed.) 1988, *Language in Geographic Context*. Clevedon: Multilingual Matters.

WILLIAMS, G. 1971, Language, literacy and nationality in Wales. *History*, 56: 1–16.

——(ed.) 1986, The sociology of Welsh. *International Journal of the Sociology of Language*, 66.

WILLIAMS, G.A. 1961, The making of radical Merthyr, 1800–36. *The Welsh History Review*, 1: 161–92.

——1981, The Merthyr election of 1835. *The Welsh History Review*, 10: 359–97.

——1982, *The Welsh in Their History*. London: Croom Helm.

——1985, *When Was Wales?* London: Black Raven Press.

WILLIAMS, J. 1985, *Digest of Welsh Historical Statistics*, (2 vols). Cardiff: HMSO, Government Statistical Service.

WILLIAMS, W.O. 1964, The survival of the Welsh language after the Union of England and Wales: The First Phase, 1536–1642. *The Welsh History Review* 2: 67–93.

WORSLEY, P. 1984, *The Three Worlds: Culture and World Development*. London: Weidenfeld and Nicolson.

3   Language Shift in Gwent, c.1770–1981

W.T.R. PRYCE

Today, Gwent is the most anglicised of all the counties of Wales.[1] Nevertheless, place-name evidence and settlement history place the county, without question, on the Welsh side of the cultural border. The principal exceptions include the Wye valley and parts of the southern Severnside shoreline where the Norman 'overprint' was to become most marked. Elsewhere, even after the Acts of Union, Welsh life, economic and social organisation and Welsh culture were to continue throughout the centuries with little disturbance (Sylvester, 1969: 105–07, 377–410; Courtney, 1983). However, as is well known, the making of iron along the northern rim of the coalfield in the later eighteenth century, the substantial development of commercial coalmining in the western valleys of the Ebwy, Sirhywi and Rhymni rivers in the nineteenth century, and the expansion of market towns and ports were all to bring changes in cultural geography which were to make Gwent fundamentally different compared with earlier times. In 1901, when the census first began to make accurate enumerations of Welsh speakers, some 35,690 persons, accounting for 13% of the county's total population of 274,415 persons aged three years and over, were returned as being able to speak Welsh. Two thousand and thirteen of them knew no other language. By 1981, when Gwent's population had increased substantially to reach 419,970, the number of Welsh speakers had declined progressively to a mere 2.5%, including 512 Welsh monoglots, residing mainly in the older industrial valley townships of the west.

The absolute numbers of Welsh speakers continued to fall throughout the nineteenth century. Thus, it is a truism that, for many years now, the language has tended to die with the people. Welsh speakers have tended to be found concentrated in the upper age groups: in 1901, 35% of them were enumerated with ages of 45 years and over. This is a significantly higher proportion than the 18% of the resident population as a whole recorded in the same age cohorts. In 1981, these age groups accounted for an even higher proportion of Welsh speakers, 47%, compared with 39% of the population generally. Now, however, for the first time the census revealed slightly higher proportions (2.56%) of bilingual Welsh children in the pre-school 3–4 age group, than in the population (2.34%). These percentages, however, are small and at this point in time not too much significance should be read into such interesting potential signs of change.

The longer-term changes that have occurred in the linguistic geography of Gwent are themselves dramatic and of very considerable interest. Indeed, as some recent commentators have pointed out, the county has experienced a complete linguistic transformation in little more than three generations, changes which, from the viewpoint of questions concerning the ultimate survival of the Welsh language, are traumatic in nature, giving rise to a very difficult context for its public usage. If history does provide object lessons, then the Gwent experience is not without significance for those other parts of the country which today are facing severe challenges to the Welsh way of life (S.R. Williams, 1985b).

Although Gwent is today the 'least Welsh' part of Wales, nevertheless the fact that these linguistic changes have all occurred so recently — that is, virtually within living memory — means that Welsh has left the county with a number of rich endowments. Its former overwhelming Welshness is revealed, not just in the very large and comprehensive array of place names, but also on the lips of its people in that they now speak a most distinctive form of colloquial English (Parry, 1985). Moreover, the residual effects of the old language have endowed them with an ethnic consciousness which, in varying ways, continues the cultural links with their fellow countrymen in the rest of Wales. Thus, although no longer widely spoken, in Gwent the Welsh language and culture continue to have long-standing significance for ordinary people.

What were the processes of language change in Gwent and why was it achieved so rapidly and so all-embracingly?

The Pre-industrial Period

No one living in Gwent before the industrialisation of its northern and western valleys could ever have contemplated the virtual disappearance of the Welsh language from everyday usage. Welsh was the language of ordinary people everywhere, throughout the greater part of the rolling countryside east of the River Usk as much as in the scattered upland communities of the west. The Welsh bardic tradition with its rich literary culture was indigenous (Bradney, 1926; G.J. Williams, 1958; see also Roderick, 1981a; 1981b). Moreover, it was within the flanking districts of the Vale of Usk — districts that were to become substantially English in speech by the late eighteenth century — that prosperous farmers and landowners embellished their manor houses and the local parish churches with inscriptions in Welsh, their own language, rather than in Latin, then the language of scholarship, or in English. Such inscriptions, commemorating a wide range of sentiments, events and personages, still survive today as at Usk (dated 1430), Coed-cwnwr in the parish of Llangyfiw (Llangeview) (1612), Cemais (Kemeys Inferior) (1623), Llanfair Discoed (1635), Tre'r-gaer (Tregare) (1638), Bryngwyn (near Raglan) (1664), Wonastow (c.1600) and at St Mellons (dating from the early 1700s).

The old Corn Market at Pontypool, built 1730, carries a bilingual sign recording details of Frances Bray, its founder. Similarly, an oak bedroom panel dated 1594 at Llanfihangel Court (Llanfihangel Crucornau), situated four miles north-east of Abergavenny, carries, appropriately, the instruction *Kofia dy ddechre* ('Remember your origins') while the Green House, a roadside inn at Llantarnam, on the southern outskirts of Cwmbrân, still displays the sign advertising *Cwrw da a seidr i chwi* ('good beer and cider for you'), dated and erected in 1719 (Evans, 1953: 27, 305, 350, 376, 383, 477, 501, 514, 522; Bradney, 1921: 60; 1923: 143, 224, 288). With, perhaps, the exceptions of the lower Wye valley and the shores of the Bristol Channel, for rich and poor, for landowner and peasant — indeed, for all conditions of men — throughout Gwent Welsh was the language of everyday life (Bradney, 1926: 3). In all likelihood English would sometimes be heard in the then small towns, most probably in Monmouth and Chepstow. But further west, even in a major regional centre such as Abergavenny, Welsh remained the dominant language — to such an extent that at least one local citizen felt compelled to settle his son in London so that he might acquire a sound knowledge of English 'without any corruption from his mother tongue which doth commonly infect men of our countree' (MacCann & Connolly, 1933: 56).

In the mid-seventeenth century Welsh still extended further east beyond Gwent into adjacent parts of England. Thus, Enderbie (1661) observed that 'the Welsh tongue is commonly used and spoken England-ward' of Offa's Dyke, extending into the adjacent parts of Herefordshire and into Gloucestershire. Indeed, the language continued to be used in the Ewyas and Archenfield districts of Herefordshire throughout much of the eighteenth century, the last native speaker finally dying at Clodock in 1883 (Enderbie, 1661: 209, 216; Charles, 1963: 88, 95–96).

It is not until 1771, however, when the Bishop of Llandaf required the parochial clergy to report on the language or languages used locally for public worship, that we have sufficient details to enable us to reconstruct the principal language zones then existing in Gwent (Figure 3.1). As we saw in the previous chapter, there are good grounds for accepting the general validity of this information. The surviving returns refer specifically to some 119 different churches which, at 87% of an estimated total of some 134 parishes, must be regarded a very high survival rate for records never intended to be anything more than ephemeral (Pryce, 1978a). These visitation records also included returns on the language of worship within the various churches of Herefordshire (then part of the Diocese of St David's) lying across the political border on the English side of the Hondda and Monnow rivers. For methodological reasons, the location and orientation of the main language divides discussed here may differ in detail from those shown for Gwent on maps of Wales as a whole (Pryce, 1978b; 1980).

The Welsh-speaking areas

From Figure 3.1 it is clear that during the later decades of the eighteenth century, the major language divides between Welsh and English coincided with the north–south orientation of the River Usk. Within this narrow sinuated zone it can be assumed that Welsh and English enjoyed roughly equal currency. From the evidence cited so far, it is clear that by 1771 the Welsh language was already in retreat. Yet, when J. Gardner toured Gwent in the 1740s he was impressed by the fact that 'the people seldom acquired English', but revealed his ethnocentricity when he stated that 'the multiplication of languages [sic] is a more immediate and perhaps a more fruitful source of moral evil than the frailty of Adam and Eve or the loves of Cupid and Psyche' (Ravenstein, 1879: 613, quoting Gardner, 1746; Ravenstein refers to this remark as 'pathetic'!).

Everywhere throughout the west, Welsh was the language of daily life and for public worship and religious instruction: even in the coastal, marshy lowlands in the vicinity of St Bride's Wentloog where, according to local records, since all the yeoman farmers spoke nothing but Welsh, they had to make special arrangements for their sons to acquire a working fluency in English (V. Thomas, 1987: 6). Already by 1771 English had been introduced for the church catechism.[2] This latter practice, designed to help the young to learn English, was an arrangement widely implemented throughout the Welsh-speaking west and was to become increasingly popular

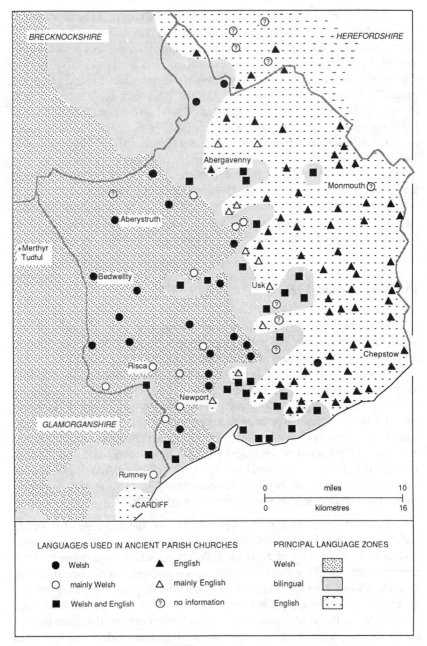

FIGURE 3.1 *Language areas, 1771*
Sources: NLW MSS. Church in Wales Records LL/QA/4–5; SD/QA/182 (1762).

during the nineteenth century — even by the nonconformist bodies who, in our own times, are often credited with having worked for the retention and promotion of Welsh.[3]

A generation later, the 1809 visitation returns show that Welsh was still retained as the sole language of worship through much of west Monmouthshire: in central districts, such as at Llanhiledd (Llanhilleth), from where the bishop was informed that worship continued to be held once on a Sunday 'in British'; at Llanddewi Fach (lying east of present-day Cwmbrân) where worship in Welsh was 'the usual custom'; and, similarly, from Aberystruth, folded, as it was, in the uplands of Blaenau Gwent, it was stated that the people worshipped 'Once in British at ten in the morning for many ages past'.[4] As Figure 3.1 shows, by this time Welsh had already contracted westwards out of Herefordshire back into Wales, and also out of the parishes of north Gwent. In reality, of course, the Archenfield district of Herefordshire had at one time been an integral part of Wales but the boundaries imposed by the Act of Union were to ensure an English future for these old Welsh communities (Rees, 1967: 29–30; Griffiths, 1980).

English-speaking areas

After reviewing all the surviving evidence, Bradney (1926: 2) concluded that the demise of Welsh as a community language everywhere seems to have commenced c.1750 and by 1771 English was the sole language used in virtually every parish church east of the Vale of Usk. Indeed, English was so deeply entrenched by 1809 that it could be reported that it was the language of worship 'by custom' (Widston), since 'time immemorial' (Undy) or 'as usual' (Llangwm).[5] The general tendency among the clergy and the minor gentry to regard English as the language of opportunity ensured that communal memories were short.

Further west, as the bilingual zone was approached, increasingly the visitation returns contain evidence that, while English dominated, the Welsh language was resorted to 'sometimes' (as at Llangatwg nigh Usk); or, alternatively, the bishop was informed much more specifically that while English dominated in church services, 'a good deal of Welch Duty' was actually performed (Llanwytherin (or Llanvetherine)). From Cemais Comawnder the local clergy reported, somewhat ambiguously, that they preached 'often in Welsh but oftener in English'![6] Of course, what these returns were trying to convey was the fact that the country parsons used both languages but with a clear preference for English.

The bilingual zone

In reality, the bilingual areas shown in Figure 3.1 were communities where Welsh and English enjoyed equal status in public activities. This should not be taken to mean, as it would in our own times, that every resident used both languages. Rather, as the documentary evidence suggests, in the bilingual areas it was much more likely that individuals spoke either Welsh or English and the parish churches sought to meet the needs of different language congregations. In short, these were the transitional zones between the two major language areas. Moreover, as anglicisation proceeded, this medial bilingual zone shifted steadily westwards. In a very real sense these bilingual areas acted as the agency of language change, heralding the onset of anglicisation which, in the context of the time, meant the operation of a one-way process of language replacement leading, eventually, to the complete disappearance of Welsh from these communities. Such schools as then existed were dedicated to the exclusive promotion of English and, outside the churches and chapels, no other institutions then existed to foster the use of Welsh.

The sinuous outline and protrusions of the bilingual zone are indicative of a diffusion situation in which English speech was slowly but progressively percolating westwards. Comments from local clergy confirm the realities of life within these communities. Thus, from Bishton, a quiet hamlet seven miles east of Newport, in 1771 the single Sunday service was sometimes in English, sometimes in Welsh, 'just as with the attendances'; and, again, at Christchurch (between Newport and Caerleon) 'sometimes Welch & sometimes in English as it suites the audience'; at Llanfihangel juxta Llantarnam (on the southern outskirts of present-day Cwmbrân) Welsh was used for the main services but catechism classes for the young were conducted in English except when a Welsh circulating school had been established. Similarly, from Tredynog (Tredunnock) in central Gwent, came the statement 'both the English & Welsh languages are equally used here'. And even from the town of Usk itself, where Divine Service was always conducted in English, they continued to preach the occasional Welsh sermon.[7]

Outside the towns the usage of the two languages was much more balanced, as at Llangatwg nigh Usk where Welsh services alternated with English ones, week by week, 'by agreement of the parishioners at a Parish meeting'.[8] It is clear, however, that towards the close of the eighteenth century English had become well established in all the towns — the first reception points in any country for new ideas and new fashions (Andrew, 1934: 278). And this is the situation confirmed by the Revd J. Mills Hoare,

Vicar of St Woolloos Church in Newport. On 21 June 1771 he wrote to his bishop, reporting that English was 'the language commonly spoken and understood' and that many found difficulty in following the Welsh sermons because 'the Welsh commonly spoken [in Newport] . . . is very corrupt'. However, the linguistic situation at Betws, a mere three miles away, was quite different: so few understood any English that the vicar found it necessary to engage a Welsh-speaking curate to minister to their spiritual needs.[9]

The observations of William Coxe (1801: 2) are in broad agreement with the regional linguistic patterns shown in Figure 3.1 and effectively sum up the linguistic situation as it had evolved by the close of the eighteenth century:

> The Welsh language is more prevalent than is usually supposed: in the north-eastern, eastern, and south-eastern parts, the English tongue is in common use; but in the south-western, western, and north-western districts, the Welsh, excepting in the towns, is generally spoken. The natives of the midland parts are accustomed to both languages: in several places divine service is performed wholly in Welsh, in others in English, and in some alternately in both. The natives of the western parts, which are sequestered and mountainous, unwillingly hold intercourse with the English, retain their ancient prejudices, and still brand them with the name *Saxons*; this antipathy, however, is gradually decreasing, by means of the establishment of English schools, and the introduction of English manners, customs and manufactures.

The Nineteenth Century

Throughout the nineteenth century the bilingual zone continued to encroach into the Welsh-speaking areas of the west, adding, through its progressive conditioning, more and more parishes to the expanding English-speaking areas (Figure 3.2). From now on all the industrial valleys of the west began to show many incipient signs of anglicisation. Evidence can be found in the returns relating to the language of 'instruction or exhortation' in the nonconformist Sunday schools (published in the famous 'Blue Books' of 1847) as well as in the arrangements for public worship in the Anglican parish churches (see Pryce, 1975). Yet, all the signs indicate that the rapidly-growing industrial communities of the Rhymni valley, along with those in the lower sections of the Sirhywi valley, at this stage remained dominantly Welsh in language, in culture and outlook. When Coxe (1801: 248, 262–63)

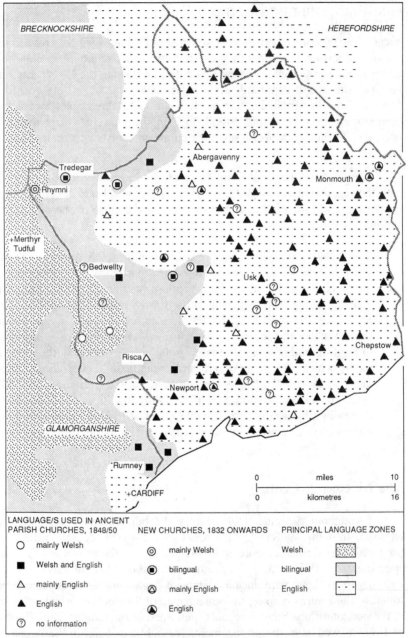

FIGURE 3.2 *Language areas in the mid-nineteenth century.*
Sources: NLW MS. Church in Wales Records LL/QA/35–37 (1848); SD/ QA/206 (1848); *Report, Commissioners of Inquiry into . . . Education*, London: HMSO, 1847, Parts I (Glamorgan, pp. 164–89); II (Brecknock, pp. 242–49; Monmouth, pp. 328–33).

visited these remote and, in the closing decade of the eighteenth century, sparsely-peopled districts, he valued the services of the Revd John Williams, his travelling companion and interpreter, because the English language was so little understood by the people he met. Fifty years later, English had arrived at Rhymni and at the ancient parish church at Aberystruth where it had been fully integrated in the public services. Nevertheless, drawing on information provided by local informants, in 1879 E.G. Ravenstein estimated that Welsh was still understood by some 74% of the population at Tredegar, Aberystruth, Mynyddislwyn and Bedwellty and, he observed, it was actively used, much more extensively than English, in churches and chapels of all kinds (Ravenstein, 1879: 614).

The underlying reasons for the dominance of Welsh in these particular areas are all tied up, intimately, with their industrialisation. All these parishes attracted great volumes of in-migrants from rural Wales — especially in the 1840s and 1850s — to the iron works and they brought with them their own language and cultural institutions (Jennings, 1934: 45, 49). As Ravenstein (1879: 614) pointed out, and as we have been reminded much more recently by Thomas (1986; 1987), without industrialisation the upper townships of these western iron- and coal-working valleys would have succumbed under the full blunt of anglicisation much earlier than they eventually did (though cf. Williams, this volume).

The buoyant, intense Welshness of western Gwent is fully evident in the famous Education Report of 1847. The Parliamentary Commissioners had been charged specifically to enquire into the state of education among the 'labouring classes', especially the means by which they could acquire a knowledge of English. Despite their controversial aspects, their final reports brought together a vast amount of descriptive and statistical information concerning the use of Welsh and the general standing of the language in the mid-nineteenth century (F. Price Jones, 1963; 1978). Officially, Monmouthshire was no longer regarded as part of Wales. Nevertheless, the Commissioners felt obliged to compile detailed information on some 18 parishes in the western part of the county because

> the great mineral basin is so thoroughly Welsh as regards the character, habits, and language of the greater part of the inhabitants, that it could scarcely have been excluded from this inquiry without injury to the comprehensiveness of the Reports.

Jelinger C. Symons was responsible for the report on Monmouthshire and he observed that these mining communities had been 'swollen by immigration', had attracted large numbers of labourers, 'induced to travel thither, lured by the golden harvest with which report invests [*sic*] mineral adventure and the wages it dispenses'. Between 1821 and 1841 the population in some of these communities had more than doubled (Education Report, 1847: 271). English was by far the main language of instruction in the 127 day schools then existing, but in the 149 Sunday schools, 80% of which were conducted by the nonconformist chapels, the linguistic situation was very different. Invariably, in these schools, the language most appropriate to the needs of ordinary people (the pupils included adults as well as children and young people) was used: 49% of these Sunday schools used both languages, in 11% Welsh was the sole language while 40% used English. It is clear that the majority of schools had made a definite decision to use Welsh because, at that time, this was the most effective way of reaching the ordinary people.

Nevertheless, equally apparent is the fact that English was deeply entrenched in all these communities: 89% of schools resorted to at least some use of that language in their work (Education Report, 1847: 289). This was very much in accord with the views of Anglican clergy, magistrates, landowners and those other leading personalities who had been invited to supply the commissioner with their own interpretation of recent linguistic trends. Invariably, all these informants replied that everywhere English was rapidly gaining ground and that this was desirable because it would make the people more deferential to their 'superiors', bring greater 'respect for the law', would make the lower orders 'more peaceful and submissive', and, on the assumption that Welsh had no literary or cultural validity, would facilitate 'their access to religious and literary works'. Welsh, it was argued, was 'a nuisance and an obstacle', imposing double burdens on the Anglican clergy (compared with their colleagues in England): 'the sooner it becomes dead, the better for the people'. Welsh, all agreed, was a secret language used by Chartists and the Rebecca rioters. Therefore, the spread of English (by providing proper schools) should be encouraged so that the law could be reinforced (Education Report, 1847: 294–95, 298, 301–04).

Yet, paradoxically, while such anti-Welsh views were being articulated, these very same western valleys were to enjoy a rich flowering of Welsh literary activities. This was a movement that appealed, essentially, to the working classes. The contributors included names that today are fully recognised among educated Welshmen far beyond the county of Gwent: Robert Ellis, a native of Montgomeryshire, known more widely by his bardic title Cynddelw; William Roberts (Nefydd), from Denbighshire; John Emlyn Jones (Ioan Emlyn), from Carmarthenshire; Evan Jones (Ieuan Gwynedd), from Merionethshire; Aneurin Jones, better known as Aneurin Fardd, a Monmouthshire man, born at Bedwas; Gwilym Ilid (Machen); and William Thomas, the famous Islwyn, who was born at Ynys-ddu in the lower Sirhywi valley (Roderick, 1981b: 9–12). The early nineteenth century also saw the establishment of the famous Cymreigyddion Society whose literary and eisteddfodic activities, under the patronage of Lady Llanofer, focused on the town of Abergavenny (M.E. Thomas, 1978). Yet, Monmouthshire's Indian summer of Welshness was to be short-lived. By 1870 most of those that had contributed to all these literary activities were dead, buried, and, locally, almost forgotten: increasingly, the Welsh language was becoming widely regarded as something of an anachronism (Roderick, 1988: 12).

The continuing demands of early iron smelting and the labour-intensive nature of the collieries were to mean that, ultimately, Wales lacked a large-enough reservoir of people to supply all the growing manpower needs (B. Thomas, 1930). And so, increasingly, labour was attracted into Gwent from adjacent parts of England, particularly Herefordshire, Gloucestershire and Somerset, and from Ireland. Kenrick's (1841) survey of the crowded social conditions in the iron-working districts includes statistics on the origins of the people and the state of the Welsh language locally. While 51% of the population of 17,196 at Trevethin were described as 'Welsh', only 106 (0.6%) were reported as unable to speak English; 44% of the population was described as 'English'; the Irish accounted for 5% (821 individuals). Unfortunately, it is not clear if the designation 'Welsh' refers to the ability to speak the language (that is, that these persons were bilingual Welshmen) or that this was merely their national affiliation. At Blaenafon, a smaller community of 5,115 persons, the Welsh formed a much larger proportion of the community: 61% were 'Welsh'; 37% were recorded as English; the Irish amounted to less than 2% of the community. Some 21 Welsh monoglots were recorded, a mere 0.4% of the population (Kenrick, 1841: 367, 373).

It is clear that as communities continued to grow, the Welsh language declined. Nevertheless, from time to time, conflicts and friction did arise between the different cultural groups, leading, sometimes, to public disturbances, particularly when English labourers had been brought in when, as Kenrick (1841: 370) stated, 'the aborigines considered it to be a wanton and unjustifiable invasion of their territory'! Ultimately, the relative isolation of these communities, exposure and the severity of the local climate, housing difficulties, the hazardous nature of work, and a community experience that blossomed into a tradition of shared hardships — eventually all these were to contribute to the evolution of an industrial proletariat and ensured that, soon, the initial cleavages between Welsh and English were to disappear. Having to live together as pioneers in a strange place affected the customs and changed the attitudes of all in-migrants, whatever their origins. By the 1920s, approaching 90% of the residents of Bryn-mawr had been born in the town but, by this time, local surveys indicate that, even though the

Welsh temperament and physical characteristics were still evident, the distinctively Welsh cultural tradition itself had been lost (Jennings, 1934: 19, 54).

The Impact of In-migration

It is clear, therefore, that commentators have placed much emphasis on the role of in-migration in bringing about the almost total anglicisation of Gwent's industrial valleys by the 1870s. Unfortunately, reliable statistical data did not become available until *after* the initial impact of industrial development had occurred. In the absence of a full statistical time series, we need to seek out surrogate information which offers broad indications of prevailing regional trends. Because of the ways in which the source data are laid out in the published census tables, we are obliged to accept registration districts (RDs)[10] as the major subdivisions of the county for analytical purposes (Figure 3.3).

FIGURE 3.3 *Registration Districts*
Sources: Census Reports, 1851–1911.

E.G. Ravenstein, in addition to his important studies concerning the distribution of the Celtic languages, also conducted pioneering research into the nature of internal migration, using the birthplace tabulations from the 1871 census reports. His famous 'laws of migration' provide a series of generalised statements based on the idea that population movements were primarily economic in origin and therefore of a selective nature. In the context of a Britain that was then undergoing rapid development, these conclusions have been widely accepted as broadly true of actual conditions and they offer us a set of useful research hypotheses (Ravenstein, 1885: 196–98; Mageean, 1982).

Iron-working districts and collieries, especially in their early developmental stages, would have experienced a strong demand for labour, giving rise, therefore, to a predominance of men in the population; when and where domestic servants were unusually numerous, as in country towns and in the larger farmhouses, we can expect to find a 'surplus' of women. Thus, Table 3.1 is based on a statistical comparison (involving the standard error for each registration area) of local sex ratios with that for England and Wales as a whole. The occurrence of significant differences (greater than

TABLE 3.1 *Sex Ratios, 1801–1851*
Per cent males in the enumerated population

	1801	*1811*	*1821*	*1831*	*1841*	*1851*
England and Wales	47.9	49.5	48.8	48.7	48.8	49.0
Monmouth Registration County	41.1*	50.1*	51.7*	51.9*	52.3*	52.1*
Registration Districts						
Chepstow	50.5*	49.5BS	50.3*	50.6*	50.0*	50.9*
Monmouth	49.1*	49.4NS	50.8*	50.1*	50.5*	50.1*
Abergavenny	49.3*	48.9NS	54.0*	53.4*	54.4*	53.6*
Pontypool	48.3*	50.2*	51.7*	53.6*	52.7*	52.0*
Newport	49.1NS	49.4NS	50.8*	50.1*	50.5*	50.1*

* significant differences at the 5% level from the sex ratio for England and Wales
BS barely significant at the 5% level
NS no significant difference
Source: Census 1851, *Population Tables 1 (Numbers of Inhabitants 1801–51), Welsh Division*. London: HMSO, 1852, pp. 6–9.

two standard deviations) points to the local importance of selective in-migration in having brought about an imbalance of the sexes.[11] It can be noted from the table that, in 1811 in particular, most areas recorded no significant differences from national trends, but all districts showed departures afterwards. Indeed, these differences increased over time and, as they became more industrialised, the Abergavenny and Pontypool RDs recorded much higher ratios of men in the population than in England and Wales generally. This evidence tends to support the fact that these communities were growing primarily by high rates of in-migration.

From 1851, a much clearer understanding of the impact of migrational change is possible because, by looking at population growth and the contribution of natural increase (the excess of births over deaths), we are in a position to calculate net migration balances into or out of a specific area, decade by decade. As can be seen from Table 3.2, the rural eastern registration districts based on Chepstow and Monmouth continued to lose population by out-migration. In the west, while the trends may appear contradictory, ultimately all the industrial areas continued to be attractive for in-migrants, especially Bedwellty where steady growth in the 1890s was to culminate in a massive 22% increase between 1901 and 1911. Similarly, Newport RD (which includes the later-developed industrial communities of the lower Rhymni, Sirhywi and Ebbw valleys) recorded substantial rates of in-migration. On the other hand, the steady decline of the older iron-working districts of Blaenafon and Abersychan is reflected in the out-migration rates for Abergavenny RD. In reality, therefore, within industrial Gwent in the later nineteenth century we see evidence of a number of complementary trends that were dependent on the waxing and waning of specific industries and localities. As one district declined, so its work-force moved on elsewhere to seek new opportunities, often just a few miles within the same or to an adjacent valley.

These statistics deal solely with net migration flows and, in themselves, indicate nothing as to the origins of migrants, nor anything concerning their cultural or ethnic identities. Not until 1891 did specific information on the languages spoken locally become available — that is, long after the industrialisation of Gwent's western valleys had been achieved. Therefore, to explore further the links between migration and the maintenance of Welshness in specific communities, we are obliged to draw on birthplace data published in the census, starting in 1851.

Sixty-five per cent of the lifetime migrants into Monmouthshire (the registration county) in 1851 recorded birthplaces in the immediately adjoining counties. A further 13% had come from other more distant parts of Wales

TABLE 3.2 *Inter-censal Net Migration Trends, 1851–1911*
This table shows net migration balances as a percentage of the enumerated population at the start of each decade. (– = out-migration; + = in-migration)

(1) Registration District	(2) 1851–60	(3) 1861–70	(4) 1871–80	(5) 1881–90	(6) 1891–1900	(7) 1901–11	(8) Summation of % decadal changes, 1851–1911
Chepstow	–17.4	–10.5	–10.7	–10.0	–12.7	–8.5	–69.9
Monmouth	–2.3	–8.4	–19.5	–18.3	–12.5	–7.8	–68.9
Abergavenny*	–1.7 {	+ 4.0	– 9.1	–10.0	–10.8	–1.1 }	+ 8.3
Bedwellty*		– 8.4	– 9.8	+ 2.2	+ 6.5	+22.2	
Pontypool	–8.8	–4.7	–14.6	– 4.2	– 1.3	+13.4	–20.3
Newport	+3.2	+3.7	– 2.5	+15.8	+ 0.3	+12.4	+32.7
Monmouth Registration County	– 3.4	– 3.7	– 9.9	+ 1.6	– 1.9	+10.9	– 6.4
*Abergavenny and Bedwellty	– 1.7	– 0.3	– 9.6	+ 1.9	+ 1.6	+16.5	+ 8.3

Sources: Census Reports 1851–1911

and about the same proportion originated in England. The English-born in-migrants, as well as the numerically much smaller numbers of Scots and Irish, tended to be concentrated in the iron-working communities of the north (in Abergavenny RD) and in Newport (see Table 3.3). Thus, as mentioned earlier, because Gwent had attracted large numbers of Welsh-speaking labourers and their families into the western valleys, industrial development delayed the full anglicisation of these communities by at least a generation. These migrants must have been drawn from those counties which, even in 1901, still recorded at least 80% of their population as speaking the Welsh language — that is, from that group of counties making up that core area of deep, inherent Welshness which has come to be known, today, as *Cymru Gymraeg* or 'Inner Wales'. The much more anglicised counties form the complementary territorial collective often referred to as *Cymru ddi-Gymraeg* or 'Outer Wales' (Pryce, 1978b: 56–60). This classification of migrant source regions is a useful device by which to obtain further insights into the ethnic and linguistic make-up of Gwent's population.

Because of data problems related to the overlap of registration areas and counties as statistical units, and also the nature of population movements during the nineteenth century, we are able to focus in detail only on aspects of longer-distance migration to the county. Thus, of the 10,810 in-migrants to Gwent with birthplaces at remote locations beyond the adjacent counties, nearly three-quarters were enumerated in Abergavenny RD which, in 1851, included all the thriving iron-making and colliery communities of the western valleys between Blaenafon and Rhymni. In the context of their all-pervading Welshness, we can highlight the fact that these particular communities accommodated 76% (some 6,275 persons in 1851) of all Gwent's in-migrants from Inner Wales — a significant and much higher proportion than those who had been born in Outer Wales (Table 3.3). In marked contrast, higher proportions of migrants from Ireland, Scotland, England, and from overseas had arrived at destinations within the Newport area.

Thus, the statistical evidence confirms the general statements of contemporary observers that it was high levels of in-migration that reinforced the Welshness of the industrial communities within the valleys of western Gwent. A similar conclusion is evident if the statistics are recast differently to show birthplace origins of the long-distance migrants within each of the registration districts (Table 3.4). The western valleys (Abergavenny RD) not only recorded the largest volume of in-migrants (12,457 persons) but also the highest proportion (63%) born in Wales. Nearly four out of every ten of these had been born within Inner Wales: almost certainly these migrants would have been natural speakers of Welsh. The communities of the Pontypool registration district (including Abersychan and Abertyleri

TABLE 3.3 *Life-time In-migration, 1851*

(1)	(2)	(3)	(4)	(5)	(6)	(7)
	Chepstow %	Monmouth %	Abergavenny %	Pontypool %	Newport %	Total (N)
Sending areas			Receiving areas			
1. Contiguous counties	15	28	30	10	17	52,137
1a Brecknock & Glamorgan	1	2	64	11	22	15,056
1b Hereford, Gloucester & Somerset	21	38	17	10	15	37,081
2. Wales (excluding 1a)	1	2	73	10	14	10,810
2a Outer Wales[1]	2	2	68	12	16	4,532
2b Inner Wales[2]	1	1	76	9	13	6,275
3. England (excluding 1b)	15	12	24	13	36	10,643
4. Scotland	8	6	20	11	55	318
5. Ireland	4	3	29	17	46	5,888
6. Foreign countries/overseas	7	10	28	11	45	584

[1] Counties of Pembroke, Radnor, Montgomery, Flint and Denbigh.
[2] Counties of Carmarthen, Cardigan, Merioneth, Caernarfon and Anglesey.
Source: Census 1851, Birthplace data, Registration Districts no. 576–580.

TABLE 3.4 *Long-distance Life-time In-migration, 1851*

	(2)	(3)	(4)	(5)	(6)
			Receiving areas		
(1)	*Chepstow* %	*Monmouth* %	*Abergavenny* %	*Pontypool* %	*Newport* %
Sending areas					
1. Wales[1]	7	10	63	31	18
1a Outer Wales[2]	4	6	25	15	8
1b Inner Wales[3]	3	4	38	16	9
2. England[4]	78	76	21	39	45
3. Scotland	1	1	1	1	2
4. Ireland	12	9	14	28	3
5. Foreign countries/ overseas	2	3	1	1	3
Total (Registration county of Monmouth)	2,031	1,697	12,457	3,605	8,453

[1] Excluding the contiguous counties of Brecknock and Glamorgan.
[2] Counties of Pembroke, Radnor, Montgomery, Flint and Denbigh.
[3] Counties of Carmarthen, Cardigan, Merioneth, Caernarfon and Anglesey.
[4] Excluding the contiguous counties of Hereford, Gloucester and Somerset.
Source: Census 1951, Birthplace Tables.

together with the lower Ebbw and the Llwyd valleys) were much less attractive to long-distance migrants, but even here 31% of them were Welsh, roughly equal numbers coming from both Inner and Outer Wales. Evidently, these trends are reflected in the much greater territorial spread of the bilingual zone by 1848 to encompass these communities (Figure 3.2).

In the research on which this chapter is based, the analysis of birthplace origins was carried forward to cover the second half of the nineteenth century and, with the exception of 1921 and 1931 (when comparable data were not published), right through to 1951. But the statistics now relate to the county as a whole and no details are given for the various registration areas as in 1851 (Table 3.5).

After 1861, as the population continued to grow, long-distance in-migration from England and elsewhere consistently out-numbered that of the Welsh. Initially, at 9% of all migrants, the supply from Inner Wales remained reasonably buoyant, but by the 1890s marginally higher proportions were being attracted from the anglicised counties of Outer Wales. Short-distance movements from the surrounding counties remained numerous. By 1911, in-movements from all parts of England had increased remarkably to account for a third of all migrants, and this continuing flow of people was maintained and is evident in the 36% of English people recorded in 1951. These accounted for a massive 69% of longer-distance migration, while during the same decades the proportions coming from remote locations in rural Wales progressively declined from one third in 1861 to a mere 10% (Table 3.6). The underlying reasons for these changes are complex, but it seems clear that they were a reflection, at least in part, of the redirection of labour flows into the expanding Glamorgan coalfield (P.N. Jones, 1969); the rapid decline and eventual collapse of the mining industry in the western valleys of Gwent in the later nineteenth century; and the revival of the market towns and especially the rise of Newport as a regional centre of growing importance for industry and commerce.

Language Areas in the Early 1900s

By the close of the nineteenth century, the bilingual zone had eclipsed all the valley communities and had been diffused further west into Glamorgan (Figure 3.4). The overall effects were that, with the exception of the upper Rhymni valley, virtually the whole of the county had now been anglicised. Many of the ancient parishes individually had passed through the complete linguistic transition — Welsh, bilingual and then English — in a matter of one or two generations (Figure 3.5). A few did retain the use of the Welsh

TABLE 3.5 *Life-time In-migration to Monmouthshire, 1861–1951*

(1)	(2)	(3)	(4)	(5)	(6)	(7)	(8)	(9)	(10)
					Receiving areas				
	1861	1871	1881	1891	1901	1911	1921	1931	1951
Sending areas	%	%	%	%	%	%	%	%	%
1. Contiguous counties	55	55	56	54	60	51	ND	ND	48
1a Brecknock & Glamorgan	23	23	23	21	26	21	ND	ND	30
1b Hereford, Gloucester & Somerset	32	32	32	33	33	29	ND	ND	17
2. Wales (excluding 1a)	15	13	12	10	10	9	ND	ND	5
2a Outer Wales[1]	6	6	6	6	6	5	ND	ND	3
2b Inner Wales[2]	9	7	6	4	4	4	ND	ND	3
3. England (excluding 1b)	17	21	23	29	23	33	ND	ND	36
4. Scotland	1	1	1	1	1	1	ND	ND	2
5. Ireland	11	10	7	4	3	2	ND	ND	2
6. Foreign countries/overseas	1	1	2	2	2	3	ND	ND	7
Total in-migration	65,036	72,932	71,964	90,202	90,948	108,655	ND	ND	111,244

[1] Counties of Pembroke, Radnor, Montgomery, Flint and Denbigh.
[2] Counties of Carmarthen, Cardigan, Merioneth, Caernarfon and Anglesey.
ND = No data
Source: Census reports 1861–1951, Birthplace Tables.

TABLE 3.6 *Long-distance Life-time In-migration to Monmouthshire, 1861–1951*

(1)	(2)	(3)	(4)	(5)	(6)	(7)	(8)	(9)	(10)
					Receiving areas				
Sending areas	1861 %	1871 %	1881 %	1891 %	1901 %	1911 %	1921 %	1931 %	1951 %
1. Wales[1]	34	29	26	22	25	19	ND	ND	10
1a Outer Wales[2]	15	14	13	13	14	10	ND	ND	5
1b Inner Wales[3]	19	15	13	10	11	9	ND	ND	5
2. England[4]	38	46	51	63	58	66	ND	ND	69
3. Scotland	2	2	2	2	3	3	ND	ND	4
4. Ireland	24	21	16	9	8	6	ND	ND	4
5. Foreign countries/ overseas	2	3	4	3	6	7	ND	ND	14
Total in-migration	29,088	33,101	31,943	41,373	36,525	53,590	ND	ND	58,436

[1] Excluding the contiguous counties of Brecknock and Glamorgan.
[2] Counties of Pembroke, Radnor, Montgomery, Flint and Denbigh.
[3] Counties of Carmarthen, Cardigan, Merioneth, Caernarfon and Anglesey.
[4] Excluding the contiguous counties of Hereford, Gloucester and Somerset.
ND = No data
Source: Census reports 1861–1951, Birthplace Tables.

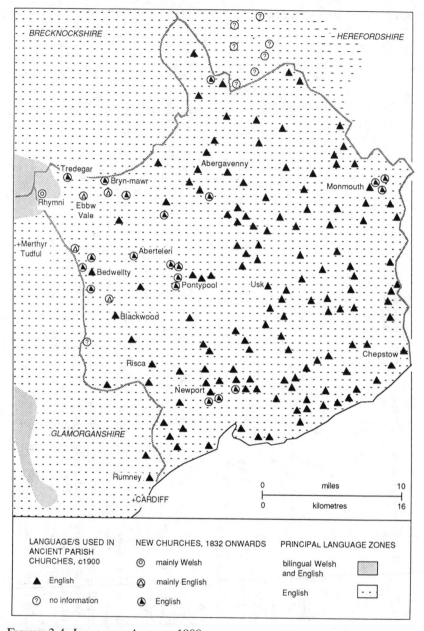

FIGURE 3.4 *Language Areas, c.*1900
Sources: *Report, Royal Commission on the Church of England . . . in . . .*
Wales. London: HMSO, 1910, Monmouthshire, pp. 368–77; Brecknockshire,
pp. 306–12; Glamorgan, pp. 347–62; NLW MSS Church in Wales Records,
SD/QA/248 (1900).

language but gradually increased the amount of English in the public services towards the end of the century. Many new churches (see Figure 3.5) were established to serve the populous communities of the valleys but, invariably, these soon abandoned the use of Welsh altogether (as at Tredegar and at Nant-y-glo) or they adopted English as the only language of worship from the outset (as at Ebbw Vale, Pontypool, Griffithstown, Fleur-de-lis).

But there are numerous signs that the language of worship in Anglican churches was not always fully representative of local conditions after the mid-nineteenth century, especially in industrial south Wales. The Report of the Royal Commission on the Church in 1911 was very critical of language policies in Llandaf diocese (which included Gwent), especially in respect of the refusal to provide services in Welsh, or partly in Welsh, for bilingual parishioners while encouraging the sole use of English everywhere (Pryce, 1978a: 19–24). Thus, it seems that the visitation returns may not be as reliable an indication of actual conditions towards the end of the century as they had been up to and including 1848 — at least, not in parishes west of the Usk River, where, to varying degrees, the Welsh language was still used by the people.

That a good deal was still being spoken is evident from the remarks of contemporary observers. George Borrow travelled through Gwent's bilingual zone in the 1850s: at Bedwas (incorrectly referred to by him as 'Pendref Bettws') in the lower Rhymni valley he came across children playing in English; a young girl informed him that she did speak Welsh 'but not very well', although it was the language of all the older people; at nearby Machen he met up with the Welsh-speaking daughter of a local landowner; east of Newport he estimated that about 10% of the population still spoke Welsh and that the language divide then lay about three miles west of Caerwent. Yet, half of all those that Borrow met on his journey replied to him in Welsh (Borrow, 1862: 709, 712–13, 723), presumably because they were people from west Gwent returning home from business in England. There can be no doubt that the linguistic situation was changing rapidly. Southall (1894: 347–48) attributed this to the departure of so many Welsh-speaking labourers from the land in the 1850s and 1860s to take up better-paid work in the mines that Englishmen and their families from Gloucestershire and from Somerset had had to be brought in as replacements.

Southall — Englishman, Quaker and publisher of Newport — was a vigorous critic of the way in which the first language census of 1891 had been organised. In his pamphlet published in 1895, he argued that, despite its shortcomings, this census showed that the monoglot Welsh remained numerous throughout west Monmouthshire and he went on to point out

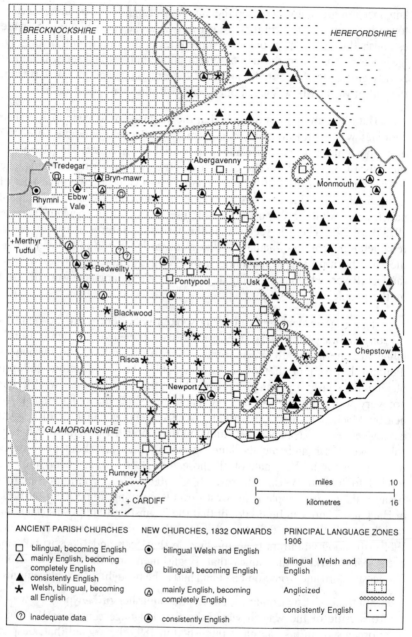

FIGURE 3.5 *Principal language zones and long-term trends at specific locations,*
*c.*1771–1906.
Sources: Based on Figures 3.1–3.4.

that the anglicised towns of Chepstow and Monmouth still returned 30 and 29 persons respectively who were 'ignorant of English'. In the Newport RD, which, as we have seen, included the communities of the lower Rhymni valley, some 2,420 Welsh monoglots were enumerated. Therefore, he argued, schools needed to teach Welsh because it was 'a desirable qualification for many public offices' and added 'even in fifty years time Welsh will be spoken in west Monmouthshire' (Southall, 1895: 11, 34–35). Despite the lengthy and forceful arguments that Southall advanced for Welsh to receive a meaningful place in schools, his advocacy met with no practical response in local schools.

All the evidence indicates that Welsh continued to be spoken widely in the western industrial valleys but it was to become more and more restricted to a colloquial context. Southall (1899:11) felt that this was insufficient 'for the preservation of the language in the century in which we live'. Because of their restricted vocabularies, he pointed out, very few young men under 40 years of age in the 1890s were equipped to appreciate the poetry of Islwyn (William Thomas, 1832–78), even in the very same area (the Sirhywi valley) where he had lived and written only a quarter of a century earlier (Southall, 1899: 19).

When the much more reliable language figures of the 1901 census enumeration were published, Southall (1904: 36) remarked that the 'continuous stream of immigration' had substantially changed the 'racial [sic] and social characteristics' of the people. After finding some solace in the fact that, because the population overall continued to grow, the absolute numbers of Welsh speakers were increasing, it is clear that Southall was bitterly disappointed in the low proportion of 13% for the county as a whole:

> A painful array of figures! Poor, miserable percentages, most of them! Where is the Patriot who will arise to save Gwent from grinding the Philistines' Corn, from losing all sight of her Cymric kinship and of Cymric ideals and speech? (Southall, 1904: 36).

The complete anglicisation of eastern Gwent had been accomplished, as we have seen, a century or more earlier (Figure 3.1). By the early 1920s, the use of Welsh in church services could not be recalled locally 'within the memory of many' and the nonconformist chapels had followed the parishes in changing to English (Bradney, 1926: 5). Those few Welsh speakers that still could be found anywhere in east Gwent usually had moved in. Southall (1894: 342), for example, reports having met an informant at Pandy railway station (actually located on the Herefordshire side of the county boundary), a native of anglicised Radnorshire, but one who had learnt Welsh in the

1850s when he worked in the Rhymni valley! So complete was the linguistic transition that many chapels in the former bilingual zone (see Figure 3.2) were experiencing 'bilingual difficulties' in 1903 before eventually making the decision to turn over to English altogether (Phillips, 1984: 4, 6; B. Davies, 1984).

Evidence examined closely by P.N. Jones shows that the advance of bilingualism had been most dramatic in the 1890s, affecting Baptist congregations first in the eastern valleys (Ebbw, Llwyd), followed later by the onset of changes further west in the Rhymni valley. According to Jones, the climax of the bilingual period was achieved in 1901. Virtually all the chapels in the Rhymni, Ebbw and Sirhywi valleys were completely English in 1914 although new Welsh causes had been started to serve local needs at Llanbradach, Cwmfelin-fach (Mynyddislwyn) and Abertyswg. Clearly, as Jones (1976: 354–55, 359) concluded, this westward retreat of Welsh was dependent on growing influences brought in by contact and hierarchical processes of diffusion.

The actual mechanisms of change have been examined closely by S.R. Williams, who points out that regional location as well as considerations of size and scale are of much relevance for explaining why some communities retained their Welshness longer than others. The eastern valleys, by virtue of their regional location, attracted, as we have seen, migrants from England and therefore were much more susceptible to early anglicisation than the western valleys. Where the flow of in-migrants was small, it could be absorbed comfortably and the new people soon adapted to the prevailing milieu and acquired a working knowledge of Welsh. But when large-scale developments were taking place, in-migrants could easily swamp a community and turn it to English, virtually overnight. Moreover, while initially the chapels functioned as bastions for the language, religious fervour on the part of patriotic Welshmen led hitherto Welsh denominations to evangelise in English. The final outcome was not, as had been intended, the conversion of the English but rather the anglicisation of the Welsh themselves (S.R. Williams, 1985b: 116)!

When, in 1882, A.J. Ellis completed his preliminary surveys for a more detailed work on English dialectology, he identified the Welsh–English line as running south from Bryn-mawr, via the Ebbw valley, west of Pontypool but passing east of Risca towards (but not quite reaching) the town of Newport. West of this line, he reported, Welsh continued to be spoken but much more widely by those who had moved in than by the 'natives' (Ellis, 1882: 192). In pointing out that everyone was strongly motivated to acquire fluency in English, his views encapsulated contemporary attitudes and feelings:

It is no longer a case of fire and sword, or of expulsion if not destruction, and it is no longer a case of conquest where the natives are forced to learn the hatred idiom. It is purely a voluntary assumption of a new language. And the motives are not far to seek. The English language opens up wide fields of employment from which the little known [sic] Welsh language shuts out a candidate. . .

. . . if a young man would 'rise', he must learn English, and he does so; and however much he may love the reminiscence of his native Welsh, and it is linguistically well worth a reminiscence, in a generation or two it slips out of his family (Ellis, 1882: 206–07).

Industrial Monmouthshire had made substantial contributions to Welsh literary culture but, in the closing decades of the nineteenth century, public opinion and popular aspirations had, in general, turned against the continued use of the old national language.

The Twentieth Century

The decline of Welsh has continued throughout the present century (see the review in Williams, this volume). In 1901, 13% of the people spoke the language but, as the population continued to grow, the proportion has halved in successive generations: 6% by 1931, 3.5% in 1951, 2.1% in 1971; and, after the slight boundary adjustments made when the new county of Gwent was created in 1974, 2.5% in 1981 (Lewis, 1980).[12]

The continuing spatial retreat is fully evident in Figure 3.6 which uses standarised shadings to show the proportions of Welsh speakers in the population of Gwent at the time of each decennial census (1901–71) in local government areas.[13] The differences between English Gwent in the east and Welsh Gwent in the west are very marked and, of course, in the context of the antecedent language geographies, are to be expected. These regional contrasts have become increasingly more pronounced over time.

Something as to the spatial processes of language change is evident in the 1921 distributions when a direct line of contiguous local government areas between Newport, in the south, and Blaenafon, in the north, recorded less than 3% as able to speak Welsh — in marked contrast to the western valleys (Figure 3.6c). Evidently, in 1921 this was the product of an emerging 'ridge' of anglicisation that was to become much more pronounced with time, leading to very low proportions throughout the whole of central Gwent in 1951 (Figure 3.6e). Yet, it must be remembered that all the signs indicate that the continued use of the Welsh language has been substantially affected

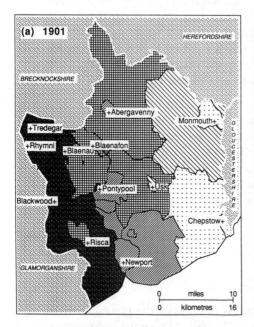

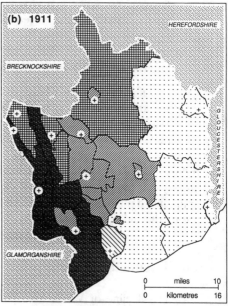

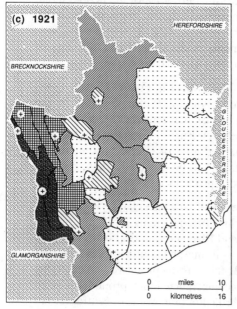

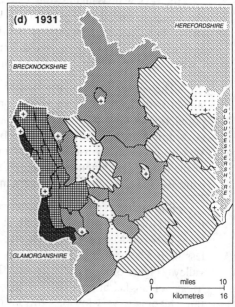

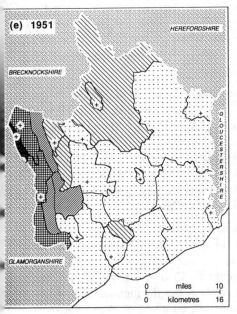

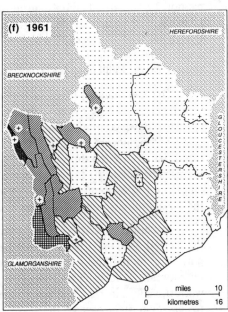

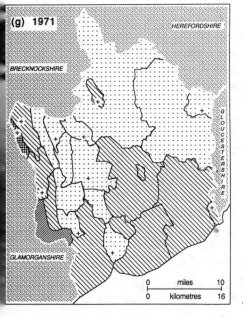

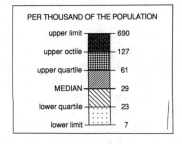

FIGURE 3.6 *Speakers of Welsh, 1901–71*
Sources: Census Reports, 1901–71

by large-scale changes taking place within Western society as a whole and cannot be regarded simply in terms of having been language-specific (Aitchison & Carter, 1985: 5–6, 40–41). We see evidence of this in the fact that towns that once occupied higher positions in the urban hierarchy became anglicised earlier than their surrounding areas and the smaller, less important centres (S.W. Williams, 1981).

The 1961 figures reveal a further series of interesting changes in the social geography of Gwent (Figure 3.6f). As the proportions of Welsh speakers have continued to decline everywhere in the industrial valleys, small but significant increases have begun to appear in lowland Gwent, a trend that continued through to 1971 (Figure 3.6g). These developments, it seems, are linked to the tendency for more and more Welsh speakers to enter the professional and administrative occupations in growth towns and their expanding satellites (Aitchison & Carter, 1987).

Aitchison & Carter's (1985) detailed analysis of linguistic trends for the period 1961–81 reveals a number of new trends in Gwent which, in part, are in marked contrast to those in neighbouring counties. As in Glamorgan, a very high proportion (over 80%) of the population in the western valleys in 1851 had been born in Wales but the number falls rapidly to less than 50% east of the Usk. Increased numbers of Welsh speakers were returned in the towns, with the largest numbers in Newport. On the other hand, a much higher proportion of Gwent's Welsh-speaking Welshmen were unable to read or write their national language, higher proportions, for example, than occur in nearby Mid-Glamorgan. Gwent also records lower proportions of schoolchildren (3–15 years of age) and also of elderly adults (65 years and over) able to speak Welsh than in the three Glamorgan counties — reflecting the long-term refusal of the local education authority to encourage the teaching of Welsh in schools. Yet, there are clear signs that absolute numbers of speakers increased slightly during 1961–71, and more noticeably during 1971–81 — especially in the western valleys and in the town of Newport (Aitchison & Carter, 1985: Maps 2, 7, 9, 11, 14, 18, 21; Lewis, 1980). In their analysis Aitchison & Carter pay special attention to the relative changes in the numbers of Welsh *and* English speakers in specific communities. Their final results indicate an overall mixed pattern of trends but their findings do reveal a clear tendency for western communities to have become slightly 'more Welsh' in the decade 1971–81 with eastern parishes becoming 'more English' (Aitchison & Carter, 1985: maps 22, 26).

All these trends are confirmed in the fact that in the mid-1980s Gwent is beginning to show public signs of the rediscovery of its Welshness. For many years (indeed, from as far back as the 1870s), the county education authority has been lukewarm in its support for the teaching of Welsh in schools. By 1988, the Welsh nursery movement, Mudiad Ysgolion Meithrin, had established well over 20 new groups in the county, mainly in the western valleys. Gradually, in response to parental pressures, some six Welsh-medium units have been started in existing English-medium primary schools; and the first fully Welsh-medium primary school has been announced, starting in September 1990, for Bryn-mawr. In August 1988 the National Eisteddfod of Wales was convened at Newport. In the following September Gwent's first Welsh-medium comprehensive secondary school was established, centrally located in Welsh Gwent at Cwm-carn in the Ebbw valley, and catering for the needs of Gwent children who previously had had to travel to Welsh-medium schools in Glamorgan. And in late February 1988, the county council announced that it would no longer oppose the use of Welsh on road signs, a change from its long-standing policy against the language that has been maintained for many years (Mudiad Ysgolion Meithrin, 1988; *Western Mail*, 1988; Roderick, 1988).

Gwent: The 'Buffer' Zone

Writing at the end of the nineteenth century, J.E. Southall (1904: 37) likened his adopted county to a sort of 'buffer state' that has received and accommodated the 'main stock of foreign [*sic*] immigration' into industrial south Wales: in playing this role Gwent saved much of Glamorgan from early anglicisation (Pryce, 1988). Southall had recognised the fact that, located as it is on the outer margins of the Welsh culture area, in terms of cultural geography Gwent could only have ever functioned as a transitional zone with England. When, in 1926, the Board of Education formulated its recommendations for the use of Welsh in schools, the members appreciated the dilemmas that arose out of this very fact. While circumstances dictated that, of necessity, English had to be the main language in the schools of west Gwent, Welsh was to be regarded as the second language 'because the local and national traditions and all that a school child has most to be proud of, belong to the second rather than the mother tongue'. In the agricultural districts east of the Usk the report recognised that 'Welsh may be said to have died actually of inanition' and here English had become the sole language in the schools.

The officials displayed considerable insight in understanding the nature of ethnic change processes: Welsh, in these rural communities, appeared in the guise of a foreign language but, in their view, English culture was, in itself, a foreign culture and this also posed a number of problems in education. Schools were advised to exercise their own judgements in teaching some Welsh according to local circumstances so that the children would be equipped for membership of a 'wider Wales' (Board of Education, 1927: 206–07, 210, 212). None of these recommendations seem to have ever been contemplated by the education authorities in the former county of Monmouthshire. In contrast, increasingly the present-day county of Gwent now shows an informed understanding of the role of the Welsh language in education and public life — an awareness that effectively begins to restore these old Welsh communities to full membership of the country of Wales.

Acknowledgements

The author is indebted to Brian LL. James, Keeper of the Salisbury Collection at University College, Cardiff, for help in locating sources. He thanks John R. Hunt, Project Officer (Cartography), Faculty of Social Sciences at the Open University, for preparing the final versions of the maps in this chapter which are based on the author's original drafts.

Notes to Chapter 3

1. This chapter adopts the new county boundaries introduced in 1974 to define Gwent but the maps and tables based on census data relate either to the old registration or to the former administrative county of Monmouth.
2. NLW MS: Church in Wales records, LL/QA/5, 1771, St Brides Wentloog return.
3. Contrast the views put forward in E.T. Davies (1977) with the empirical evidence discussed by P.N. Jones (1976) and S.R. Williams (1985a).
4. NLW MS LL/QA/23, 1809.
5. NLW MS LL/QA/23, 1809.
6. NLW MS LL/QA/5, 1771.
7. NLW MS LL/QA/5, 1771.
8. NLW MS LL/QA/23, 1809.
9. NLW MS LL/QA/5, Newport St Woolloos.
10. Registration Districts (RDs) had been drawn up in 1837 for the purpose of recording births, marriages and deaths. A number of problems occur in the use of these areas, not least the fact that the Chepstow and Monmouth RDs overlapped the River Wye to include a few parishes in the counties of Gloucester and Hereford; the north Monmouthshire parishes of Grosmont and Llangua were included in Hereford registration county, while St. Mellons and Rumney parishes were included in the tabulations for adjacent parts of Glamorgan.
11. For methods of calculation see Pryce (1982: 77–80).
12. The proportion of the population speaking Welsh in 1981 reaches 2.7% in the area covered by the former county of Monmouth. See Aitchison & Carter (1985: 20).
13. The published census tables do not provide an adequate time series of language data for territorial units smaller than rural and urban district authority areas. A few boundary changes did occur, decade by decade, but, because the maps in Figure 3.6 refer to proportions of speakers in the local population at specific

dates (and *not* to changes between one census and the next), these can be disregarded for practical purposes. For details of census coverage, see Pryce (1986).

References

AITCHISON, J. and CARTER, H. 1985, *The Welsh Language 1961–1981; An Interpretative Atlas*. Cardiff: University of Wales Press.
——1987, The Welsh language in Cardiff: a quiet revolution. *Transactions of the Institute of British Geographers*, new series 12: 82–92.
ANDREW, C.B. (ed.) 1934, *The Torrington Diaries: Vol. 1*. London: Eyre and Spottiswoode.
BOARD OF EDUCATION 1927, *Welsh in Education and Life: Report of the Departmental Committee on Welsh in the Education System of Wales*. London: HMSO.
BORROW, G. 1862, *Wild Wales: Its People, Language and Scenery*. London: John Murray (5th edn, reprinted 1907).
BRADNEY, J.A. 1921, *A History of Monmouthshire, Vol. III, Pt.1*. London.
——1923, *A History of Monmouthshire, Vol. III, Pt 2*, London.
——1926, *A Memorandum, Being an Attempt to Give a Chronology of the Decay of the Welsh Language in the Eastern Part of the County of Monmouth*. Abergavenny: Minerva Press.
CARTER, H. and GRIFFITHS, H.M. (eds) 1980, *National Atlas of Wales*. Cardiff: University of Wales Press.
CHARLES, B.G. 1963, The Welsh, their language and place names in Archenfield and Oswestry. In H. LEWIS (ed.) *Angles and Britons: the O'Donnell Lectures*. Cardiff: University of Wales Press, 85–110.
COURTNEY, P. 1983, The rural landscape of eastern and lower Gwent, *c*.AD 1070–1750, PhD thesis, University of Wales (Cardiff).
COXE, W. 1801, *An historical tour in Monmouthshire* (2 vols). London.
DAVIES, B. 1984, Churches and chapels of Tredegar. *Gwent Local History*, 57: 14–22.
DAVIES, E.T. 1977, The census of religion in Monmouthshire. *Gwent Local History*, 43: 14–15.
EDUCATION REPORT 1847, *Reports, Commissioners of Inquiry into the State of Education in Wales. Part II: Brecknock, Cardigan, Radnor, and Monmouth*. London: HMSO: 269–334.
ELLIS, A.J. 1882, On the delimitation of the English and Welsh languages. *Y Cymmrodor*, 5: 173–208.
ENDERBIE, P. 1661, *Cambria Triumphans or Brittain in its Perfect Lustre*. London.
EVANS, C.J.O. 1953, *Monmouthshire: Its History and Topography*. Cardiff: William Lewis.
GARDNER, J. 1746, *The History of Monmouthshire*. London.
GRIFFITHS, H.M. 1980 Administrative areas, 1284–1980. In CARTER and GRIFFITHS (1980: Section 2.1).
JENNINGS, H. 1934, *Brynmawr: A Study of a Distressed Area*. London: Allenson & Co.

JONES, F. PRICE, 1963, Effaith brad y Llyfrau Gleision. *Y Traethodydd*, 118: 49–65.

——1978, The Blue Books of 1847. In J.L. WILLIAMS and G.R. HUGHES (eds), *The History of Education in Wales*. Swansea: Christopher Davies: 127–44.

JONES, P.N. 1969. Some aspects of immigration into the Glamorgan coalfield between 1881 and 1911. *Transactions of the Honourable Society of Cymmrodorion*, Session 1969: 82–98.

——1976, Baptist chapels as an index of cultural transition in the south Wales coalfield before 1914. *Journal of Historical Geography*, 2: 347–60.

KENRICK, G.S. 1841 Statistics of the population in the parish of Trevethin (Pontypool) and at the neighbouring works of Blaenavon in Monmouthshire. *Journal of the Royal Statistical Society*, series A, 3: 366–75.

LEWIS, H. 1980, Monmouthshire and the Welsh language census 1901–1971. *Gwent Local History*, 48: 18–24.

MAGEEAN, D. 1982, Principal themes in migration studies. In D. MAGEEAN and W.T.R. PRYCE, *Patterns and Processes of Internal Migration*, Units 9–10 of *D301: Historical Sources and the Social Scientist*. Milton Keynes: Open University Press, 6–41.

MACCANN, J. and CONNOLLY, H. 1933, *Memorials of Father Augustine Baker and Other Documents Relating to the English Benedictines*. Catholic Record Society Publications (Vol. 33).

MUDIAD YSGOLION MEITHRIN, 1988, Information from the Director, 10 Park Grove, Cardiff, 25 January.

PARRY, D. 1985, English dialects in Gwent. *Planet: The Welsh Internationalist*, 53: 82–90.

PHILLIPS, R. 1984, Religion on the moors: nonconformity and education at Castleton and the Wentloog Moors in the nineteenth century. *Gwent Local History*, 57: 2–10.

PRYCE, W.T.R. 1975, Industrialism, urbanization and the maintenance of culture areas: north-east Wales in the mid-nineteenth century. *Welsh History Review*, 7: 307–40.

——1978a, Welsh and English in Wales, 1750–1971: a spatial analysis based on the linguistic affiliation of parochial communities. *Bulletin of the Board of Celtic Studies*, 28: 1–36.

——1978b, Wales as a culture region: patterns of change 1750–1971, *Transactions of the Honourable Society of Cymmrodorion*, Session 1978: 229–61. Revised and reprinted in I. HUME and W.T.R. PRYCE (eds), 1986, *The Welsh and their Country: Selected Readings in the Social Sciences*. Llandysul: Gomer Press: 26–63.

——1980, The Welsh language, 1750–1961. In CARTER and GRIFFITHS (1980: Section 3.1).

——1982, Migration in pre-industrial and industrial societies. In D. MAGEEAN and W.T.R. PRYCE, *Patterns and Processes of Internal Migration*, Units 9–10 of *D301: Historical Sources and the Social Scientist*. Milton Keynes: Open University Press, 45–103.

——1986, The British census and the Welsh language. *Cambria: a Welsh Geographical Review*, 13 (Proceedings of the E.G. Bowen Memorial Conference): 79–100.

——1988, Language areas and changes, c.1750–1981. In P. MORGAN (ed.), *Glamorgan County History, Vol. VI: Glamorgan Society, 1780–1980*.

Swansea: The Glamorgan County History Trust: 265–313.

RAVENSTEIN, E.G. 1879, On the Celtic languages of the British Isles: a statistical survey. *Journal of the Royal Statistical Society*, 42: 579–636.

—1885, The laws of migration. *Journal of the Royal Statistical Society*, 48: 167–235.

REES, W. 1967, *The Union of England and Wales*. Cardiff: University of Wales Press.

RODERICK, A. 1981a, A history of the Welsh language in Gwent, Part 1. *Gwent Local History*, 50: 13–39.

—1981b, A history of the Welsh language in Gwent, Part 2. *Gwent Local History*, 51: 2–32.

—1988, *The Music of Fair Tongues: The Story of the Welsh Language in Gwent*. Newport: National Eisteddfod Committee.

SOUTHALL, J.E. 1894, *Wales and her Language*. Newport: Southall.

—1895 *The Welsh Language Census of 1891*. Newport: Southall.

—1899 *Preserving and Teaching the Welsh Language in English Speaking Districts*. Newport: Southall.

—1904, *The Welsh Language Census of 1901 . . . also a Coloured Linguistic Map of Wales with a Chapter on Welsh in the Schools*. Newport: Southall.

SYLVESTER, D. 1969, *The Rural Landscape of the Welsh Borderland: A Study in Historical Geography*. London: Macmillan.

THOMAS, B. 1930, The migration of labour into the Glamorganshire coalfield, 1861–1911. *Economica*, 10: 275–92. Reprinted in W.E. MINCHINTON (ed.), *Industrial South Wales 1750–1914*. Newton Abbot: David & Charles, 1969: 37–55.

—1986, The Industrial Revolution and the Welsh Language. In C. BABER and L.J. WILLIAMS (eds), *Modern South Wales: Essays in Economic History*. Cardiff: University of Wales Press: 6–21, 279–83.

—1987, A cauldron of rebirth: population and the Welsh language in the nineteenth century. *Welsh History Review*, 13: 418–37.

THOMAS, M.E. 1978, *Afiaith yng Ngwent: hanes Cymdeithas Cymreigyddion y Fenni, 1833–1854*. Cardiff: University of Wales Press.

THOMAS, V. 1987, Communities of the Wentloog Levels, Monmouthshire, 1650–1800. MA dissertation, University of Wales (Cardiff).

Western Mail 1988: 'New Welsh secondary school is Gwent's first', 26 February: 17; 'Welsh milestone', 2 March: 11.

WILLIAMS, G.J. 1958, *The Welsh Tradition of Gwent*. Cardiff: Plaid Cymru.

WILLIAMS, S.R. 1985a, Rhai agweddau cymdeithasol ar hanes yr iaith Gymraeg yn ardal ddiwydiannol Sir Fynwy yn y bedwaredd ganrif ar bymtheg. PhD thesis, University of Wales (Aberystwyth).

—1985b, Welsh in the valleys of Gwent. *Planet: The Welsh Internationalist*, 51: 112–18.

WILLIAMS, S.W. 1981, The urban hierarchy, diffusion and the Welsh language: a preliminary analysis, 1901–71. *Cambria: A Welsh Geographical Review*, 8: 35–50.

Part 2
Descriptive Sketches

4 The Phonetics of Cardiff English[1]

BEVERLEY COLLINS and INGER M. MEES

Cardiff English (CE) is taken here to be the accent used by working-class speakers in the city of Cardiff and surrounding areas. The extent of the accent in one direction is sharply defined by the geographical barrier of the hilly country to the north of the town; Tongwynlais, although inside the city boundary, is outside the accent area. To the west and east the spread of the accent is greater, covering much of the county of South Glamorgan and in addition the adjacent area of south-west Gwent, including the town of Newport, which has a form of speech which is in most respects similar to CE. The speakers of CE and related accents probably number just under half a million people.

General Characteristics of CE

The low-lying coastal region of south-east Glamorgan and south-west Gwent has in all likelihood been largely English-speaking for more than 500 years (Windsor Lewis, 1964: 4–5; Chapters 2, 3, 7, this volume). Probably as a result of this, the speech of these areas differs considerably from the neighbouring accents of the south Wales valleys region. A frequent reaction from people who encounter the accent of the Cardiff–Newport area for the first time seems to be that it scarcely sounds like a 'proper Welsh accent' at all.

In fact, there is much justification for this lay judgement inasmuch as, though there are certainly connections between CE and the accents of the adjacent formerly Welsh-speaking valleys, the speech of the Cardiff region also shares many phonetic/phonological features with the accents of the English Severnside area of Gloucestershire, Avon and Somerset. This can be seen in, for example: the presence of a clear/dark 'l' allophonic patterning; the general absence of the so-called 'lilting' intonation tunes typical of southern Welsh English (Wells, 1982: II, 392); the lack of certain vowel contrasts (particularly the absence of /ɪu/ in the JUICE lexical set); and the extensive use of assimilation and elision. But, on the other hand, CE differs from the neighbouring English varieties in being non-rhotic — a characteristic which is common to the overwhelming majority of south Wales accents (cf. Windsor Lewis, Chapter 6).

Setting

'Setting' is used here as a term to cover the general posture of the vocal organs as they are held throughout the speech process (Honikman, 1964; Laver, 1980); it is known to vary from one accent to another (Knowles, 1978: 89). What follows is a largely impressionistic account of the setting of CE.

The accent is characterised by an overall lack of lip-rounding. The lips are tense and the corners of the mouth are noticeably retracted. Lip-rounding in CE is socially determined. In the broadest forms of the accent, vowels which are typically rounded in other types of English are unrounded, e.g. the THOUGHT and LOT vowels. Even the approximant /w/ may be realised without lip-rounding [ɯ̈], especially before /iː/, e.g. *sweet, wheel*. Middle-class CE tends to have neutral lip-setting, with the THOUGHT vowel having the marked lip-rounding found in many other British accents, including RP, and the NURSE vowel also being rounded [ø:], as is typical of Welsh varieties of English (Wells, 1982: II, 381). Broader varieties of CE appear generally to realise NURSE without, or with only slight, lip-rounding.

The CE tongue shape can be characterised as 'alveolarised'. There is general tongue advancement; the front/blade of the tongue is tense and held close to the alveolar ridge with the sides tending to be raised. The posterior of the tongue is lax, producing a rather enlarged pharyngeal cavity. The soft palate is partly lowered throughout the process of articulation giving rise to semi-continuous nasality in running speech.

In CE, the vocal folds appear to be tenser than in RP with a strong tendency to anterior voice. Creak, as typical of RP, is largely absent and, where found, is characteristic of the more sophisticated middle-class varieties of CE. The tenseness of the vocal folds is often combined with a noticeably husky, breathy quality. The overall effect is of greater resonance and tension, combined with an impression of hoarseness; the accent is sometimes pejoratively labelled 'harsh' or 'grating'.

The general pitch of the voice is probably somewhat lower than in RP, with the exception of an affective high pitch register (see below).

Consonants

Consonant system of CE

In systemic terms, the CE consonants are essentially the same as RP. The only differences lie in the absence in CE of a consistent use of /h/, and the addition of marginal /x/ and /ɬ/ (see Table 4.1 and below).

Stops

The plosives /p,t,k/ are strongly aspirated in initial position in stressed syllables. There is a tendency for medial voiced plosives to weaken to fricatives; it is especially noticeable with /b/, which may be realised as [β], e.g. *horrible* ['ɑrəβl̩]. /b,d,g,dʒ/ are markedly devoiced in final position and the contrast with /p, t, k, tʃ/ is mainly indicated by the length of the preceding vowel. These features, though found in other forms of English, including RP, are more exaggerated and consistent in CE. In unstressed position, the fortis–lenis contrast is frequently lost in running speech, e.g. the opposition between *paint it green* and *painted green*. Certain words also have common variants with fortis consonants as alternatives to lenis, e.g.

Table 4.1

	Bilabial	Labio-dental	Dental	Alveolar	Post-alveolar	Palato-alveolar	Palatal	Velar	Glottal
Plosives	p b			t d				k g	
Affricates						tʃ dʒ			
Fricatives		f v	θ ð	s z (ɬ)		ʃ ʒ		(x)	(h)
Nasals	m			n				ŋ	
Approximants	w			l	r		j	w	

1) Marginal phonemes shown in brackets. For the status of /ɬ/ and /x/, see below.
2) Note that /w/ is labial-velar.

wardrobe /'wʌ:drəup/, *second* /'sɛkənt/, *husband* /'əzbənt/; note also stressed *and* /'ant/ when used as a hesitation marker.

In the broadest forms of the accent, /p,t,k/ lack glottalisation in final position, though more sophisticated speakers tend to adopt glottalisation along the lines of mainstream RP (Mees, 1983: 84; 1987). Elision of final alveolar stop consonants in a small set of high-frequency words is described below. In medial position between voiced sounds, /t/ is generally voiced, typically being realised as a tap [ɾ], e.g. *better* ['bɛɾə], *hospital* ['ɑspɪɾl̩]. Between a vowel and syllabic /l/, [ʔ] occurs regularly only in the word *little*. As in RP, the sequence /tn/ is frequently [ʔn], e.g. *kitten* ['kɪʔn̩]. Note that glottalisation is weaker in the broader forms of the accent. Unlike RP, words like *Canton, lantern* are realised as ['kanʔn̩], ['lanʔn̩] with glottal stop followed by syllabic nasal (RP = /'kæntən, 'læntən/). Thus, in CE, syllabic /n/ is found in certain contexts in which it does not occur in RP. Note also the sequence /ndn̩/, e.g. *London* /'ləndn̩ / (RP = /'lʌndən/).

As in many accents of English, the sequences /tj/, /dj/ are alien to CE; *tube, due* are invariably /tʃu:b, dʒu:/ (never /tu:b, du:/ as in some accents).

Fricatives

/ð/ is normally approximant rather than fricative and frequently suffers assimilation or elision (see below), e.g. *that, there* [at, ɛ:]. Probably as a result of setting characteristics (see above), with some speakers /ʃ, ʒ/ may lack the lip-rounding generally found in other types of English; /s/ and /z/ tend to somewhat sharper friction, especially before close front vowels, e.g. *seat, sister*. Lenis /z/, especially, is strikingly devoiced in final position, so that in running speech *plays* may appear to be homophonous with *place*. However, because of duration differences in the preceding vowel (or nasal or lateral), complete neutralisation of final /s ~ z/ is rare.

As in most English and Welsh accents, /h/ is marginal in CE. /h/-dropping suffers the usual social stigmatisation described in, for instance, Wells (1982: I, 254). /hj/ is /j/ in the broadest forms of the accent, e.g. *human* /'ju:mən/, *huge* /ju:dʒ/. Note also *here, hear* as /jø:/. More sophisticated speakers replace this by [ç], e.g. ['çum:ən], a pronunciation also found as a realisation of /hj/ in RP. The CE [ç] appears, however, to have a rather more front articulation and closer narrowing. These features (and possibly slightly longer duration) makes CE [ç] sound rather prominent to the RP speaker.

It is questionable whether /ɬ/ should be considered even as a marginal phoneme of the dialect since it is found rarely and only in the speech of individuals from Welsh-speaking backgrounds or those with strong feelings of Welsh language loyalty. It is used exclusively in Welsh personal and place names, e.g. *Llewelyn*, *Llandaff*, *Castell Coch*. Mainstream CE speakers will anglicise such names /lə'wɛlɪn/, 'landəf, 'kasl 'kʌ:k/ and many Cardiffians find it difficult — in most cases impossible — to produce a convincing /ɬ/, substituting /kl, θl/ or /xl/ instead (cf. Coupland, 1988).[2]

/x/ appears more established in the accent than /ɬ/. Many CE speakers produce /x/ in place names of Welsh origin, e.g. *Mynachdy* /mə'naxdi:/, Pantbach /pant'ba:x/ (though /mə'nakdi:, pant'ba:k/ are more commonly attested). /x/ is also found in a couple of expressions of disgust, e.g. *ugh* /əx/; *ach-y-fi* /əxə'vi:/.

Nasals

As in most basilectal types of English, the ending *–ing* is generally pronounced as /ɪn/, e.g. *singing*, *ceiling* /'sɪŋɪn/, /'si:lɪn/. This feature suffers mild social stigmatisation, but is nevertheless to be heard even from otherwise fairly sophisticated speakers of middle-class varieties of CE. The morpheme - *thing* in the items *something*, *nothing*, *anything*, *everything* is occasionally /θɪŋk/; this seems most common in the speech of working-class children (cf. Mees, 1983: 90; 116–7; this volume).

Approximants

There is no trace in CE of rhoticism; /r/ is pronounced only before vowels on a pattern similar to that of RP. As in most other non-rhotic accents, intrusive 'r' (Gimson, 1980: 208–9; Wells, 1982: I, 222–7) is regularly heard, e.g. *draw attention* /'drʌ:r ə'tɛnʃn̩/, *drawing* /'drʌ:rɪn/.

CE /r/ is generally a post-alveolar approximant, but in the broadest accents, it is realised as a strong alveolar tap [ɾ], particularly in intervocalic position. It is well-known that in old-fashioned types of RP (Noel Coward is often quoted as an example), tap realisations of /r/ are also heard (Wells, 1982: II, 282) but the RP taps sound very different from the Cardiff ones. In CE, a larger portion of the tongue is involved than in RP, and the articulation is less rapid, and therefore the effect is of a sound of longer duration, rather like a type of /d/. Since /t/ in CE is also often realised as an alveolar tap [ɾ] (or even as a post-alveolar approximant [ɹ]) before /ə/

and unstressed /ɪ/, this results in a potential reduction of contrasts such as *starting* ~ *starring*, *butter/but a* ~ *borough*, *hotter* ~ *horror*.

Unlike other south Wales varieties, CE /l/ exhibits the same allophonic patterning as RP, namely with clear [l] before vowels and [j], and dark [ɫ] before other consonants and pause. As in RP, dark [ɫ] may be vocalised and realised as a high back vowel. CE frequently has obvious 'breaking' before dark [ɫ] (Wells, 1982: II, 298), e.g. *meal* [mi:əɫ], *school* [sku:əɫ], *old* [əuəɫd].

/w/ and /j/ are on the whole similar to RP, though, as stated above, setting characteristics can produce an unrounded variety of /w/, whilst /j/ often has slight palatal friction in CE. /j/ is elided before /i:/, e.g. *yeast*, *yield* /i:st, i:ld/. See below for /jø:/ as an alternative to /i:ə/ in words of the NEAR type.

Vowels

Vowel system of CE

The vowel system of CE, as shown in Table 4.2, is systemically closer to RP than are most accents of Welsh English. RP /ɪə/ and /ʊə/ are replaced in CE by the sequences /i:ə/ and /u:ə/. Since the SQUARE vowel is typically pronounced without any glide at all, this means that in our analysis CE is regarded as having no centring diphthongs. The STRUT vowel is represented as /ə/ (RP /ʌ/), but it is questionable whether the distribution of /ə/ and /ʌ/ in RP is as dissimilar from CE /ə/ as this notation suggests.

In realisational terms, however, the vowels of CE and RP are very different. Compared with RP, many CE vowels have a more centralised articulation (the LOT, FOOT, TRAP, DRESS, and THOUGHT vowels) and the starting points of most of the diphthongs (see below) are also considerably more central. Furthermore, it is striking that most vowels in CE, at least in broad varieties, seem to lack lip-rounding (see above). This is most noticeable with the THOUGHT vowel, but also with LOT and FOOT. If rounded at all, they have tight inner lip-rounding.

Note that Table 4.2 contains two keywords which have /ɪə/ in RP: NEAR and BEER. NEAR represents a small set of words: *near*, *mere*, *year*, *ear*, *here* and *hear* (and their derivatives). These words may either be /i:ə/ or pronounced with a rising diphthong [ɪø:] (phonemicised as /jø:/), e.g. *near*, *mere* njø:, mjø:/.[3] It is not unusual for *year*, *ear*, *here* and *hear* to be pronounced in the same way /jø:/. BEER represents all other words

Table 4.2

CE	RP	Keyword	CE	RP	Keyword	CE	RP	Keyword
ɪ	ɪ	KIT	iː	iː	FLEECE	ei	eɪ	FACE
ɛ	e	DRESS	ɛː	ɛə	SQUARE	əu	əʊ	GOAT
a	æ	TRAP	aː	ɑː	PALM	əi	aɪ	PRICE
ɑ	ɒ	LOT	ʌː	ɔː	THOUGHT	ʌu	aʊ	MOUTH
ə	ʌ	STRUT	uː	uː	GOOSE	ʌi	ɔɪ	CHOICE
ɣ	ʊ	FOOT	øː	ɜː	NURSE	iːə~jøː	ɪə	NEAR
a~aː	ɑː	BATH				iːə	ɪə	BEER
ə	ə	commA				uːə~ʌː	ʊə~ɔː	CURE
iː	ɪ	happY						

which have /ɪə/ in RP. These, contrary to the NEAR words, are heard only with the vowel sequence /iːə/, e.g. *Ian, idea, real* /ˈiːən/, /əiˈdiːə/, /ˈriːəl/. Before /r, l/ followed by a vowel, where RP has /ɪə/, CE exhibits /iː/, e.g. *cereals, really* /ˈsiːriːəlz/, /ˈriːliː/.

Checked vowels

The steady-state checked vowels are shown in Figure 4.1. CE front vowels tend to be more open than their counterparts in RP. KIT is somewhat more open than the average of RP — though a realisation similar to CE /ɪ/ is heard from many younger RP speakers. DRESS and TRAP are more open than RP and typically somewhat retracted. CE TRAP is very similar to the type of vowel heard from many younger RP

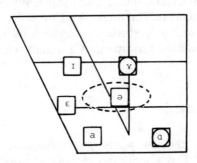

Figure 4.1 *Checked Vowels*

speakers, particularly females (Gimson, 1980: 109). As has been noted for other varieties of English, including RP (Fudge, 1977; Jones, 1956: 235–36), CE has a prolonged variety of the TRAP vowel in a small number of lexical items (e.g. *man, mad, bad, bag*). Despite the lengthening, this prolonged /a/ appears to be clearly distinct from the PALM vowel. Notwithstanding Lediard (1977: 264), *bag* does not appear with the PALM vowel in our informants' speech.

The LOT vowel /ɑ/ is unrounded and noticeably more front than RP /ɒ/. FOOT /ɣ/ is unrounded and somewhat more centralised than RP /u/. Again, a vowel of similar type seems to be gaining ground with the younger RP population. Though certain workers (e.g. Windsor Lewis, 1964: 11) have taken CE to have a contrast /ə ~ ʌ/, we shall here regard these vowels as having an allophonic relation, i.e. /ə/ is employed here to cover both RP /ə/ (i.e. commA) and also, when stressed, the RP vowel /ʌ/ in STRUT. It is problematical, even in RP, whether the stressed variant should be considered as a separate phoneme or not, because of the absence of minimal pairs — see the discussion in, for example, Jones (1967: 58–62); Wells (1970: 233–5); and Wells (1982).

CE stressed /ə/ covers a wide area of vowel space and shows considerable idiolectal variation. It is, however, strikingly closer than average RP /ʌ/, being typically half-open or above. This vowel seems also (on average) closer than its counterpart in most other south Wales accents.

Incidential variation

The final vowel in happy words is /i:/ and never /ɪ/ as in the traditional description of RP — though the /i:/ variant seems now to be well established in the speech of younger RP speakers (Gimson, 1980: 105; Wells, 1982: II, 294). As with the RP /i:/ users, the CE vowel in happY is generally short and often more open, being realised as [ɪ]; a few (broader) CE speakers, however, consistently retain close but shortened [ï] in this context. The internal unstressed vowel in examples such as *anniversary, universe, elephant, television*, is realised as /i:/ by some broad CE individuals. Mainstream CE usually chooses /ə/ in these cases.

Free steady-state vowels

The free monophthongal steady-state vowels are shown in Figure 4.2. The /i:/ in FLEECE is a noticeably closer and more front vowel than RP, and generally lacks any glide. GOOSE is also closer, somewhat advanced from back, but typically lacking the glide variants found in

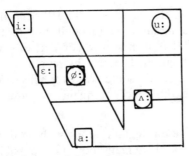

FIGURE 4.2 *Free Monophthongal Vowels*

mainstream RP and many other accents of England. The vowel /ɪu/, found in most other varieties of Welsh English, thus providing a contrast /u:~ɪu/ in GOOSE and JUICE, is unknown in Cardiff, though it is apparently to be heard in the speech of Newport (Windsor Lewis, personal communication).

The SQUARE vowel, CE /ɛ:/, corresponds to RP /ɛə/, the latter usually being treated as a centring glide — although nowadays in RP a steady-state vowel is common, a fact discussed by numerous scholars (Ball, 1984: 43; Brown, 1977: 36; Gimson, 1980: 144; Windsor Lewis, 1964: 21). In CE /ɛ:/ is always a steady-state vowel and is strikingly raised, as compared with RP, being generally well above half-open. Many speakers realise /ɛ:/ with a vowel of about the same height as their DRESS vowel, differentiating only by means of length.

The THOUGHT vowel, /ʌ:/, is unrounded, half-open and centralised in the broadest forms of CE (though more sophisticated forms of the accent have a closer vowel with the strong rounding typical of modern RP; see above). In the speech of younger informants, we have not been able to find evidence for the NORTH–FORCE distinction (Wells, 1982: I, 159–62) mentioned by Windsor Lewis (1964: 11) and described by Tench and by Connolly elsewhere in this volume as occurring in other south Wales dialects. However, there is evidence that such a distinction was common and indeed lives on in the language of older CE speakers.[4]

The NURSE vowel, /ø:/, is more front and closer than RP /ɜ:/. Mainstream CE has a strongly rounded vowel of about half-close tongue height (see above for sociolinguistic variation of lip-rounding resulting from setting characteristics).

The PALM vowel, /a:/, is undoubtedly considered to be the most characteristic vowel of the accent. In broad CE it is generally a front open vowel (about cardinal vowel 4) and may have some raising. This vowel is often noticeably longer than the RP equivalent and is frequently realised with some nasalisation (even if not in the vicinity of nasal consonants). It is not true, however, for CE, to say that TRAP /a/ and PALM /a:/ are distinguished merely by length, as stated by Hughes & Trudgill (1979: 51–52) for south Wales English. There would appear always to be some difference of quality in addition to any duration contrast.

CE /a:/ is the accent feature, along with /h/ dropping, which suffers the most apparent social stigmatisation. One possible form this can take was reported to us pithily by a young informant: 'If I say ['kæ:dɪf] my Mummy 'its me. She says I've got to say ['kɑ:dɪf] and talk properly.'

Incidential variation

CE has an apparently confusing pattern of alternation between /a/ and /a:/ in words such as *class, pass, grass, bath, laugh, answer, chance, dance*, which have /ɑ:/ in RP and have been classified by Wells (1982: I, 133–35) as BATH-type. The TRAP vowel /a/ appears to be favoured before nasal plus consonant while the PALM vowel /a:/ is the preference before fricatives. Certain words, e.g. *bath, laugh, ask, rather, father, master* and the suffix *-graph* in *photograph* etc., appear hardly ever to have /a/. Other items, e.g. pre-nasal *answer, chance, dance* (and also pre-fricative *castle, nasty* are overwhelmingly said with /a/.

However, apart from a degree of social pressure to produce PALM in these words in middle-class CE (presumably under the influence of RP), broad and mainstream Cardiff speakers show confusing idiolectal variation and the same speaker may even produce TRAP and PALM varieties in succeeding sentences (e.g. *France* as /frans/ and /fra:ns/). Therefore the CE distribution is quite unlike that of northern English accents (see Wells, 1982: II, 353–56; 387); on the other hand, there does appear to be some similarity between CE and the patterning in south-western varieties of English.

Diphthongs

The FACE vowel, /ei/ (Figure 4.3), has a closer and more centralised starting-point than RP /eɪ/. The off-glide is more prominent and reaches a closer tongue position. Though a few conservative speakers of the older generation may have very narrow glides (allowing /ei/ to be regarded as a potential diphthong), this traditional pronunciation has now virtually disappeared. Unlike most other Welsh accents of English, CE FACE is

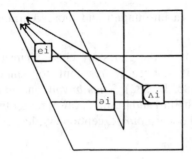

FIGURE 4.3 *Fronting Diphthongs*

nowadays clearly a full diphthong.[5] There is no trace of a *mail–male* contrast found in some south Wales accents (Connolly, 1981: 52–3; this volume).

The corresponding back vowel GOAT /əu/ (Figure 4.4) has two realisations. Traditionally, GOAT in CE was a potential diphthong of an [oᵘ] type; it is nowadays replaced by a back/central glide [ÿü], particularly in the speech of younger Cardiffians (see Coupland, 1980: 6). Like FACE this vowel tends to have a noticeably closer end-point than its RP counterpart /əu/.

Again, CE shows no trace of a *toe–tow* contrast as found in some other south Wales accents (Connolly, 1981: 53).

Apart from the diphthongs /ei/ and /əu/, CE has three other closing diphthongs: /əi/ (PRICE), /ʌu/ (MOUTH) and /ʌi/ (CHOICE). /əi/ and /ʌu/ correspond respectively to RP /aɪ/ and /au/. In CE /əi/ has a noticeably closer and /ʌu/ has a somewhat closer starting-point than their RP counterparts. (Since the starting point of /ʌu/ is back rather than truly central we have chosen not to represent it as /əu/, which would otherwise

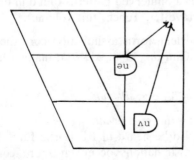

FIGURE 4.4 *Backing Diphthongs*

mislead.) CE /ʌi/ has an unrounded and more centralised first element than RP /ɔɪ/.

The final elements of the glides are closer than in RP. Like other Welsh accents, CE is noticeably resistant to 'smoothing' of these diphthongs (Wells, 1982, II, 382). Thus *buying* and *tower*, for instance, will be said as ['bəiɪn, 'bəijɪn] and ['tʌuə, 'tʌuwə] rather than ['baːɪn, 'tɑːə]. Note, however, that the word *our*, exceptionally, has an alternative form /aː/.

Incidential variation.

It is well-known that RP has a phenomenon (Wells, 1982: I, 163) whereby in words such as *sure, cure, tour*, etc. /ɔː/ replaces /ʊə/. This is also common in CE — far more so, it would seem, than in most regional English or Welsh varieties. The patterning is difficult to analyse, but it would appear (Mees, 1983: 78–9) that in CE /ʌː/ replacement is frequent for certain words, e.g. *tour, sure, insure*. Other words, e.g. *pure, cure* (i.e. words containing a consonant + /j/) are found with the THOUGHT vowel in the speech of middle-class Cardiffians (possibly even more frequently than /ɔː/ replaces /ʊə/ in RP).

Features of Connected Speech

Assimilation and elision

CE is characterised by remarkably extensive assimilation and elision. Much of this is found in other types of English, including RP (see, for example, Brown, 1977). It is the extent and consistency of assimilation and elision — even at relatively slow rate of delivery — which is notable in CE. It is striking that CE forms are of typical English type. There is no evidence of the Welsh-influenced patterns found in other south Wales accents such as Abercrave (cf. Tench, this volume).

CE has place and lenis/fortis assimilation corresponding closely to that found in RP (see Gimson, 1980; 289–91); manner assimilation most frequently affects /ð/:

/ð/ → [l] following /l/, e.g. *all that*

/ð/ → [n] following /n/, e.g. *in the*

Similar patterns may also be heard in RP (Ortiz Lira, 1976). However, in CE such manner assimilations occur far more consistently, being extended to even strongly stressed contexts, e.g. *in these, although* [ɪn 'niːz, ʌ:'ləu].

In the words *wasn't, doesn't, isn't*, /z/ is often realised as [d] under the influence of the following nasal: ['wɑdn̩, 'dədn̩, 'ɪdn̩]. This may be further reduced to [wɑn:, dən:, 'ɪn:].

Final /t/, or /t/ in a final /ts/ cluster, is sometimes realised as the corresponding homorganic fricative [s], resulting in the case of /ts/ in elision, e.g. *about Secret Seven* [ə'bʌus 'si:krɪs 'sɛvn̩] *it's dead* [ɪs 'dɛd], *gets some chips* ['gɛs səm 'tʃɪps] (see below).

Elision is also found in patterns similar to colloquial RP (e.g. Gimson, 1980; Brown, 1977), though to a far greater degree of predictability, and even at slow, careful rates of delivery. A selection of examples is given below. Consonant elision includes:

1. Syllable-final pre-consonantal /t,d/, e.g. *United States* [ju:'nəitɪ 'steits], *started collecting* ['stɑ:tɪ kə'lɛktɪn], *but we* [bə wi:], *pocket money* ['pɑkɪ məni], *about four* [ə'bʌu 'fʌ:]. Elision is particularly common with a set of high-frequency words, including *it, bit, get, but, lot, that, quite, said* (for full list, see Mees, 1983: 120), where /t,d/ may also be elided pre-pausally (e.g. *that's right* ['ðas 'raɪ]) and intervocalically (e.g. *but I* [bə əi]). In addition, /t/ may be deleted in final /-nt/ clusters, not only before consonants as in colloquial RP, e.g. *don't drive* [dəun 'draiv], but also before vowels, e.g. *can't handle* [ka:n 'andl̩], *went up* ['wɛn 'əp].
2. /r/ is occasionally elided in intervocalic position, e.g. *very* [vɛ:i:], *America* [ə'mɛ:ɪkə]. A 'remnant' of the /r/ is seen in the lengthening of the preceding vowel. (We suspect that Dannie Abse's representation of his father's constantly saying 'venyer' (*very near*) is an attempt to convey /r/ elision.)
3. Elision of initial /ð/, e.g. *that, there* /at, ɛ:/.

With vowels, elision mainly involves the deletion of /ə/ and /ɪ/, e.g. *except, electric, eleven, police, gorilla* [sɛpt, 'lɛktrɪk, 'lɛbm̩, 'pli:s, 'grɪlə]. Examples similar to these are of course found in RP. Again, it is the extent and the consistency which is characteristic of CE.

Intonation and rhythmic features

In general, it is true to say that CE shows more resemblances to English dialects in its intonation patterns than it does to other accents of Wales. In particular, CE lacks the close correlation with the pitch patterns of Welsh which is such a striking feature of the neighbouring accents of Glamorgan and Gwent.

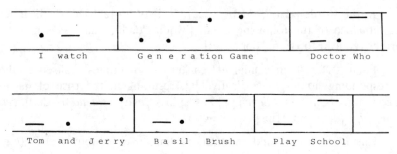

FIGURE 4.5

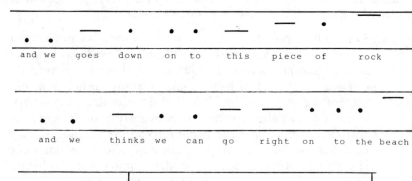

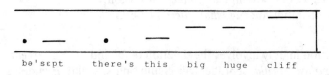

FIGURE 4.6

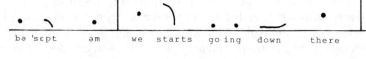

FIGURE 4.7

It's love ly

[ɪts 'ləvli]

FIGURE 4.8

Though the pitch range is somewhat more extended than in RP, it is nevertheless considerably more compact than in the above-mentioned south Wales accents. Overall, the average CE pitch is lower than other south Wales accents and also appears to be lower than the average for RP. However, CE consistently has stretches of speech at a higher affective range coinciding with excitement, annoyance, emphasis, etc. The characteristic nuclear tunes of CE have counterparts in RP. The accent is notable for extensive use of rise-fall and fall-rise patterns; both of these are somewhat more extended than their RP counterparts.

CE intonation is curious in one tune which is not only characteristic of lists, as in RP, but also strikingly of narrative mode, consisting of a high-pitch terminal rise to each intonation group[6] — cf. Coupland (1988: 31) who refers to this pattern as Tone Group 6 (see Figures 4.5 and 4.6). In both of these cases, the terminal rises reach a far higher pitch than in RP.

CE has vowel length patterns which are closer to RP than they are to the rather more syllable-timed effect of much south Wales English. A feature of the accent which is reminiscent of some south-western varieties of English is the extended length of certain free vowels, especially /a:/, /ʌ:/ and /ø:/. On the other hand, the close vowels /i:, u:/ are noticeably shorter than the corresponding sounds in RP.

Though CE does not appear to exhibit consonant lengthening (Connolly, 1981: 59) there is frequently noticeable extra weight given to unstressed syllables often combined with a rising pitch on the syllable concerned, *he's landed, it's lovely* (see Figures 4.7 and 4.8).

It is perhaps in certain of these rhythmic features that CE can be shown to have most in common with other south Wales accents.

Notes to Chapter 4

1. We wish to acknowledge the detailed and helpful observations made by Jack Windsor Lewis on an earlier draft of this article; responsibility for the content remains, of course, our own.
2. Native Cardiffians do not appear commonly to replace /ɫ/ with /fl/, as discussed in Wells (1982: II, 389). Replacement with /θl/ appears to be confined to post-vocalic context, e.g. *Gelligaer* [Street]: /gɛθli:'gɛ:/ (though cf. Coupland, 1988: 40–6).
3. Pronunciations of this type are in fact not uncommon in RP. Editions of the *English Pronouncing Dictionary* produced before A.C. Gimson took over as editor from Daniel Jones show all the NEAR words (except *mere*) with /jɜ:/-type alternatives for RP. Furthermore, /jɜ:/ is even given for *ear*, with the label 'rarely' (Jones, 1960). Brown (1977: 76) points out that /ɪə/ is frequently replaced by a vowel 'sometimes indistinguishable' from the realisation of /ɜ:/.
4. Windsor Lewis (personal communication) states that this distinction was 'common in my day' and 'only the least sophisticated ran them together'. We have found evidence of a NORTH–FORCE opposition in the speech of an older CE informant (80 years at time of recording). The Cardiff-born co-author of this article (BC) was not aware of any distinction in his own childhood speech or in that of his contemporaries. It is possible that this is a feature which is subject to age variation and may be in the process of being lost from the accent.
5. Mees (1977; 1983) showed the FACE vowel as /e:/ and the GOAT vowel as /o:/, which reflect the more conservative pronunciations of these diphthongs.
6. A strikingly similar pattern can be heard in Bristol dialect, for example from the speaker on the BBC record *English with an Accent*.

References

BALL, M.J. 1984, The centring diphthongs in southern English — a sound change in progress. *Journal of the International Phonetic Association* 14, 1: 38–44.
BROWN, G. 1977, *Listening to Spoken English*. London: Longman.
CONNOLLY, J.H. 1981, On the segmental phonology of a south Welsh Accent of English. *Journal of the International Phonetic Association* 11, 2: 51–61.
COUPLAND, N. 1980, Style-shifting in a Cardiff work-setting. *Language in Society*, 9: 1–12.
——1988, *Dialect in Use: Sociolinguistic Variation in Cardiff English*. Cardiff: University of Wales Press.
FUDGE, E. 1977, Long and short [æ] in one southern British speaker's English. *Journal of the International Phonetic Association* 7, 2: 55–65.
GIMSON, A.C. 1980, *An Introduction to the Pronunciation of English* (3rd edn). London: Edward Arnold (1st edn, 1962).
HONIKMAN, B. 1964, Articulatory settings. In D. ABERCROMBIE, D.B. FRY, P.A.D. MacCARTHY, N.C. SCOTT and J.L.M. TRIM (eds), *In Honour of Daniel Jones*. London: Longman, 73–84.
HUGHES, A. and TRUDGILL, P. 1979, *English Accents and Dialects*. London: Edward Arnold.

JONES, D. 1956, *An Outline of English Phonetics* (8th edn). Cambridge: University Press (1st edn, 1918).

—— 1960, *English Pronouncing Dictionary* (11th edn). London: Dent (1st edn 1917).

—— 1967, *The Phoneme: its Nature and Use* (3rd edn). Cambridge: Heffer (1st edn, 1950).

KNOWLES, G.O. 1978, The nature of phonological variables in Scouse. In P. TRUDGILL (ed.), *Sociolinguistic Patterns in British English*. London: Edward Arnold, 80–90.

LAVER, J. 1980, *The Phonetic Description of Voice Quality*. Cambridge: Cambridge University Press.

LEDIARD, J. 1977, The sounds of the dialect of Canton, a suburb of Cardiff. In D. PARRY (ed.), *The Survey of Anglo-Welsh Dialects. Vol. 1, The South-East*. Swansea: University College, Appendix A.

LEWIS, J. WINDSOR 1964, Glamorgan Spoken English, Unpublished manuscript.

MEES, I.M. 1977 Language and social class in Cardiff: a survey of the speech habits of schoolchildren. Master's dissertation, University of Leiden.

—— 1983, The speech of Cardiff schoolchildren: a real time study. Doctoral dissertation, University of Leiden.

—— 1987, Glottal stop as a prestigious feature in Cardiff English. *English World-Wide* 8, 1: 25–40.

ORTIZ LIRA, H. 1976, Some phonetic correlates of the rapid colloquial style. *Journal of the International Phonetic Association* 6, 1: 13–22.

WELLS, J. 1970, Local accents in England and Wales. *Journal of Linguistics* 6: 231–52.

—— 1982, *Accents of English* (3 vols). Cambridge: Cambridge University Press.

5 Transcribed Specimen of Cardiff English[1]

J. WINDSOR LEWIS

ðə fɒlwɪŋ vəːʒn əv "ðə nɒθ wɪnd ən ðə sʌn" reprəzents ən ʌnsəfɪstɪkeɪtɪd *kadɪf (CARDIFF) prənʌnsɪeɪʃn.

ʌ ɪz sentrl, ə haf klǝɯs, a(ː) = ä, u = üꞈ, aɤ = äɤ, w = wꞈ, ɔ̈ = ɔ̈ꞈ, i = ï, ɔɯ = ɔ̈ɯ, ɔ̈ = ɔ̈ꞈ, aɪ = äɪ, l = lə ..., ... lᵛ, r = alvjələ ɹ ɔ ɾ, eː = eꞢ, ɛɪ = ɛɹɪ ; ʌðə valjuz ər ɔl əbaɯt kadnl.

ə 'nɒːθ 'wɪn(d) ən nə 'sʌn wəz avɪn 'aːg(ju)mənt baɤ 'wɪtʃ 'wʌn əv əm wəz ə 'strɒŋŋəs. ɛn ʌp kʌmz ɪs 'travlər 'ɒːl 'rapt 'ʌp ɪn ə 'wɒːm 'klɔ̈k. sö ðɛɪ ə'griz əʔ ðə'wʌn ək kəg 'gɛr ɪm tə 'tɛɪk ɪr' ɒːf 'fəːs əb bi 'rɛkŋ 'strɒŋŋər ən ni 'ʌðə. ɛn ðə'nɒːθ 'wɪm blɔɯz 'aːdz i 'kan. bəʔ ðə 'mɔːr i 'blɔɯz (ð)ə'taɪtə ðə'travlə pɤlz ɪz 'kɔ̈ɯʔ 'raɤn(d) ɪm, ən ɪn i ɛn(d) ðə 'nɒːθ 'wɪŋ gɪvz ʌp 'traɪɪn. ɛn ə 'sʌn 'ʃãĩz 'aɤʔ 'wɒːm ən 'streːrəwɛɪ ðə'travlə tɛɪs 'ɒːf ɪz kɔ̈t. sɔ(ɯ) ðə 'nɒːθ 'wɪŋ 'gɒr əb'mɪt ðəʔ ðə 'sʌm wəz ə 'strɒŋŋəs.

dʒak wɪnzə lʊɪs.

Note to Chapter 5

1. This transcription first appeared in *Le Maître Phonétique*, 1964, 121: 6–7, and is reproduced here in its original form. Phonetic symbols differ, in some respects, from the IPA conventions generally used elsewhere in the volume. Phonetic values represented are summarised at the head of the fragment.

6   The Roots of Cardiff English[1]

J. WINDSOR LEWIS

In south Pembrokeshire and in the county of Glamorgan in the rural parts of the Gower peninsula a type of English developed more similar to the south-western English spoken on the opposite side of the Bristol Channel than to the English of the rest of the historic county of Glamorgan. At the present time English is the predominant language of all historic Glamorgan except chiefly for an area in the extreme north-west bordering on historic Carmarthenshire and west Breconshire (cf. Williams, this volume). But we find two quite distinct types of English within the county, with a vaguely defined transitional zone between them. One of these is heard in the area between and around the two urban centres of Barry and Cardiff; the other appears to have resulted largely from the spread of the first type into the hill areas, which were almost entirely Welsh in language before the Industrial Revolution, and into the rest of the coastal 'Vale' of Glamorgan which has suffered a great deal of ebb and flow of English and Welsh. This ebb and flow is strikingly demonstrated by some of the Vale place names such as Brynhill Fach and Penhill Fawr, which show three tiers of occupation, and Welsh St Donats, Hampston Fach, Rhiw Saeson, Broadland Fawr, Michaelston-y-fedw, and Monkton Ganol, which point to Welsh reoccupation of medieval English settlements. The Cardiff variety of Welsh English extends into coastal Monmouthshire at least as far as Newport; the other, 'Cymric', variety extends into parts of Monmouthshire, Breconshire and Carmarthenshire, and English of a quite similar type may be heard even in parts of Cardiganshire, Pembrokeshire and Montgomeryshire.

A.J. Ellis was so completely mistaken about almost all Glamorgan that he placed it all within his Celtic border, which he took into the sea three miles south-west of Swansea, not resuming it till two miles south-west of Newport. The suggestion that any form of Glamorgan English can be called 'book English' — which was how Ellis described what he thought to be the only kind within his Celtic Border, defining it as 'Learned by instruction and not communication, or . . else spoken by the children, perhaps even the grandchildren, of those who thus learnt it' — is very wide of the truth. As he said in his article 'On the Delimitation of the English and Welsh Languages' (1882), he obtained his information only by means of a postal questionnaire sent to 'clergymen of the parishes along or near the supposed route'. Unfortunately he had only two Glamorgan informants, one at Merthyr and the other at Llantrisant whose incumbent, though it is only ten miles from Cardiff, offered the amazing observation 'I can name no particular place within many miles of this place, where the natives speak English'. It was a pity that nobody brought to his notice the investigations of E.G. Ravenstein (1879) for Ellis (1889) repeated his mistakes.

Ravenstein, who traversed the areas himself, observed that

> Cardiff forms the centre of an extensive district in eastern Glamorgan-shire within which Welsh is no longer [sic] spoken by a majority, and which is separated from the more thoroughly Welsh part of the county by a line commencing on the R. Rumney, above Machen, and running thence to the north of Whitchurch between Cardiff and Llandaff, past Leckwith, St. Lythans, Barry, Porthkerry, St. Athan and Llantwit Major, to the coast near St. Donats.

Apart from the fact that the line would now at least run well north of Llandaff and that we have transitional areas at the northern and western ends of his area, Ravenstein's description might well stand as an account of where the Cardiff variety of English is spoken today. He also mentioned another English-speaking area, extending roughly from Margam to Pyle and south to the coast, which today is almost entirely indistinguishable linguistically from the rest of surrounding Glamorgan. An important historical account of the English language in Glamorgan was given in a Celtic-Border survey by Williams (1935), in which he remarked that the 'modern linguistic distribution is primarily the result of the medley of peoples and races drawn into Glamorgan by its recent industrialisation [cf. Pryce, and again Williams, this volume] and, secondarily, the effect of long historical fusion within the area in pre- and post-Norman times'. He expressed the opinion that in the fifteenth century the lowlands of south Glamorgan were English in speech, and pointed out that, although 'before the industrial epoch' north Glamorgan was entirely Welsh in speech, 'the zone lying mainly between Swansea–Neath–Resolven–Aberdare, Merthyr Tydfil–Rhymney on the north, and Port Talbot–Bridgend–Pontypridd on the south became populated by peoples of mixed language affinities, though Welsh was undoubtedly the speech of the majority of its inhabitants'.

Here we have the explanation of the rapidity with which a genuine non-book-learnt dialect of English has become the speech of this area today: there always was a very substantial minority of English speakers in the area from the time of the first immigrations. The resultant Cymricised variety of English shows considerable signs of Welsh influence, more phonologically than grammatically or lexically. The really outstandingly significant feature of Cardiff English is the totally non-south-western quality and distribution of its 'r' sound, which is the commonest 'Danelaw' variety. In un-Cymricised South Pembrokeshire, West Gower and East Monmouthshire 'r' is usually distinctly retroflex and survives before consonants. As a non-retroflex alveolar sound is also the usual value of 'r' in the area surrounding Cardiff it may occur to some to suggest that the Cardiff 'r' is due to the influence of Welsh. However, there are serious objections to this explanation. First, we should expect that it should be a flapped or possibly trilled sound initially before vowels in strong syllables as in the adjacent varieties of Welsh, but Cardiff speakers never ordinarily flap or trill 'r' in such a position. Only a very small minority of Cymric Glamorgan English speakers may be heard to do so, chiefly those who are bilingual. Second, we should expect that at the time of the suggested substitution of the Welsh 'r' for the English, the previous (retroflex) sound would have been in use before consonants, and therefore that an 'r' sound would be retained there. In fact there do seem to be some signs of such a development surviving between Margam and Neath where a flapped 'r' was often to be heard in such words as 'thirty' and 'dirty', at least until recently. This is not surprising because we have evidence for the existence of a south-western type of dialect in the Vale of Glamorgan almost as far east as Cardiff, just west of which we have in the place-name *Drope*, a strikingly typical south-western phonological development (of *thorpe*). Trevelyn (1910) gave the form *drepence* for 'threepence' and Pierce (1968) shows 'v'/'f' alternations in several Dinas Powis names. Phillips (1956) records *vally*, an obvious adoption of 'felly', for the Ely valley dialect of Welsh.

Before the Norman occupation of the Glamorgan lowlands a few years after the Doomsday Book, we have very little information on language distribution in Glamorgan, but it is clear from place-name evidence that there was a considerable amount of Scandinavian settlement there. Charles (1934) concluded that 'in Glamorgan there existed a stronger Norse agricultural community than in south Pembrokeshire'. Ekwall (1918) said that 'Some settlement certainly took place in Glamorgan, especially round Cardiff'. There is certainly no extensive non-standard Scandinavian lexical element in the present-day dialect but this is hardly surprising in view of the tremendous rate of the nineteenth-century immigrations — as Dieth said: 'in the mixing of dialects the lexical differences are usually the first to be levelled out'. However, if we presume that the Anglo-Norman settlers were outnumbered linguistically by natives of Scandinavian origin, it is perfectly feasible that the 'r' sound of the latter could have prevailed in the ensuing linguistic assimilation. This would suggest that a Teutonic dialect has been the language of the Cardiff area for well over 1,000 years. Certainly, as far as influence from what is properly describable as the Welsh language is concerned, there is no single item of general everyday vocabulary, syntax, morphology or phonology in the dialect which can certainly be assigned to a Welsh-language origin and which is not shared with the general forms of English.

Note to Chapter 6

1. JWL's descriptive observations on contemporary Cardiff English here can be usefully cross-referenced with Collins & Mees's contribution to this volume, and with Coupland (1988: Ch. 2) [ed.].

References

CHARLES, B.G. 1934, *Old Norse Relations with Wales*. Cardiff.
——1938, *Non-Celtic Place-Names in Wales*. London Medieval Studies.
COUPLAND, N. 1988, *Dialect in Use: Sociolinguistic Variation in Cardiff English*. Cardiff: University of Wales Press.
EKWALL, E. 1918, The Scandinavian Settlements. In H.C. DARBY (ed.), *An Historical Geography of England before 1800*. Cambridge: Cambridge University Press.
ELLIS, A.J. 1882, On the Delimitation of the English and Welsh Languages. *Y Cymmrodor*.
——1889, *Early English Pronunciation Vol V*.
PHILLIPS, V.H. 1956, 'Astudiaeth o Gymraeg Llafar Dyffrin Elai a'r Cyffiniau'. Unpublished University of Wales thesis.
PIERCE, G.O. 1968, *The Place-Names of Dinas Powys Hundred*. Cardiff: University of Wales Press.
RAVENSTEIN, E.G. 1879, On the Celtic Languages of the British Isles. *Journal of the Royal Statistical Society*.
TREVELYN, M. 1910, *Old Llantwit Major*.
WILLIAMS, D.T. 1935, Linguistic Divides in South Wales. *Archaeologia Cambrensis*.

7   Syntax and Lexis in Glamorgan English

J. WINDSOR LEWIS

In 1964 I completed a manuscript entitled 'Glamorgan Spoken English' of over 400 typewritten pages. It had been put together with many interruptions over the previous 15 years and consisted of phonetic, grammatical and lexical observations on those features which distinguished the English of Glamorgan (as it then was but minus Gower) from most of the varieties spoken elsewhere in the English-speaking world.

Having been born in Cardiff and lived there 25 years and having many contacts in the rest of the county, I found such a compilation a natural exercise to undertake for someone attracted to the study of language. Its glossary of over 2,600 entries was based on general observations and informal discussions with no use of systematic questionnaire-based interviews. It included word forms not witnessed elsewhere, pronunciations and semantic values not found in the standard language, 300 or so local place-name and personal-name pronunciations, and many 'reverse' entries recording the fact that certain expressions or forms in general everyday use in most of the rest of the English-speaking world were 'alien' to Glamorgan English. The **lexical** comments that follow are a selection from the contents of that glossary.

The following abbreviations have been used: 'CE' for the variety of English heard between and around Cardiff and Barry (and along to Newport); 'Cmr' for the 'Cymric' variety of English (see p. 105) heard in the rest of the historic county of Glamorgan (excluding Gower); and 'Gm' for the name of that county. I have usually omitted any comment on the wideness of currency of the items. This is extremely variable, some being apparently universally known in Wales and others being of very restricted occurrence, in some cases by now possibly obsolete. Some were exclusively CE and some exclusively Cmr. I have excluded most place names, nicknames, slang, catchphrases, stock metaphors and similes and proverbialisms and have in general not included the numerous references to occurrence in Anglo-Welsh literature made in the original text.

The expression 'cf.' is used to indicate vowel agreement or rhyming value in reference to the parallel portions of the words in question. Some glosses are close synonyms; others are only explanatory descriptions. The sign ' is the International Phonetic Association's marker of principal stress in the following syllable, though I have not on this occasion made systematic use of phonetic transcription. ' marks an omitted segment.

The Welsh-language Element in Gm Vocabulary

CE yielded no words of Welsh-language origin not shared with general English except for the mildly pejorative term for a Cymric south Walian *shonny*, the Cymricised form of *Johnny* and its derivatives. *Daio* from *Dai*, i.e. David, was similarly used. Probably the latter placing of the second element of *shoni-onions*, the term for the once very familiar itinerant Breton onion-seller, betokens original formulation in Welsh and subsequent passage into English.

Even Cmr Gm English provided only a few widely used items. *Gymanfa ganu* and *cawl* were naturally used, like *eisteddfod*, for identifiably Welsh phenomena. The commonest Welsh word in daily use seemed to be the oath *Duw*. Variants of this as *Jiw*, *Jawch*, *Jawl* and other items like *darro*, *Jesu (mawr)*, *arglwydd (mawr)*, *nefoeth (mawr/wen)* and *myn uffern i* were confined to fairly consciously picturesque speaking, as were most of *cariad* (darling), *bach* and *fach* (male and female address endearments), *conin* (grouser), *crachach* (élite), *diprish* (lethargic), *didorath* (shiftless), *groven* (rind), *mochyn* (term of abuse) and *wuss* (contemptuous term of address). Less self-consciously used were *bopa* (auntie), *cam* (step, pace), *kibe* (hoe), *milgi* (whippet), *shwmai* (the greeting) and *teishen lap* (layer cake). Not all of these are of certain Welsh-language origin.

Welsh-language influence on the forms of originally non-Welsh words seemed at least possible in a number of Cmr items. These included *braddish* and *brattish* (both 'brattice'), *coppish* ('trouser-fly' evidently from *codpiece*), *cornish* (cornice), *loshin* (Cmr for 'lossin', i.e. sweetmeat, from *lozenge*), and *slyshe* (slice) all possibly showing Gwentian palatalisation. The vocalic elements of *croot* (puny fellow) and *cloock* (broody, etc.), both with the FOOT vowel, and particularly those of *Lewis*, *Llew* and *mew* as heard in Cmr with the first vowel of Welsh *Dewi* seem to point clearly to Welsh-language influence.

The Flemish Element in Gm Vocabulary

A well-known expression *ach-y-fi* (also *ych-y-fi*) shown by its usual spelling to be generally taken for Welsh, rather naturally on account of its usually containing a voiceless velar fricative, is curiously enough most likely to be of Flemish origin. It has a CE variant *akkavee* and Wright (1905a) at *accabe* suggests for that a derivation in common with closely similar forms quoted from Bremen, Holstein and Flemish sources. It has to be remembered that the same fricative value can be associated with the general English exclamation *ugh*, exclamatory noises falling frequently outside the normal phonetic repertoire of a language (see Jones, 1977: s. *ugh*).

Of likely Flemish origin are the word *reeve* (gather, of fabric) and the Cmr items *culf* (hunk, of bread) and *pimp* in its sense of Peeping Tom (and corresponding verb) as used by Dylan Thomas in *Portrait of the Artist as a Young Dog*. So is Cmr *bosh* for a kitchen sink (but known to Murray *et al.*, 1884, and Wright, 1905a, only as a mining term).

The Scandinavian Element in Gm Vocabulary

The surnames *Skyrme* and *Skrine* are more likely to owe their non-Saxon-seeming /sk-/ to Flemish than to Scandinavian origin but, as with the standard language, the intermingling was such that attempts at disentangling origins are pretty futile. Thus despite the prevalence of 'Danelaw' /r/ quality and distribution in south Wales (as suggested at p. 107) it is only possible to point to a handful of items that could have descended from the lowest Germanic substratum. One such is *teem* whose now-forgotten metaphor is paralleled in the synonymous Gm usage *empty* (come down hard, of rain). The literal sense 'cuckoo' of *gook* (cf. *spook*, *fool*) is also apparently no longer used. A similar term *toop* (cf. *took*) for 'stupid' (person)', limited to Cmr and widely taken as a Welsh-language loan, and spelt *twp* accordingly, seems to equate to *tup* (ram). Other possible items are *eckle* (spy, peep, see Wright, 1905a, at *ettle*), *flake*, *flick* (both 'flitch', 'side of bacon'), *gilt* (young sow), *gossup* (gossip), *niggle* (nag), *sket*, *skit* (both: spot, splash; scoot), *skip* (basket), *scram* (scratch), *scranky* (scraggy), *scrink* (runt; niggardly) *scruggins* (bacon bits) and two items which seem to have entered general English slang only relatively recently, *cag-handed* and *gaumless*. Some of these are not very widespread and any of them might have entered Gm from south-western or more northerly dialects.

Various word forms and senses were recorded which, though not necessarily even of likely Scandinavian origin, are yet characteristic of the

Danelaw rather than Saxon areas of England. Among these were *again* in the sense of 'later', *aisy* (easy), *bap* (kind of loaf), *better* (recovered), *bowly* (child's hoop), *boogy* (cf. *book*; bogey, nit; nasal-mucous particle), *clatch* (clout; doughy), *clotch* (clot), *cokum* (cunning; stupid), *daft, danted* (daunted), *devilskin* (naughty child), *hunker down* (crouch), *mam(my)* (mum(my)), *mange* (cf. *flange*), *poin* (whine), *run* (race, another person), *scruff* (scrape), *sniffles* (snuffles), *soddened* (soaked), *sodgy* (soggy), *tash* (throw roughly), *up in years* (elderly), *wan* (cf. *ran*; won), etc.

The South-Western Element in Gm Vocabulary

It is usually impossible to determine, of any one of the fairly considerable number of south-western contributions to the south Wales vocabulary, whether it is attributable to pre-industrial times or later. Among forms and senses recorded in Wright (1905a) for south-western counties are the following Gm expressions: *cree* (respite), *daps* (plimsolls), *bulk* (belch), *dram* (tram), *fousty* (fusty), *golden chain* (laburnum), *handsome* (as regular term of address), *heck* (hop), *lootch* (cf. *butch*; filthy liquid), *mob* (a game of hide and seek), *navel* (cf. *gravel*), *nippy* (cold), *pink* (chaffinch), *pink up* (cheer; adorn), *pine end* (gable end), *scag* (catch thread of garment), *scud* (scab; sleet), *skit* (splash), *smeech* (smell), *sprayed, spreathed, spreed* (all: chapped), *stingy-nettles* (stinging nettles), *shoe-nut* (Brazil-nut, from resemblance to a clog), *reeve* (gather fabric), *tump* (hillock), *whimberry* (bilberry), *wisp* (sty on eyelid), *wit-wat* (cf. *cat*, foolish), etc.

Some of these were more West Midland rather than purely south-western items, e.g. *tump*. To this grouping we can probably also assign *pikelet* (muffin) and the Shakespearian verb *to mich* (play truant). Besides this last thoroughly characteristic south Walian word there is another which in its exact form is apparently to be found nowhere else but is surely derived from French via western English: *jibbon* (spring onion). The nearest Wright (1905a) has to it is *gibble* (which like *jibbon* is obviously a descendant through Old French from Latin *cepa*) with a record of that form in Gm as 'seaside plantain' which I was unable to vouch for as still current.

Various domains of use might well have repaid more systematic investigation, including some of the following:

Mining Terms

Among the handful of such expressions which came to my notice, all belonging to the Cymric area, of course, were: *bond* (pit-cage), *bonked* (left above ground having missed descent of cage), *braddish, brattish* (draught-curtain), *butty* (workmate; chum); *dram* (tram), *journey* (set of trams), *pitch* (slope), *stent* (work area).

Countryside Terms

The glossary was no doubt particularly short on farming expressions. I had little or no contact with farmers, fishermen, and the like. Among nature terms noted were *boy's ribbon* for a plant with green-and-white striped leaves, *golden chain* (laburnum), *shivvy* (wild strawberry), *shoes and stockings* (yellow trefoil), *tongue-fern* (hart's tongue) and *whimberry* (bilberry). Terms for or connected with animals included *coob* (cf. *book*, 'coop'), *coot* (cf. *book*, 'sty'), *crink* (runt), *goody-hoo* (owl), *honey-coomb*, *in kindle* (pregnant), *sheep-tod* (dropping), *wizzen* ('weasand' i.e. windpipe, etc.), *yucker* (nestling bird).

Games Terms

Most of those who discussed the region's English with me had vivid recollections to offer of their childhood usages especially the names of games they played and other games terminology, some of which varied widely. There were eight different terms for *fivestones* (also *gobstones, pitstones, dandies*), several for *strong horses* (a rough boy's game also called *bomberino*), and variants of hide-and-seek (including *mob*), chasing games including *copper-slopper* (played with truncheons), *shoocky* (cf. *cook*, played with knotted scarves), ballgames including *queenie-o-coco* (played with boys against girls) and various games with marbles, to which term *allies* (cf. *alleys*) was much preferred. There was careful preservation of 'correct' traditional expressions such as *adging* (edging forward), *barm* (favourable position), *camel* ('knuckle-hold', very probably a Welsh-language loan known only in Cymric) and *fen mennance* (a call to prohibit the next), *fornollacking* (surreptitious improvement of position). The individual whose turn it was to be the seeker was *on it*. The claim for immunity from being caught twice in succession was *no killing the butcher* and the derisive reply of a participant addressed by the wrong name was quaintly *Barley-man's name!* An appeal to be temporarily excused from participation in a chasing game was *cree!* Wright (1905a) had it only for Salisbury but Opie & Opie (1959) showed how incomplete such records were, finding it the 'prevailing term on both sides of the Bristol Channel' besides at Worcester and Birmingham.

Other Children's Expressions

Expressions used by and to young children included *acky* (disgust), *babba* (baby), *boogyman* (cf. *book*, bogeyman), *cacker* (defecate), *coopy down* (crouch), *loller* or *lossin* (sweetmeat), *oo* (you), *poop* (cf. *book*, defecate), *tats* or *tatters* (for babies' 'walkies' from *ta-ta*), etc.

Older children's expressions included much conscious slang such as *guff* (challenge), *cleck* (tell tales), *half-snacks* (shares), *impot* (imposition) and *goosegog*, *razgog* for gooseberry and raspberry which gave rise to the even more extravagant *liegog* (library, i.e. 'lie-berry')!

General Expressions

There were many other usages not felt to be either childish or slangy but ordinary everyday colourless expressions most unlikely to be recognised by their users as regionalisms. They included: *aye* (yes, not homophonous with *eye*), *back and fore* (i.e. forth), *bad-in-bed* (ill), *beeswax* (to polish), *birdlime* (i.e. bird droppings), *boughten* (attributive, 'bought'), *bracers* (braces), *by here* (here), *chesty* (boastful), *cootch* (cf. *butcher*: snuggle, etc.), *dirt* (as verb), *drib-drab* (piecemeal), *dull* (stupid), *eggbound* (constipated by eating eggs), *empt* (empty, verb), *grain* (original fabric colour), *grouts* (tea-leaves), *ingrimed* (ingrained with, of dirt), *kid* (informal friendly term of address), *latebird* (compare *homebird*), *like* (so to speak), *man* (term of address to either sex with neutral vowel), *pith* (the crumb of bread), *trimmings* (Christmas decorations), *tricky* (ingeniously devised) and many others.

Gm Pronunciations of Individual Words

The distinction between a pair of 'different' though related words and a pair of variant pronunciations of the 'same' word is of course in fact a gradient one. The following items were all included as occurring either usually or to some extent in forms different from those of the most general varieties of current British English: *adver'tisement, af''noon, alablaster, almond* (cf. *Alma*), *a'thritis, ashphalt, aspidestra, ast* (*ask* and *asked*), *ba's* (baths), *bay'net, blackbeedle, Bri'dgend (not Bridg'end), Cammell* (Campbell in 'the Campbells are coming'), *car'board, castle* (as *Cassell*), *casterate, casuality, catacomb* (cf. *tomb*), *celery* (as *salary*), *cellu'loid, cementery* (compare the standard Spanish form), *cheffonier* (chiff-), *choir* (as *coir* and also so but with *w*), *coll'ery*, *colloq'ial*, *comb* (cf. *doom*), *com'ment* (verb), *coveteous*, *cookoo*, *darling* (Cmr as *dullin*), *demerara* (cf. *dumb*), *deevorce*, *domineer* (cf. *air*), *drownded*, *err* (as *air*), *Eu-rope*, *excape*, *fish'op*, *fi'epence*, *foolish* (Cmr as *fullish*), *gangerene*, *girl* (Cmr as *gel*), *Giberaltar*, God (as *gawd*), *gone* (as *gawn*), *gransher* (i.e. 'grandsire'), *Griffiths* (as *Griffiss*), *grove* (as *groove*), *gully* (cf. *bully*), *gypsophila* (cf. *lobelia*), *half-past* (as *ap-arse*), *handbag* (as *ambag*), *hear* and *here* (as *year*, rhyming with *fur*), *heighth* (consonants as *eighth*), *Hirwaun* (as *Urwin*), *hold* (as *holt*, as noun only), *hose* (as *whose*), *isn't* (as *in* or *idn*), *jaunders* (i.e. *jaundice*), *jujube* (as *jube*), *ladened*, *lamp'ost*, *laurel* (Cmr, cf. *law*), *leave* (noun as *leaf*), *liquorice* (as *lickerish*), *maroon* (the colour, as *marone*), *mar'lous* (i.e. *marvellous*), *mazzipan*, *mastiff* (as *mastive*), *Maureen* (as *marine*), *merc'ry*, *mischievious*, *mind* (as *mine*), *motor* (Cmr as *moto*), *moustache* (cf. *stash*), *nearly* (cf. *curly*), *Neba-cha'nezzar*, *night-dress* (as *nitrous*), *nougat* (as *nuggat*), *nought* (for 'nothing' — but not for 'zero' — as *nowt*), *now'days*, *or'chestra*, *orniment*, *pantomine*, *papier mâché* (as *paper mashy*), *paraffin* (as *parafeen*), *partic'lar*, *pavement* (as *payment*), *pearmain* (cf. *remain*), *peep-bo* (as *peep-oh*), *pep'mint*, *p'roxide*, *petticoat* (cf. *delicate*), *photo* (cf. *motor*), *picture* (as *pitcher*), *pillow* (as *pillar*; and so most such *-ow* words), *pincers* (as *pinchers*), *plen'y*, *p'escription*, *p'etend*, *progr'mme* (Cmr only), *pudding* (as *pudden*), *pumice-stone* (as *pummy*, etc.), *Rab'iotti*, *raddish* (as *reddish*), *rear* (i.e. 'raise' as *rare*), *rec'rd* (Cmr: noun only), *rhubarb* (as *-bab*, *-bob*, *-b'b*), *ridic'lous*, *rind* (as *rine*), *'robust*, *salad* (cf. *pallid*), *Sarah-Ann* (as *Sar'ann*), *sarsaparilla*, (as *sasparella*), *sauce* (Cmr, cf. *loss*), *saucepan* (as *sosp'n*), Scotch Highlander (as *Scotchy-lander*), *Si'mese*, *siren* (as *sy'reen*), *some'dy*, *something* (as *summin*), *somewhat* (as noun only, regularly *summat*), *stirrup* (as *sturrup*), *student* (as *studient*), *syrup* (cf. *Surrey*), *s'ringe*, *tarpaulin* (as *tarpolin*), *ta-ta* (as *t'ra*), *taters* (i.e. *potatoes*), *theatre* (cf. *better*), *tooth* (cf. *book*), *tortoise* (cf. *noise*), *twen'y*, *umberella*, *vase* (cf. *gauze* and *phase*), *vi'let*, *wad* (cf. *fad*), *wan* (past of *win*, cf. *pan*), *wasn't* (as *wodden*, *wan*), *wasp* (cf. *asp*), *weir* (as *ware*), *Wenceleslas*, *whore* (as *who're*), *woman* and *won't* with no /w/, *yeast* (as *east*), *yest'day* and many others.

Syntax and Morphology

The 1964 MS acknowledged that Gm shared with most popular forms of English such features as double comparatives and negatives, demonstrative *them*, the regularised possessives *hisself* and *theirselves*, uninflected adverbs as in, for example, *it hurts awful bad*, unmarked plurality after numerals, unsanctioned past-tense expressions as in, for example, *we've ate 'em, he come, they done it, she never*, etc., and present-tense forms with *-s* for all persons. It also listed a number of to some extent more peculiarly Gm features among which were the following.

Substantives

It noted various plural-form substantives regularly treated as singular, including *baths, bracers, pinchers, scissors, scales, trousers* and *tweezers*, and other plural nouns with collective senses also so treated, e.g. as in *not this ages, not much hopes/thoughts, eggs is no good, apples is best* besides the widespread popular *orders is orders*.

Pronouns

Besides the generally familiar sentence-final vocative *you* of admonitory commands, it found *you* so added in encouraging ones, as in e.g. *carry on, you; sit down, you*. The notorious Cmr *look you* seemed to have become rare if not quite obsolete.

It was pointed out that the initial *do* of emphatic general educated commands (e.g. as in *do sit down*) was alien to unsophisticated Gm usage.

Masculine and feminine pronouns were noted as very often used to refer to what Wright (1905b: §393) termed 'formed, individual objects', as in, for example, *she's a lovely job that bike* and *that stone's a big 'un, idn' he?*.

Old-fashioned Cmr speakers were recorded as sometimes using *which* instead of the usual Gm *who* or *that* as in e.g. *my sister which lives in Pengam*. Widely popular *what* in such use was not recorded.

Adjectival usages

The adjectival suffixes *-y* and *-ified* were noted as occurring in items like *burny, fainty, goldy, liquidy, mocky, picky, pointy, pound-notey, stingy* (from *sting*), *reddy, Welshy, whitey*, etc., and *cheesified, shonnified, summerified, Welshified*, etc.

Paratactic adjectival clauses were fairly commonly recorded as in *I gets I can't help it, it do make me I don't know where I am* and *I'm gone I don't know how to get through my work*.

Adverbial and prepositional, etc. usages

Certain participial adjectival forms were noted as employed adverbially, notably in *it's raining pouring*.

Only temporal uses of *since* were commonly found. *Since* was not much used for 'because', being replaced by *'cause*, *seeing-as* or *being-as*. Temporal *since* could be followed by present-tense verb forms, e.g. *not since I'm back home*.

The general educated *as if* was noted as often replaced by *like if* or *like as if*, e.g. in *they treated him like as if he was dirt*.

The replacement of *to* by *and* found in the general educated usage *try and* was observed as extended to *start* and *mind* as in *mind and look after yourself* and *don't start and make trouble*.

The preposition *for* was noted as sometimes heard before an object in connection with *like to* as in *I wouldn't like for him to know it*.

The reduction of complex prepositions by omission of the second element increasingly observable in general educated usage was found to be very prevalent in Gm as in *out the window, round the back, over the shop* (which thereby was ambiguous).

One of the most characteristic features of Gm English proved to be the avoidance (in all but rather sophisticated speakers) of exclamatory *how* with adjectives and adverbs. The most typical equivalent of this is *there's*, e.g. *there's lovely*! General educated colloquial usage has only commendation (and discommendation) using *there's* before substantival expressions, e.g. *there's a fine sight* or *there's a good boy*, of which the Gm pattern is probably a development.

It seemed that the least sophisticated Gm speakers showed much greater preference for the *a* form over the *an* form of the indefinite article before words beginning with vowel sounds. This frequently resulted in loss of the article altogether through elision of the rhythmically weak schwa, thus making *have a heart* and *give us a hand* indistinguishable from *have heart* and *give us hand*, since generally in unsophisticated Gm no aspirates would figure in such expressions.

Verbal usages

Highly characteristic of Gm English proved to be its employment in most situations by the least sophisticated speakers of the *-s* form of the present tense not only for the third person singular as in general educated usage but for all the other persons singular and plural as well. This is a characteristic shared with various, especially southern and south-western, areas at least as far east as Reading. (It is found very widely indeed in popular usage over the English-speaking world in what we may call the present historic or narrative style notably with the verb *say*, as in *so I says to him*.)

However, and in this respect it does not accord with the distinctions reported in Cheshire (1978) for the Reading area, Gm seems to have semantic distinctions between *iterative* and *non-iterative* uses of present tense forms, the latter not taking the *-s* inflection. The non-iterative forms appear to express a non-conclusive state of mind while the s-inflection forms refer mainly to repeated activities, continued conditions or express futurity. The iterative forms are generally interchangeable with progressive-tense forms. For example *he always doubts my word* and *he's always doubting my word* can be interchanged with little difference of meaning, but *I doubt it* can hardly be exchanged for *I am doubting it* without a much stronger sense contrast.

In some of the following contrastive examples, the choice of the s-inflection form is more or less equivalent to the addition of an adverb such as 'always' in general educated English. Sometimes it endorses the iterative meaning of an accompanying adverb:

> I agree . . . I agrees with you usually.
> I ask you! . . . I always asks you first.
> I bet he don't . . . I bets on horses.
> I believe you . . . I never believes horoscopes.
> I doubt it! . . . I never doubts your word.
> I forget for the minute . . . I forgets people's names.
> I forgive you . . . your mother and father always forgives you.
> I guess you're right . . . I guesses the answers.
> I mean to say . . . . . . I means well but I puts my foot in it.
> I notice you got a new car . . . I notices things like that.
> I reckon that'll do . . . I reckons up the totals.
> I see . . . I sees her home.
> I tell you what . . . I tells him where he gets off.

I would not wish to claim that the kinds of usages illustrated above were never departed from by any speakers; but the pattern was far too frequently observed in the least sophisticated speakers for the uninflected forms to be put down simply to standard-usage influence; and the use of inflection in some non-iterative types was not surprising in view of the subtlety of the distinction in many situations.

This feature of Gm grammar is probably the most strongly stigmatised of all and is generally avoided by lower-middle-class speakers. Even so, it was curious to observe it cropping up from time to time in various speakers who had positive ideas on correctness of usage that might be expressed for example by insistence on the desirability of sounding one's 'aitches'.

In Cmr only, the unemphatic periphrastic present with unstressed *do* proved very common, possibly more eastward from Rhondda than westward, e.g. *they do 'do it 'for you.*

The prefix *a-* was never noted to occur before present participles in living use though *a-past* and participial adjective *a-willing* were reported to have been in recent use among older folk in the north-west of Glamorgan. Although the non-standard past-tense forms heard were mostly the ones shared with popular English world-wide, some use of *brung* was noted and of *swole* and *snook (cf. book)* instead of *sneaked*, but the latter at least seemed to be mainly jocular. Quite commonly *hurted* was noted in serious use.

In Cmr alone the future tense form was very frequently observed in temporal subordinate clauses, e.g. *wait till she'll have him home.* This no doubt reflected Welsh-language influence.

Present and past participles were quite frequently observed as postponed to the final position in the sentence, as in e.g. *he's a nice lad getting, it's a good size coming, isn't it cold gone!* Such occurrence would usually treat the participle as post-tonic but it could be the tonic or have its own separate tonic as in *it's six o'clock gone.*

Finally, comparing the 'Glamorgan Spoken English' record with the most recent account of CE morphology and syntax in Coupland (1988: 33–37), the following points occur. No confirmation can be offered for the verb usage of *they's awful.* Besides *we has,* the form *we haves* was well attested. The verb form /du:z/ *does* was recorded for speakers born in Cardiff who had never lived elsewhere, but only for the iterative-type semantic applications, never as an auxiliary. The absence of *were* in first and third singular forms was confirmed. So was absence of various generalised non-standard *-ed* forms. So was the existence in Gm of the invariant tags *is it* and especially *isn't it,* but the point was made that they were vastly more characteristic of Cmr than of CE. Predicate fronting was so little observed as not to be recorded for CE, being taken to occur there no more than in general educated usage.

References

CHESHIRE, J. 1978, *Present tense verbs in Reading English*. In P. TRUDGILL (1978).
COUPLAND, N. 1988, *Dialect in Use: Sociolinguistic Variation in Cardiff English*.
    Cardiff: University of Wales Press.
JONES, D. 1977, *Everyman's English Pronouncing Dictionary*. (ed. A.C. Gimson)
    London: Dent.
MURRAY, SIR JAMES A.H. *et al* 1884, *The Oxford English Dictionary*. London:
    Oxford University Press.
OPIE, I. and OPIE, P. 1959, *The Lore and Language of Schoolchildren*. London:
    Oxford University Press.
THOMAS, DYLAN 1940, *Portrait of the Artist as a Young Dog*. London: Dent.
TRUDGILL, P. (ed.) 1978, *Sociolinguistic Patterns in British English*. London:
    Edward Arnold.
——1984, *Language in the British Isles*. London: Cambridge University Press.
WRIGHT, J. 1905a, *The English Dialect Dictionary*. Oxford: Oxford University
    Press.
——1905b, *The English Dialect Grammar*. Oxford: Oxford University Press.

8 Port Talbot English

JOHN H. CONNOLLY

Port Talbot is an English-speaking industrial town with a population of approximately 50,000, situated on the coast of West Glamorgan some seven miles east of Swansea. The present description presents an outline of the local variety of English (of which the author possesses a native knowledge), and is based throughout on first-hand experience. The description will focus upon working-class speech, in order best to bring out the distinctive characteristics of Port Talbot English (PTE).

Segmental Phonology[1]

Consonants

PTE manifests the following consonant system. Plosives: /p,b,t,d,k,g/; affricates: /tʃ, dʒ/; fricatives: /f,v,θ,ð,s,z,ʃ,ʒ,h/; approximants: /w,r,l,j/; nasals: /m,n,ŋ/. Note, however, that /h/ is not always pronounced in contexts where it would be expected in standard varieties, and it is common to hear the participial suffix *-ing* rendered as /ɪn/ rather than /ɪŋ/. Occasionally the indefinite article is pronounced /ə/ rather than /ən/ before a vowel, e.g. *a airport* /ə 'ɛ:po:t/. PTE is non-rhotic, except that a small minority of speakers employ /ər/ rather than /ø:/ in words like *work*. With regard to allophonic variation, /l/ is realised as a clear lateral approximant in all environments, while /r/ is usually pronounced as a tap, except in the clusters /tr/ and /dr/, which are normally realised phonetically as post-alveolar affricates. The aspiration of plosives is comparatively strong, and is often manifested as weak affrication, especially in the case of alveolars. Consonant lengthening also occurs in many contexts (see below). Glottal realisation of /t/ in word-final position is atypical but by no means unknown in PTE. Finally, it may be noted that PTE speakers are generally able to pronounce the sounds [x] and [ɬ], which are found in various local Welsh place names.

Vowels

The vowels which constitute the PTE system are presented in the following lists, along with exemplificatory words taken as far as possible from Wells's (1982: I, 120) reference set.

> Checked monophthongs: /ɪ/ *kit*, /ɛ/ *dress*, /a/ *trap*, /ɒ/ *cloth, lot*, /ʊ/ *foot*, /ə/*strut*, comma.
>
> Free monophthongs: /iː/ *fleece*, happy, /eː/ *face*, /ɛː/ *square*, /aː/ *bath, palm, start*, /ɒː/ *north, thought*, /oː/ *goat, force*, /uː/ *goose*, /øː/ *nurse*.
>
> Diphthongs: /eɪ/ *ray*, (/aɪ/*aye*), /ɒɪ/ *choice*, /ʌɪ/ *price*, /ɪu/ *glue*, /ʌu/ *mouth*, /ou/ *flow*.

A number of matters call for comment here, beginning with two observations relating to the system as a whole. Firstly, the system contains no centring diphthongs, since /ɛː/ is monophthongal while the vocalic elements of words like *near* /ˈniːə/ and *cure* /ˈkɪuə/ are disyllabic. Secondly, the vowel /aɪ/ has only a marginal status within the system, being found only in a very small number of words. (Hence it has been placed in brackets in the above list.) However, it does contrast with /ʌɪ/ in the pairs *aye*/ɪ and *Dai*/*Di* (the abbreviated forms, respectively, of *Dafydd* and of *Diana* or *Diane*).

The distinction between the vowels /u/ and /ɪu/ gives rise to minimal pairs such as *through*/*threw* and *blue*/*blew*. To some extent the appropriate vowel can be predicted from the spelling, in so far as where the orthographic form contains 'o' (as in *through* or *pool*) the corresponding phonological representation contains /uː/. Otherwise the spoken vowel is generally /ɪu/ (as in *threw, blew* or *muse*), except that 'u', 'ue' or 'ui' are typically pronounced /uː/ when preceded by /r/ (as in *Ruth, rue* or *cruise*). The /uː/ vowel is also found immediately following /l/ in *blue* and typically also in *flute, Lucifer, lunar, lunatic, lupin, Luther, plume, plural* and *Pluto*, but is atypical in other comparable words, such as *clue* or *glue*. In addition, /uː/ occurs typically in the words *insurance* and *surety*. A further point is that /ɪu/ is not generally preceded by /j/, so that, for instance, /ˈkɪuə/ is a more typical rendering of *cure* than /ˈkjɪuə/. However, /j/ may precede /ɪu/ in word-initial position, so that, for example, *use* may be either /ɪus/ or /jɪus/; and when the word begins with 'y' (as in *youth* /jɪuθ/) the /j/ is nearly always present, except that in *you* and its derivatives the semivowel may or may not be included.

The distinctions between /eː/ and /eɪ/ and between /oː/ and /ou/ again give rise to minimal pairs, such as *laze*/*lays* and *groan*/*grown*. Here too, as Wells (1970) has noted, the correct vowel can generally be predicted from the orthography. The /eɪ/ vowel is generally appropriate only if the spelling contains 'i' or 'y' but not otherwise, while /oʊ/ is generally appropriate only where the orthographic representation contains 'u' or 'w'. Hence we find /eɪ/ in *tail, lays, veil* and *grey*, /e:/ in *laze, bass, gauge* and *halfpenny*, /oʊ/ in *boulder, grown* and *sewn*, and /o:/ in *groan, go, foe, rove* and *brooch*. However, there are numerous exceptions. First of all, /e:/ is subject to certain distributional restrictions. It does not appear in word-final position or before a vowel, so that words like *ballet* and *mosaic* contain /eɪ/ instead. Nor does /e:/ normally occur before a nasal, so that words such as *strange* again display /eɪ/, though the proper names *Cambridge* and *James* do have /e:/. In addition, /eɪ/ is found where the orthographic sequence '-ation' appears, as in *creation* or *nation*, and also in *patient* and *patience*. On the other hand, it is /e:/ that occurs in *bait, gait, gaiter, Jamaica, raisin, traipse* and *waist*. As for /o:/ and /oʊ/, the general rule is violated in the words *though* and *although*, which contain /o:/ rather than /oʊ/, and also in unstressed morph-final '-ow' in words like *elbow* /'ɛlbo:/. The other exceptions arise chiefly where the vowel is followed by /l/. Where this consonant is spelt 'll', although the appropriate vowel is normally /o:/, as in *poll* and *toll*, nevertheless the words *roll, stroll* and their derivatives have /oʊ/. Where the consonant is spelt 'l', /oʊ/ appears where a further consonant follows the /l/, as in *old* or *molten*.

A further point to note about /o:/ concerns the pronunciation of the orthographic sequence 'or'. The normal PTE pronunciation of this sequence is /ɒ:/, as attested in words like *cord* and *sort*, but in some words /o:/ is found instead. The latter pronunciation is regular where the sequence is followed by a vowel, as in *story* and *glorious*, and it is found, too, in the participial forms *borne, sworn, torn, worn* and *shorn*. In addition, /o:/ is common in syllables introduced by /f/, /s/ or /sp/ and ending in an obstruent, and especially within monosyllabic roots conforming to this description, such as *force, ford, fort, forth, porch, pork* and *sport* (though *fork* has /ɒ:/). Longer words containing syllables that satisfy the above description and similarly display /o:/ include not only derivatives of the items just listed, such as *forceful*, but also the words *afford, forceps, fortress, import, importance, important, portent, portion* and *proportion*. /o:/ is found as well in the words *horde, sword* and *divorce*, even though the syllables concerned do not match the specified description. Furthermore, it is /o:/ which appears in words like *boar, core, floor* and *four*, where the vowel is rendered orthographically by the sequences 'oar', 'ore', 'oar' or 'our'. On the other hand, as implied earlier, the vowel in words like *thought* and *lawn* is /ɒ:/.

Turning to the vowel pair /ɒː/ and /ɒ/, PTE generally displays the checked rather than the free member in the context of a following /l/ plus consonant; hence *fault*/fɒlt / and *salt* /sɒlt/. However, /ɒː/ is normal where the consonant sequence /ld/ follows, as in *bald* or *cauldron*, and is also found in *palsy*. It should be noted, too, that /ɒ/ rather than /ɒː/ appears before the cluster /st/ in *Austin* and *Austria*, and it also occurs in the first syllable of *saucepan*.

Some comments are in order as well in respect of the vowel pair /a/ and /aː/. Although, as noted earlier, the word *bath* contains /aː/ rather than /a/, this does not mean that the lexical incidence of these two words is in general the same as in southern English. In fact, in words like *chance* and *demand*, where the vowel spelt as 'a' precedes a consonant cluster introduced by a nasal, PTE always selects the checked vowel, in a manner comparable with northern English. The same is true in respect of most words such as *graph* /graf/, *lath* /laθ/ and *glass* /glas/, where the vowel is followed by a fricative, but /aː/ does occur in *laugh* and *laughter*, in *bath* and *path*, and in *ghastly* and *last(ly)*. /aː/ is also frequently found in *man*, *bag* and *bad*, especially when the latter has its dialect meaning of 'ill'.

The vowel /ɪ/ is more restricted in its distribution in PTE than in traditional RP. In unstressed word-final position /iː/ is found instead, e.g. in *greedy* and *softly*; and neither /ɪ/ nor /ʊ/ occurs before a vowel in the same word (cf. Wells, 1970: 241), so that, for instance, *hurrying* is /ˈhəriːɪŋ/ not /ˈhərɪɪŋ/ and *doing* is /ˈduːɪŋ/ rather than /ˈduɪŋ/. /iː/ is also found in preference to /ɪ/ in prefixes like *anti-* and *poly-*, while in the suffix *-est* the PTE vowel is /ə/. On the other hand, /ɪ/ does appear in the inflectional suffix allomorphs /ɪd/ and /ɪz/).

The monophthong /iː/, rather than the diphthongal sequence /iːə/, occurs in the tonic syllable of polysyllabic words like *bleary* and *imperial*, where /r/ follows. /iː/ is also typical in the first syllables of adverbs like *nearly* and *really*. However, in monosyllables like *beer*, *fear*, *mere* and *near*, the diphthongal sequence /iːə/ generally appears, though *ear*, *hear* and *year* manifest the sequence /jøː/. In the cases of *mere* and *near*, there is therefore an interesting contrast with the situation in Cardiff as described by Collins & Mees (this volume).

In addition to the general rules and exceptions listed above, there are a few points to note in relation to individual words. *Tooth* is pronounced /tuθ/, the strong form of *their* is /ˈðeɪə/, *motor* is /ˈmoːtoː/ and *mauve* is usually /mɒːv/. The commonly employed forms of address *man* and *girl* are pronounced /mən/ and /gəl/ in this particular usage. *Own* is /oːn/ when accompanied by a possessive determiner (as in *my own*), but /oun/

when used as a verb. In addition, some speakers have /a/ in *daunt* and *jaunt*, /u:/ in *hose* and *whole*, /ə/ in *want*, and /e:/ in the first syllable of *area*.

Finally, some brief notes are in order on the phonetic realisations of the vowels in the PTE system. /i:, u:/ are very close, /ɪ,ʊ/ are between close and half-close, /e:, ø:, o:/ are half-close, /ɛ/ is half-open, and /a,a:,ɒ,ɒ:/ are fully open. /ə/ is half-open when stressed, but may be slightly closer when unstressed. On the front-back axis, all the monophthongs are articulated at or near the periphery of the vowel area, except for /ə/ which is central and /ɪ,ʊ/ which are slightly centralised. The starting and finishing points of the diphthongs are fairly near to the qualities of the corresponding monophthongs; in the case of /ʌɪ/ and /ʌʊ/ the monophthong corresponding to the first element is, of course, /ə/.

Assimilation and elision

PTE exhibits assimilation and elision processes in much the same way as other accents of English, with elision being a particularly common phenomenon. The consonants which are most liable to elision are word- or morpheme-final /t,d/ and word-initial /ð/; e.g. *not fair* /nɒ 'fɛ:/, *handbag* /'hambag/ (with assimilation of the nasal as well as elision of the plosive), *what's this?* /'wɒs 'ɪs/. Among the vowels, unaccented /ə/ is the most likely to be elided, e.g. *factory* /'faktri:/, *perhaps* /praps/, though renderings like /'faktəri:/, in which the vowel is retained, are quite normal. Elision involving a reduction in the number of syllables is, however, very common in the following expressions: *there you are* /'dɛ: 'wa:/, *isn't it?* /'ɪn ɪt/, *never mind* /'nɛ 'maɪn/ and *why* + negative form of *do*, as in *why don't/didn't you?* /'waɪn ɪu/, *why doesn't/didn't he* /'waɪn i:/. The reduction of *Co-op* to /kɒp/ is a characteristic south Wales feature found in PTE.

Non-segmental Phonology[2]

Stress

PTE, like other Welsh accents, tends to avoid double stress within a single word; hence such characteristic accentual patterns as *Bridgend* /brɪdʒ'ɛnd/, *ice-cream* /'ʌɪskri:m/ and *free-wheel* /fri:'wi:l/. However, vowels in unaccented syllables are more liable to obscuration of quality than is the case with many Welsh accents; for example, *moment* is typically /'mo:mənt/ and *by there* is usually /bə'ðɛ:/, though *Welshmen* is /'wɛlʃmɛn/, perhaps because *men* is a separate root from *Welsh*.

In PTE, as in Welsh accents generally, there is a particularly strong connection between stress and syllable-length. Unaccented syllables tend to be short even when they contain free vowels; thus, for instance, the first vowel in /fri:'wi:l/ is phonetically not [i:] but [i]. Accented syllables, on the other hand, are characterised by lengthening effects in which the part played by postvocalic consonants is of special note. When any accented vowel other than /e:,ɛ:,a:,ɒ:,o:,ø:/ is followed by one or more consonants, there is a strong tendency for consonantal lengthening to take place. For example, the plosive in all of the following words tends to be lengthened: *lob, lobby, sit, city, shunt, shunting*. The effect is most noticeable in relation to fortis plosives, and when these occur intervocalically, as in *city* or *shunting*, it is comparable to consonantal doubling. In cases where the lengthening affects a cluster, it focuses upon the first of any fortis segments (e.g. the /t/ in *shunting*, the /p/ in *lipstick* or the /s/ in *nasty*), or otherwise simply upon the first consonant of the cluster (e.g. the /v/ in *lovely*, where the cluster concerned contains no fortis consonants). As an alternative to consonant lengthening, however, one sometimes hears the lengthening of an accented checked vowel instead, for example if *casserole* is pronounced ['ka:səro:l].

Intonation

There is an old joke which runs, 'The trouble with the Welsh is that they never stop singing, even when they're talking'! Part of this impression may be due to the tendency for the nuclear pitch movement not to be confined to the tonic syllable of the tone unit but to be distributed over the tail as well. The head of the tone unit, too, can exhibit a fair amount of pitch movement. Details of the melodic patterns are still in need of investigation, but a notable characteristic is the nuclear pitch-pattern low level + rise + fall, which is common in emotively neutral statements. In both falling and rising tones the range of pitch movement is often considerable. Thus, there are notable similarities between PTE and Abercrave English in respect of prosodics; see the very interesting discussion of rhythm and intonation in the latter variety offered by Tench (this volume).

Grammar

Several of the salient dialectal features of PTE at the grammatical level concern verbs. First, the auxiliaries *do* and *have* are often uninflected in the third person singular of the present tense, e.g. *do she want any? he have taken the lot*. Second, declarative affirmative sentences are frequently constructed with the auxiliary *do*, as in sentences like *they do put up with it*, where *do* is unaccented and no sense of rebuttal of an earlier utterance is intended. Alternatively, the auxiliary may be dispensed with but the main verb take an *-s* inflection in all forms of the present tense, e.g. *I likes it, they drinks gallons*. Third, main verbs are readily topicalised and fronted along with the rest of the predicate, as in *sitting in his chair he was*.

A further characteristic feature is the use of the third person singular neuter tag questions *is it?* and *isn't it?* in relation to superordinate clauses in which the subject is not third singular neuter; for example, *opening a shop you are, is it? he's gone to Cardiff, isn't it?* Another feature is the use of *there* to introduce exclamations, as for instance in *there's posh you do look!* The word *there* can, of course, also be used to open existential statements, and in such constructions it is possible for a relative pronoun to be omitted, e.g. *there's a syndicate in the office have come up on the football pools*. An additional characteristic is the use of the expression *that one* as a resumptive pronominal intensifier, e.g. *he's a scream, that one*.

In addition to the above, PTE exhibits a number of characteristics which are also quite common in non-Welsh dialects. These include double negation; the use of *never* to mean 'didn't'; the occasional employment of *as* as a relative pronoun; the use of *them* as a determiner (e.g. *them boys*); the omission of the *-ly* suffix from adverbs, especially the intensifier *real* (e.g. *real great*); the use of singular noun forms after numerals higher than one (e.g. *three foot*); the treatment of certain plural-only words as singular (e.g. *a scissors*); the simplification of complex prepositions (e.g. *down Margam* rather than *down to Margam*); the use of the reflexive forms *hisself* and *theirselves*; the occurrence of the verb form *ain't*; and the employment of past participles as preterites, as in *I done it yesterday*.

Lexis

PTE exhibits several lexical items which are not found in Standard English, though in many cases the same words also occur in other south Wales dialects.[3] Some are direct borrowings from Welsh, such as *cam* ('stride') and *crachach* ('posh people') or are derived from Welsh words, for example *poin* ('pester', cf. Welsh *poeni*, 'torment') and *venter* ('bet', cf. Welsh *fentro*, a mutated form of *mentro*, 'venture'), while others are

English-based, such as *ashman* ('dustman') and *troughing* ('guttering'). Moreover, a number of words which do occur in Standard English have additional, non-standard usages in PTE, for instance *after* ('later') and *scram* ('scratch'). In some cases of this kind, Welsh influence can be detected; an example is the use of *lose* in the sense of 'miss' (a bus). Again, similar usages can be found in other dialects of south Wales.

PTE also has a number of idioms which contribute significantly to its south Welsh flavour. Certain of these involve characteristic use of prepositions, especially *on* and *by*. The Welsh-influenced usage of *on* in sentences like *what is on this?* ('What is the matter with this?'), *there's times on him* ('He is moody') or *there's no shape on this* ('This is totally unsatisfactory') is found in PTE, while dialectal uses of *by* are found in the phrases *by here* and *by there*, and as well in such expressions as *what's the time by you?* and *you can't go by him* ('You cannot depend on him'). Also characteristic is the usage of *for* in expressions like *there's gratitude for you!*

In addition to these particular prepositional usages, PTE has a number of other idioms. Examples include *burnt to glory* ('burnt to a cinder'), *gone home* ('worn out', said of a garment), *possible if . . .* ('surely it is not the case that . . .') and *sure to be* ('undoubtedly').

Transcribed Specimen of Port Talbot English

/soː 'wʌɪn ɪu 'goː tə pə'tɒlbət 'səm tʌɪm ən 'lɪsn tə ðə 'piːpl 'tɒːkɪn? ɪs 'nɒ sətʃ ə 'baːb 'pleːs, əz'lɒŋ əz ɪu 'doː mʌɪn ðə 'smɛldʒəs 'rʌum bʌɪ ðiː 'abiː 'wøːks, ɪu 'nou lʌɪk, ən ðɛːz 'ɒlwɪz ðə 'biːtʃ, ə koːs, wɛː ðiː 'ɛːr ɪz nʌɪs ən 'frɛʃ, ən ɪu kən 'siː rʌɪt ə'krɒs ðə 'beɪ tə 'məmblz 'lʌɪtʌus. 'greːt ɪt 'ɪz, mən./

Notes to Chapter 8

1. This section is based largely on Connolly (1981). Other existing descriptions of south Wales English pronunciation can be found in Hughes & Trudgill (1979); Parry (1979); Trudgill & Hannah (1982: 27–29); Wells (1982: II, 377–93); Thomas (1984) and Coupland (1988); and allusions to the subject are also made in Wells (1970); and O'Connor (1973). Some criticisms of certain of these other references are found in Connolly (1981; 1983).
2. This section is in substantial agreement with Wells (1982: II, 391–92) and Thomas (1984: 183).
3. An extensive collection of expressions characteristic of south Wales English generally is found in Edwards (1985; 1986), though these booklets contain a fair proportion of material that is by no means particular to Welsh English.

References

CONNOLLY, J.H. 1981, On the segmental phonology of a south Welsh accent of English. *Journal of the International Phonetic Association*, 11: 51–61.

——1983, Review of Wells (1982). *English World-wide*, 4: 103–06.

COUPLAND, N. 1981, *Dialect in Use: Sociolinguistic Variation in Cardiff English*. Cardiff: University of Wales Press.

EDWARDS, J. 1985, *Talk Tidy: The Art of Speaking Wenglish*. Cowbridge: Brown & Sons.

——1986, *More Talk Tidy*. Cowbridge: Brown & Sons.

HUGHES, A. and TRUDGILL, P. 1979, *English Accents and Dialects: An Introduction to Social and Regional Varieties of British English*. London: Edward Arnold.

O'CONNOR, J.D. 1973, *Phonetics*. Harmondsworth: Penguin.

PARRY, D. 1979, *The Survey of Anglo-Welsh Dialects 2: The South-West*. Swansea: University College.

THOMAS, A.R. 1984, Welsh English. In P. TRUDGILL (ed.), *Language in the British Isles*. Cambridge: Cambridge University Press, 178–94.

——1985, Welsh English: a grammatical conspectus. In W. VIERECK (ed.), *Focus on: England and Wales*. Amsterdam: Benjamins, 213–21.

TRUDGILL, P. and HANNAH, J. 1982, *International English: a Guide to Varieties of Standard English*. London: Edward Arnold.

WELLS, J.C. 1970, Local accents in England and Wales. *Journal of Linguistics*, 6: 231–52.

——1982, *Accents of English* (3 vols). Cambridge: Cambridge University Press.

9 The Pronunciation of English in Abercrave

PAUL TENCH

Abercrave (Welsh: Abercraf) is the northernmost industrial village in the Swansea Valley.[1] It has had an industrial tradition for two hundred years, first in lime quarrying and, in this century, in coalmining. Abercrave lost the last of its three coalmines in 1967, with the depressing consequences that have been experienced widely in south Wales — nothing has taken its place.

Abercrave is distinct in two ways from the nearest localities described elsewhere in this volume. It is distinct from Port Talbot (Connolly, this volume) in that it was entirely Welsh-speaking until the Second World War, when evacuees were settled there. English speaking is therefore confined to the last two generations. Much of the village life is conducted in Welsh, but it is noticeable that the younger generation generally use English far more than they do Welsh.

The other near locality described elsewhere in this volume is Myddfai (Parry, this volume) in north Carmarthenshire; Abercrave is separated from Myddfai by the Black Mountain (Bannau Brycheiniog and Bannau Sir Gaer) which has constituted an enormous barrier to communication between the two communities. Abercrave speech shares a good deal with the rest of the upper part of the Swansea valley, from Ystalyfera and Ystradgynlais northwards. Interviewees conceded that they could not identify the precise origin of speakers between Ystradgynlais and Abercrave, but they could distinguish speakers from Cwmtwrch and the villages of that valley.

The following description of the pronunciation features of the people of Abercrave is based on observations during a period of stay in the summer of 1986, and tape-recordings of conversations and word-lists from men in their fifties and sixties who had been born and brought up in Abercrave all their lives.[2]

Perhaps the best method of presentation is to follow Connolly's clear and concise description of West Glamorgan English (Connolly, 1981; this volume), for although Abercrave is situated in the county of Powys, culturally and socially it belongs to the Swansea valley, most of which lies in West Glamorgan. Connolly's description is based on the model established by Wells (1970; 1982).

Consonants

It is commonly reported that the consonants of regional accents in the UK differ remarkably little from the consonant system of RP; that is certainly the case in Abercrave. /h/ is lacking regularly in informal conversations, although it is present in emphatic utterances and in the reading of word-lists. /l/ is clear throughout; consequently, there is no hint of 'breaking' before /l/ (see Wells, 1982: II, 298). /r/ is regularly a tap [ɾ] and is distributed as in RP. /ŋ/ is regularly replaced in final unaccented -ing by /n/; the phonemic status of /ŋ/ in Abercrave is determined solely by the cases of /n/ and /ŋ/ contrasting in final position of accented monosyllabic words, e.g. *thin* and *thing* (*nothing* is rendered with a final /n/). Aspiration of /p,t,k/ is fairly strong in initial position of accented syllables. The Welsh consonants /ɬ, x, r̥/ are marginal, appearing, as expected, in proper nouns and common Welsh expressions; /r̥/ is nevertheless also often heard in the word *right*, when used as a discourse marker.

The final /z/ of RP in the -*es* morphemes is regularly replaced in the speech of many by /s/ in Abercrave, as in, e.g. *tomatoes*. The plural forms of *path*, *bath* and *mouth* contain /θs/ rather than the /ðz/ of England. /j/ replaces /h/ in *here*, *hear* and *heard* and precedes the vowel in *ear;* thus *here*, *hear*, *ear* and *year* are homophones.

/n/ regularly assimilates to /m/ and /ŋ/ in appropriate bilabial and velar environments as in RP; however, the /n/ before /m/ in *government* is elided. /d/ and /t/ do not assimilate to the same extent. Indeed, the released alveolar articulation of /t/ in places where it would be replaced by an assimilated form or a glottal stop in RP is a conspicuous feature; *department* is pronounced with an obviously [tʰ] articulation, rather than the [p] or [ʔ] of RP; similarly in *rat cage*. Elision of /t/ and /d/ after a consonant and before an initial consonant of another word is by no means as regular a feature as it is in informal speech in England. In the recordings, /t/ was elided in *next week*, *first job*, but retained in *soft wood*. /d/ was retained in *binds*, *old boy* and very rarely elided; a clearly released alveolar articulation was kept in sequences like *standard one, could be, headmaster*. /s/ assimilated to /ʃ/ in *bus shelter*, but not in *this yard*. The patterns of assimilation and elision in Abercrave English are clearly Welsh (language) in character and are distinctively different from those of most types of native British English.

The consonant lengthening that is typical and well known in south Wales English speech is not so much a segmental phenomenon as prosodic (see Connolly, 1981: 59–60; this volume) and is dealt with later on in this description.

The consonant system of Abercrave English can be charted as in Table 9.1.

TABLE 9.1   The consonant system of Abercrave English

	Bilabial	Labio-dental	Dental	Alveolar	Palato-alveolar	Palatal	Velar	Labio-velar	Uvular	Glottal
Nasals	m			n			ŋ			
Plosives	p b			t d			k g			
Affricates					tʃ dʒ					
Fricatives		f v	θ ð	s z	ʃ ʒ				(x)	(h)
Lateral					(ɬ) l					
Tap					(r̥) r					
Approximant						j		w		

Vowels

In contrast to the relative stability of the consonant system in British varieties of English, the vowel system is subject to a great deal of variation, both systemically and realisationally. Again, Abercrave English is no exception.

Informants were requested to read a list of words after they had been engaged in relaxed informal conversation for about half an hour. The intention was to treat this part of the interview as an appendage to what had been presented as the main purpose, the recording of the conversation. In this way, it was hoped that the reading of the list would be as 'normal' as possible and would reflect genuine Abercrave pronunciation and not an affected, over-formal pronunciation. Some differences were, however, noticeable — principally the production of /h/ — but vowel qualities remained pretty consistent with the production of vowels in the conversations. The usefulness of word-lists is that they provide a convenient means of comparison between informants in a locality in order to establish a norm, and also a convenient means of comparison of norms of different localities. Wells (1982) has used this technique very effectively.

My word-list was Wells's 'standard lexical sets' (Wells, 1982: I, xviii–xix), augmented by keywords that Connolly (1981) showed to be relevant. The vowel qualities from Wells's 'standard lexical sets' in Abercrave English are given below, in phonetic transcription:

KIT	[ɪ]	NURSE	[ɜ:]	PRICE	[ai]		
DRESS	[ɛ]	FLEECE	[i:]	CHOICE	[ɒi]		
TRAP	[a]	FACE	[e:]	MOUTH	[au]		
LOT	[ɒ]	PALM	[a:]	NEAR	[i:ə]		
STRUT	[ʌ]	THOUGHT	[ɒ:]	SQUARE	[ɛ:]		
FOOT	[u]	GOAT	[o:]	START	[a:]		
BATH	[a]	GOOSE	[u:]	NORTH	[ɒ:]		
CLOTH	[ɒ]			FORCE	[o:]		
				CURE	[ɪu:ə]		

Wells added the following in his presentation of a south-east Wales variety of English (Wells, 1982: II, 380):

happY [i:]

lettER [ə]

commA [ə] (I used sofA instead, as being a more familiar word.)

I added the following, after Connolly (1981):

HERE	[i:ə]	THROUGH	[u:]
STALE	[e:]	GO	[o:]
TAIL	[ei]	CONE	[o:]
KNOW	[ou]	THREW	[ɪu]
THOUGH	[ou]	CORN	[ɒ:]
SHORE	[o:]	GOING	[o:ɪ]

The following systemic differences from the RP vowel system are to be noted. First, there is no phonemic difference between [ʌ] and [ə]; the latter is confined to unaccented syllables, the former to accented. The vowel phoneme will be transcribed, in this description of Abercrave English, with the symbol for the accented variety: /ʌ/.

Second, RP centring diphthongs are lacking: /ɪə/ and /ʊə/ are represented by a disyllabic articulation, involving a long, monophthongal, vowel followed in the next, unaccented, syllable by [ə], i.e. /ʌ/; thus *near* is, phonemically /'niː:ʌ/ and *cure* /'kɪuː:ʌ/; the other centring diphthong of RP, /ɛə/, is represented by a long monophthongal vowel of approximately cardinal vowel 3 quality: /ɛː/.

Third, Abercrave English possesses three vowel phonemes that do not exist in RP, which distinguish pairs of words which are homophonous in RP. Besides /ei/ as in *tail*, Abercrave has /eː/ as in *stale*; they, therefore, do not rhyme, as they do in RP and a distinction is made in otherwise homophonous pairs like *waist*, with /ei/ and *waste*, with /eː/. The basic guide to the differentiation between them was given by Wells (1970: 238): /ei/ is found where the vowel is rendered orthographically by a digraph whose second element is *i* or *y*, and /eː/ elsewhere. This was neatly illustrated by one informant's reference to a *play place*: /pleiple:s/. Connolly (1981: 52–3; this volume) notes some exceptions to this rule in West Glamorgan English, but there appear to be fewer exceptions in Abercrave. For instance, /eː/ *is* generally found before a nasal, e.g. *range, strange,* etc., and *is* used generally in the sequence *-ation*; in each case, unlike in Port Talbot and West Glamorgan.

Similarly, /oː/ is found besides /ou/, so that *no* /noː/ is not a homophone with *know* /nou/ in Abercrave. The same basic guide to differentiation between the two is valid for this pair: /ou/ is found where the vowel is rendered orthographically by a digraph whose second element is *u* or *w*, and /oː/ elsewhere. Again, there do not appear to be deviations from this rule to the extent that Connolly (1981: 53) has described for Port Talbot and West Glamorgan.

In addition, /ɪu/ is found besides /uː/ for RP /uː/; thus *threw* /θrɪu/ is not a homophone with *through* /θruː/. The basic guide to differentiation in this case also appears to be principally orthographical. Where RP /uː/ and /juː/ correspond to orthographic *ew*, they are rendered in Abercrave English consistently as /ɪu/, thus Abercrave *threw* and *blew* /blɪu/ rhyme with Abercrave *new, few,* etc. /nɪu/, /fɪu/ and not with Abercrave *true* /truː/, *blue* /bluː/. Indeed, RP post-consonantal /juː/ seems to be consistently rendered as /ɪu/ in accented syllables as in *suit, beauty, duty, tune*; also recorded were the words *individually* and *actually* with /ɪu/ after the /d/ and /t/ respectively in unaccented syllables; however, *popular* and *particular* had /ʊ/, not /ɪu/. Word-initially, where no *y* occurs, e.g. *use, Europe* /ɪu/ occurs; however, the form /juː/ is used where *y* appears initially before an /uː/ vowel, as in *you, youth,* as in RP.

Figures 9.1–9.4 represent the Abercrave English vowel system and provide an idea of the phonetic realisation of it. Two things are immediately apparent about the system: first, the high degree of symmetry; and second, the close parallelism with south Walian Welsh. There is a higher degree of symmetry in the Abercrave English vowel system than in the RP one. There are six short vowels: two front, two central and two back. /ɪ/ is close to the RP norm; /ɛ/ is more open than RP and approximately equivalent to cardinal

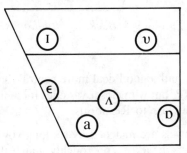

FIGURE 9.1 *Short monophthongs*

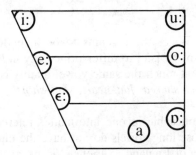

FIGURE 9.2 *Long monophthongs*

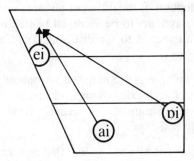

FIGURE 9.3 *Fronting diphthongs*

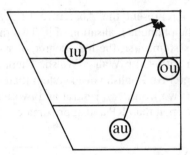

FIGURE 9.4 *Backing diphthongs*

vowel 3; /a/ is opener and a good deal more central than the RP /æ/; /ʌ/ is relatively open, like RP, but with closer varieties [ə] in unaccented syllables; finally, /ʊ/ and /ɒ/ are close to RP norms.

The six short vowels are matched by six long vowels, plus two more. The long vowels /iː, ɛː, ɜː, aː, uː, ɒː/ roughly match the six short vowels; and in addition, we have /eː, oː/. Abercrave bears out Wells's (1982: II, 381) general claim that:

> In all parts of Wales there seems to be a tendency for the pairs /ɛ, ɛː/, /a, aː/, /ɒ, ɔː/ [*sic*] to differ principally in length, rather than in quality; so that much the same vowel quality is often to be heard in the pairs *shed–shared*, *hat–heart*, *shot–short*.

This became very noticeable in one informant's reference to an *ash cart* (/a, aː/). The two close long vowels do not have the diphthongal tendency associated with many of England's varieties. /iː, eː, ɛː, uː, oː/ are more or less identical to their cardinal equivalents. /ɒː/ is noticeably more open than RP /ɔː/, hence the adoption of the different phoneme symbol; /aː/ is clearly central, not back; /ɜː/ appears to be identical to English /ɜː/, without any of the lip-rounding attributed to Cardiff and Port Talbot renderings of the vowel.

Three fronting diphthongs are matched systemically, though not quite phonetically, with three backing diphthongs. /ei/ and /ou/ have less movement than is reported for other south Walian accents (Wells, 1982: II, 384); the first element is clearly half-close.

Abercrave English has a vowel system that matches Abercrave Welsh in all respects except that the former lacks four diphthongs of the latter (see Jones, n.d.). Jones identifies a symmetrical pattern of ten diphthongs in the

Welsh of the Ystradgynlais area which can be displayed in the following manner:

ei		ʊi		ɪu		ou
	ei				eu	
	ai		ɒɪ		ɛu	ʌu

Abercrave English lacks /əi,ʊi/ and /ɛu,əu/, leaving a system of three fronting and three backing diphthongs.

It is also worthwhile noting where Abercrave English differs from Port Talbot and West Glamorgan English. Systemically, the only difference seems to be the lack of the contrast that Connolly (1981:54; this volume) reports for West Glamorgan, between /aɪ/, as in *Dai, aye,* and/ ʌi/ as in *die, dye, Di* and *I.* There does not appear to be any such contrast in Abercrave; the first element of the Abercrave diphthong is open enough to justify the symbol /ai/. All the diphthongs in Abercrave end fairly close, to justify the use of [i] and [u] in their symbolisation, rather than the [ɪ] and [ʊ] that Connolly employs for West Glamorgan.

The vowel in *strut* is too open to justify the use of [ə]. Incidentally, Parry uses the /ʌ/ symbol for the equivalent vowel in Myddfai. Also, as mentioned above, no lip-rounding appears to be involved in the articulation of /ɜ:/, which makes the Abercrave version closer to that of Myddfai in that respect too.

Transitional insertion of /j/ and /w/ between respective close vowels (and closing diphthongs) and a following vowel is a good deal less marked than it is in other south Walian English accents.

Finally, before leaving this consideration of the vowels, certain distributional features need to be mentioned. First of all, the phonological distribution of Abercrave /i:/ includes final unaccented syllables as in *happy*, where conservative RP has /ɪ/; this replacement is total.

In addition, there are certain lexical (or 'incidental') features of distribution. Abercrave follows the northern pattern of *bath* and *dance* words by selecting the short vowel totally; items recorded included *bypass, passed, grass, class, fast, last, master, path, bath, laugh, after.* Connolly (1981) and Collins & Mees (this volume) report various exceptions to the northern pattern in West Glamorgan and Cardiff; but in Abercrave, no single instance of the long vowel was recorded in these sets of words.

Abercrave also follows the West Glamorgan pattern of *north* and *force* words (Connolly, 1981: 56–57). *North, thought, corn, small, dawn,* have /ɒ:/; *force, course, door, four storey* have /o:/. Thus, whereas in RP *doe* is homophonous with *dough*, in Abercrave it is homophonous with *door*. Abercrave selects /iː/ and /uː/ regularly before /r/, e.g. *period*, *security*. The vowel selection in other individual lexical items was noted as follows: *one* has /ʌ/; *off*, /ɒ/; *our*, /auʌ/; *really* is pronounced /riːliː/; *area* has initial /eː/; *their*, /eɪʌ/; *haulier* /a/ for /ɔː/. *Co-op* loses a syllable and becomes /kɒp/. *Renowned* was pronounced with /ou/. *Tooth* has /ʊ/, *whole* /uː/. *Want* has RP /ɒ/, although one informant noted that a pronunciation with /ʌ/ was known among non-Welsh speakers of English.

Rhythm and Intonation

The rhythm and intonation of Welsh English speech are perhaps the most conspicuously different features from accents of England. These differences are what strike an Englishman's ear as the most characteristic features in identifying Welsh forms of English. These, the most prominent features, are often totally ignored in accent studies, since most of them concentrate almost exclusively on segmental items. The difference in rhythm accounts for the phenomenon of consonant lengthening, as well as other factors mentioned below. Connolly (1981: 59–60; this volume), as noted above, drew attention to prosodic phenomena, and it is not surprising to discover that the rhythmic characteristics of Welsh are transferred directly to the English spoken in those parts of Wales that have traditionally been Welsh-speaking.

Williams (1986) has presented an excellent and thorough investigation of the cues that identify 'stress' in Welsh. The differences between Welsh and English stress are illustrated by a remarkably opposite perception by English- and Welsh-speakers of stressed syllables in Welsh words and sentences read aloud. The Welsh-speakers' perception was confirmed in respect of spontaneous, continuous speech, too. Basically, English-speakers perceive stress in terms of pitch prominence, aided by greater duration and/or greater amplitude. Welsh-speakers, on the other hand, perceive as stressed vowels vowels that have no pitch change, have short duration and lower 'envelope amplitude', although greater peak and mean amplitude. In regular words, the stressed syllable is penultimate; the ultimate contains vowels of longer duration, pitch glide and greater 'envelope amplitude' — no wonder that English speakers are misled into thinking that these final syllables are stressed! Welsh stressed vowels are accompanied by a following consonantal lengthening. (Incidentally, it was found that Welsh vowels do not vary in length as a result of stress, in the way that English vowels do.)

Native speaker intuition, the coincidence of stressed (usually penulti-mate) syllables with the beat of music, and immunity to sound change, all conspire, according to Williams, to set up this syllable with short vowel duration and no pitch prominence as the stressed syllable. If acoustic prominence is not the cue to Welsh stress, what is?

One major clue is the degree of 'foot isochrony' based on this syllable. If isochrony is measured on the English-type process, no significant tendency towards isochrony is detected. On the other hand, measured on those syllables perceived by Welsh-speakers to be stressed, a very strong tendency to isochrony is detected. In other words, Welsh stress — far from being associated with loudness and pitch prominence — is the carrier of rhythmic prominence. 'The realisation of stress in Welsh depends far more on rhythmic and perceptual phenomena' (Williams, 1986: 48).

Williams raised an interesting suggestion from a consideration of the Old Welsh Accent Shift in the late eleventh century. Word stress shifted from final to penultimate syllables. Whereas a 'pitch element' was retained on the final syllable, a 'stress element' was transferred to the penultimate. (Thus it might be legitimate to consider the final *pair* of syllables as a single unit for prosodic analysis in Welsh, with a conflation of prosodic effects in the case of stressed monosyllables).

The lengthening of a consonant is an inherent feature of an accented syllable in Welsh and is not confined to cases of such consonants in intervocalic position, since it also occurs in monosyllabic words. This phenomenon is transferred to Welsh English *in toto*. Connolly (1981: 59) comments:

> Lenis as well as fortis consonants may be affected when preceded by a short monophthong (e.g. in *ladder*, *busy*), though in such cases the increase in duration is generally less than the equivalent of doubling. Furthermore, even in the absence of a following syllable a comparable lengthening effect is again detectable on lenis consonants after any vowel except the long monophthongs /e:, ɛ:, a:, ɒ:, o:, ø:/. (The vowels in this list . . . do not include /i:, u:/ or any of the diphthongs . . .).

Connolly's description seems to fit Abercrave English precisely.

The accent timing (i.e. 'foot isochrony') of Welsh works differently from that of English. In English, the 'squashing' of unaccented syllables within a foot results in a high incidence of the neutral vowel and also accounts for special weak forms of certain words. These two features are noticeably absent in Abercrave English. It was often noticed that the orthographic vowel in an unaccented syllable provided the basis for a non-neutral articulation. For instance, the unaccented vowel in *cricket, buckets, fastest, model, movement, jewel* was /ɛ/; in *instance, crystal* the vowel had a quality between [a] and [ʌ]. Neutral vowels were usually retained in contexts where RP loses them regularly in informal speech, e.g. *factory, delivery, reference.* Unaccented pronunciations of *to* were regularly /tu/ even before a consonant; unaccented *them* retained /ɛ/.

The most notable intonational features are the high degree of pitch movement on an unaccented post-tonic syllable, as noted above (which leads to the impression of a high proportion of rise-falls), and the high degree of pitch independence of unaccented syllables in pre-tonic position — glissando rising is very common. These two features lie behind the claim that Welsh people have a 'sing-song' or 'lilting' intonation. Their 'neutral' intonation patterns have a good deal more pitch movement than those of English 'neutral' patterns. Rising tones marking incomplete information seem to rise higher than they do in the corresponding English RP form.

Overview

Abercrave English is young; it is but two generations old. The articulation is clear and precise; there is less elision and assimilation than in the accents of England or the accents of non-Welsh-speaking areas of south Wales (Cardiff, Newport). English has been taught as a second language in Abercrave, and Wells's (1982) references to the effect of English language teaching in Welsh-speaking are well borne out there.

Wells suggests that the non-rhoticity of most Welsh English accents can be accounted for in this way. In the nineteenth century, when English became thoroughly established in Wales, lack of post-vocalic /r/ was already part of 'received' pronunciation in England. (It must be noted, however, that English words containing post-vocalic /r/ had been borrowed into Welsh at a much earlier stage, e.g. *nurse, farm, skirt, discourse, storm, sport* became Welsh *nyrs, fferm, sgurt, sgwrs, storm, sbort.*) Wells also noted that during the nineteenth century English had still not acquired fully open starting points in *price* and *mouth* vowels, which accounts for West Glamorgan's adoption of /əɪ/ and /əu/ — as witnessed for instance, in the borrowing of *nice,* as Welsh *neis.*

Spelling pronunciations involving /ei/ and /ou/ also suggest the effect of English being taught as a second language, as do pronunciations of words like *renowned* with /ou/, *cricket*, etc., with /ɛ/ and *instance*, etc., with a vowel varying between /a/ and /ʌ/.

However, the full-scale introduction of English as a second language came to Abercrave much later than in other parts of south Wales, with the effect that later developments in RP are reflected. This would explain Abercrave's preference for /ai/ and /au/ for West Glamorgan /əi/ and /əu/, and Abercrave's preference for the opener articulation /ʌ/ for West Glamorgan /ə/. Furthermore, Abercrave's narrower diphthongs /ei/ and /ou/ reflect present RP rather than West Glamorgan's /ɛɪ/ and /ɔu/, and the quality of teaching may have produced better renderings of RP /ɜ:/ than the stigmatised /ø:/ of West Glamorgan.[3]

Abercrave English thus represents a more modern form of acquired English than Connolly's West Glamorgan English. Where the former differs from the latter, it shows links with north Carmarthenshire (e.g. Myddfai), principally in the vowel qualities of /ʌ/, /ɜ:/, /ai/ and /au/.

Notes to Chapter 9

1. National Grid reference SN 8112.
2. Special thanks are due to Mr Bernard Parsons, Mr Vivian Jones and Mr Len Price, all of whom have lived their whole lives in Abercrave and kindly consented to be recorded.
3. Wells (1982: II, 383) is of the opinion that 'it would not be unfair to say that to an Englishman, it [the auditorily unusual quality of /ɜ:/ in many Welsh accents] is often reminiscent of the slightly inaccurate attempts at this vowel made by learners of English as a foreign language'.

References

CONNOLLY, J.H. 1981, On the segmental phonology of a south Welsh accent of English. *Journal of the International Phonetic Association*, 11, 2: 51–61.
JONES, A. (n.d.), Tafodiaith Ystradgynlais.
WELLS, J. 1970, Local accents in England and Wales. *Journal of Linguistics*, 6: 231–52.
——1982, *Accents of English* (3 vols). Cambridge: Cambridge University Press.
WILLIAMS, B. 1986, An acoustic study of some features of Welsh prosody. In C. JOHNS-LEWIS (ed.), *Intonation in Discourse*. London: Croom Helm, 35–51.

10   The Conservative English Dialects of North Carmarthenshire

DAVID PARRY

The material discussed here and in the description of south Pembrokeshire in Chapter 11 is drawn from that collected in fieldwork for the *Survey of Anglo-Welsh Dialects* (University College, Swansea), in this case in 1974 (Parry, 1977; 1979).[1] The informants in both cases were chosen to represent the older generation of dialect-speakers; all were natives of their respective villages, had spent little or no time away, and had worked on the land for most of their lives. The six north Carmarthenshire localities investigated were Cenarth (Cen), Llansawel (Ll), Myddfai (My), Login (Log), Newchurch (Nch) and Gelli Aur (GA).[2]

Phonology

The questionnaire[3] by which the material was elicited does not provide for the setting-up of 'minimal pairs' for phonemic analysis; consequently, the phonemic systems proposed in this and the following discussion have been arrived at instinctually rather than scientifically.

Consonants

The six north Carmarthenshire dialects investigated appear to share a consonant system differing little from that of RP as regards its component phones and phonemes, although there are some differences in their distribution, the most important cases being noted below.

/l/ is realised very nearly always as clear [l] in all six dialects, dark [ɫ] being attested only very sporadically and unpredictably.

/r/ commonly appears corresponding to orthographic 'r' before consonants and in word-final position, though this is not consistently true in all the dialects for any particular word. Examples: /r/ occurs medially in *farmer* (Ll, My, Log, GA), *farthing* (Log), *first* (My, GA), *forks* (Ll, My), *heard* (My, Log), *morning* (My), *third* (My, GA); finally in *boar* (Cen, Ll, Nch), *butcher* (Cen, My), *butter* (My, Log, Nch), *door* (Ll, My, Log, Nch), *chair* (Cen, My, Nch), *farmer* (Ll, My, Log, GA), *flour* (My, Log), *hour* (Cen, GA), *ladder* (Cen, Log, Nch), *hare* (My, Log, Nch), *hear* (My), *mare* (My, Log), *sugar* (Nch), *year* (Cen, My, GA).

/j/ appears initially in *ears* /jə:(r)z/ (Ll, My, GA), but is lacking in such forms as *dew* (Ll, Nch, GA), *Tuesday* (Cen, Ll, Log, Nch, GA), *yeast* (Log, Nch).

Among the fricatives, we occasionally find voiceless forms in north Carmarthenshire corresponding to their voiced counterparts in RP, e.g. /s/ appears medially in *thousand* (My, Nch, GA), *Tuesday* (GA), also in all dialects with some speakers corresponding to RP /z/ in the plurals of nouns; and /θ/ appears medially in *farthing* (Cen, My, Log), finally in *with* (Log).

/n/ commonly corresponds to RP /ŋ/ in the combination /ɪŋ/ in words such as *evening, morning*, and present participles.

Vowels

The vowel phonemes proposed for the six dialects investigated, with their respective phonetic realisations, are shown in Table 10.1. All dialects have nos 1–19, but no. 20 is not found in the Myddfai system. The following is an outline of the distribution of the sounds in the six dialects under discussion:

/ɪ/, realised as [ɪ], corresponds to the RP /ɪ/ of stressed syllables.

/ɛ/, realised as [ɛ], corresponds generally to RP /e/, also to RP /i:/ in *grease* (Cen). The combination /ɛr/ corresponds to RP /ɛə/ in such forms as *chair* /tʃɛr/ (Ll, My, Nch), *pears* /pɛrz/ (Cen). Unstressed /ɛ/ may correspond to RP /ə/ or zero in such forms as *squirrel* (all dialects), as does unstressed /ɛr/ in such forms as *butcher* (GA), *butter* (Nch), *ladder* (Log), *sugar* (My).

/a/, realised as [a], corresponds generally to RP /æ/, also to RP /ɒ/ in *wasps* (Cen, Ll, Nch, GA); to RP /ɑ:/ in *branch* (all dialects), *calf* (Cen, My, Nch, GA), *chaff* (Cen, Ll, My, Log, Nch), *draught* and *grass* all dialects. The combination /ar/ corresponds to RP /ɑ:/ in *farmer* (Ll,

TABLE 10.1 *North Carmarthenshire Vowel Phonemes*

Phoneme No. Designation	Reali- sations	Dialects	Phoneme	Reali- sations	Dialects
1 /ɪ/	[ɪ]	All	12 /ɔ:/	[ɔ:]	All
2 /ɛ/	[ɛ]	All	13 /o:/	[o:]	All
3 /a/	[a]	All		[əu]	All
4 /ʌ/	[Ä]	All	14 /u:/	[u:]	All
	[ə]	All		[uə]	All
5 /ɔ/	[ɔ]	All	15 /ai/	[ai]	All
6 /ʊ/	[ʊ]	All		[əi]	All
7 /i:/	[i:]	All	16 /ɔi/	[ɔi]	All
8 /e:/	[e:]	All	17 /au/	[au]	All
	[ei]	All	18 /iə/	[iə]	All
9 /ə:/	[ə:]	All	19 /ɔə/	[ɔə]	Cen, My, Log,
	[œ:]	All			Nch, GA
10 /ɛ:/	[ɛ:]	All		[oə]	Ll, My
	[ɛə]	Cen, Ll, Log, GA	20 /iu/	[ɪu]	Cen, Ll, Log, Nch, GA
11 /a:/	[a:]	Cen, Ll, My, Nch, GA			
	[ɑ:]	Ll, Log			

My, Log, GA), *farthing* (Cen, Log). Unstressed /a/ corresponding to RP /ə/ or zero is attested in *sugar* (GA), *thousand* and *woman* (My).

/ʌ/ corresponds generally to RP /ʌ/ and /ə/, also to RP /ʊ/ in *put* [pÄt] (Nch, GA). The realisation in stressed syllables is [Ä] except for one attestation of [ə], in *uncle* (Cen); conversely, [Ä] is attested in the stressed and unstressed syllables of *butter* (Cen). The combination /ʌr/ sometimes occurs as reflex of RP /ə:/; for instance [Är] is attested in *first* and *third* (My, GA).

[ə] in unstressed syllables corresponds generally to RP /ə/, and occurs additionally in the second (unstressed) syllables of what in RP are monosyllabic forms with triphthongs, e.g. *fire* /ˈfaijʌ(r)/ (all dialects), *flour* /ˈflauwʌ(r)/ (all dialects); similarly *hear* /ˈhi:jʌ(r)/ (Cen, My, Log, Nch, GA), *hour* /ˈauwʌ(r)/ (Cen, Ll, Log, Nch, GA), *iron* /ˈaijʌ(r)n/ (Cen, Ll, My, Log, Nch). Also, [ə] corresponds to RP zero in *apples* /ˈapʌlz/ (Cen, GA), *weasel* (Cen, My, Log).

/ɔ/, realised as [ɔ], is generally a reflex of RP /ɒ/ (but for exceptions in *wasps* cf. above). Additionally, /ɔ/ is attested as reflex of RP /ʌ/ in *onions* (Cen, Log); and of RP /əu/ in *yolk* (Cen). The combination /ɔr/ corresponds to RP /ɔ:/ in such forms as *forks* (Cen, My), *slaughter* (My, Nch, GA).

/u/, realised as [ʊ], corresponds generally to RP /u/ except in *put* (Nch, GA). Additionally, /u/ corresponds to RP /ʌ/ in *uncle* (Log), and to RP /u:/ in *goose* (Log), *hoof* (Cen, My, Log, Nch, GA), *tooth* (Cen,Ll, My, Log, Nch).

/i:/, realised as [i:], corresponds generally to RP /i:/, and is attested also in *hear* /'hi:jʌ(r)/ (all dialects). Unstressed /i:/ corresponds to RP /ɪ/ in words with final orthographic -*y*, e.g. *ready, holly* (all dialects).

/e:/ corresponds generally to RP /eɪ/. The realisation [e:] is attested in all dialects in *break, gate, spade*. Otherwise, [e:] and [ei] are in apparently random distribution.

/ə:/ corresponds generally to RP /ə:/. [ə:] is by far the commoner realisation, [œ:] being attested more sporadically, as in *work* (Log), *first* and *third* (Nch). Additionally, /ə:/ in the combination /jə:r/ corresponds to RP /ɪə/ in *ears* (Ll, GA), realised as [œ:] in the former, [ə:] in the latter.

/ɛ:/ corresponds generally to RP /ɛə/ (but note also the north Carmarthen combination /ɛr/ in *chair, pears*, above). All dialects have the realisation [ɛ:]; this and [ɛə] are in apparently random distribution in the dialects of Cenarth, Llansawel, Login and Gelli Aur, which have both.

/a:/ (varying with /ar/) is a reflex of RP /ɑ:/, the realisation being usually [a:], though [ɑ:] is also attested at Llansawel and Login. The following phonetic forms are attested in four of the relevant words:

	Cen	Ll	My	Log	Nch	GA
arm	a:	a:	a:	ɑ:	a:	a:
calf	a	ɑ:	a	ɑ:	a	a
farmer	a:	ar	ar	ar	a:	ar
farthing	ar	a:	a:	ar	a:	a:

/ɔ:/, realised as [ɔ:], corresponds generally to RP /ɔ:/. Additionally, /ɔ:/ corresponds to RP /ɒ/ in *quarry* (Ll); RP /u:/ in *root* (My); RP /ɔə/

in *boar* (Ll), *door* (Cen, Ll, Log), *four* (Log, GA). For /ɔr/ corresponding
to RP /ɔ:/ see *forks, slaughter,* above.

/o:/ corresponds to RP /aʊ/ and RP /əʊ/, and occasionally to RP /ɔə/.
When /o:/ corresponds to RP /ɔə/ the realisation is [o:], as in *boar* [bo:r]
(Cen). When /o:/ corresponds to RP /aʊ/ the realisation is always [əu].
This is attested *generally* in the dialects of Cenarth, Llansawel and
Myddfai, and *sporadically* in the other dialects in such forms as *plough*
(Log, Nch), *snout* (Log, GA), *sow* (noun, Nch, GA), *thousand* (Log,
Nch). When /o:/ corresponds to RP /əʊ/ the realisation may be either
[əu] or [o:]. The following are the phonetic forms attested in a sample
of six words:

	Cen	*Ll*	*My*	*Log*	*Nch*	*GA*
coal	o:	əu	o:	o:	o:	o:
cold	əu	əu	o:	o:	əu	əu
oak	əu	o:	o:	o:	o:	əu
snow	əu	əu	o:	o:	əu	o:
spokes	o:	o:	o:	əu	o:	o:
yolk	əu	o:	o:	o:	o:	o:

The above table may give the impression that Myddfai has only [o:] as
reflex of RP /əʊ/, but [əu] is in fact attested there in *colt. Shoulder* is
one word that has [əu] in all six dialects. Other attestations of north
Carmarthen /o:/ include [əu] in the combination [əuwər] corresponding
to RP /aʊə/ in *hour* (Cen, Log, GA), and [əu] corresponding to RP /ɒ/
in *trough* (My).

/u:/ occurs as a reflex of RP /u:/, but this function is shared with
/ɪu/ (cf. below) and in some dialects with /ʊ/ (cf. above). Additionally,
north Carmarthen /u:/ corresponds to RP /əʊ/ in *comb* (Ll, My, Log,
Nch, GA). The realisation is generally [u:], but [uə] is attested in all
dialects in *stool.*

/ai/ corresponds generally to RP /aɪ/ and additionally to RP /eɪ/ in
such forms as *clay* (Cen, Nch), *drain* (GA). The combination /aijʌ(r)/
corresponds to RP /aɪə/ in such forms as *fire* (Ll, Log, Nch). [ai] is much
the commoner of the two realisations; [əi], with which it is in apparently
random variation, is attested more sporadically, in such forms as *eye*
(Cen, Log, GA), *fight* (Nch, GA), *hive* (My, Nch, GA), *ivy* (Ll, My,
GA), *mice* (Ll, Nch), *white* (Ll).

/ɔi/, realised as [ɔi], corresponds to RP /ɔɪ/ in all six dialects.

/au/, realised as [au], corresponds generally to RP /au/, although this function is shared with north Carmarthen /o:/, cf. above. Attestations of /au/ are in fact somewhat sporadic; a sample of five words shows /au/ in *cow* (Cen, Log, Nch, GA), *plough* (My, GA), *snout* (Ll, Nch), *sow* (noun, Log), *thousand* (GA). The combination /auwʌ(r)/ corresponds to RP /ʊə/ in *flour* (Cen, Log), *hour* (Ll).

/iə/, realised as [iə], is recorded sporadically as a reflex of RP /ɪə/ as in *ears* (Cen, My, Log, Nch), *year* (Cen, Ll, Log, Nch, GA); but a far more common reflex of RP /ɪə/ in the north Carmarthen dialects is the combination of /i:jʌ(r)/.

/iə/ corresponds to RP /i:/ in *wheel* (Cen. Log. GA).

/ɔə/ corresponds to RP /ɔə/, as in *boar*, *door*, *four* etc. The realisation is [ɔə] at Cenarth, Login, Newchurch and Gelli Aur, [ɔə] and [oə] in apparently random distribution at Myddfai, [oə] only at Llansawel.

/ɪu/, realised as [ɪu], is attested as a reflex of RP /u:/ in some forms with orthographic *ew*, *ue*, such as *dew* (Ll, Log, Nch, GA), *ewe* (GA), *suet* (Nch), *Tuesday* (Cen, Ll, Log, Nch, GA). /ɪu/ is not found in the Myddfai system.

Grammar

Noun-plurals often have /s/ suffixed even to singulars ending in voiced sounds, such as *peas* /pi:s/ (My), *shoes* (Cen), *flies* (Cen), *chains* (My, GA), etc. *Calf* has plural /kafs/ (My), *sheaf* has plural /ʃi:fs/ (GA).

The indefinite article is attested sporadically in the contexts illustrated in *Have you got a toothache?* (Log), *a tongs* (Log, Nch, GA); *a hames* (GA); *a leggings* (Nch); *a scissors* (Log); *a stockings* (Nch); *a straps* (on a harness) (Nch).

In exclamatory sentences, *there's* followed by adjective is common, e.g. *there's funny questions!* (Nch); *there's twp I am!* ('How foolish I am!') (GA).

To express habitual action or continuing states, the dialects commonly use continuous forms of the verb where Standard English uses indefinite forms (present tense) or imperfect forms (past tense). Examples: *she's wearing the trousers* ('she wears the trousers', said of a domineering wife); *they have a shed in which they're keeping chickens; I'm not thinking much of it* ('I don't think much of it', i.e. 'I'm unimpressed by it'); *they were leaving them out about two o'clock to water* (i.e. 'they used to let them out'); *after you was going to finish that stack you was rising the middle part up a bit* (i.e. 'you would raise').

Inflected past-tense forms include *creeped* (Ll, Nch); *reach* (Cen, Ll); *swole* 'swelled' (GA); *teached* (My). Past participles include *ate* /eit/ 'eaten' (My); *broke* (Ll); *drank* (GA); *drunked* (Cen); *eat* (Cen); *stole* (Ll).

A word can be given special emphasis by placing it at the beginning of its sentence; e.g. *'axle' they were calling it* (i.e. 'People used to call it "axle"'); *a weed it is; tabs* ('inferior cigarettes') *they were*; *"The gargat" I'm calling it* (i.e. 'I call it "the gargat" [a disease affecting animals]'); *coal they're getting out mostly* (answer to the question: 'What do miners get from the ground?').

Stop may be followed by *to* plus verb-stem where Standard English has *from* plus gerund, as in *The horse is stopping the cart to go up* (i.e. 'The horse has the function of stopping the cart from going up'): *to stop the wood to wear out*; *To stop the wheels to go back; we were stopping them to do that.*

Indirect questions retain the order verb + noun/pronoun found in direct questions in such forms as *I don't know what time is it; I don't know is there a name on it; I don't know what is that, neither.*

Dialectal uses of prepositions are illustrated as follows: *of* in *It's not very big of a farm* (i.e. 'It's not a very big farm'); *on* in *the name on it* ('the name of it'); *on times* ('at times'); *for* in *I know for one farmer by Carmarthen who* . . . ('I know of . . .'), *we know for places now that haven't got pans* ('We know of . . .'); *to* in *I'm very cross to you* (' . . . with you'); *with* in *with hand* ('by hand'). Also, *with* is used to denote 'possession' of various circumstances, attributes, etc., as in *there's no horns with the cattle round this way; they're cracking with you* (referring to chapped hands); *it was warm with the cowshed always; there's a lot of work about the wheat with you; they'll go rot with you* ('they'll rot on your hands').

Lexis

In some cases the answers to lexical questions consisted in Welsh words that the informants said were the only ones they knew to express the notions concerned. A few examples out of many are *mwnci* 'hames', *bwbach* 'scarecrow', *bargod* 'eaves of a haystack', *turio* 'to root' (of pigs), *cardodwyn/cardidwyn* 'the smallest pig of a litter'. These are presumably explained by the fact of their being rather specialised, agricultural terms that the informants (all of whom had Welsh as their first language) use in conducting their business without the need arising for English equivalents. Likewise *ty-bach* ('small house') is such a well-established euphemism for 'lavatory' that there is no need to adopt an English one in its place when speaking English.

A few words are English translations of their Welsh equivalents, e.g. *dog's grass* 'couch grass' (*porfa ci*); *white lady* 'bindweed' (*ladi wen*); *the candle of the eye* 'pupil' (*cannwyll y llygad*).

Some words are Welsh stems with English plural-morphemes, e.g. *pentans* 'hobs', *trogs* 'ticks' (Welsh *trogen*, sg.).

Another group of words, English in origin, appear in the dialects sometimes with a Welsh pronunciation, sometimes an English one. For instance, the gangway in a cow-house, from which the animals are fed, is known variously as the *walc* /walk/ or the *walk* /wɔːk/; the hub of a wheel is the *bwl* /buːl/ or the *bowl* /boːl/; a bread-bin is a *crochon* /ˈkrɔxɔn/ or a *crock* /krɔk/.

Other words occur in north Carmarthen and relatively widely in dialects in England; such are *dribbles* 'cart-ladders'; *moil* 'a hornless cow' which, though Welsh in origin, is recorded also in the border-counties of Herefordshire and Shropshire; *gilt* 'a young sow'; *lip/lipe* 'basket'; *flask* 'basket'; *rig* 'ridgel'; *tun-dish* 'domestic funnel'; *spreckles* 'freckles'; *hanch* 'a bite' (from a plum, etc.); *golden chain* 'laburnum'; *peal* 'one-year-old salmon'. The Norse word *haggard*, unlike other Norse words such as *gilt* mentioned above, is found in north Carmarthen and in Scotland, Ireland, and the Isle of Man, but not, apparently, in England, in its sense of 'stack-yard'.

Lockses ('whiskers on a man's face') and *pine-end*, on the other hand, that are apparently English terms, are recorded only very sparsely, if at all, in England; Orton *et al.* (1962–71) apparently found no instances of the former, and only five instances (out of a possible 313) of the latter — in Gloucestershire, Somerset and Wiltshire.

Overview

A few of the features of the dialects under consideration may have reached north Carmarthenshire through the influence of the dialects of such English counties as Cornwall, Devon and Somerset — features such as initial /j/ in *ears*, final /-ɪn/ corresponding to RP /-ɪŋ/, /a/ in *wasps*, final unstressed /i:/ corresponding to RP /ɪ/, and the lexical items *gilt, lip(e), flask, rig, tun-dish, hanch, golden chain* and *peal*. All these phonological and lexical features are recorded not only in south-western England but in other parts of England as well. So, too, are the past tense verb-forms *creeped*, *teached*, and the past participle *stole*.

Other forms recorded in England apparently do not occur in the south-west but do occur further afield, especially the West Midlands and/ or the north. Such are /a/ in *branch* and before /f, s/; /ʊ/ in *goose, hoof, tooth*, and the lexical items *dribbles* and *moil*.

Apart from the features noted above, and apart from features that are in more-or-less general usage in English, just about all the *distinctive* characteristics of the English spoken in north Carmarthenshire are examples of borrowings from the sounds, the syntax, the idioms or the lexis of the Welsh language.

Notes to Chapter 10

1. The fieldworker to whom I am indebted for the collection of the material is William Bundy Esq., M.A.
2. National Grid references; Cenarth, SN 2641; Llansawel, SN 6136; Myddfai, SN 7730; Login, SN 1623; Newchurch, SN 3824; Gelli Aur, SN 5919.
3. Eugen Dieth and Harold Orton, *A Questionnaire for a Linguistic Atlas of England* (1952), modified for use in Anglo-Welsh Localities by Anne Chesters, Clive Upton and David Parry (Swansea 1968).

References

ORTON, H. *et al* (eds) 1962–71, *The Survey of English Dialects* (13 vols). Leeds: E.J. Arnold.

PARRY, D. 1977, *The Survey of Anglo-Welsh Dialects, Vol. 1: The South-East*. Swansea: University College.

——1979, *The Survey of Anglo-Welsh Dialects, Vol. 2: The South-West*. Swansea: University College.

11 The Conservative English Dialects of South Pembrokeshire

DAVID PARRY

Data for this description were gathered between 1969 and 1975.[1] The six localities investigated, all south of the Pembrokeshire landsker, were Camrose (Cam), Wiston (Wis), Marloes (Mar), Llangwm (Lla), Angle (Ang) and St Florence (St).[2]

Phonology

Consonants

The six south-Pembrokeshire dialects investigated appear to share a consonant-system differing little from that of RP as regards its component phones and phonemes, although there are some differences in their distribution, the most important cases being noted below.

/l/ is almost always realised by clear [l]. Dark [ɫ] is attested, but only sporadically, among some speakers in the word-final combination /ʊl/ as in *bull, wool*, or syllabically as in *kettle, thimble*.

/n/ regularly corresponds to RP /ŋ/ in the word-final combination /ɪŋ/, as in *evening, morning* and present participles.

A south Pembrokeshire voiced sound sometimes corresponds to its voiceless counterpart in RP. For instance:

/v/ = RP /f/ in *fellies* (all dialects), *furrow* (Mar, Lla, Ang)
/z/ = RP /s/ in *see-saw* (Mar), *sink* (Lla); *mistletoe* (Mar), *basin* (Ang); *rinse* (Wis)
/ð/ = RP /θ/ in *thatch* (St); *anything* (Lla); *broth* (Mar), *mouth* (noun, Wis)

/g/ = RP /k/ in *naked* (Ang), *spokes* (Mar); *poke* (Mar)
/dʒ/ = RP /tʃ/ in *butcher* (Lla).

On the other hand, a south Pembrokeshire voiceless consonant occasionally corresponds to its voiced counterpart in RP. For instance:

/t/ = RP /d/ in *second* (Cam, Ang), *hundred* (Ang)
/s/ = RP /z/ in *cousin* (Mar), *Tuesday* (St)
/θ/ = RP /ð/ in *farthing* (Cam, Wis, St).

Also attested are correspondences such as these:

/d/ = RP /θ/ in *thistle* /'daisl/ (all dialects)
/sk/ = RP /ʃ/ in *skred* 'shred' (Lla)
/v/ = RP /ð/ in *scythe* (Lla, Ang, St)
/f/ = RP /θ/ in *swath* (Ang, St).

Sometimes south Pembrokeshire consonants have *no* reflex in RP; for instance, *ears* has initial /j/ (Lla, St). But the reverse of this is attested more widely: for instance *trough* /trou/ lacks final /f/ (Wis, Mar); /j/ is lacking in *yeast* /i:st/ (Mar, Lla, Ang), *dew* /dɪu/ (Ang), *ewe* /ɪu/ (Ang), *Tuesday* /'tɪuzdɪ/ (Ang).

Vowels

The vowel phonemes proposed for the six dialects investigated, with their respective phonetic realisations, are shown in Table 11.1. All six dialects have nos 1–17. No. 18 is confined to Camrose, Marloes, Llangwm and Angle; no. 19 to Camrose and Angle; no. 20 to Wiston, Llangwm and Angle. The distribution of the vowels is as follows:

/ɪ/, realised always as [ɪ], corresponds generally to RP /ɪ/ in stressed syllables. For south Pembrokeshire /i:/ corresponding to RP /ɪ/ in unstressed syllables, see below.

/ɛ/, realised always as [ɛ], corresponds generally to RP /e/, and occasionally to RP unstressed /ə/, /ɪ/, as in *ladder, suet* (Wis); *butter* (Mar).

/a/ corresponds generally to RP /æ/, and may also correspond to RP /ɑ:/, as in *chaff* (Cam, Wis, Mar, Lla, St), *draught* (Cam, Wis, Mar, Lla), *grass* (Cam, Wis, Lla, St), *branch* (Wis, Mar, Lla, Ang, St). /a/ corresponds also to RP /ɒ/ in *wasps* (Wis, Ang). The phonetic realisation is [ä] in all the dialects, but Camrose has additionally [ɑ] attested in *rat, saddle,* and [æ] attested in *branch, rabbits.*

/ʌ/ corresponds largely to both RP /ʌ/ and RP /ə/ (note however that RP /ʌ/ often has south Pembrokeshire reflex /ʊ/, and sometimes reflex /ɔ/, cf. relevant sections below). /ʌ/ occurs also in south Pembrokeshire words of the pattern (C) + V + /j/ or /w/ + /ʌ/ + (C), e.g. *hear, hour, iron* that in RP have (C) + triphthong + (C). Hence south Pembrokeshire *flour* /'flauwʌ/, *fire* /'faijʌ/, *iron* /'aijʌn/ in all dialects, also *hear* /'h)i:jʌ/ (Cam, Mar, Ang), *hour* /'auwʌ/ (Cam, Mar, Lla, St). Each of the six dialects has the three realisations [ʌ], [ə] and [ə']. Of these, [ə'] is attested only in unstressed final syllables, as in words with final orthographic 'er', also *fire* (Cam, Ang), *flour* (Wis, Ang), *hear* (Mar, Ang), *hour* (Cam, Mar, Lla), *iron* (Cam, Mar), *sugar* (Cam, Mar, Lla). [ʌ] is attested mainly in stressed syllables, as *butter* (Cam, St), *furrow* (Wis, Ang, St), *jump* (Cam, Ang, St), *mushrooms* (Mar, St), *none* (Cam, St), *nothing* (Ang, St), *onions* (Cam, Wis, St), *uncle* (Cam, Wis, Mar, Ang, St). [ə] may occur in stressed syllables, e.g. *furrow* (Cam), *onions* (Mar, Ang), *shovel* (Ang); also, corresponding to RP /ɒ/, in *dog* (Wis). But [ə] is far commoner in unstressed syllables, especially in words with final orthographic '-er', and in the final syllables of words such as *fire, flour, hour, iron*, etc. (see above) as a variant of [ə'].

/ɔ/, realised always as [ɔ], corresponds generally to RP /ɒ/ — except in *wasps* (Wis, Ang) — and occasionally to RP /ʌ/, as in *couple* (Cam), *nothing* (Cam, Mar), *gloves* (Wis, St), *onions* (Lla, St), *oven* (Cam, Wis), *rungs* (Wis, Lla, Ang), *shovel* (St). Also, /ɔ/ occasionally corresponds to RP /əu/, as in *colt* (Mar, Ang), *groat* (Wis), *oats* (Ang).

/ʊ/, realised always as [ʊ], corresponds generally to RP /ʊ/, and sometimes to RP /ʌ/, as in *butter* (Wis, Mar, Lla, Ang), *cud* (Wis, Lla, St), *cut* (Wis, Lla, Ang), *furrow* (Mar, Lla), *jump* (Wis, Mar, Ang), *Monday* (Cam, Wis), *mother* (Wis, Lla, Ang), *mushrooms* (Cam, Wis, Lla, Ang), *none* (Mar, Lla), *nothing* (Wis, Lla), *oven* (Lla), *shovel* (Cam, Wis, Lla), *uncle* (Lla). And sometimes /ʊ/ corresponds to RP /u:/, as in *hoof* (Wis, Mar, Ang), *root* (Wis), *tooth* (Mar, Lla, Ang).

/i:/, realised always as [i:], generally corresponds to RP /i:/ and sometimes to RP unstressed /ɪ/, as in *ready* and other words with final orthographic '-y', at Camrose, Wiston, Llangwm and St Florence.

/ei/ corresponds generally to RP /eɪ/ and sporadically to RP /aɪ/, as in *eye, flies* (plural noun), *hive, ivy* (all at Cam, Ang), *white* (Ang). It is attested also as a reflex of RP /ɑ:/ in *chaff* (Ang), and of RP /ɪ/ in *holly* (Ang).

The commonest realisation is [ei], the *only* attested form at Wiston and Llangwm. Marloes has only [ei] and [e:]; here and in Camrose, Angle and St Florence, which have [ei], [e:] and [ɛi], there is no clear rule

TABLE 11.1 *South Pembrokeshire Vowel Phonemes*

Phoneme	Realisations	Dialects	Phoneme	Realisations	Dialects
1 /ɪ/	[ɪ]	All	9 /əː/	[ɜˑ]	All
2 /ɛ/	[ɛ]	All		[əː]	Lla, St
3 /a/	[ä]	All		[œː]	Wis, Lla, Ang, St
	[æ]	Cam	10 /ɛː/	[ɛː]	Cam, Wis, Lla, St
	[ɑ]	Cam		[ɛˑː]	Cam, Wis, Lla, Ang, St
4 /ʌ/	[ʌ]	All		[ɛə]	Cam, Lla
	[ə]	All		[ɛəˡ]	Cam, Mar, Lla, Ang
	[əˡ]	All		[eə]	Mar
5 /ɔ/	[ɔ]	All		[eəˡ]	Mar
6 /ʊ/	[ʊ]	All	11 /aː/	[äː]	All
7 /iː/	[iː]	All		[ɑː]	Cam, Wis, Lla, Ang, St
8 /ei/	[ei]	All		[ɑˑː]	Cam, Ang
	[eː]	Cam, Mar, Ang, St		[aˑː]	Mar
	[ɛi]	Cam, Ang, St	12 /ɔː/	[ɔː]	All
				[ɔˑː]	All

Phoneme	Reali-sations	Dialects	Phoneme	Reali-sations	Dialects
13 /ou/	[ou]	All	16 /ɔi/	[ɔi]	All
	[ɔu]	All		[oi]	Wis, Lla, Ang, St
	[o:]	Cam, Ang	17 /au/	[au]	All
	[əu]	Mar, St		[əu]	Cam, Ang
14 /u:/	[u:]	All		[æu]	Cam, Wis, Mar
	[ʊ:]	St		[ɛu]	Cam, Lla, Ang, St
	[uu]	Cam	18 /iə/	[iəʳ]	Cam, Mar, Lla
15 /ai/	[ai]	Cam, Wis, Mar, Lla, Ang		[iə]	Ang
	[ɑi]	Wis, St	19 /ɔə/	[ɔəʳ]	Cam, Ang
	[æi]	Mar, Ang	20 /u/	[u]	Wis, Lla, Ang
	[ɐi]	St			

NB. The superscript character [ʳ] is here used to express *retroflex* r-colouring.

determining which realises /ei/ corresponding to RP /eɪ/ in any given word. In Camrose, [ɛi] is attested only as reflex of RP /aɪ/, in *eye* and *flies* (plural noun).

/ə:/ corresponds generally to RP /ə:/, also to RP /ɪə/ in *ears* /jə:z/ (Wis, Lla, St). The realisation [əˑ:] occurs in all six dialects and is indeed the only one attested at Camrose and Marloes. On the other hand [əˑ] is attested only once at Wiston, where all other recordings of /ə:/ are realised as [œ:]. The form [ə:] is attested only at Llangwm and St Florence, in both cases rather sporadically.

/ɛ:/ corresponds generally to RP /ɛə/. The phonetic realisations are comparatively numerous and of apparently random distribution, as in the following examples:

	Cam.	Wis.	Mar.	Lla.	Ang.	St.
chair	ɛəˑ	ɛ:		ɛə	ɛˑ:	ɛ:
hare	ɛˑ	ɛˑ:	ɛəˑ	ɛəˑ	ɛəˑ	ɛˑ:
mare		ɛˑ:	ɛəˑ	ɛəˑ:	ɛəˑ	ɛˑ:
pears		ɛ:	eə	ɛ:		ɛ:

/a:/ corresponds generally to RP /ɑ:/ except in *chaff, grass* and other words that had Middle English /af/ or /as/, which generally have south Pembrokeshire /a/, cf. above. The commonest realisation is [ä:]. Of the others, [ɑ:] is attested in *calf* (Cam), *arm* (Wis, Ang), *farmer* (Wis), *farthing* (Lla, Ang, St), [aˑ:] in *arm* and *farthing* (both at Mar); [ɑˑ:] in *arm* (Cam), *farmer* (Ang).

/ɔ:/ corresponds generally to RP /ɔ:/ and commonly also to RP /ɔə/ in those dialects that have no /ɔə/ phoneme. Occasionally too /ɔ:/ corresponds to RP /əu/ as in *cold* (Lla), *spokes* (St); and to RP /ɒ/ as in *wrong* (Ang), *off* (Ang, St).

All the dialects have both realisations, [ɔ:] and [ɔˑ:]. Of these, [ɔˑ:] is much the commoner at Camrose, Marloes and Angle, [ɔ:] at Wiston, Llangwm and St Florence.

/ou/ corresponds generally to RP /əu/, also occasionally to RP /ɒ/ as in *trough* /trou/ (Wis, Mar); to RP /u:/ as in *stool* (Wis); *goose* (St); and to RP /ɔ:/ as in *straw* (Ang). Of the four realisations, [ou] and [ɔu] are attested in all six dialects, [o:] only at Camrose and Angle, [əu] only in the one word *snow* at Marloes and St Florence. Distribution is apparently random.

/u:/ corresponds generally to RP /u:/ but there are exceptions in those dialects that have a separate /ɪu/ phoneme (discussed below) and also in the cases of *tooth, hoof,* cf. above. Additionally, /u:/ occasionally corresponds to RP /əu/ as in *yoke* (Mar), *yolk* (Cam, Ang), *oats* (St), *toad* (Lla, Ang), *go* (St), *coal* (Ang), *rope* (Ang, St); and to RP /ʊ/ as in *sugar* (Wis, Lla). The realisation is always [u:] except for [ʊu] in *ewe* (Cam) and [ʊ:] in *hoof, oats* (St).

/ai/ corresponds to RP /aɪ/ and is found also in words that in RP have /aɪə/ — such words as *fire, iron,* which in south Pembrokeshire have two syllables, structured as (C) + /ai/ + /j/ + /ʌ/ + (C). [ai] is the sole realisation attested at Camrose and Llangwm. [ɑi] appears at Wiston only in *ivy, fire,* but at St Florence it is the *chief* realisation, in a dialect in which the only other attested realisation is [əi], recorded only in *eye, ivy, mice.* At Marloes, [æi] is much commoner than [ai], which is the exact opposite of the situation at Angle.

/ɔi/ corresponds generally to RP /ɔɪ/. Of the two attested realisations, Camrose and Marloes have only [ɔi], the other dialects having both [ɔi] and [oi], in apparently random distribution.

/au/ corresponds generally to RP /aʊ/ and is found also in words that in RP have /aʊə/ — words such as *hour, flour, flower,* which in south Pembrokeshire have two syllables, structured as (C) + /au/ + /w/ + /ʌ/ + (C). Additionally, at Angle, /au/ corresponds to RP /əu/ in *oak* and RP /u:/ in *goose.* The commonest realisation is [aʊ], found in all six dialects, always with at least one other realisation. The distribution of these realisations is apparently random.

/iə/ is attested only in Camrose, Marloes, Llangwm and Angle, where it corresponds to RP /ɪə/, the reflex of which in the other dialects is the two-syllable combination /'i:jʌ/ (as in *beer*) or the monosyllabic /jə:/ as in *hear* /hjə:/, *ear* /jə:/, *year* /jə:/. /iə/ is realised as [iəʲ] (Cam, Mar, Lla), [iə] (Ang).

/ɔə/, realised always as [ɔəʲ], is found only at Camrose and Angle, corresponding to RP /ɔə/ in words such as *boar, door, floor, four.*

/ɪu/, realised always as [ɪu], is found only at Wiston, Llangwm and Angle, corresponding to RP /u:/ or /ju:/ in words such as *ewe* /(j)ɪu/, *dew* /d(j)ɪu/, *suet* /'s(j)ɪuɪt/, *Tuesday* /'tɪuzdi:/.

Grammar

Shaft (Wis), and *year* and *acre* (Ang), have plural forms with zero inflexion following numerals. *Shaft* makes plural /ʃa:vz/ or /ʃavz/ (Cam, Ang, St), /ʃa:fs/ or /ʃafs/ (Cam, Mar).

The indefinite article appears in *a tongs* (Cam, Wis), similarly *a scales* 'a pair of scales' (Lla), *a scissors* (Cam, Wis, St), *a shears* (St), *a stairs* (Lla), *a dripples* 'a set of cart-ladders' (Cam).

The definite article is recorded before following vowels in the forms [ðə] in *the animals* (Mar), *the interior* (Cam); [ð] in *the earth* (Cam, St), *the eye* (Cam), *the horse* /ð ɔːs/ (Mar).

The article is absent in the expression *to cast calf* 'to calve before time' (Cam, Lla).

The old second person singular pronoun *thou*, with verb-form in *-est*, is attested in *How couldst thou* /kʊst ðʌ/ *make that out?* (Wis, Lla), and the corresponding objective form in *It's ages since I saw thee* at the same localities.

He has unstressed form /ʌ/ attested at Mar, St, and unstressed objective /n/ (Old English *hine*) (Mar, Ang). *It* has unstressed form /t/, nominative and objective, attested in *'t wasn't* (Cam, Mar); *do 't* (Mar); and unstressed objective form /n/ (Cam, Mar, Ang, St).

Possessive forms (conjunctive) include second singular *thy* /ði/ (Lla, St); third singular neuter /ɪt/ in *on it back* (Mar). Disjunctive forms include *yourn* (Ang).

Relatives *as* and *what* are attested at Angle in *the man as/what looks after the cows*, also *as* with neuter antecedent at Camrose and Marloes.

First person singular present tense habitual forms *I knows, I takes* and the like occur in all six dialects. Third person singular present tense habitual forms with zero inflexion are recorded at Marloes, e.g. *she want the bull, at four o'clock school finish*. Periphrastic third person singular and plural forms such as *We do* /dʌ/ *call it* . . ., *the cows do* /dʌ/ *graze in the field* are recorded at Angle.

Past tense forms include *creeped* (Mar); *come* (Mar, Lla), *catched* (Wis), *growed* (Wis, Lla), *heat* /hɛt/ 'heated' (Cam, Ang), *keeped* (Mar), *lied* 'reclined' (Ang), *seen* (Mar, Ang), *teached* (Mar), *throwed* (Mar).

Past-participial forms with prefixed /ʌ/ are attested in *a-fetched* (Lla), *a-been* (Ang), *a-found* (Wis), *a-lost* (Ang), *a-passed* (Ang).

Other past-participial forms include *drank* (Cam, Mar, Lla, Ang), *ate* (Cam), *aten* /'ɛtn/ (Ang), *beat* /bɛt/ 'beaten' (Cam), *saw* 'seen' (Lla), *took* 'taken' (Wis).

Indirect questions retain the order verb + noun/pronoun found in direct questions in such forms as *What's he studying I don't know* (Cam); *I'm not sure is it Caerleon or not* (Ang).

Be has first person singular present-tense negative *I aren't* (unstressed) (Ang). Old second person singular forms are attested in *Where beest-thou* /bɪst ðʌ/ (Cam); *Art thou* /aːt ðʌ/ *coming home?* (Lla). Past tense (auxiliary) forms include second person singular *you was thirsty* (Mar, Ang), third person singular *she were colted* (Cam); first personal plural *we was thirsty* (Ang); third person plural *they was thirsty* (Ang).

Auxiliary *do* in clause-final position has third person singular present tense *he do* (Mar, Lla, Ang), third person plural *they does* /duːz/ (Ang, St) and negative third person singular *he don't* (Mar, Lla, Ang, St).

Auxiliary *have* has third person singular present tense *he have* (Mar); negative *he haven't* (Cam, Mar, Ang).

Of follows *enough* in *enough of teats, enough of sticks* (Wis). *On* is attested in *there's no name on them* (i.e. 'they have no name') (Ang).

The compound preposition *for to* is attested in *I went to town for to see the doctor* in all six dialects.

Lexis

Only a few south Pembrokeshire words appear to be Welsh, e.g. *cardodwyn* and related phonetic forms 'the smallest pig of a litter'; *sile* 'base of a haystack' (Welsh *seiliad*?); *pompren* 'wooden bridge'; *twp* 'stupid'; *bragget* 'mead'; *skew* 'a settle' (Welsh *ysgiw*); *teckle* 'tea-kettle'; *robin-the-driver* 'gadfly' (Welsh *robin-y-gyrrwr*).

English dialect-words attested in south Pembrokeshire include some that are recorded by Wright (1898–1905) or Orton (1962–71) mainly in the West Midlands, e.g. *ranch/range* 'gangway in a cow-house', *evil* 'agricultural fork', *cratch/cretch* 'tailboard of a cart', *dribbles* 'cart-ladders'.

Of wider currency in England, including the south-west, are such south Pembrokeshire forms as *ails* 'bristles of barley'; *offis/oavese* 'eaves of a stack'; *poll* 'hornless cow'; *gilt* 'young sow'; *withy* 'willow'; *grouts* 'tea-leaves'; *twitch* 'couch-grass'; *seed-lipe* 'seed-basket'; *rig* 'ridgel'; *emmock-hills* 'ant-hills'; *eft* 'newt'; *quot* 'to squat on the heels'; *mind* 'to recall'; *diddikies* 'gipsies'; *flake* 'a hurdle'; *fog* 'long grass'; *all abroad* 'all to pieces'; *hunch* 'a large slice'; *miskin/mixen* 'dung-heap'; *galeeny* 'guinea-fowl'; *goslings* 'willow catkins'; *slop* 'gap in a hedge, an opening'.

Whereas the south Pembrokeshire words in the preceding paragraph are recorded in both south-western and other parts of England, the following are recorded, outside south Pembrokeshire, *only* in south-western England, i.e. the area covered by Dorset, Cornwall, Devon and Somerset as constituted before 1974: *foriers* /'vʌri:jʌz/ 'headlands of a field'; *pilk* 'to butt'; *cawel* 'basket'; *frithing* 'fence made of wattled thorns'; *belge* 'to bellow'; *notlins* 'chitterlings'; *culm* 'slack coal'; *kift* 'clumsy'; *nuddock* 'neck'; *pin-bone* 'hip-bone'; *murfles* 'freckles'; *lab* 'to gossip'; *springle* 'trap for catching birds'; *fox-day* 'a single fine day in a spell of bad weather'; *skit* 'to seep'.

A number of other south Pembrokeshire words are apparently unattested anywhere else in Britain, some being of unknown derivation. This group includes *hantrees* 'hames'; *swang* 'stretcher on a harness'; *mally-/molly-lamb* 'pet lamb'; *moil* 'to root' (of pigs); *traloo* 'bindweed'; *preen* 'to butt'; *by-holt* 'hired hand'; *lonker* 'shackle with which animals are hobbled'; *brimsy* 'on heat' (of sows); *noy* 'wooden box'; *cruglins* 'chitterlings'; *shoal* (adj.) 'shallow'; *gant* 'gander'; *cutty evet* 'newt'; *trapple* 'threshold'; *looch* 'porridge-stick'; *shug* 'tremors'; *labigan* 'a busybody'; *squitways* 'diagonally'; *cats' nails* 'small pieces of skin at the base of the finger-nail'; *cranted* 'stunted'; *spewk* 'to vomit'; *binch* 'the thatch of a rick'; *bleaze* 'the bladder of a pig'; *boosack* 'half-castrated pig'; *graidies* 'traces on a plough'; *pilvelgin* 'a ridge where there was a furrow the previous year'; *druke* 'a crank, or anything with a sharp corner'; *easy-come-scwt* 'slow in movement'; *enfensile* 'an outcast'; *all by leisures* 'gently, in leisured manner'; *scaddly* 'greedy'; *spaked* 'leaking, swollen'; *wish* 'to throw out'; *ball-fire* 'a fire made from balls of small coal mixed with clay'; *culf* 'hunk of bread'; *to key* 'to lock a door'; *kiddle* 'cauldron' (in the sense of Old Norse *ketill* whence *kettle*); *stum down* 'to slow down a fire by putting *culm* on it'; *wall-plot* 'the part of a cottage wall immediately under the roof'; *elligug* 'the guillemot'; *rab* 'yellow rock-soil'; *squiff* 'short shower of rain'; *staniel* 'stallion'; *tufty* 'desiring the bull' (of cows).

Overview

Little in the south Pembrokeshire dialects seems to derive from Welsh. The preference for clear [l], the voiceless consonants in the contexts mentioned in *second, cousin*, etc. (cf. above), the single phoneme /ʌ/ corresponding to both RP /ʌ/ and RP /ə/, and Wiston/ Llangwm/Angle /ɪu/ are perhaps all that seem possibly to be due to Welsh influence (even so, /ɪu/ is attested sporadically in Cornwall and other English counties) so far as sounds are concerned. In the grammar, the order verb + noun in indirect questions and the use of *on* in *there's no name on them* are perhaps due to Welsh influence; in the lexis, we have only the few forms listed above (*cardodwyn*, etc.).

As is well known, many features of the dialects of this area are shared with those of south-western England. Examples include voiced consonants in at least the /v/ for /f/, /z/ for /s/, and /ð/ for /θ/ contexts, along with /d/ for /θ/ and /v/ for /ð/, and /j/ in *ears*. *r*-coloured vowels are of course not peculiar, in England, to the south-west, but they are widely attested there. The Marloes [æi]-reflexes of RP /aɪ/ are attested by Orton *et al.* (1962–71) in Somerset and (in some cases) Devon, the only other English places where these are attested being as far away as Herefordshire, Cheshire, Yorkshire, Durham, and the Isle of Man. Almost all the grammar discussed is attested in the dialects of England, including the south-west, but the periphrastic present-tense habitual with *do* /dʌ/ does appear to be specifically south-western. In addition we have the otherwise uniquely south-western English lexis listed above.

Traces of Old Norse influence appear slight: /sk/ in *skred* 'shred for animal fodder', perhaps, and one or two lexical items such as *haggard* (Old Norse *hey-garðr)* 'stackyard' and *kiddle* 'cauldron'.

The longish list of words not attested elsewhere in Britain suggests that a sizeable part of the south Pembrokeshire dialects may be peculiar to this area.

Notes to Chapter 11

1. The fieldworkers to whom I am indebted for collecting the material are Miss Theresa Dacey, Miss Francesca Ayres, Clive Upton and Robert Goss.
2. National grid references: Camrose, SM 9320; Wiston, SN 0318; Marloes, SM 7908; Llangwm, SM 9909; Angle, SM 8703; St Florence, SN 0801.

References

ORTON, H. *et al* (eds) 1962–71, *The Survey of English Dialects* (13 vols). Leeds: E.J. Arnold.
WRIGHT, J. (ed.) 1898–1905, *The English Dialect Dictionary* (6 vols). Oxford: Oxford University Press.

12 Accents of English in Wales: A Postscript

J.C. WELLS

Alan Thomas (1984: 178) was right in his comment that 'the subject of Welsh English is inadequately documented'. Nevertheless it is pleasing to see the progress in the documentation of English in Wales that has been achieved in the past few years. The Wales chapter of my own general survey of English accents (Wells, 1982: II, Ch. 5.1) now needs a number of corrections and amplifications, not least in the light of the articles published in the present most welcome compilation.

It is gratifying to find that the descriptions offered by Thomas (1984), by Trudgill & Hannah (1982), and by me (Wells, 1982) (descriptions written, I think, largely independently of one another) have on the whole been borne out by later research. We would now, however, be able to be more specific about the details of different varieties within south Wales; one hopes that it may soon be possible to say the same about mid- and north Wales.

Cardiff is the city in which two of the phoneticians represented in this book grew up (Collins, Windsor Lewis) and to which two more have given close professional attention (Mees, Coupland). As a result, both its accent and its sociolinguistics are now rather well documented (for the latter, see Mees, 1983, and particularly Coupland, 1988). Collins & Mees remind us that to visitors the accent of the Cardiff–Newport area may scarcely sound like a 'proper Welsh accent' at all, and have gone some way towards explaining why this should be so.

As we move from Cardiff towards Port Talbot and Swansea and then into the areas where the use of Welsh remains, or at least has recently been, a reality among the general population, the picture changes. The phonetics of Welsh, which in Cardiff is at best a distant substratum and perhaps not even that, in the upper Swansea valley is an ever-present factor, as Tench demonstrates in Chapter 9. Port Talbot, as Connolly makes clear in Chapter 8, occupies an intermediate position. In Cardiff (and Newport?) we find the same patterning of clear and dark /l/ as in RP; elsewhere in south and mid-Wales /l/ is always clear. While [x] appears to be available in the phonetic repertoire of speakers in all three places, the characteristically Welsh [ɬ] is used only in Port Talbot and Abercrave, and does not belong to ordinary Cardiff speech — at least, randomly selected Cardiff people do not use it in most of the proper names that might seem to call for it (Coupland, 1988: 41–46).

A phonetic account of a given accent must obviously include a statement of the segmental phonemes and the allophonic rules determining their realisation. But it is also important to consider the nature of the phonological processes of connected speech. Collins & Mees show that in Cardiff speech these may be of a nature and an extent rather different from RP and perhaps from accents of England in general. Connolly demonstrates that some of the Cardiff specialities extend to Port Talbot, while Tench shows that things are rather different in Abercrave, where 'the patterns of assimilation and elision . . . are clearly Welsh and are distinctively different from those of most types of native British English'.

It is also important to give due attention to rhythm and intonation (an area where I am only too aware that my own work has tended to fall short). For these aspects of Welsh and Welsh English we now have the important and interesting experimental work carried out by Williams (1986) and summarised by Tench in this book. It turns out that native speakers of Welsh use quite different auditory cues from English people for their perception of stress.

The two chapters by Parry offer valuable summaries of the materials collected in south-west Wales in fieldwork for the *Survey of Anglo-Welsh Dialects* (Parry, 1979). They tend to show that in parts of Dyfed we may be dealing with a traditional-dialect situation comparable to that found in rural England and very different from the post-EFL situation that obtains in the upper Swansea Valley and no doubt in much of Gwynedd. Other Parry (1979) findings are as yet available only in the form of unpublished dissertations, (e.g. Penhallurick, 1978; 1980; 1986). Parry is alert to the shortcomings for phonemic analysis of the questionnaire, derived from Orton *et al.* (1962–71), on which the Parry (1979) fieldwork is based: if more data collection in this framework is envisaged, will it now be possible to modify the questionnaire in such a way as to remedy this lack?

The sociolinguistic approach inspired among others by Labov and Trudgill has borne fruit, as we have seen, in Cardiff; let us now look for the carrying out of similar survey work in the other large urban centres, namely Swansea and Newport. And why not in Aberystwyth, Wrexham, or Llandudno, too?

Linguistic publishing has been slow to incorporate modern sound recording and reproduction techniques. But an increasing range of linguistic and dialectological materials may now be expected to become available in audio form. The Welsh Folk Museum is to be congratulated on its pioneering work in this field: I hope that their recently published cassette of Merthyr Tydfil speech (Awbery and Thomas, 1987) will be the first of many. In a few years from now, when the primary medium of publication ceases to be print and instead takes some kind of digital magnetic form, let us hope that authentic recordings of the language variety under description will be taken for granted as an essential component of any scholarly article in our field.

Let us hope, too, that the English speech of other parts of Wales soon receives attention of the same scholarly quality, attention to phonetic detail, and insight as this book furnishes for much of South Wales. It puts us English to shame.

References

AWBERY, G.M. and THOMAS, B. (eds) 1987, *On the Best Side: Memories of Life in Rhyd-y-car*. Sound recording on cassette. St Fagan's: Welsh Folk Museum, WFM 001.

COUPLAND, N. 1988, *Dialect in Use: Sociolinguistic Variation in Cardiff English*. Cardiff: University of Wales Press.

MEES, I.M. 1983, The speech of Cardiff schoolchildren: a real time study. Doctoral dissertation, University of Leiden.

ORTON, H. *et al.* (eds) 1962–71, *The Survey of English Dialects* (13 vols). Leeds: E.J. Arnold.

PARRY, D. 1979, *The Survey of Anglo-Welsh Dialects, Vol. 2: The South-West*. Swansea: University College.

PENHALLURICK, R.J. 1978, The Anglo-Welsh dialect of Llandebie, Dyfed. BA dissertation, University College, Swansea.

——1980, A phonological comparison of two villages of the Gower peninsula, MA dissertation, University College, Swansea.

——1986, A phonological, lexical, morphological and syntactic survey of the Anglo-Welsh dialects of Gwynedd and Clwyd. PhD dissertation, University College, Swansea.

THOMAS, A. 1984, Welsh English. In P. TRUDGILL (1984).

TRUDGILL, P. (ed.) 1984, *Language in the British Isles*. Cambridge: Cambridge University Press.

TRUDGILL, P. and HANNAH, J. 1982, *International English: A Guide to Varieties of Standard English*. London: Edward Arnold.

WELLS, J.C. 1982, *Accents of English* (3 vols plus cassette). Cambridge: Cambridge University Press.

WILLIAMS, B. 1986, An acoustic study of some features of Welsh prosody. In JOHNS-LEWIS, C. (ed.), *Intonation in Discourse*. London: Croom Helm, 35–51.

Part 3
Sociolinguistic Processes

13 Patterns of Sociophonetic Variation in the Speech of Cardiff Schoolchildren[1]

INGER M. MEES

This chapter discusses some patterns of sociophonetic variation in the speech of 36 Cardiff schoolchildren who were tape-recorded at two points in time. The data are drawn from a larger-scale study (Mees, 1983) of Cardiff English (CE) conducted within a Labovian framework (Labov, 1966). Work on the survey started in 1976. At that time there was a clear need for sociolinguistic research on child populations. Little information was available on how patterns of sociolinguistic variation reported in adult speech communities develop in the speech of children and teenagers. Studies which did include a discussion of the language of younger speakers tended to do so as part of a larger survey dealing with adult age-groups as well, the main emphasis being on the adult population.

Among the first to focus more specifically on children's speech were Romaine (1975) and Reid (1976). These two surveys of Edinburgh schoolchildren suggested that the acquisition of sociolinguistic variation may take place long before adolescence. My own Cardiff study (Mees, 1977) showed similar patterns of variation in the speech of pre-adolescent Cardiff schoolchildren. Having found this variation in the speech of 9–11-year-olds, my next step was to find out how these patterns develop during adolescence. There were two ways of doing this: a study in real time or a study in apparent time. Real-time studies simply take the speech of the same people at different points in historical time. Apparent time studies compare the language of two or more groups of people of different ages, usually at the same point in time. The obvious advantage of an apparent-time study is that one does not have to wait a number of years before being able to investigate the differences. However, a real-time study is clearly more reliable and this was the approach adopted in the Cardiff survey.

In this chapter some of the results of Mees (1983) will be reported. But I shall also focus on certain methodological features, since many of the difficulties encountered in the course of the study were of a methodological nature. Most importantly, a need was felt for a higher level of precision in the identification of the phonological variables and their variants. By taking into consideration factors such as linguistic context, position of the variable in the word, and different lexical categories, additional information on speech variation is obtained which would otherwise not have emerged from the analysis of the material.

Research Design and Phonological Variables

The first of the two recordings took place in December 1976 when the children — chosen non-randomly — were between the ages of 9 and 11. The second was performed somewhat more than four years later; by then, the informants were in their early teens. The subjects were divided into three social classes on the basis of father's occupation (Class 1: professional and managerial; Class 2: white-collar, intermediate non-manual; Class 3: skilled, semi-skilled and unskilled manual). There were six boys and six girls in each class sample. Two speech styles were elicited: 'reading passage' style and 'interview' style.

The phonological variables analysed were:

1. (r), i.e. the pronunciation of intervocalic /r/: [ɹ] or [ɾ].
2. (h¹), i.e. the pronunciation of /h/ in lexical words: /h/ or Ø.
3. (h²), i.e. the pronunciation of /h/ in grammatical words and the full verb *have*: /h/ or Ø.
4. (ng), i.e. the pronunciation of unstressed *-ing*: /ŋ/ or /n/.
5. (t), i.e. the pronunciation of word-final /t/ in a small set of common monosyllabic words: [t], [ʔt], [ʔ], [t̬] or Ø.
6. (T), i.e. the pronunciation of post-tonic /t/ in words other than those covered by (t): [t], [ʔt], [ʔ] or [t̬].

The variables were analysed in terms of social class, style and sex differentiation. In addition, the data collected in 1976 were compared with those of 1981.

Before discussing some of the results of the survey, I shall focus on certain methodological questions. Hudson (1980: 144) has identified five stages in sociolinguistic work in which methodology is 'important and problematic': selecting speakers, circumstances and linguistic variables; collecting the texts; identifying the linguistic variables and their variants;

processing the figures and interpreting the results. Hudson (1980: Ch. 5) and Romaine (1980) give a good account of the difficulties encountered in each phase. In what follows, I shall be concerned chiefly with the problems I was faced with in Hudson's third stage, i.e. the identification of the phonological variables and their variants. Three sets of considerations will be discussed. Establishing the possible phonetic realisations of the variables and finding a sensible way of grouping them is not always as straightforward as it may seem. Further, a decision has to be made as to whether all occurrences of a particular pronunciation feature (e.g. h dropping) should be considered as belonging to a single variable or to two or more variables. Finally, it may be important to consider the phonetic context in which each instance of a variable occurs since the selection by the informants of one variant rather than another is frequently determined by this.

Identification and grouping of variant forms

Let us first consider some of the difficulties involved in identifying and grouping the possible phonetic realisations of a variable. Phonological variables may be either discrete or gradient. Variation in the pronunciation of consonants tends to be in terms of clearly distinguishable alternatives (though see below), whereas variation in vowels has a more continuous nature. For instance, [t] and [ʔ] — two possible variants of post-tonic /t/ in Cardiff English (cf. Collins and Mees, this volume) — have completely different articulatory descriptions and are auditorily distinct, while [aː] and [a̠ː] — two possible realisations in CE of the PALM vowel — involve much smaller articulatory differences and are auditorily less distinct. The more continuous nature of the variation in vowels makes it much more difficult to establish discrete categories for vowels than for consonants and consequently also much more difficult to score the vocalic variables. The phonetic continuum has to be divided up in an arbitrary manner (see Knowles, 1978). The researcher has to make sure that the division is the same for all informants and that borderline cases (e.g. vowels between [a̠ː] and [aː]) are consistently assigned the same numerical value.

To avoid such problems connected with the listing of the variants of vowels, it was decided to concentrate only on consonantal variables in the Mees (1983) study. (See Mees, 1977, and Coupland, 1988, for an analysis of some vocalic Cardiff variables.) The relatively discrete nature of consonantal variables makes it easier to set up distinct categories and thus restricts the number of inaccurate observations.

However, even consonantal variables are not as discrete as one might first be inclined to think. One problem is that one is sometimes faced with intermediate variants. In the case of the two (h) variables, for instance, a weakly voiced allophone [ɦ] was occasionally heard. This was assigned to /h/ rather than Ø. But at times the allophone was so weak that it was difficult to decide where it should be classed. Similar problems emerged in the case of the (r) and (ng) variables. Fortunately, there were very few marginal pronunciations of this type, which meant that such doubtful cases could be omitted without distorting the results.

The most difficult variable of all to deal with was the realisation of post-tonic /t/, e.g. *that, matter*. This was due mainly to the large number of possible phonetic variants and the distribution of these variants, which made it necessary to set up several extra variables (see below). For instance, in the case of word-final /t/ before a vowel — (t^V) — it was necessary to consider five variant pronunciations:

1. [t]
2. [ʔt]
3. [ʔ]
4. [t̬]
5. Ø

Pronunciation type (1) included all realisations of /t/ which were not voiced and not glottally reinforced, i.e. aspirated and unaspirated /t/. Pronunciation type (2) included all articulations where an alveolar closure was accompanied by a glottal closure, i.e. pre-glottalised and post-glottalised /t/ ([ʔt, tʔ]) and also ejective /t/: [t']. Pronunciation type (3) represented a glottal stop without the addition of an alveolar closure. Pronunciation type (4) included [t̬], [ɾ] and [ɹ]. These all represent voiced articulations (in contrast to all the others mentioned). They are articulatorily and auditorily similar and can be said to move along a single phonetic dimension (degree of stricture); thus there seems ample justification for grouping them together. Finally, type (5) involved complete elision of /t/.

The matter was complicated further by the fact that /t/ had fewer variants before a consonant or pause than before a vowel. The voiced allophones (type 4) were found before a vowel only and therefore type (4) was excluded in the other two contexts (before a pause and before a consonant). Even these two environments could not be treated identically, since it is difficult to hear the difference between [ʔt] (type 2) and [ʔ] (type 3) before plosive consonants (e.g. *got better, got two*), as a result of which it was decided not to distinguish these two variants before a consonant. Thus types (2) and (3) were conflated in pre-consonantal context.

Having identified and grouped the variants of post-tonic /t/, one final problem remained, namely whether the pronunciation types established should be analysed using a continuous scale. As Milroy (1984: 210) states, 'variants may sometimes not be analysable on a continuum at all'. In his index scale Macaulay (1977) distinguished two pronunciations of post-tonic /t/ only: [t] and [ʔ]. And although Romaine (1975) identified five variants in her Edinburgh study, she too collapsed these into two in her (t) index scale. As a result, there were no problems in scoring the forms, since both researchers could simply work out the percentage of non-standard forms. Trudgill (1974), on the other hand, recognised three main variants, scoring the values as one continuous variable:

(t) — 1 [tʰ~ t]
(t) — 2 [tʔ]
(t) — 3 [ʔ]

In this case, Trudgill's variants can 'quite naturally be arranged in order, since (t) — 2 is articulatorily intermediate between the other two variants' (Chambers & Trudgill, 1980: 61). In the Cardiff material, however, it is difficult to see how the five variants ([t], [ʔt], [ʔ], [t] and Ø) can be arranged in a continuum. An additional problem relating to variables treated as continuous variables is that 'an average score may reflect consistent use of the median value, or more variable use of extreme values' (Milroy, 1984: 210).

Because of these problems (the large number of variants for (t), the difficulty in ordering the forms in an articulatorily natural manner, and the fact that a continuous variable scale reflects variation less precisely) it was decided to follow the approach adopted by Romaine (1978) in the calculation of the (r) variants ([ɹ], [r] and Ø) in her Edinburgh study. This consisted of working out a percentage score for each variant. Even if it had proved possible to arrange the (t) variants on a continuum, there would have been one final major problem, namely whether the social facts corresponded with the phonetic facts (see also Romaine, 1980: 189). A gradient score would have presupposed a knowledge of how each of the variants relates to the standard which serves as a target for the speakers. Whereas the other variables studied in the Cardiff survey—(r), the (h) variables and (ng) — all had a prestigious and a non-prestigious form, it was not immediately apparent in the case of the (t) variables which of the realisations were associated with high and which with low status. And even if the social significance of the variants had been known to me, this might well have conflicted with the articulatory ordering of the forms.

Establishing the phonological variables

So far we have mainly been concerned with the problems involved in the identification and grouping of the variant forms. Below, we shall focus on the identification of the phonological variables themselves. As the Cardiff survey progressed, it became clear that variation in the pronunciation of /h/ could not be captured properly by setting up a single variable. The same was true of the pronunciation of post-tonic /t/. Both will be discussed below.

On the whole, h-dropping has been treated as a single variable (e.g. Trudgill, 1974; Coupland, 1980; Petyt, 1980). In the Cardiff study, two variables were established: (h^1) and (h^2). (h^1) symbolises the use of /h/ or Ø in the category of lexical words, (h^2) deals with grammatical items beginning with /h/, plus the full verb *have*. The reason for this division was that in RP, which is the prestige accent which speakers move towards in their more formal speech styles, these two classes of words behave differently with respect to the use of /h/. Lexical items tend to receive stress and retain /h/, whereas grammatical items (e.g. auxiliary verbs, pronouns) 'regularly lose /h/ in RP in unaccented, non-initial situations in connected speech' (Gimson, 1980: 192). Thus *he's nine* is /hi:z'naɪn/, but in *I think he's nine* (h) may be either /h/ or Ø. In other words, h-dropping is acceptable in RP in certain environments. For this reason, I would argue that the realisation of /h/ in these contexts should be excluded from the calculations (see also Wells, 1982: I, 254–55).

The following pronouns were covered by (h^2): *he, his, him, her, who, how*. The number of instances of *he* outnumbered the occurrences of the other pronouns by far. All stressed forms were included in the calculations. Of the unstressed forms, only the occurrences following pause were considered, that is, all environments where h-dropping is unacceptable in RP. In the calculation of the (h^1) words it was decided never to count the same item more than three times (Macaulay, 1977: 31, note 1), whereas (h^2) items, which consisted of a very limited number of items with a high frequency of occurrence, were counted whenever they occurred. As well as covering the pronouns mentioned above, (h^2) was also taken to include most forms of *have*.[2]

Table 13.1, which presents the 1981 indices for (h^1) and (h^2) by social class and style, illustrates that, at least in CE, there is a difference between the two classes of words with respect to h-dropping. A single lexeme category

Table 13.1   *(h¹) and (h²) Indices by Social Class and Style, 1981 Scores*

	Class 1		Class 2		Class 3	
	(h^1)	(h^2)	(h^1)	(h^2)	(h^1)	(h^2)
Interview style	4.2	37.8	7.4	49.5	36.1	80.1
Reading passage style	0.0	2.4	0.0	5.0	2.3	7.9

would have failed to reveal such information. A comparison of the two types of (h) words reveals that children of all social classes are strongly aware of the social significance of both (h^1) and (h^2). In the more monitored speech style of the two, the reading passage style, there is virtually no h-dropping, in either the lexical or the grammatical words. In the interview style, there appears to be a major difference between the two classes of words. The speakers of classes 1 and 2 have extremely low scores for (h^1), but a noticeably higher percentage of /h/-elision for (h^2). Class 3 speakers also exhibit an enormous difference between (h^1) and (h^2). In (h^1) words, h-dropping is 36%, while in (h^2) words the percentage is as high as 80. Note that the distribution of the scores across the classes is in the expected direction: the lower the social class, the higher the percentage of zero forms.

From a sociolinguistic point of view, there is no need to establish two categories; the trends are identical in both types of word. (Though note that until we have tested whether the two categories of words produce similar or different results, we have no way of knowing whether they are subject to the same social constraints.) However, from a phonetic point of view, the information is valuable in that it tells us something about the linguistic constraints operating on the use of /h/.

As the reading passage style indices for both (h^1) and (h^2) were remarkably low in all three classes, I decided to work out the percentage of h-dropping in this style for those grammatical words (i.e. (h^2) words) where /h/ may be elided in RP. The reading passage provided a number of such occurrences, e.g. *feeling sure of himself, on his left, because he had heard.* These (h^2) words were termed (h^3). Table 13.2 shows the reading passage style indices for (h^3) by social class. It is noticeable that the percentage of h-dropping is much higher in (h^3) than in (h^1) and (h^2) in this speech style. However, this is to be expected since h-dropping is optional in (h^3) words in RP.

TABLE 13.2 *Percentage Indices for (h³) by Social Class, Reading Passage Style, 1981 Scores*

Class 1	Class 2	Class 3
59.5	46.6	46.6

Since the difference between the three groups of informants was not statistically significant, we can conclude that (h^3) does not show clear social class stratification in the reading passage style. We saw in Table 13.1 that the (h^1) and the (h^2) variables hardly exhibit class differentiation in the reading passage style either. Thus, all Cardiff speakers appear to be strongly aware of the social significance of (h). A probable explanation for the pattern of /h/-elision found with (h) is that h-dropping — 'the single most powerful pronunciation shibboleth in England' (Wells, 1982: I, 254) — is subject to overt criticism in Cardiff. Chambers & Trudgill (1980: 84) suggest that one of the main reasons why certain variables are more likely to suffer overt stigmatisation than others is 'the divergence between pronunciation and orthography'. In my conversations with schoolteachers and pupils, reference was often made to 'dropping one's aitches'. This strong awareness of the social significance of /h/ may be the reason for the very low percentage of /h/-elision in the reading passage style in (h^1) and (h^2) in all classes. It may also have resulted in making the children of the lower class groups particularly careful to sound /h/ in *all* linguistic contexts, even those where elision is optional in RP.

These differing patterns in the pronunciation of /h/ would have been obscured if h-dropping had merely been considered as a single variable. The decision to operate with three different categories of h-dropping (based on the patterns of /h/-pronunciation in RP) means that the variation of /h/-elision in CE is reflected more accurately than it would otherwise have been.

Another example of a variable which is more conveniently split into two categories is the pronunciation of non-syllable-initial /t/, e.g. *bit, bitter*. As stated above, it appeared that /t/ had a large number of variant forms. On the basis of other surveys (e.g. Macaulay, 1977; Reid, 1976; Romaine, 1975; Trudgill, 1974) I had expected to find two significant variant pronunciations only: glottalised and non-glottalised /t/, e.g. [nɒʔ, nɒʔt] and [nɒt] for *not*. As a non-native of Cardiff, I was not prepared for a zero realisation of /t/. It was only when I started listing words and counting the variants of /t/ that I realised that elision of /t/ was very common, although it was restricted to a small number of high-frequency words: *it, bit, get, let, at, that, got, lot, not, what, put, but, might, right, quite, out, about*. Nevertheless, these words constituted between 85% and 90% of the recorded instances with /t/. The remaining words with post-tonic /t/, e.g. *street, light, notice*, were dealt with separately (symbolised as (T)). It is not possible to exclude the possibility that /t/ in these (T) words may also occur with zero forms in CE, but except for a very small number of instances /t/ was never elided in these words in my material. However, given more informal speech styles (as in Reid, 1976) than the ones obtained, I think it possible that /t/ may be elided in words other than the ones listed above, particularly if /t/ occurs in an unstressed syllable, e.g. *favourite, jacket* (two of the very few examples from my material where this was the case).

Apart from the difference with respect to the zero form, the two variables also exhibited differences with respect to the other realisations. Compare, for instance, the results in the interview style for (t) and (T) words word-finally before a vowel (represented as (t^V) and (T^V) respectively) in Table 13.3. In the high-frequency words (i.e. (t^V) words, e.g. *bit of*), the voiced allophones [t̪,ɾ,ɹ] are clearly the most frequently used variants, whereas in the remaining words (i.e. (T^V), e.g. *bought it*) [t] is the most common variant. The division into two variables instead of one is capable of revealing these types of difference.

TABLE 13.3   *Percentage Indices for (t^V) and (T^V) by Social Class, Interview Style, Five Variants, 1981 Scores.*

	Class 1		Class 2		Class 3	
	(t^V)	(T^V)	(t^V)	(T^V)	(t^V)	(T^V)
[t]	18.7	56.5	15.0	57.2	10.4	57.5
[ʔ]	38.4	23.6	22.1	8.4	4.2	2.1
[ʔt, t̪ʔ]	6.7	14.7	11.7	31.7	5.9	31.6
[t̪]	29.4	3.9	44.0	2.8	62.7	8.9
Ø	6.9	0.0	7.3	0.0	17.1	0.0

Phonetic context

The final methodological problem concerning the identification of the variables which will be discussed in this chapter is that of phonetic context. One example of a case where the phonetic environment is important is that of unstressed -*ing* (i.e. the (ng) variable). The two variants selected by the informants were of course /ŋ/ and /n/. Generally, there were few difficulties in assigning the variants to these two types. However, sometimes a bilabial [m] was heard for (ng), e.g. *swimming pool* ['swɪmɪm puːl]. All such occurrences of [m] were assigned to the /n/ category, as it is usual for final alveolars to assimilate to the place of the following word-initial consonant, whereas syllable-final velars are normally stable in such contexts. On the other hand, a decision was made to exclude all -*ing* forms before a velar consonant (e.g. *nightingale, magnifying glass, watching cartoons, quick-drying glue*), since in these cases there is no way of knowing whether an [ŋ] heard on the tapes was the result of an assimilation rule applied to an initially selected /n/, or whether /ŋ/ was selected in the first place. The problem is illustrated below:

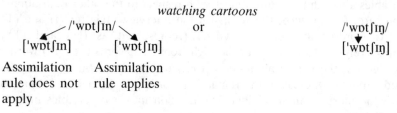

watching cartoons

	/'wɒtʃɪn/	or	/'wɒtʃɪŋ/
['wɒtʃɪn]	['wɒtʃɪŋ]		['wɒtʃɪŋ]
Assimilation rule does not apply	Assimilation rule applies		

In the case of the (t) and (T) variables, context also played a significant role. The frequency of occurrence of a particular variant could to a certain extent be predicted on the basis of what followed word-final /t/, i.e. whether /t/ was followed by a consonant (e.g. *bit more*), a pause, or a vowel (e.g. *bit of*). For instance, glottalised and elided forms were much less likely to occur before a vowel than in the other two environments (see Table 13.4.).

Of course, there is no need to stop at three contexts. Romaine (1975: 115–16) considered seven environments altogether; for instance, she distinguished between word-final position before a following pause and utterance-final position. The only difficulty in considering a large number of contexts might be that one ends up having very few instances of each variant. Ideally, one should start off by analysing a certain number of categories which seem relevant, and then later conflate the categories for which there seems a basis for doing so. In other words, if one's analysis of word-final and utterance-final position yields similar results,

TABLE 13.4 *Percentage of Glottalised and Elided Forms by Context, Interview Style, All Speakers, 1981 Scores*

Context	Consonant	Pause	Vowel
[ʔ, ʔt]	53.5	46.5	33.5
Ø	31.3	32.6	10.4

then one would be justified in conflating these two contexts in the final analysis of the material. In the Cardiff study, the main finding obtained by splitting up the (t) variables into three contexts was that certain variants are restricted to certain positions, such as (t̞, ɾ, ɹ], which occur before a vowel only. Unless such a breakdown of the variables is made, this type of information is lost.

In addition to considering the segments preceding and following a variable, one might also examine the actual position of the variable itself. For instance, although (h¹) — the category of lexical words — occurs in prevocalic position only, it is possible to divide this variable into a number of different categories. The most common occurrence of /h/ is stressed, word-initial position, e.g. *home, hospital, high*. But /h/ may also be:

1. stressed, but not word-initial, e.g. *behave, rehearse*.
2. unstressed, word-initial, e.g. *however, historical*.
3. non-word-initial and not carrying the main stress, e.g. *grass-hoppers, skinheads, lighthouse*.

A subdivision of this kind was carried out in the Cardiff study. It should be noted that the above three types formed only a small fraction of the total occurrences of (h¹). Nevertheless, differences emerged between the three types. h-dropping was least common in unstressed, word-initial position (i.e. type 2). In stressed, non-word-initial position it was also infrequent, but in type 3 /h/ was elided relatively often (see Mees, 1983: 107–10 for full details).

However, subcategorisations do not always show important results. For instance, I attempted to analyse the amount of h-dropping in the three most common types of *have* (Cheshire, 1982: 32):

1. *have* as a full verb, e.g. I had a bike.
2. *have* as an auxiliary, e.g. I haven't got a clue.
3. *have* with a following *to* + infinitive, to express obligation, e.g. we had to leave.

TABLE 13.5   *Percentage of Elided Forms for Three Types of Have, 1976 and 1981*

	have as a full verb	*have* as an auxiliary	*have* + *to* + infinitive
1976	61.5	69.5	64.1
1981	63.3	49.6	68.4

(Note that for *have* as an auxiliary only those *have* forms were counted which were stressed and those which were unstressed, post-pausal.)

Table 13.5 shows the percentage of zero forms in 1976 and 1981 for the three types of *have*. With the exception of the 1981 score for *have* as an auxiliary, which is lower than the other indices for *have*, h-dropping does not differ greatly in the three types of *have*. (Since no statistical tests were performed on these figures, it is not clear whether the 1981 score for *have* should be interpreted as a decrease in h-dropping in adolescence as compared with pre-adolescence.)

The above is an example where a further breakdown of the variable does not reveal a change in the pattern of h-dropping, and if one were only interested in establishing the amount of h-dropping in Cardiff speech, this subcategorisation would not be necessary.

Some Results of the Cardiff Study

The rest of this chapter will be devoted to a discussion of some of the results of the Cardiff survey, notably the trends identified diachronically and in the sex dimension. The analysis will focus on two groups of variables: first, (r), (h^1), (h^2) and (ng), which all have a standard and a non-standard variant; second, word-final /t/ in the 17 words mentioned on p. 175, i.e. the (t) variables, which have three or more variants.

The variables (r), (h^1), (h^2) and (ng)

As a first step the correlation of the four phonological variables with class, sex and style was worked out for the 1981 results. Then, these figures were compared with those obtained in 1976. First, we shall look at the covariation with social class and style.

The patterns which emerged for class and style for (r), the (h) variables and (ng) were similar to those obtained in other British sociolinguistic studies, i.e. non-standard forms were more common in the speech (1) of the lower than of the higher classes and (2) in the interview style than in the reading passage style. The results are summarised in Table 13.6. In virtually all cases the class differences were statistically significant.[3] The variables (r) and (ng) show what has been termed gradient stratification, i.e. a 'progressive increase in the frequency of occurrence of a variant when compared for various social groups' (Wolfram & Fasold, 1974: 79–80). The (h) variables, however, exhibit *sharp* stratification, i.e. there is a clearer demarcation between the classes. Here, the two middle-class groups are sharply marked off from the working-class group. Why should there be a clear separation between the middle and the working classes in the case of (h^1) and (h^2) and not in the case of (r) and (ng)? I suspect this is connected with the extent to which the variables are overtly stigmatised in the speech community. As stated earlier, h-dropping was frequently criticised by teachers and children, whereas the use of [ɾ] and, surprisingly, also of /n/[4] was rarely commented upon. Thus it would appear that members of the Cardiff speech community are more aware of the social significance of /h/-elision than of [ɾ] and /n/.

Some support for this view can be found in the (h) figures showing stylistic differentiation. In all three classes the differences between the two styles were statistically significant for both types of (h). Table 13.6 illustrates that h-dropping is reduced to a minimum in the reading passage style for all speakers. In the case of (ng) the differences between the styles are also statistically significant in all three classes. It is noticeable, however, that the (ng) scores are much higher in both styles than those

TABLE 13.6   *Percentage of Non-standard Forms for (r), (h^1), (h^2) and (ng) by Social Class and Style, 1981 Scores*

	(r)		(h^1)		(h^2)		(ng)	
	Inter-view style	Reading passage style	Inter-view style	Reading passage style	Inter-view style	Reading passage style	Inter-view style	Reading passage style
Class 1	6.6	6.8	4.2	0.0	37.8	2.4	48.3	20.9
Class 2	37.3	32.0	7.4	0.0	49.5	5.0	79.3	49.6
Class 3	74.4	69.7	36.1	2.3	80.1	7.9	96.0	60.4

for any of the other variables. This would appear to signify that although the speakers are aware of the social significance of (ng) — as shown by the decrease in the use of /n/ in the reading passage style — this variable does not suffer strong stigmatisation. (This is confirmed by the results showing sex differentiation; see below.)

Conversely, there is little or no stylistic variation for the (r) variable (the differences were not statistically significant). In other words, the speakers are relatively unaware of the social significance of (r). Note that there is no 'help' to be derived from the orthography in terms of increasing the speakers' awareness of (r). This there is, of course, for the (h) variables and (ng).

In summary, we can illustrate the degree of stigmatisation apparently associated with the four variables as follows:

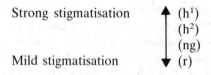

We shall now turn to the scores showing sex differentiation in the four variables. Tables 13.7 and 13.8 summarise the correlation with social class and sex for (r), (h¹), (h²) and (ng) in two speech styles. Far fewer statistically significant differences were found between the sexes than between the classes and speech styles. With the exception of (ng) the general trends, however, seem to support the findings of other workers, with fewer low-status forms in the speech of females than of males. Romaine (1984: 113) observes that in her study of Edinburgh school-children she 'found some evidence for sex differentiation in the use of certain variables by children as young as six years old'. But she goes on to say that 'although all of the phonological variables I examined (with

TABLE 13.7   *Percentage Indices for (r), (h¹), (h²) and (ng) by Social Class and Sex, Interview Style, 1981 Scores*

	(r)		*(h¹)*		*(h²)*		*(ng)*	
	Girls	*Boys*	*Girls*	*Boys*	*Girls*	*Boys*	*Girls*	*Boys*
Class 1	5.4	7.8	3.5	4.9	31.1	44.4	56.5	40.0
Class 2	27.5	47.1	1.9	12.9	41.5	57.5	81.4	77.1
Class 3	68.5	80.3	27.6	44.5	75.5	84.6	98.1	93.8

TABLE 13.8   *Percentage Indices for (r), (h¹), (h²) and (ng) by Social Class and Sex, Reading Passage Style, 1981 Scores*

	(r)		(h¹)		(h²)		(ng)	
	Girls	Boys	Girls	Boys	Girls	Boys	Girls	Boys
Class 1	2.1	11.5	0.0	0.0	0.0	4.8	27.4	14.3
Class 2	14.6	49.3	0.0	0.0	3.3	6.7	68.7	30.4
Class 3	55.2	84.1	0.0	4.5	0.0	15.7	69.1	51.6

the exception of (ing)) showed a trend towards sex differentiation, the results are not statistically significant'. I find this statement interesting in two respects. First, it is striking that, both in Romaine's study and my own, (ng) was the only variable where female speakers appeared to use the same or a higher percentage of non-standard forms than male speakers.[5] It was remarked earlier that (ng) scores were on the whole higher than scores for other variables and this was taken to indicate that this variable does not suffer strong stigmatisation. The fact that the girls exhibit a trend towards using more low-status variants than the boys seems to confirm this view. Thus at least in *two* British communities (ng) appears to be less strongly stigmatised in the speech of children and teenagers than in the speech of adults. (Note that Fischer's (1958) results for (ng) in a New England village show clear sex differentiation of the usual type at an early age.)

The second interesting fact about Romaine's observation is the following. Clear patterns of sex variation have frequently been established for adults. In all cases, females were shown to use more prestige variants than males; 'indeed, this is perhaps the most strikingly consistent finding of all to emerge from sociolinguistic dialect studies in the industrialised western world' (Chambers & Trudgill, 1980: 72). As we have seen, neither the scores for the Cardiff teenagers nor those for the Edinburgh children exhibited consistent statistically significant differences between the sexes, although the trends for most variables were in the same direction as those identified for adult speakers in numerous studies. Instead of stressing that the pattern of sex differentiation in childhood and adolescence is similar to that of adulthood, we should perhaps turn things round and emphasise that linguistic sex differentiation is not so clearly manifested in the speech of children and teenagers as in the speech of the adult population. It is interesting to speculate as to why this should be the case.

The tendency for women to use a higher percentage of prestigious forms is generally attributed to the fact that they are more status-conscious than men. Chambers & Trudgill (1980: 98) suggest some reasons why this should be the case (see also Trudgill, 1983: 161–68, for a more detailed discussion). Two of these explanations are relevant for our purposes:

1. In our society, women have fewer opportunities, still, for achievement, and are therefore more likely to signal their social status by how they appear and behave (including linguistically) than by what they do.
2. Women tend, perhaps as a result of fewer occupational opportunities and a greater tendency to remain at home, to participate in less cohesive social networks. They are therefore less subject to peer group pressure than men, and at the same time are more used to finding themselves in situations that are 'formal' in the sense that they are not particularly well-acquainted with the people they are talking to. Formal speech styles therefore result.

It is evident that these factors apply much more strongly to adults than to teenagers and children, and I suggest that this is why there was no marked sex differentiation in the speech of the adolescents of this survey. They were all still at school, so that the social pressures from the peer group were similar for both sexes. Neither the boys nor the girls derived their status through their occupations. Consequently, their social position was more or less equal, and this is reflected in their linguistic behaviour. If the informants had been recorded after they had left school, we would probably have found that the speech differences between the sexes had increased (see Coates, 1986: 121–34 for an interesting discussion of the way in which children acquire sex-appropriate language).

The last part of this section will be devoted to the diachronic dimension. Tables 13.9 and 13.10 compare the 1976 indices for (r), (h^1), (h^2) and (ng) with those of 1981 in each of the two speech styles. The most striking thing about the indices in these tables is the general absence of differences between pre-adolescence and adolescence. None of the four variables reveal major changes between 1976 and 1981. Thus the patterns of speech seem to be more or less fixed by the age of ten. After that there are minor fluctuations in the speech of the children, but there is nothing which points to a complete reversal of the patterns of variation once the language system has been acquired.

Despite the fact that the differences between 1976 and 1981 are on the whole small, there are in some cases statistically significant differences

TABLE 13.9   *Percentage Indices for (r), (h¹), (h²) and (ng) by Social Class and Time, Interview Style*

	(r)		(h¹)		(h²)		(ng)	
	1976	1981	1976	1981	1976	1981	1976	1981
Class 1	18.8	6.6	1.1	4.2	36.3	37.8	38.9	48.3
Class 2	49.0	37.3	6.3	7.4	49.9	49.5	88.7	79.3
Class 3	75.0	74.4	29.1	36.1	76.3	80.1	90.9	96.0

TABLE 13.10   *Percentage Indices for (r), (h¹), (h²) and (ng) by Social Class and Time, Reading Passage Style*

	(r)		(h¹)		(h²)		(ng)	
	1976	1981	1976	1981	1976	1981	1976	1981
Class 1	9.7	6.8	0.0	0.0	1.7	2.4	27.4	20.9
Class 2	45.4	32.0	0.0	0.0	2.8	5.0	67.9	49.6
Class 3	73.4	69.7	0.6	2.3	1.7	7.9	53.6	60.4

between the two points in time. For both middle-class groups (i.e. classes 1 and 2), there are statistically significant differences between the (r) scores of 1976 and 1981, the 1981 percentages being lower than those of 1976. This could point to two things. Either the scores indicate a sound change in progress, whereby tap realisations are becoming less common in Cardiff speech, or they reflect the phenomenon of age-grading, of the 'characteristic linguistic behaviors appropriate for different stages in the life history of an individual' (Wolfram & Fasold, 1974: 89). Age-grading differences tend to be repeated in every new generation. In this particular case, this would mean that it is 'appropriate' for middle-class speakers to employ fewer tap realisations as teenagers than as pre-adolescents. Or, to put it differently, that the Cardiff speakers' awareness of the social significance of certain variables (e.g. (r)) emerges at a later stage than that of others (e.g. the (h) variables). It is difficult to say which of the two possibilities we are dealing with here, but I suspect the age-grading explanation is the most likely one in this case.

Apart from the (r) variable, the (ng) variable also exhibits statistically significant differences between the 1976 and 1981 reading passage style scores of these two class groups. Again, there is a decrease in the use of non-standard forms. On the other hand, these speakers show a statistically significant increase in the use of (h^1) in the interview style and of (h^2) in the reading passage style. Note, however, that the differences between the two points in time are minimal.

In class 3, three variables show statistically significant differences between the two recordings. In the interview style, there is an increase in the use of (ng) and the same is true of (h^1) and (h^2) in the reading passage style.

Although the overall changes between the stages of pre-adolescence and adolescence are slight and far from all the differences are statistically significant, two trends seem to recur in each variable. The indices of the working class tend to remain stable or move *away* from the standard as the children grow older. Conversely, the percentage scores of the lower middle class (class 2) remain stable or move *towards* the prestige norm. These features are apparent in both speech styles (see Tables 13.9 and 13.10). Thus these two classes are more clearly separated in adolescence than in childhood.

If the sex dimension is also taken into account, it becomes evident that it is the lower-middle-class *girls* and the working-class *boys* who are largely responsible for the increasing divergence between the two classes. In both styles, the class 3 boys consistently have more non-standard forms in 1981 than in 1976, whereas the class 2 girls (with one exception) consistently show a movement towards the prestige norm. (Again, the scores are far from always statistically significant, but the pattern is so regular that I think it should be pointed out.) The development is illustrated in Table 13.11, which shows for both speech styles the *mean* of the group scores for the four variables by class, sex and time.

TABLE 13.11   *Mean of the Group Scores for (r), (h^1), (h^2) and (ng) by Class, Sex and Time*

	Interview style				Reading passage style			
	Girls		Boys		Girls		Boys	
	1976	1981	1976	1981	1976	1981	1976	1981
Class 1	19.0	24.1	28.5	24.3	8.5	7.4	10.9	7.7
Class 2	47.9	38.1	49.0	48.7	27.5	21.7	30.6	21.6
Class 3	67.1	67.4	68.5	75.8	35.4	31.1	29.2	39.0

A possible explanation for the movement shown by the lower-middle-class girls towards the prestige norm is the following. On the whole, the upper middle class tends to be responsible for setting standards of behaviour, including standards of speech behaviour. Members of this class are linguistically secure: there is no need for them to modify their speech. The lower middle class, however, tends to be less secure, socially *and* linguistically. Members of this class (notably the females) typically wish to be identified with the upper middle class, and one of the ways of achieving this is by imitating the speech behaviour of this class. The figures in Table 13.11 show that the lower-middle-class girls are closer to the prestige variety as teenagers than as children and this could indicate that their class consciousness increases as they grow older. However, it is perhaps debatable whether awareness of class differences is actually present at the age of 14.[6] Certainly, it cannot be established by linguistic criteria alone; it must be determined on the basis of independent criteria.

It is also possible that the greater gap between the middle and working classes in adolescence is connected with the extent to which the speakers are influenced by their peers. It has been suggested that pressures from the peer group are strongest in pre-adolescence. Hockett (1950: 451) draws attention to 'the outstanding importance of other children among the environmental forces which condition the emerging dialect of a child'. Labov (1972: 138) claims that from about 4 to 13 years old the child's speech pattern

> is dominated and regulated by that of the preadolescent group with which he plays. These are the peers who are able, by their sanctions, to eliminate any deviations from the dialect pattern of the group . . .

> It is in the first year of high school that the speaker begins to acquire the set of evaluative norms . . . He becomes sensitive to the social significance of his own form of speech, and other forms; complete familiarity with the norms of the community seems to be attained at the age of 17 or 18. On the other hand, the ability to *use* prestige forms of speech . . . is not acquired until relatively late: the youngster seems to begin this process at 16 or 17 (emphasis added).

Both Mees (1983) and several others (e.g. Macaulay, 1977; Reid, 1976; Romaine, 1975) have shown that the ability to use prestige forms may be acquired much earlier than the age of 16 or 17. The wide range of stylistic variation demonstrated in primary schoolchildren shows that young children are indeed aware of prestigious forms. (We have seen, though, that awareness of the social significance of some variables is acquired later than that of others.) Now it is possible that peer-group pressure prevents pre-adolescent children from employing their full range of stylistic variation. During adolescence, the growing class consciousness and increasing linguistic awareness may, in the case of the lower-middle-class girls, override the influence of the peer group. On the other hand, it seems plausible that the peer group pressures exerted on the working-class males become stronger rather than weaker in adolescence. Cheshire (1982), for instance, has shown that the degree of adherence to the peer group and the norms of the vernacular culture affected the extent to which teenagers in Reading used non-standard forms. Working-class males are more likely to be influenced by the covert prestige connected with the use of non-standard forms, i.e. 'prestige in the sense of being favourably regarded by one's peers, and of signalling one's identity as a member of a group' (Chambers & Trudgill, 1980: 99).

The (t) variables

The (t) variables — the realisation of word-final /t/ in a small set of common words — were more difficult to handle than the variables discussed so far. Instead of simply having a standard and a non-standard form, depending upon the context up to five different variants were noted for these variables (see above). First we shall consider the covariation with class and style.

Tables 13.12 and 13.13 show the percentage indices for each variant of word-final /t/ in three contexts (before a consonant, a pause and a

TABLE 13.12 *Percentage Indices for (tᶜ), (tᵖ) and (tᵛ) by Social Class, Interview Style, 1981 Scores*

	(tᶜ)			(tᵖ)			(tᵛ)		
	Class 1	Class 2	Class 3	Class 1	Class 2	Class 3	Class 1	Class 2	Class 3
[t]	11.3	26.8	31.9	15.8	27.1	15.5	18.7	15.0	10.4
[ʔt]	79.1	47.5	9.9	56.6	44.4	9.0	38.4	22.1	4.2
[ʔ]				21.3	9.8	3.1	6.7	11.7	5.9
[t̬]							29.4	44.0	62.7
Ø	9.7	25.8	58.3	6.4	18.8	72.6	6.9	7.3	17.1

TABLE 13.13   *Percentage Indices for (t^C), (t^P) and (t^V) by Social Class, Reading Passage Style, 1981 Scores*

	(t^C)			(t^P)			(t^V)		
	Class 1	Class 2	Class 3	Class 1	Class 2	Class 3	Class 1	Class 2	Class 3
[t]	10.0	35.5	57.1	25.0	79.2	95.9	85.4	75.0	75.0
[ʔt]	86.7	64.6	37.5	4.2	12.5	0.0	6.3	8.4	0.0
[ʔ]				70.8	8.3	4.2	4.2	12.5	25.0
[t]							2.1	4.2	0.0
Ø	3.4	0.0	5.5	0.0	0.0	0.0	0.0	0.0	0.0

vowel), symbolised as (t^C), (t^P) and (t^V). Note that the scores for [ʔt] and [ʔ] were not distinguished before a consonant (see pp. 170–71, above). Three conclusions can be drawn. First, elision is a low-prestige variant. The use of zero forms decreases from low to high social status. In the interview style it is an extremely common variant for working-class speakers. Hardly any forms occur in the reading passage style. Second, [t] is found only before a vowel. This variant, too, is virtually restricted to the interview style and here it shows the same distribution as Ø. Thus [t] is also a low-status variant. Third, glottalisation (both [ʔ] and [ʔt]) appears to be a prestigious feature in CE. Its usage increases as we move up the social scale in all contexts in both speech styles except in the reading passage style before a vowel. This is a completely different pattern from that found by other researchers in other speech communities (e.g. Norwich, Edinburgh and Glasgow), where pre-glottalisation and glottal replacement are associated with low prestige rather than high prestige.

I have argued elsewhere (Mees, 1987) that (1) casual observations suggest that in Cardiff glottalisation is more prevalent among younger than older speakers; (2) glottalisation for Cardiffians is a high-status rather than a low-status variant; and (3) the model of glottalisation of the Cardiff middle-class speakers is very similar to that found in mainstream RP. All these factors make it seem highly likely that glottalisation is an innovation in CE introduced by the higher socio-economic classes in imitation of RP. As can be seen in Tables 13.12 and 13.13, glottalised forms are most common before a consonant and least so before a vowel (see also pp. 176–77, above). The only context in which [t] realisations are found more frequently than glottal realisations in the highest social class is in the reading passage style before a vowel (see below).

We shall now turn to the covariation of (t) with sex and time. Since Chambers & Trudgill (1980: 97) state that unusual patterns of sex differentiation may indicate that a linguistic change is in progress, it is worth investigating this possibility for the Cardiff data. To illustrate clearly the covariation of (t) with sex and time, it is easier to start with the 1976 results (rather than the 1981 scores which have been used to demonstrate the patterns of sociophonetic variation discussed so far).

On first listening to my 1976 recordings of the Cardiff children two things struck me with respect to the use of the glottal stop before a vowel. First, there was a striking difference between the male and female speakers of class 1 in the percentage of [ʔ] used in the interview style for (t^V), as in *but I, bit of*, etc. The second interesting pattern was the much higher percentage of glottally reinforced allophones found in all intervocalic contexts in the speech of the males (notably those of classes 2 and 3). The girls used far more [t] forms. We shall begin with a discussion of the first of these two patterns (see Table 13.14).

The upper middle class girls employ a higher percentage of glottal stops than the boys. No statistical tests were performed on the 1976 scores, but it would appear from the scores that [ʔ] for (t^V) is a variant characteristic of the highest social class and of female speech. We have seen above that there is some evidence that glottalisation of word-final /t/ is an innovation in Cardiff speech. It appears to have been introduced by speakers of the higher classes in imitation of RP. It is heard frequently before a consonant and a pause. Wells (1982: I, 261) observes that [ʔ] for word-final pre-*vocalic* /t/ is a recent development in the speech of younger RP speakers. This suggests that the feature has now acquired a certain degree of prestige in this environment. Since it is said to be the case that 'if a linguistic change is taking place in the direction of the prestige variety it will be spearheaded by middle class women' (Chambers & Trudgill, 1980: 97), it does not seem unlikely that use of [ʔ] is an

TABLE 13.14   *Percentage of [ʔ] for (t^V) by Social Class and Sex, Interview Style, 1976 Scores*

	All	Girls	Boys
Class 1	21.5	27.7	15.2
Class 2	4.1	1.7	6.5
Class 3	2.3	4.3	0.3

innovation introduced by this group of speakers. It is simply the extension to another context (namely that before a vowel) of a feature which has earlier been adopted in other environments (i.e. those before a consonant and a pause). As yet, it has only filtered into the less formal speech styles; the reading passage style scores (not reproduced here) show that it is not established in careful speech.

A comparison of the 1976 scores with those of 1981 (Table 13.15) shows that use of [ʔ] is on the increase. There is a marked increase in the use of full glottalisation in the middle classes, the differences being statistically significant. In the working class this new feature appears not to have caught on yet. Although there was only a gap of just over four years between the two recordings, our 1981 figures appear to lend support to the supposition made on the basis of the 1976 scores, namely that use of [ʔ] represents a sound change in progress initiated by the upper middle class (notably the girls) and now spreading to the lower middle class.

TABLE 13.15   *Percentage of [ʔ] for (t^V) by Social Class, Sex and Time, Interview Style.*

	All		Girls		Boys	
	1976	1981	1976	1981	1976	1981
Class 1	21.5	38.4	27.7	52.1	15.2	24.6
Class 2	4.1	22.1	1.7	23.6	6.5	20.5
Class 3	2.3	4.2	4.3	2.0	0.3	6.3

The pattern described above applied to the small list of very common words listed on p. 175. Interestingly, the same pattern is repeated in all other words containing word-final /t/ before a vowel. However, it is not found in medial intervocalic position (e.g. *fighting, started, matter*) and this again corresponds with the situation in RP. Nor, as stated earlier, has the phenomenon spread to careful speech styles. Although I believe the increase in the use of [ʔ] to be a sound change, we should not rule out the possibility that the variation described is merely a reflection of age-grading differences (see above). If it is a sound change in progress, then it is not surprising that it should be led by the upper middle class. The speech of the members of this class enjoys *overt* prestige: it is judged by speakers of standard and non-standard varieties alike to be the 'proper' way of speaking. As a result, the accent of the upper classes — in England and south Wales (at least in the Cardiff area) this will usually be a type of RP — exerts great pressure on non-standard varieties.

However, linguistic changes do not always begin in higher-class groups. The use of glottally reinforced allophones before a vowel appears to be a change led by the males of the lower classes. Since the use of [ʔt, tʔ] was seen in all intervocalic contexts before a vowel (i.e. all word-final /t/ items before a vowel, and word-medial /t/), we shall here not restrict ourselves to the common items ending with /t/, but show the results for *all* intervocalic tokens (see Table 13.16). In both speech styles, the girls use [ʔt, tʔ] less frequently than the boys. The difference is most marked in the working class. In RP, glottal reinforcement is *not* heard with intervocalic /t/. In CE it is rare in the higher social classes. Unlike [ʔ], discussed above, it does not enjoy overt prestige. Thus it is a change *away* from the prestige norm. The fact that such a high percentage of [ʔt, tʔ] was found in the speech of the working-class boys suggests that it is an innovation introduced by this group. This seems all the more likely if we take into consideration that 'changes away from the prestige norm . . . will have working class . . . men in the vanguard' (Chambers & Trudgill, 1980: 97–98). Changes away from the prestige variety tend to occur as a result of *covert* prestige associated with the use of non-standard forms. Since men are typically more favourably disposed towards the use of non-standard forms than women (see p. 186, above) the concept of covert prestige could also explain the spread of [ʔt, tʔ] from the working-class males to the males of the other classes.

Tables 13.17 and 13.18 take the time dimension into account as well as the sex dimension. It is evident that especially the working-class boys show a marked increase in the use of glottally reinforced allophones. Thus this appears to be a sound change led by this group. The fact that

TABLE 13.16   *Percentage of [ʔt, tʔ] for All Intervocalic Tokens by Social Class and Sex, 1976 Scores*

	Interview style			Reading passage style		
	All	*Girls*	*Boys*	*All*	*Girls*	*Boys*
Class 1	6.4	1.9	10.8	3.5	2.4	4.5
Class 2	8.2	3.8	12.5	10.3	4.5	16.0
Class 3	17.3	4.4	30.2	13.0	5.7	20.3

TABLE 13.17   *Percentage of [ʔt, tʔ] for all Intervocalic Tokens by Social Class, Sex and Time, Interview Style*

	All		Girls		Boys	
	1976	*1981*	*1976*	*1981*	*1976*	*1981*
Class 1	6.4	10.8	1.9	5.4	10.8	16.2
Class 2	8.2	22.3	3.8	15.8	12.5	28.7
Class 3	17.3	23.1	4.4	3.1	30.2	43.2

TABLE 13.18   *Percentage of [ʔt, tʔ] for all Intervocalic Tokens by Social Class, Sex and Time, Reading Passage Style*

	All		Girls		Boys	
	1976	*1981*	*1976*	*1981*	*1976*	*1981*
Class 1	3.5	3.3	2.4	0.0	4.5	6.6
Class 2	10.3	10.5	4.5	0.0	16.0	20.9
Class 3	13.0	27.4	5.7	2.1	20.3	52.7

in 1981 they used more than 50% of [ʔt, tʔ] in the reading passage style perhaps confirms our suggestion that covert prestige is attached to this feature.

Except for the glottally reinforced allophone for intervocalic /t/, all glottal realisations appear to be characteristic of the higher social classes rather than the lower in CE. Thus CE runs counter to most other accents of British English, where the glottal stop allophone 'appears to have begun amongst lower class groups' (Chambers & Trudgill, 1980: 88).

Concluding Remarks

The Cardiff survey has shown that a child's sociolinguistic competence may develop much earlier than originally suggested by Labov. It would appear that patterns of class and style variation in the speech of children are similar to those generally found in adult speech communities. On the other hand, sex differences are not as clearly established as in adult populations. The inclusion of a diachronic dimension has demonstrated that there are possibly grounds for assuming that working-class males move away from the standard during adolescence whereas lower middle-class females tend to move towards the prestige variety.

It is impossible to generalise on the basis of a single study in real time. Additional longitudinal studies are called for, both in Cardiff and in other speech communities, to find support for the conclusions drawn here. New surveys should preferably start with even younger (pre-school) children and continue far into adulthood in order to establish the age at which sociolinguistic variation emerges and when, if ever, it ceases to develop.

Notes to Chapter 13

1. I am grateful to Nikolas Coupland and Beverley Collins for their helpful comments on an earlier draft of this chapter. In addition, I wish to thank Lesley Milroy, who read the final version, suggesting some interesting alternative interpretations of the findings; these have been incorporated in footnote form, below.
2. See Mees (1983: 111–15) for the reasons for including both the full verb *have* and auxiliary *have* in the (h^2) counts.
3. The results of the statistical tests are not reported here. The reader is referred to Mees (1983).
4. This might be because /n/ was common until the early 19th century (Prins, 1972: 229) and is still heard occasionally in conservative U-RP (Wells, 1982: II, 283).
5. Lesley Milroy (personal communication) remarks that there is no principled reason why the two speaker variables of sex and class should *always* interact (as they often do in data from Western societies), i.e. just because (ng) exhibits clear class stratification, it does not necessarily follow that it is also a sex-marked variable. She points out that (ng) has been identified as a marker of social class in just about every community in which it has been studied and that its further function as a sex marker is likely to depend to a certain extent on how other features of the phonology in given communities function to mark out sex differences.
6. I have always felt a little unhappy about this explanation, but have not been able to come up with an alternative. Milroy (personal communication) is not keen on this interpretation either, but suggests that 'one could argue rather more simply that emerging male norms are embodied by WC boys and female norms by LMC girls. It is the social values associated with these classes which are also associated with masculinity and femininity respectively'. Milroy favours an approach which focuses initially on sex differentiation and considers how it might be associated with class differentiation, rather than seeing it as following on from class differentiation.

References

CHAMBERS, J.K. and TRUDGILL, P. 1980, *Dialectology*. Cambridge: Cambridge University Press.

CHESHIRE, J. 1982, *Variation in an English Dialect: A Sociolinguistic Study*. Cambridge: Cambridge University Press.

COATES, J. 1986, *Women, Men and Language*. London & New York: Longman.

COUPLAND, N. 1980, Style-shifting in a Cardiff work-setting. *Language in Society*, 9: 1–12.

——1988, *Dialect in Use: Sociolinguistic Variation in Cardiff English*. Cardiff: University of Wales Press.

FISCHER, J.L. 1958, Social influences on the choice of a linguistic variant. *Word*, 14: 47–56.

GIMSON, A.C. 1980, *An Introduction to the Pronunciation of English* (3rd edn). London: Edward Arnold (1st edn, 1962).

HOCKETT, C.F. 1950, Age-grading and linguistic continuity. *Language*, 26: 449–57.

HUDSON, R.A. 1980, *Sociolinguistics*. Cambridge: Cambridge University Press.

KNOWLES, G.O. 1978, The nature of phonological variables in Scouse. In P. TRUDGILL (1978): 80–90.

LABOV, W. 1966, *The Social Stratification of English in New York City*. Washington, DC: Center for Applied Linguistics.

——1972, *Sociolinguistic Patterns*. Philadelphia: University of Pennsylvania Press.

MACAULAY, R.K.S. 1977, *Language, Social Class, and Education: A Glasgow Study*. Edinburgh: Edinburgh University Press.

MEES, I.M. 1977, Language and social class in Cardiff: a survey of the speech habits of schoolchildren. Master's dissertation, University of Leiden.

——1983, The speech of Cardiff schoolchildren: a real time study. Doctoral dissertation, University of Leiden.

——1987, Glottal stop as a prestigious feature in Cardiff English. *English World-Wide*, 8, 1: 25–39.

MILROY, L. 1984, Urban dialects in the British Isles. In P. TRUDGILL (ed.), *Language in the British Isles*. Cambridge: Cambridge University Press, 199–218.

PETYT, M. 1980, *The Study of Dialect: An Introduction to Dialectology*. London: Deutsch.

PRINS, A.A. 1972, *A History of English Phonemes*. Leiden: Leiden University Press.

REID, E. 1976, Social and stylistic variation in the speech of some Edinburgh schoolchildren. M.Litt. thesis, University of Edinburgh.

ROMAINE, S. 1975, Linguistic variability in the speech of some Edinburgh schoolchildren. M.Litt. thesis, University of Edinburgh.

——1978, Postvocalic /r/ in Scottish English: sound change in progress? In P. TRUDGILL (1978): 144–57.

——1980, A critical overview of the methodology of urban British sociolinguistics. *English World-Wide*, 1, 2: 163–98.

——1984, *The Language of Children and Adolescents*. Oxford: Basil Blackwell.

TRUDGILL, P. 1974, *The Social Differentiation of English in Norwich*. Cambridge: Cambridge University Press.

——(ed.) 1978, *Sociolinguistic Patterns in British English*. London: Edward Arnold.

——1983, *On Dialect*. Oxford: Basil Blackwell.

WELLS, J.C. 1982, *Accents of English* (3 vols). Cambridge: Cambridge University Press.

WOLFRAM, W.A. and FASOLD, R.W. 1974, *The Study of Social Dialects in American English*. Englewood Cliffs, NJ: Prentice Hall.

14   Welsh Influence on Children's English[1]

BOB MORRIS JONES

The aim of this study is twofold: it seeks to assess the influence of Welsh on the English of young children and it attempts further to analyse this influence within a sociolinguistic framework. Features of English which show the influence of Welsh will be referred to as Welsh-influenced English (WI), while non-Welsh-influenced English (non-WI) will be used to refer to equivalent patterns which do not exhibit Welsh influence. Before looking at the details of the analysis, several preliminary issues will be examined.

Thomas (1984) rightly points out that Welsh is not the only influence on English in Wales, as various regional and social varieties of English also exert a powerful influence. Like Bowen (1969; 1986) and Pryce (1986; this volume), he highlights the effect of geography on Wales and suggests that English influence is more evident in the industrial south and the eastern counties along the Wales–England border, while Welsh influence is more pronounced in the north and the west of Wales. The geography of the former areas links Wales with England and allows face-to-face interactions of people of different linguistic backgrounds (but see further discussion under 'Region' below). Essentially, however, as is evident in Thomas's interpretation, geography is also related to bilingualism — monolingual English speakers being more numerous in the south and east while bilingual speakers are more numerous in the west and the north. The bilingual–monolingual contrast is important for this study, and we can now outline its significance.

This study examines the influence of Welsh on the spontaneous colloquial English of children aged between five and seven years. The vast majority of the children in the sample speak English as a first language (see Table 14.11 below). Thus, using distinctions which are found in Baetens-Beardsmore (1982: 37–68), any influences from Welsh found in this study do not arise because of the current mediation of bilingual speakers (through *interference* or *code-switching*) but have been acquired as *integrations* in the acquisition of English as a first language (L1). Originally, of course, these integrations would have arisen in the English of bilinguals. Thomas (1984: 176–79) uses the term 'evolved' to characterise this type of integrated Welsh influence and suggests that southern and eastern English varieties in Wales are in this respect more evolved than the English of bilingual speakers in the northern and western areas. He also adds the following interesting observation about evolved Welsh English (mainly the English of monolinguals):

> These dialects are now independent of contemporary Welsh influence, and we must expect them progressively to shed indigenous Welsh characteristics, since their model is the same as that of other varieties of British English — Received Pronunciation and Standard English.

This is a central concern in this study, and the investigation of the language of young children is of relevance to the 'shedding' or otherwise of WI features. It is suggested that the occurrence of WI features in the English of very young L1 speakers during the early years of language development will be a good indication of the durability of the Welsh nature of English in Wales.

Investigating child language also allows an attempt to consider the influence of the school. It should be noted, however, that schools in Wales can vary according to the medium of instruction (the details are given in a later section), and this in its turn calls for an awareness of different linguistic types of L1 English children.

Thus, a distinction should be made here between two types of Welsh influence on L1 English: integrated WI features, as already discussed; and Welsh transfers as used by L1 speakers of English who are learning Welsh as a second language (L2) in school — that is, L2 code-switching or interference (in turn, this type of L2 influence must be distinguished from Welsh influence in the English of L1 speakers of Welsh). Common examples of the second type of Welsh influence on L1 English are the use of Welsh colour-terms when speaking English. This type of transfer might be due to situational code-switching rather than interference as, for instance, with the use of the word *canol* (middle) in the example *put it in the canol, shall we*. This type of L2 Welsh influence is an interesting phenomenon in itself but will not be considered in this study — it does not represent integrated transfers.

This study concentrates upon lexical and syntactic features and asks whether WI exists at the level of dialect as opposed to that of accent. Although the majority of sociolinguistic studies have concentrated primarily on phonological features, there have been a number of observations on syntactic and morphological variables. Cheshire (1982), in particular, shows that the latter can be fruitfully used in sociolinguistic studies. It is interesting to consider whether lexical and grammatical distinctiveness can endure or whether users conform more to the influences of wider English usage (both standard and non-standard). The lexical and grammatical variables are outlined in greater detail in the next section.

The analysis is based on a corpus of child language which is located in the Department of Education, UCW, Aberystwyth, and was originally collected during the 1970s for an educational project funded by the Welsh Office. Details about the nature of the corpus are given in the various sections below which present different aspects of the study, but a brief outline of its main characteristics may be useful at the outset. Pairs of children were recorded in a play situation (mainly around a sandbox containing silver sand and a variety of play objects) in infant and primary schools throughout Wales. The material under consideration is spontaneous speech and not speech elicited by interview techniques (exchanges between the children and a researcher supervising the recording occasionally take place, but the language of the children remains spontaneous). This in itself adds interest to the investigation, given that many sociolinguistic studies use the interview technique and analyse formal data to some degree (Trudgill, 1974: 45–54 discusses degrees of formality).

Some idea of the size of the corpus can be given by the following statistics. There are 68 children aged five, 67 aged six, and 67 aged seven. In terms of frequencies of word-form occurrences, there are 59,795 from the five-year-olds, 61,029 from the six-year-olds, and 67,573 from the seven-year-olds. The play-sessions lasted for roughly half an hour and, for each age, there are approximately 22.5, 21.5 and 18 hours of recording — a substantial collection of spontaneous speech.

In addition to the recordings, the original project also collected background information about the children, and details are again given in the relevant sections below. The recordings and background details were originally intended to analyse language from an educational point of view and were not based on sampling techniques to achieve sociolinguistic analyses. But despite some methodological difficulties created by the original manner of data collection, the data are a rich resource for sociolinguistic interpretation. Of particular interest is that data were collected from many parts of Wales, allowing regional factors to be considered.

The Syntactic and Lexical Variables

Taken together, Parry (1972), Thomas (1984) and Coupland (1988) are valuable sources for the grammatical and lexical characteristics of WI (but it should be emphasised that they are not uniquely concerned with WI as they also consider many wider aspects of English in Wales). In the analysis given here, only those grammatical and lexical features which it has been practical to analyse in the corpus have been investigated. In effect, this means that the lexical variables give a fairly comprehensive account of the vocabulary used; any WI lexical features which are not discussed simply do not occur in the corpus (but see later remarks about the limitations of corpora in investigating competence rather than performance). But there are two notable syntactic omissions (both mentioned by Thomas, 1984: 191–92), namely the possibly more frequent use of fronting in English in Wales, and the use of the present and past progressive patterns for generic reference. The status of fronting is difficult to assess because, as Coupland (1988: 36–37) points out, fronting also occurs in other varieties of English. Its status as a WI variant would thus seem to depend upon its greater frequency in English in Wales, and this could only feasibly be established by a contrastive study involving another corpus of other varieties of English. Alternatively, if the current corpus were used, some method of distinguishing WI and non-WI users might support a comparison of the frequencies of fronting in the two groups. As can be seen, the study of fronting raises considerable methodological difficulties which it has not been possible to treat adequately for the preparation of this study. Consequently, it has been deemed wiser to leave its investigation for future research. Beyond these two features, it is again felt that the grammatical variables considered give a relatively comprehensive characterisation of WI in the data.

There is one other general point that should be considered. In some instances it is possible to find a source for a WI variant not only in Welsh but also outside Wales. In these instances the Welsh source can be favoured as the more obvious choice. Or, alternatively, Welsh influence can be seen as a probable contributory factor rather than the sole influence. Individual instances are detailed below.

Table 14.1 lists the variables under consideration, giving the WI and non-WI realisations in each case; the capitalised forms are abbreviated labels which it is convenient to use in tables later in the discussion. As can be

TABLE 14.1   *The Lexical and Syntactic Variables*

	WI variants	non-WI variants
TAG	is it / isn't it / yes	shall we / I
MUST	mustn't	can't
PAR	mam; mamgu; nain; taid	mum / mummy / mammy / mama / mother; gran / granny / granma / nanna / grandmother; grandad / grandfather; dad / daddy / father
EXP	ugh; duw	shucks; (good) gosh; wow; yuck; crumbs; blimey; cor; yikes; crikey; (good/my) god; bother; dear (me)
STIR	turn	stir
SPILL	lose	spill
MISS	lose	miss
DO	do	make
JOK	joking	pretend
VOC	man; boy(s)	silly (thing / nut(ter) / bugger); stupid; girl; lad; baby; mate

seen, there are two syntactic variables, TAG and MUST, while the remainder are lexical ones. Of the latter, two are based on direct borrowing, namely, PAR and EXP, while VOC, SPILL, MISS, and DO are loan translations. JOK is problematic, as is discussed below.

TAG refers to the distinctive use of *isn't it, is it* and *yes* as tags to sentences where their occurrences would not be predicted by regular tag formation. Thomas (1984: 192) and Coupland (1988: 36) mention the use of *isn't it* as in *you're going home now, isn't it?*. Thomas suggests that it is generalised in place of regular tags. He also mentions the tag use of *yes* to which he attributes a question function (e.g. *you're at university, yes?*). Coupland develops the functional approach differently by suggesting that *isn't it* is equivalent to *isn't that so?* and is thus functionally different to the regular tags. Although not mentioned by Thomas or Coupland, the corpus indicates that *is it* is also used as a tag (in fact, it is more frequent than *isn't it*). In this study, only those instances of the WI tags which are equivalent to *shall I/we?* are considered, as in:

> *make a big castle, i'n' it*
> *let's finish this off, isn't it*
> *we'll just leave that there like that, yeah*

These can be compared with:

> *put the house like that, shall we, Stephen*
> *let's take all the animals out, shall we*
> *then we'll take everything out, shall we*

Although there are additional instances of the WI tags where *shall I/we* would not be used, they are not considered. This restriction allows more accurate interpretations of the data and, as far as this corpus is concerned, it accounts for the majority of the instances of the WI tags.

We must now turn to consider whether we can view the WI tags to be the result of the influence of Welsh. They may have developed in English in Wales originally through bilinguals translating non-verbal tags which are found in the Welsh language:

	northern	*southern*
positive	*ie*	*efe*
negative	*ynte*	*yntefe*

(The negative forms are reduced to *tefe* and *te*.) It is not within the scope of this study to give a detailed account of their occurrences in Welsh (an outline of verbal and non-verbal tags can be found in Jones & Thomas, 1977: 302–03, 316). Of particular significance is that they can occur in contexts where *shall* would be used in standard English:

> *rhoi hwn i lawr, ie/efe*   put this down, yes/is it   (=shall we)
> *awn ni yn ôl, ie/efe*   we'll go, yes/is it   (=shall we)

The negative Welsh tags are also used frequently in other contexts in Welsh conversational discourse. (In this respect, it is significant that this writer is familiar from his youth with speakers from Rhos near Wrexham in north-east Wales who actually use the local Welsh language version *inau* in English discourse.) In addition, we should also bear in mind that positive and negative responsives in Welsh are based on the verb:

> *oedd John yn canu?* –   *oedd / nac oedd*
>
> (was John singing   was / NEG was   = yes / no)

It might be that incipient bilinguals generalised the use of the answer words *yes* and *no* to the formation of tags, where the verbal material is very similar. Although the above remarks do not represent direct evidence for Welsh non-verbal tags as a source of the WI tags, there is sufficient similarity in their respective usages to support such a view.

The label MUST refers to the use of either *must* or *can* in negative forms in their epistemic modal uses. In non-WI, *can't* is used as the negative equivalent of *must* ('logical necessity') (see Palmer, 1974: 137); e.g. *she must be leaving — she can't be leaving*. This author has heard *must* being retained in the negative version to give *she mustn't be leaving*. The equivalent Welsh pattern uses a nominal *rhaid* (necessity) and not a verb. But the significant point is that Welsh uses the same form in positives and negatives: *mae'n rhaid ei bod hi'n gadael* (it is necessary that she is leaving) and *mae'n rhaid ei bod hi ddim yn gadael* (it is necessary that she isn't leaving). The use of *must* quoted above may thus be the result of the influence of Welsh. In fact, however, we face here a good example of the difficulty of precisely establishing Welsh as a source, for Trudgill (1984: 33) tells us that *mustn't* is used epistemically in the north-west of England. Of course, it is not claimed that the latter is a source, but its existence there may suggest that it could have arisen in English in Wales through generalisation. However, the availability of the Welsh model which operates a similar generalisation can be claimed as at least a contributory factor in the development of epistemic *mustn't*.

The label PAR refers to the words used for parents and grandparents. As well as the English forms, there are occurrences of the Welsh words for parents and grandparents, namely: *mam* for mother; *taid* (north Wales) or *tadcu* (south Wales) for grandfather; and *nain* (north Wales) or *mamgu* (south Wales) for grandmother. The analysis includes their use as general nouns as well as specific use to refer to a child's individual parent or grandparent. As can be seen from Table 14.1, there is a greater range of forms in the non-WI examples. The words for parents are the most frequently used. It should be noted that there is a problem with identifying which variety some of the forms belong to. The form *dad* is very similar to the Welsh *tad*, and *dad* is itself used by Welsh speakers (*tada* is also to be heard in some areas). But *dad* is used extensively in English outside Wales. The form *mammy* is clearly similar to *mam* and WI membership is possible, but the use of the -*y* ending is typically non-WI and is accordingly assigned to the latter. The *Shorter Oxford English Dictionary* (*SOED*) tends to suggest that *dad* and *mam* in non-WI have developed out of child language; the various entries for the *mother* variants suggest a development as follows: *mam* > *mammy* (diminutive) > *mummy* > *mum*. *SOED* does not detail this development and it is unclear how *dad* and *mam* would thus arise. In contrast with this developmental explanation, there is also the possibility that Welsh (or Celtic) has been a substratal influence on English in what is now England and that *mam* and *dad* have been borrowed from early Welsh. All this is speculative but is no less plausible than the child language approach. Readers who are interested in the Celtic substratal explanation might like to consider similar remarks by Thomas (1984: 191–92) about the origin of *do* as a non-emphatic auxiliary in positive declarative sentences (*I do like jelly* — cf. standard *I like jelly*).

The label EXP refers to words used as expletives. Instances of expletives in the corpus which are related to Welsh are *ugh* and *duw* (god). *Ugh* is the spelling sometimes used to suggest (unconvincingly) the rendering of Welsh *ychafi* ['əxa'vi] (or just *ych* [əx]) which indicates a distasteful reaction to something unpleasant. *Duw* is sometimes realised as *jiw*, as happens in Welsh. The study of expletives has concentrated on those which have conventionalised spellings and has not included the full range of paralinguistic noises such as [ew] a noise commonly used by Welsh speakers to precede their utterances.

Welsh words can be translated into English, sometimes producing distinctive results where a Welsh word has more than one English equivalent. The label TURN refers to the use of either *turn* or *stir* as in *have you turned/stirred the tea?* The use of *turn* for *stir* is based on the use of the Welsh word *troi* (turn, stir). The label SPILL refers to the use of *lose* or *spill* as in *you're losing/spilling the milk on the floor*; and the label MISS refers to the use of the same verb *lose* or *miss* as in *I've lost/missed the bus*. In Welsh *colli* is the equivalent of *lose, spill* and *miss* (in the above senses).

The label DO refers to the use of *do* or *make* with objects of result as in *let's do/make a sandcastle*. Welsh uses *gwneud* for both *do* and *make*. In assessing this variable, it is important to stress that we are concerned with objects of result. *Do* can be used with other types of objects in non-WI as in *after playtime we do sums* or *I'm going to do a jigsaw*. Here *do* indicates 'being involved in the performance of an activity' (such as mathematics or jigsaw-solving) and would not be replaced by *make* in this sense.[2]

The label JOK refers to the use of *joking* or *pretend* as in *joking/pretend that this is a castle* or *this is a joking/pretend bomb*. The word *joking* obviously occurs in English but its use in this sense is typical of parts of south Wales. It occurs in southern Welsh in this sense as *jocan*. It is not easy to plot relationships here. It may be that *joking* has been borrowed into Welsh at some early stage, as is suggested in *Geiriadur Prifysgol Cymru*, part XXXII. But *SOED* does not give any instances of *joking* with the WI usage as an equivalent of *pretend*. It is therefore unclear whether this meaning has developed in Welsh after borrowing the form, or whether the form and the meaning have been borrowed from some source (possibly one of the dialects of English). Nor is it clear whether its current WI use has been transferred from Welsh or whether it has developed within English in Wales from some other source. In the absence of evidence to the contrary, it is assumed to be a product of the influence of Welsh.

The label VOC refers to the various types of vocatival addresses. The WI variants compare with the use in Welsh of such forms as *bach'an* (boy) and *'wr* (man) and can be taken as loan translations. As can be seen, there are far more non-WI forms than WI forms. Interestingly, the use of *baby* is quite frequent and reflects the usage of the television fictional character, Kojak (*who loves you, baby*), who was particularly popular in the 1970s.

A Quantitative Analysis

A purely taxonomic account can gradually gather a list of points which can create the impression that WI is a very distinctive variety (this is particularly true of the mainly anecdotal but very popular *Talk Tidy* series by Edwards (1985; 1986)). But it leaves unanswered a number of questions such as: the extent to which WI features are employed; who uses them; and whether they are always used to the exclusion of the non-WI equivalents. These questions will be considered, in relation to the corpus referred to above, in this and the following sections.

Using computer programs written in SPITBOL, the WI and non-WI versions of the selected variables were collected in the sentences in which they occurred; an indication was also given of the child who used them. Subsequently, each child was given two scores for each variable: one score counting the number of WI versions and another for the number of non-WI versions. If a child had not used any version of a variable a score of zero was entered for both the WI count and the non-WI count. The individual performances were then collated to give an overall picture, and it is with this aspect that we can begin the quantitative analysis.

A general statistical profile: Frequencies and methodology

In this subsection, we will consider some methodological issues that arise from using corpora of spontaneous speech as data bases in the study of linguistic usage. We will examine the range of frequencies that the variables produce and the consequences this has for quantitative analyses.

Table 14.2 gives an overall statistical profile of the variables, irrespective of the variant used. The variables are ranked by frequency. The numbers of users would have given a very similar rank-order (this is confirmed by high Spearman correlation coefficients of the rankings of frequencies and users: 0.997 for the five-year-olds, 0.976 for the six-year-olds, and 0.954 for the seven-year-olds).

The data in Table 14.2 are arranged in ten ranks, in ascending order. These ten points can be conflated in more general groupings although, as is often the case in these matters, establishing the boundaries between groups can be difficult. There would appear to be five clusterings of frequencies over the three year groups: 0–14; 29–45; 72–77; 126–171; and 274–403. On this basis, the relative classification given in Table 14.3 can be suggested. There are four methodological implications which emerge from the frequencies, relating to the lower frequencies.

First, it should be noted that the frequencies reflect performance and not competence. In this respect, it should be noted that some lexemes are typically low-frequency in performance — thus the infrequent occurrence of variables like SPILL, MISS and STIR is characteristic of the vast majority of lexemes in the corpus (and, indeed, in general). In particular, zero frequency does not necessarily mean that an item is not a part of a child's linguistic ability — it may be better regarded, like low frequency, as being a product of the infrequent use of an item in actual performance.

Second, frequencies are relevant to assessing the usefulness of corpora of spontaneous unelicited language in sociolinguistic analyses (as compared with the use of the interview technique). Low-frequency items do not supply sufficient examples to allow reliable generalisations. In the main, this is only possible in this study with JOK, DO, PAR, EXP, possibly TAG, and less possibly VOC.

Third, however, there are some fluctuations in the frequencies. Generally speaking, the statistical arrangement on the basis of rank in Table 14.2 follows the same pattern over the three years, as Spearman correlations of rank in respect of the three ages indicate: 0.851 for the five- and six-year-olds, 0.915 for the six- and seven-year-olds, and 0.863 for the five- and seven-year-olds. DO is consistently high-frequency in all three ages and is thus a key marker in the discussion of WI. However, certain of the variables change ranks. PAR is also very prominent but declines over the years until it is forced down to rank 7 with a much reduced frequency. EXP increases

TABLE 14.2 *Statistical Frequencies of the Patterns, in Ascending Rank-order*

	Five-Year-Olds			Six-Year-Olds			Seven-Year-Olds	
	Frequency	(Users)		Frequency	(Users)		Frequency	(Users)
SPILL	0	(0)	STIR	0	(0)	MISS	1	(1)
MISS	1	(1)	MUST	0	(0)	MUST	3	(2)
STIR	2	(2)	MISS	4	(4)	STIR	3	(1)
MUST	3	(3)	SPILL	6	(3)	SPILL	6	(5)
VOC	9	(6)	VOC	12	(8)	VOC	29	(10)
JOK	12	(6)	TAG	14	(12)	TAG	30	(16)
TAG	30	(11)	EXP	45	(23)	PAR	72	(33)
EXP	35	(15)	JOK	77	(20)	JOK	73	(17)
PAR	313	(51)	PAR	171	(38)	EXP	126	(30)
DO	403	(53)	DO	274	(55)	DO	303	(55)
Total	808	(62)	Total	603	(64)	Total	646	(64)

TABLE 14.3   *Frequency Classes of the Variables*

	Five-year-olds	Six-year-olds	Seven-year-olds
Very low frequency	SPILL, MISS,	SPILL, MISS,	SPILL, MISS
	STIR, MUST,	STIR, MUST,	STIR, MUST
	VOC, JOK	VOC, TAG	
Low frequency	TAG, EXP	EXP	VOC, TAG
Moderate frequency	—	JOK	JOK, PAR
Fairly high frequency	—	PAR	EXP
High frequency	PAR, DO	DO	DO

in use over the three years, particularly at age seven. JOK is another variable which increases its ranking with the six-year-olds through a rise in its own frequency. Smaller movements are found with TAG and VOC in the lower ranks. (It is not the aim of this study to assess child language in developmental terms. But the decline of PAR may be related to the children's gradual development away from the home environment in the early years of schooling, and this point is relevant to observations about school influence discussed later in the analysis). In this limited way, there are changes in performance over the three years. The study of language variety in developmental terms should thus be prepared to make use of different markers of variation at different ages.

Fourth, it is evident from Table 14.2 that different numbers of users are involved with the different variables. Although not apparent in Table 14.2, it is also the case that individual users produce different numbers of examples. Consequently, corpora cannot be relied upon to produce samples, as can be achieved with the interview method. This point is important for statistical analyses performed upon corpus data, as is briefly discussed below in the analysis of school types.

These methodological problems are referred to again at various points below and, depending upon the aims of the analysis, decisions have to be made as to whether to examine individual variables or to look at them overall.

Proportions of WI features

This subsection examines the central issue of the relative strengths of the WI and non-WI realisations of the variables in the corpus. Table 14.4

TABLE 14.4 Proportions of WI Features for Each Pattern, in Ascending Rank-order

Five-year-olds

	Frequency, WI variants	Frequency, both variants	WI variants (%)
MISS	0	1	0
MUST	0	3	0
STIR	0	2	0
PAR	4	313	1.28
DO	110	403	27.30
EXP	10	35	28.57
JOK	4	12	33.33
VOC	4	9	44.44
TAG	26	30	86.67
SPILL	0	0	—
TOTALS	158	808	19.55

Six-year-olds

	Frequency, WI variants	Frequency, both variants	WI variants (%)
MISS	0	4	0
JOK	4	77	5.19
PAR	13	171	7.60
SPILL	1	6	16.67
DO	47	274	17.15
EXP	9	45	20
VOC	5	12	41.67
TAG	11	14	78.57
MUST	0	0	—
STIR	0	0	—
TOTALS	90	603	14.93

Seven-year-olds

	Frequency, WI variants	Frequency, both variants	WI variants (%)
JOK	0	73	0
MUST	0	3	0
STIR	0	3	0
MISS	0	1	0
PAR	4	72	5.56
VOC	3	29	10.34
DO	34	303	11.22
EXP	21	126	16.67
TAG	24	30	80
SPILL	5	6	83.33
TOTALS	91	646	14.09

gives the details by year group for the individual variables and the totals of their combined occurrences. In this table, the variables are sorted in ascending order of the ranks of the proportions of WI variants. In terms of the totals, the figures show that overall the incidence of WI variants for the variables under consideration in this corpus is quite small — 19.55% for the five-year-olds, 14.93% for the six-year-olds and 14.09% for the seven-year-olds. Moreover, bearing in mind that the above variables are only a small proportion of the total number of grammatical patterns and vocabulary items found in the corpus (i.e. of the total speech produced and not just the specific variables under consideration), we would have to conclude that WI features at the level of dialect are not prominent in the language of these children. This conclusion needs to be qualified in view of the fact that, as previously stated, not all possible WI grammatical variables have been considered, although, impressionistically, I feel that the picture would not alter substantially except to increase the proportions of non-WI variants. Furthermore, of course, this analysis does not take account of WI influence in terms of phonological factors.

However, if we examine particular items a different picture emerges. Here the incidence of WI can vary from 0% to over 80%. But it must be emphasised that a consideration of the individual proportions is meaningless without taking into account the total frequencies for a particular variable. Take, for example, MISS with the five- and seven-year-olds — the total absence of a WI variant is hardly significant given that only one instance of the variable occurs. It is only with the higher-frequency groups that we have sufficient numbers to justify more meaningful analysis. With these points in mind, we can consider some of the individual variables.

Intuitively, an analyst may expect the names for parents or grandparents, PAR, to show marked Welsh influence. Here is an area of strong emotional ties which might encourage the maintenance of the old Welsh names through the medium of English. It is therefore very surprising to find that the incidence of Welsh names is very slight (but the problems of accurately identifying these forms, discussed above, should be borne in mind — particularly the status of *dad*). The fact that this variable belongs to the higher-frequency groups means that this conclusion is a reliable one. It would seem, therefore, that the Welsh names have been rejected. This author can supply an anecdote to throw some light on this. On one occasion in the 1950s, a child addressed his mother with *mam* in a public place and was reprimanded by her for doing so. The conclusion here is that the mother felt that *mam* was a low-status item and conferred low status on her and her family or, in more colloquial terms, 'showed her up'. In this particular case, a WI feature is clearly being stigmatised as many non-standard English features are.

EXP does rather better as a marker of WI but this may be due to the interpretation of the [x] *ugh* sound as being related to *ychafi*. But as can be seen, the strength of the WI forms does decline slightly over the years.

JOK is an interesting example. As already indicated, there is a marked increase in the use of this variable with the six- and seven-year-olds. But from the figures given, it would appear that this applies to *pretend* because the WI proportion falls from 33.33% with the five-year-olds to 5.19% with the six-year-olds, and with the seven-year-olds *joking* does not register. Here there would appear to be a complete rejection of the WI variant. However, as is discussed below, there are regional factors to consider. Moreover, the WI influence may continue in the morphology of *pretend* — the use of the -*ing* form *pretending* may reflect the -*ing* form *joking*, as in for instance *pretending this is a farm*. It may be that we have a development as follows:

$$joking \rightarrow pretending \rightarrow pretend.$$

VOC is a very low-frequency item until seven years of age. But it is interesting to note that the proportions of WI variants are fairly high, although they do tend to decrease over the years.

DO presents a consistent and reliable measure of WI. It is high-frequency with all age groups and there is a reasonable proportion of the WI *do*; as with other variables, the proportion of the WI variant tends to fade over the years.

The variable which shows the clearest and most consistent WI influence is TAG. It is the only variable where the WI variant is in the majority and it remains so over the three years. Unfortunately for sociolinguistic studies, it belongs to the low-frequency category of variables, particularly with the six-year-olds when it dips into the very-low-frequency group, and cannot supply sufficient data to analyse large numbers of users. This would appear to be a classic sociolinguistic methodological problem of observation: we have an apparently significant variable but it would appear that conventional sampling methods of data collection (the interview technique) are inappropriate because its use would seem to be limited to spontaneous speech where its occurrences are infrequent. Perhaps more extensive or more ingenious future research may overcome these frustrations.

Table 14.4 would appear to invite developmental comments. But real-time comparisons of the three age groups are limited by the fact that losses and gains of children occurred during the years of data collection. Table 14.5 gives the number of children who were involved in different longitudinal groupings: the sequence 51 51 51 indicates that there were 51 children who were present in all three years, while the sequence 10 10 – indicates that there were 10 children who were present at five and six years of age but

TABLE 14.5 *Longitudinal Comparisons of Numbers of Children*

Five-Year-Olds	Six-Year-Olds	Seven-Year-Olds
51	51	51
10	10	—
—	5	5
1	—	1
6	—	—
—	1	—
—	—	10
68	67	67

who were absent at seven years of age; and so forth. In comparing ages it is important to remember the losses and additions. As can be seen, there is a considerable new intake with the seven-year-olds and this should be borne in mind when suggesting any possible developmental trends.

Concentrating on the major items, there are three trends over the three ages which can be summarised as follows:

1. a decrease over the three ages

    DO   27.30% > 17.15% > 11.22%
    EXP   28.57% > 20.00% > 16.67%
    JOK   33.33% > 5.19% > 0.00%
    VOC   44.44% > 41.67% > 10.34%

2. an overall increase but a decease from age six to age seven

    PAR   1.28% < 7.60% > 5.56%

3. a decrease from five to six but an increase from six to seven

    TAG   86.67% > 78.57% < 80.00%

In the main, the WI features decline in terms of proportions of the variables over this age-range and, on this basis, it would seem that WI in the language of primary schoolchildren is gradually replaced by non-WI, particularly at six years of age. On the face of it, this supports the view of Thomas outlined above, that the influence of Welsh does not endure in the evolved English dialects in Wales. It also compares with other studies surveyed by Romaine (1984: 104–11) which indicate that non-standard variants are more frequent with younger speakers. This interpretation is re-examined from another standpoint in the next section.

Given that this development occurs over the early years of schooling, it is reasonable to suggest that the commencement of formal education may be a factor in this process. There is no direct evidence for this view in the data under consideration but it can be speculated that there are two forces at work in school. First, the gradual expansion of the child's world away from the immediate influences of the family introduces exposure to the non-WI usage among other children. The general decline in frequencies of the variable PAR, noted earlier, can be interpreted as an indication of the reduction of the central role of the home in the face of the child's greater involvement with institutions and activities outside. Second, in the absence of empirical data on the nature of teacher and classroom language in Wales, the influence of teachers and teaching is unknown, but two points can be made: the gradual development of literacy surely promotes non-WI variants; and traditional notions of correctness are typically associated with teachers (who have themselves experienced the forces of prescriptivism at school and college) and it can be speculated that teachers would be inclined to promote the non-WI variants. This, however, needs to be confirmed or denied by empirical research into the attitudes and classroom practices of teachers in Wales. Of these two views, the first conforms with general sociolinguistic beliefs. Trudgill (1986: 31) reasserts that the major influence on children is that of other children of the same peer-group. In this light, the role of the school in language change is that it acts as a location for peer-group mixing and, again following Trudgill (1986), allows accommodation during face-to-face interactions by WI speakers to the majority usage of non-WI speakers.

The variables and individual variation

This subsection looks again at the relative strengths of the WI and non-WI variants of the variables, but this time from the point of view of the choices that users make. That is, we will consider whether a child is monostylistic or whether he/she can control both the WI and non-WI variants. This analysis can then be interpreted in terms of either trends in language change or, more speculatively, the development of style-switching.

The discussion of the variables in terms of the contrast of WI and non-WI features may create the impression that, for any one variable, users can be divided into two general groups: those who use the WI variant and those who use the non-WI variant. An analysis of the corpus shows that there are three possible groups: (i) those children who use non-WI variants only; (ii) those who use WI variants only; and (iii) those who use both types of variant. The existence of the third type means that there is variation within the usage of certain individuals. Thus, users can be described in terms of the proportions of WI and non-WI variants in their usage. This approach is adopted in terms of various groups of users in the following sections. In this subsection, the variables themselves will be described in terms of these three types.

Table 14.6 gives the details for the individual variables in the three age groups. Take, for instance, the variable DO as used by the five-year-olds. There are 19 children who use the non-WI variant *make* to produce 100 instances; there are only 6 children who use the WI variant *do*, producing 12 instances; and there are 28 children who use both variants, producing 193 occurrences of non-WI *make* and 98 instances of WI *do*. Table 14.6 also gives the details for usage over all the variables taken together — indicated by the label ALL. Note that ALL is not a simple total of the individual variables but indicates usage over all the variables — thus, although there are 48 five-year-olds who use only the non-WI variant of PAR (278 times), there are only 22 users who consistently select the non-WI variant of each variable that they have used. It should be borne in mind that not all these users have necessarily chosen the same variables — as previously emphasised, we are dealing with 'naturalistic' data and not controlled sampling.

Table 14.6 is detailed in that it gives users and frequencies. This is particularly useful with mixed usage where the relative strengths of the WI and non-WI frequencies can be seen. The table may be overdetailed for ready absorption and a briefer summary using percentages of users is given in Table 14.7. These percentages are based on the total number of users for each age group in order to maintain some idea of the relative strengths of the variables. Further, in order to simplify the picture, the lower-frequency variables have been omitted in Table 14.7. But ALL still refers to the total usage of the children.

With the five-year-olds, there are three variables which have mainly non-WI-only users, namely, PAR, EXP, and VOC. At this age, DO is mainly mixed usage, TAG is mainly WI-only usage and JOK sees equal proportions of non-WI-only and WI-only users. However, a clear pattern emerges with the six- and seven-year-olds: each variable has mainly non-WI-only users except for TAG which is mainly WI-only usage. With the exception of TAG, then, there is a movement to strengthen non-WI-only usage. Thus, TAG again emerges as a prominent marker of WI with all three ages.

TABLE 14.6 *Individual Variation among the Variables*

| | Non-WI | | WI | | Non-WI and WI | | |
| | | | | | | Frequency | |
	Users	Frequency	Users	Frequency	Users	Non-WI	WI
Five-year-olds							
							0
TAG	1	4	10	26	0	0	0
MUST	3	3	0	0	0	0	0
SPILL	0	0	0	0	0	0	0
MISS	1	1	0	0	0	0	0
STIR	2	2	0	0	0	0	0
JOK	3	8	3	4	0	0	98
DO	19	100	6	12	28	193	4
PAR	48	278	0	0	3	31	2
EXP	10	24	4	8	1	1	0
VOC	4	5	2	4	0	0	154
ALL	22	160	2	4	38	490	
Six-year-olds							
TAG	3	3	9	11	0	0	0
MUST	0	0	0	0	0	0	0
SPILL	2	4	0	0	1	1	1
MISS	4	4	0	0	0	0	0
STIR	0	0	0	0	0	0	0
JOK	16	73	4	4	0	0	0
DO	27	107	4	7	24	120	40
PAR	29	120	2	3	7	38	10
EXP	15	32	5	6	3	4	3
VOC	5	7	3	5	0	0	0
ALL	19	145	1	2	44	368	88
Seven-year-olds							
TAG	5	5	10	22	1	1	2
MUST	2	3	0	0	0	0	0
SPILL	1	1	4	5	0	0	0
MISS	1	1	4	5	0	0	0
STIR	1	3	0	0	0	0	0
JOK	17	73	0	0	0	0	0
DO	37	170	4	8	14	99	26
PAR	29	62	2	2	2	6	2
EXP	18	45	4	7	8	60	14
VOC	7	22	1	1	2	4	2
ALL	23	164	1	3	40	391	88

TABLE 14.7   *Individual Variation (Percentages of Users)*

| | Five-year-olds | | | Six-year-olds | | | Seven-year-olds | | |
	Non-WI	WI	Both	Non-WI	WI	Both	Non-WI	WI	Both
TAG	1.61	15.63	0.00	4.69	14.06	0.00	7.81	15.63	1.56
JOK	4.83	4.83	0.00	25.00	6.25	0.00	26.56	0.00	0.00
VOC	6.45	3.23	0.00	7.81	4.69	0.00	10.94	1.56	3.13
DO	30.65	9.68	45.16	42.19	6.25	37.50	57.81	6.25	21.88
EXP	16.13	6.45	1.61	23.44	7.81	4.69	28.13	6.25	12.50
PAR	77.42	0.00	4.83	45.31	3.13	10.94	45.31	3.13	3.13
ALL	35.48	3.23	61.29	29.69	1.56	68.75	35.94	1.56	65.50

Of particular interest are those instances with a straightforward contrast of WI and non-WI users. This indicates monostylistic usage for both groups. Such usage occurs only with the five- and six-year-olds, and is further limited to certain variables, namely TAG, JOK, and VOC. At this age, WI speakers with these variables are unaffected by the competing non-WI variants. However, by the age of seven, the strength of the WI-only usage for these variables seems to begin to diminish, being replaced by the non-WI usage (as in the case of JOK) or joined by mixed usage (as in the case of TAG and VOC).

In terms of overall usage, given by ALL in Tables 14.6 and 14.7, we see that there are very few WI-only users — that is, there are very few users who for every variable they use (however many that may be) consistently choose the WI variant. However, it is not the case that non-WI-only usage is in the majority. In the main, we have mixed usage, but it can be seen from Table 14.6 that the non-WI variants are the favoured option: WI selection in the same individuals occurs as a small proportion of a mainly non-WI usage. In this light, WI users cannot be isolated in homogeneous linguistic terms.

There would appear to be two ways of interpreting these trends. First, there is the face-value interpretation that WI usage declines as the children get older. As suggested earlier, this confirms Thomas's judgement. From the point of view of language change, this may be a significant observation as it confirms a view of change which is transitional through mixed usage: i.e. WI → WI+non-WI → non-WI. This process of dialect change is historically a part of the much wider process of language shift: Welsh →

WI → WI+non-WI → non-WI. Language bilingualism (Welsh/English) begins a shift from Welsh to English which is eventually completed by dialectal bilingualism (WI/non-WI).

Second, we can consider the view of Romaine (1984: 100–02) that the children are developing style-switching — that they are gradually realising that the WI and non-WI variants are appropriate in different contexts. Romaine's study of Edinburgh schoolchildren shows that six-year-olds exhibited 'a great deal of inherent variability i.e. variation that takes place while the linguistic and extra-linguistic context remain the same' in an interview situation (paradoxically, there is a suggestion that her interview may have contained casual and more careful variation). Appropriately for this study, this variation involved the use of negative formation from either Scottish English (e.g. *didnae*) or English English (e.g. *didn't*). Romaine then claims, although she does not empirically justify, that the non-standard variants would still be quite frequent outside the interview context in peer-group activities. (Reid, 1976, referred to by Romaine, 1984: 97–99, demonstrates phonological style-switching with eleven-year-olds, much older than the children being studied here, in relation to social class.) Thus, according to Romaine, the different frequencies of standard and non-standard variants in the interview and the playground would indicate the gradual acquisition of style-switching.

There is one important difference between Romaine's study and the present one, namely that the children in this study are already in a peer-group situation. As suggested earlier, the only possible contextual influence here might be the wider setting of the school. In the absence of any direct observations of peer-group interaction on the playground and in the home environment, it remains an open question whether the trends in Tables 14.6 and 14.7 indicate the decline of WI or the development of style-switching. The available facts, however, suggest that, between the ages of five and seven, WI usage is gradually replaced by non-WI usage in peer-group interaction in the school. Moreover, the fact that variability also occurs with some of the variables at five may indicate that variability is already established in the home environment. In this light, it would appear that the influence of the parents has already introduced variability and the developmental trends at school are facilitated by pre-school usage.

Region

Region is the traditional distinguishing criterion for dialectological accounts of variation. But the corpus raises some interesting issues for defining WI in terms of traditional dialectology. Over recent decades English people from England have moved into various parts of Wales, particularly many of the Welsh-speaking areas, and also into the English-speaking development areas (such as the Newtown area of eastern mid-Wales). In some Welsh-speaking areas, English L1 speakers are sometimes to be found only among those families who have moved from another area. (Of course, this same dialectological problem also applies to the movements of Wales-born people within Wales). Is the English of these newcomers to be included? If so, we will see the characteristics of English English in what we may call 'Welsh English'. On the other hand, should we seek out only certain informants on the basis of the usual dialectological principles of region and long-standing residence? A traditional, strict dialectological approach would not entertain using child data, so it must be obvious that this study is not a dialectological one in the conventional manner. Moreover, the ethos of contemporary sociolinguistic approaches would view population movements as an interesting area of study. Further, within an approach which sees Welsh influence and English influence as the forces which have shaped the character of English in Wales, it is not inappropriate that children of different backgrounds should be included (indeed, in terms of future research, a specific study of the varieties of English of the *mewnlifiad* (inflow), as this population movement is described in Welsh, would be interesting research). Also, there is a general view that young children can accommodate to the local dialect of an area to which their families may move (see Trudgill, 1986: 28–38). In this light, the following analyses are based on all the children in the corpus, thus giving a comprehensive account of the variables as they are realised in Wales today.

There are two ways of looking at the data in regional terms: by examining school types; and by looking at the individual locations of the schools. We will consider school types first and examine individual schools in the next subsection.

School types: WI versus non-WI

There are three types of school which can be set up on the basis of the medium of instruction:

1. Those schools in which English is the medium of instruction and Welsh, if it figures at all, occurs only as a taught subject; we will refer to these as 'English' schools.
2. Those schools in which Welsh is the designated medium of

instruction for children in the nursery range (aged between three and seven) although English is introduced after age seven; these schools are referred to either as 'Welsh' schools or 'bilingual' schools.

3. Those schools in which the medium of instruction is mixed according to the L1 of the children (in some instances, separate streams are set up, but we will not go into this amount of detail); we will refer to these as 'mixed' schools.

A two-sample *t*-test assuming unequal variances is used to compare each type with each of the other types separately (the TWOT procedure of MINITAB, as described in Appleton, 1982: 81–82, is the actual test used). Before looking at the results, several restrictions relating to the data will be explained. They are relevant not only to this comparison between school types but also to comparisons discussed in the remaining subsections.

First, children for whom there are missing data for background details are excluded from the test (fortunately, this does not apply to the comparisons of school type). Second, only those children who actually use at least one of the variants of a variable are included — this excludes non-users of the variable. Third, the statistical test used below is based on the proportion of WI variants for the variables. Fourth, the statistical analysis is based on the WI proportions of individual children and not the total proportions for groups of children — in this way individual variance can be taken into account. Fifth, in order to ensure the largest possible numbers of children and frequencies, the totals for all the variables are taken as the basis of the analysis. Although we may lose sight of individual variables, the greater numbers allow more reasonable generalisations.

Table 14.8 shows that the mixed schools have higher WI means than the other two types. At first sight, school type is an educational category and these results could be used to assess the influence of the school on the language of the children. Of particular importance would be the contrast of the Welsh schools with the mixed and English schools — the former being Welsh-medium and the latter being English-medium (at least, in the case of the mixed schools, for the L1 English speakers). But it can be seen that the means of the Welsh schools are lower than those of the mixed schools and that there is only one statistically significant difference between the Welsh and the English schools (with the seven-year-olds). Overall it is the mixed schools which show higher proportions of WI features.

TABLE 14.8   *Two-sample t-test for School Types and WI Proportions*

Five-year-olds

SCHOOL	N	MEAN	STDEV	SE MEAN
1 (Welsh)	12	0.164	0.129	0.037
2 (Mixed)	12	0.357	0.339	0.098
6 (English)	38	0.157	0.236	0.038

95 PCT CI FOR MU 1 − MU 6: (−0.102, 0.115)   (Welsh vs English)
TTEST MU 1 = MU 6 (VS NE): T=0.12 P=0.90 DF=35.0

95 PCT CI FOR MU 2 − MU 6: (−0.026, 0.424)   (Mixed vs English)
TTEST MU 2 = MU 6 (VS NE): T=1.90 P=0.079 DF=14.5

95 PCT CI FOR MU 1 − MU 2: (−0.417, 0.032)   (Welsh vs Mixed)
TTEST MU 1 = MU 2 (VS NE): T=−1.84 P=0.087 DF=14.1

Six-year-olds

SCHOOL	N	MEAN	STDEV	SE MEAN
1 (Welsh)	9	0.140	0.127	0.042
2 (Mixed)	17	0.229	0.270	0.065
6 (English)	38	0.185	0.173	0.028

95 PCT CI FOR MU 1 − MU 6: (−0.153, 0.064)   (Welsh vs English)
TTEST MU 1 = MU 6 (VS NE): T=−0.88 P=0.39 DF=15.9

95 PCT CI FOR MU 2 − MU 6: (−0.104, 0.192)   (Mixed vs English)
TTEST MU 2 = MU 6 (VS NE): T=0.62 P=0.54 DF=22.1

95 PCT CI FOR MU 1 − MU 2: (−0.250, 0.072)   (Welsh vs Mixed)
TTEST MU 1 = MU 2 (VS NE): T=−1.14 P=0.27 DF=23.8

Seven-year-olds

SCHOOL	N	MEAN	STDEV	SE MEAN
1 (Welsh)	11	0.223	0.154	0.047
2 (Mixed)	20	0.250	0.293	0.066
6 (English)	33	0.105	0.148	0.026

95 PCT CI FOR MU 1 − MU 6: (0.005, 0.231)   (Welsh vs English)
TTEST MU 1 = MU 6 (VS NE): T=2.22 P=0.042 DF=16.6

95 PCT CI FOR MU 2 − MU 6: (−0.000, 0.291)   (Mixed vs English)
TTEST MU 2 = MU 6 (VS NE): T=2.06 P=0.050 DF=25.0

95 PCT CI FOR MU 1 − MU 2: (−0.192, 0.137)   (Welsh vs Mixed)
TTEST MU 1 = MU 2 (VS NE): T=−0.34 P=0.73 DF=29.0

We can explain these (at first sight, strange) differences if we turn away from school type as an educational category. Their significance as far as this study is concerned is that the school tends to reflect the linguistic character of the area in which it is located. Thus, the English schools are located in the so-called anglicised areas, the mixed schools are to be found in areas where Welsh is used. The Welsh schools are unusual in that they tend to be found also in the anglicised areas, particularly in the towns which throughout Wales are strong centres of anglicisation (even within Welsh-speaking areas). Thus, although Welsh is used within the school, the community outside the school is predominantly English-speaking. This study thus suggests that Welsh and English schools have more in common from the point of view of WI than the mixed schools: it is the latter which tend to be correlated more with WI.

Individual locations: Variation within WI

Table 14.9 gives the locations of the schools used in the analysis and the numbers of children in each year group. The original project which selected these schools did not have dialectological aims, and some locations are notably absent (particularly in the southern valleys and the area around Llanelli). Nevertheless, the locations are spread throughout Wales and allow some geographical comparisons. This distribution of the locations also avoids the possibility of overconcentration on a Wenglish Geltacht.

There are three variables which indicate regional differences — TAG, JOK and words for PAR.

The tags are particularly interesting because they demonstrate a number of choices, as already illustrated: *is it* versus *isn't it* versus *yes* versus *shall*. Of particular interest is the observation by Thomas (1984), noted earlier, that *yes* is essentially northern and *isn't it* is essentially southern. The corpus confirms that there is a noticeable tendency for the use of the WI tag *yes* to occur in the north (at Llanberis, Penrhyndeudraeth and, especially, Llansannan) while the choice of either *is it* or *isn't it* occurs mainly in the south (at Aberystwyth, Brynaman, Carmarthen, Swansea, Ebbw Vale, Brynderi, Pontypridd, Cardiff and Newport). There are two exceptions to this regional distribution in that an example of *yes* is found at Aberystwyth (which is not surprising in view of its central position) and another example at Cardiff (which is unexpected). The bulk of the examples follow the north–south distribution. This dialectal distribution correlates markedly with the regional differences in Welsh, discussed earlier, in that *is it* (in particular) and *isn't it* can be related to

TABLE 14.9   *Geographical Locations of the Schools*

		Five-year-olds	Six-year-olds	Seven-year-olds
South-East Wales	Cardiff	10	10	8
	Pontypridd	4	4	4
	Newport	4	4	3
	Ebbw Vale	4	3	4
	Brynderi	4	4	3
South-West Wales	Llandysul	2	2	2
	Brynaman	2	2	2
	Carmarthen	4	4	3
	Swansea	8	6	6
Mid-West Wales	Aberystwyth	10	10	8
	Tregaron	1	–	–
Mid-East Wales	Knighton	2	2	2
North-West Wales	Caernarfon	2	2	2
	Bethesda	1	–	–
	Rhosgadfan	1	1	1
	Penrhyndeudraeth	–	–	4
	Llanberis	–	4	4
North-East Wales	Bala	4	4	3
	Colwyn Bay	–	–	2
	Llansannan	1	1	2
	Wrexham	4	4	4

southern *efe* while *yes* can be related to northern *ie*. This suggests that we have here an example of the Welsh dialects influencing the existence of dialects within WI.

The WI form *joking* is recorded at Brynaman and Carmarthen. There is also one instance in a Welsh school in Cardiff. But this instance does not reflect any consistent usage there (it may be the result of outside influence on the child or even population movement referred to earlier). *Joking* emerges as a regionally restricted feature of WI. Unlike the WI tags, it has no other WI equivalent which contrasts with *pretend*. Overall, the frequencies show that *joking* has not been prominent and does not develop as extensively as *pretend* (see Table 14.2).

A further regional distinction is found in the use of the WI words for grandparents. As already seen, the WI versions do not figure prominently but *nain* and *taid* are found in northern locations (*nain* at Wrexham, Bala, Llanberis, Llansannan; and *taid* at Wrexham, Llansannan); *mamgu* and *dadcu*, with even more restricted usage, are found at Aberystwyth, a more southern area. The data are very limited but these incidences do meet the known facts about the regional distribution of the Welsh forms.

Sociolinguistic Aspects

In this section, four factors will be examined: sex, the linguistic backgrounds of the parents, the socio-economic backgrounds of the parents, and the educational backgrounds of the parents. All the relevant details about the parents were obtained by questionnaires completed by them. (As already mentioned, children for whom there are missing data are excluded from the analysis. The other restrictions on the use of the TWOT test, as described above, are also applied.)

Boys and girls

Sex differences have been a popular factor in sociolinguistic research and it is interesting to see whether it has any bearing on the use of WI or non-WI variants. Romaine (1984: 113–23) surveys a number of studies of children and adolescents which show sex differences and she states that her own study of Edinburgh children showed differences between boys and girls as young as six.

The results of this current study are given in Table 14.10. The figures show that the boys are in the majority in all three ages. In no case does the *p*-value show that the results are statistically significant at the 5% level. Contrary to expectations on the basis of more general studies, the table shows that the means of the girls' WI proportions are higher than those of the boys' WI proportions. There would appear to be no explanation for this in the data as neither the lexical items nor the grammatical variables appear to have any sex distinctions, with the possible exception of expletives, *man* and *boy(s)* (see Table 14.1), which favour the boys anyway. It would, therefore, be interesting to see whether this tendency is found in older age groups.

TABLE 14.10   *Two-sample t-test for Sex and WI Proportions*

Five-year-olds

SEX	N	MEAN	STDEV	SE MEAN
2 (GIRLS)	27	0.223	0.265	0.051
1 (BOYS)	35	0.178	0.244	0.041

95 PCT CI FOR MU 2 − MU 1: (−0.086, 0.177)
TTEST MU 2 = MU 1 (VS NE): T=0.69 P=0.49 DF=53.5

Six-year-olds

SEX	N	MEAN	STDEV	SE MEAN
2 (GIRLS)	30	0.227	0.229	0.042
1 (BOYS)	34	0.158	0.161	0.028

95 PCT CI FOR MU 2 − MU 1: (−0.032, 0.169)
TTEST MU 2 = MU 1 (VS NE): T=1.37 P=0.18 DF=51.2

Seven-year-olds

SEX	N	MEAN	STDEV	SE MEAN
2 (GIRLS)	29	0.214	0.256	0.048
1 (BOYS)	35	0.135	0.166	0.028

95 PCT CI FOR MU 2 − MU 1: (−0.032, 0.191)
TTEST MU 2 = MU 1 (VS NE): T=1.44 P=0.16 DF=46.3

Linguistic background of the parents

The linguistic backgrounds of the parents would seem to be a reasonable source as a correlation with WI elements. It should be emphasised that we are concerned here with the L1 of the parents and not with the language that the parents speak with the children. Thus, it is possible to have an L1 Welsh parent who speaks English with the child. In the majority of cases, the language of the family is English and the first language of the child is English, too, as Table 14.11 shows.

TABLE 14.11   *L1 of the Children*

	five	*six*	*seven*
English	66	64	64
Welsh	2	3	3
	68	67	67

TABLE 14.12 *Two-sample t-test for L1 of Father and WI proportions*

Five-year-olds

L1	N	MEAN	STDEV	SE MEAN
2 (ENGLISH)	44	0.208	0.246	0.037
1 (WELSH)	7	0.194	0.361	0.14

95 PCT CI FOR MU 2 − MU 1: (−0.332, 0.36)
TTEST MU 2 = MU 1 (VS NE): T=0.10 P=0.93 DF=6.9

Six-year-olds

L1	N	MEAN	STDEV	SE MEAN
2 (ENGLISH)	42	0.171	0.177	0.027
1 (WELSH)	10	0.240	0.149	0.047

95 PCT CI FOR MU 2 − MU 1: (−0.185, 0.047)
TTEST MU 2 = MU 1 (VS NE): T=−1.27 P=0.22 DF=15.7

Seven-year-olds

L1	N	MEAN	STDEV	SE MEAN
2 (ENGLISH)	47	0.126	0.152	0.022
1 (WELSH)	11	0.223	0.269	0.081

95 PCT CI FOR MU 2 − MU 1: (−0.281, 0.089)
TTEST MU 2 = MU 1 (VS NE): T=−1.15 P=0.28 DF=11.5

The purpose of this part of the discussion is, then, to investigate a possible correlation between those L1 Welsh parents who speak English with their children and WI usage. The results are given in Tables 14.12 and 14.13. The figures show that children whose parents' first language is Welsh are a small proportion of the total. In no case are the differences between the two groups of children statistically significant. However, with one exception (namely, the five-year-olds who have Welsh-speaking fathers), there is a trend for the children who have at least one Welsh speaking parent to have higher means of WI features.

Socio-economic background of the parents

Romaine (1984: 83–94) reviews a number of studies which investigate social class differentiation and highlights a number of positive findings.

TABLE 14.13   *Two-sample t-test for L1 of Mother and WI Proportions*

Five-year-olds

L1	N	MEAN	STDEV	SE MEAN
2 (ENGLISH)	45	0.185	0.228	0.034
1 (WELSH)	9	0.306	0.365	0.12

95 PCT CI FOR MU 2 − MU 1: (−0.407, 0.16)
TTEST MU 2 = MU 1 (VS NE): T=−0.96 P=0.36 DF=9.3

Six-year-olds

L1	N	MEAN	STDEV	SE MEAN
2 (ENGLISH)	46	0.171	0.169	0.025
1 (WELSH)	9	0.196	0.197	0.066

95 PCT CI FOR MU 2 − MU 1: (−0.182, 0.132)
TTEST MU 2 = MU 1 (VS NE): T=−0.36 P=0.73 DF=10.4

Seven-year-olds

L1	N	MEAN	STDEV	SE MEAN
2 (ENGLISH)	51	0.140	0.177	0.025
1 (WELSH)	8	0.179	0.206	0.073

95 PCT CI FOR MU 2 − MU 1: (−0.216, 0.138)
TTEST MU 2 = MU 1 (VS NE): T=−0.51 P=0.62 DF=8.7

In this subsection, we shall investigate whether social class controls the use of WI and non-WI features.

The results of the analysis based on the socio-economic backgrounds of the fathers and the mothers are given separately in Tables 14.14 and 14.15. Two groups are used which are based on the higher and lower classes of the Registrar General's classification, class 3 being split on the basis of the nature of the occupation — those akin to classes 1 and 2 are assigned to the higher class along with 1 and 2, and those more akin to classes 4 and 5 are assigned to the lower class along with 4 and 5.

Looking at Tables 14.14 and 14.15, it is interesting to note that the upper group is the larger group with the mothers whereas the lower group is the larger group with the father — a fact which probably reflects

TABLE 14.14   *Two-sample t-test for Socio-economic Class of Father and WI|Proportions*

Five-year-olds

SOC	N	MEAN	STDEV	SE MEAN
1 (UPPER)	24	0.125	0.218	0.044
2 (LOWER)	33	0.241	0.264	0.046

95 PCT CI FOR MU 1 − MU 2: (−0.244, 0.013)
TTEST MU 1 = MU 2 (VS NE): T=−1.81 P=0.076 DF=54.1

Six-year-olds

SOC	N	MEAN	STDEV	SE MEAN
1 (UPPER)	26	0.148	0.158	0.031
2 (LOWER)	32	0.215	0.181	0.032

95 PCT CI FOR MU 1 − MU 2: (−0.156, 0.022)
TTEST MU 1 = MU 2 (VS NE): T=−1.51 P=0.14 DF=55.7

Seven-year-olds

SOC	N	MEAN	STDEV	SE MEAN
1 (UPPER)	26	0.135	0.174	0.034
2 (LOWER)	32	0.127	0.150	0.026

95 PCT CI FOR MU 1 − MU 2: (−0.079, 0.095)
TTEST MU 1 = MU 2 (VS NE): T=0.18 P=0.86 DF=49.6

different job opportunities. Thus, within a family, there may be different socio-economic factors at work from the father and the mother.

Both tables reveal that the differences are not statistically significant at the 5% level (the nearest occurs with the fathers of the five-year-olds). Both tables, however, show the same developmental trend. At five and six, the children of the upper-group mothers or fathers have lower means of WI proportions. But the means of the lower group decline in both analyses until, surprisingly, they are lower than the upper group means at age seven. On this basis it can be suggested that the decline of WI features in general revealed by Table 14.4 is due to the gradual rejection of these features by the children of parents who belong to the lower socio-economic group. As earlier suggested, the fact that this occurs

TABLE 14.15   *Two-sample t-test for Socio-economic Class of Mother and WI Proportions*

Five-year-olds

SOC	N	MEAN	STDEV	SE MEAN
1 (UPPER)	27	0.190	0.251	0.048
2 (LOWER)	22	0.251	0.282	0.060

95 PCT CI FOR MU 1 − MU 2: (−0.217, 0.094)
TTEST MU 1 = MU 2 (VS NE): T=−0.79 P=0.43 DF=42.6

Six-year-olds

SOC	N	MEAN	STDEV	SE MEAN
1 (UPPER)	32	0.143	0.152	0.027
2 (LOWER)	20	0.230	0.200	0.045

95 PCT CI FOR MU 1 − MU 2: (−0.193, 0.020)
TTEST MU 1 = MU 2 (VS NE): T=−1.66 P=0.11 DF=32.6

Seven-year-olds

SOC	N	MEAN	STDEV	SE MEAN
1 (UPPER)	31	0.162	0.192	0.034
2 (LOWER)	24	0.130	0.176	0.036

95 PCT CI FOR MU 1 − MU 2: (−0.068, 0.131)
TTEST MU 1 = MU 2 (VS NE): T=0.63 P=0.53 DF=51.4

during the primary school age range may suggest the influence of the school peer-groups as opposed to the home environment. These results tend to suggest that WI is a low-status variety which is initially used by the lower socio-economic groups but is gradually forsaken. If this trend is maintained as the children get older, it bodes ill for the continued use of WI features. On the other hand, there may be some evidence here for style-switching. It has been observed in style-switching investigations that some lower socio-economic groups tend to hypercorrect. There is, therefore, a remote possibility that the children of mothers or fathers of lower socio-economic groups style-switch in school to such an extent that their non-WI usage exceeds that of the upper group. But this is speculation which is not as yet supported by direct evidence.

Educational background of the parents

In order to achieve a different view, details were also obtained about the educational background of the parents. Again, two classes were established which took into account the secondary and higher education of the parents. The higher class was established on the criteria of having attended a grammar school, or having gone on to higher education. The lower class included all others.

An analyst would intuitively expect a result which is similar to that found with the socio-economic groupings — that is, that WI features (at least initially) be related to the lower educational group. Tables 14.16 and 14.17 show that there are no statistically significant differences at the

TABLE 14.16 *Two-sample t-test for Educational Class of Father and WI Proportions*

Five-year-olds

EDUC	N	MEAN	STDEV	SE MEAN
1 (UPPER)	25	0.203	0.297	0.059
2 (LOWER)	24	0.185	0.207	0.042

95 PCT CI FOR MU 1 − MU 2: (−0.129, 0.166)
TTEST MU 1 = MU 2 (VS NE): T=0.25 P=0.80 DF=43.0

Six-year-olds

EDUC	N	MEAN	STDEV	SE MEAN
1 (UPPER)	29	0.186	0.171	0.032
2 (LOWER)	23	0.157	0.161	0.034

95 PCT CI FOR MU 1 − MU 2: (−0.065, 0.121)
TTEST MU 1 = MU 2 (VS NE): T=0.61 P=0.54 DF=48.5

Seven-year-olds

EDUC	N	MEAN	STDEV	SE MEAN
1 (UPPER)	30	0.136	0.197	0.036
2 (LOWER)	25	0.173	0.166	0.033

95 PCT CI FOR MU 1 − MU 2: (−0.135, 0.062)
TTEST MU 1 = MU 2 (VS NE): T=−0.75 P=0.46 DF=53.0

TABLE 14.17   *Two-sample t-test for Educational Class of Mother and WI Proportions*

Five-year-olds

EDUC	N	MEAN	STDEV	SE MEAN
1 (UPPER)	25	0.243	0.297	0.059
2 (LOWER)	25	0.181	0.223	0.045

95 PCT CI FOR MU 1 − MU 2: (−0.088, 0.211)
TTEST MU 1 = MU 2 (VS NE): T=0.83 P=0.41 DF=44.6

Six-year-olds

EDUC	N	MEAN	STDEV	SE MEAN
1 (UPPER)	29	0.167	0.150	0.028
2 (LOWER)	24	0.194	0.202	0.041

95 PCT CI FOR MU 1 − MU 2: (−0.127, 0.074)
TTEST MU 1 = MU 2 (VS NE): T=−0.54 P=0.59 DF=41.6

Seven-year-olds

EDUC	N	MEAN	STDEV	SE MEAN
1 (UPPER)	26	0.140	0.160	0.031
2 (LOWER)	30	0.165	0.200	0.037

95 PCT CI FOR MU 1 − MU 2: (−0.121, 0.072)
TTEST MU 1 = MU 2 (VS NE): T=−0.50 P=0.62 DF=53.7

5% level. But they do indicate a surprising trend, at least with the fathers. With the latter, it is the children of fathers who belong to the higher educational group who have the higher mean of WI proportions. Their mean, however, declines until at age seven it is lower than the children who have lower-group fathers. In the case of the mothers, the children of the upper group use more WI features only at age five; the mean declines over the next two years and at both later ages is less than the mean of lower-group children.

It is not surprising that the WI mean declines — that is predictable from earlier analyses. By seven years of age, a consistent pattern emerges — the children of the status groups are choosing the status non-WI features. The remarkable point is that the socio-economic class standpoint and the educational standpoint produce different results for the five- and six-year-olds. At face value, we seem to have contradictory forces at work — the higher-status educational group tend to choose the lower-status WI, while the higher-status socio-economic group more predictably tend to choose the higher-status non-WI. At face value, parents' educational backgrounds do not seem to attribute low status to WI; or alternatively, educational background is not a good indicator of social status. But we should bear in mind that each of the factors, including region on the basis of school type, has been analysed separately. Thus, we have no way of assessing the interaction of the various factors. Unfortunately, the data are unlikely to tolerate further divisions to study the interactions of factors. The analysis as it stands raises possibilities which may help to promote further discussion and comment in this field.

Summary and Conclusions

Although spontaneous corpora introduce methodological problems for statistical analyses, they have the enormous benefit of actually revealing the functional load of the variables under investigation in actual discourse. In this light, we have seen that the frequency of WI features of dialect is relatively slight overall, but that the variable TAG, although its frequency is not high, is a prominent and consistent marker of WI. There appears to be a trend for the small amount of WI to decline at age six and less so at age seven. The most obvious conclusion here is that the minority WI speakers accommodate to their non-WI peers at school. But the existence of individual variability allows speculation about the development of style-switching. The analysis has suggested, however, that variability already exists in the home so that the developments in school were already anticipated in the family usage. In terms of predicting the types of speaker that would use WI, the statistical analyses revealed trends rather than firm statistically significant differences. In general, a WI speaker may have at least one L1 Welsh-speaking parent, attend a mixed school and therefore be an L1 English speaker in a Welsh-speaking area, and have a father or mother who belongs to the lower socio-economic group. The latter characterisation reflects the distribution of non-standard English speakers but, surprisingly, it was contradicted by the educational backgrounds of the parents. By age seven, however, the socio-economic differences had declined, which may suggest that it is the lower socio-economic groups that change from WI to non-WI. It emerges that region, in more than one way, is an influence on WI — in the first place, an analysis of school types revealed that WI is stronger in the less-anglicised areas; and in the second place, region produces variety within

WI. The first point is important. If WI is located mainly in the Welsher regions then it may be that WI is following the path of Welsh — contraction to certain regions. Ultimately, there thus exists the possibility that WI will be subject to the same demographic pressures as Welsh and will suffer the same fate unless, like Welsh, it is actively supported by its own users and influential institutions. Finally, it should be noted that we have only studied users at an early age. Developmental factors may alter the distribution of WI and non-WI variants, particularly as more adult discourse factors exert their influence, and studies of later ages, particularly adolescents, may produce different results.

Notes to Chapter 14

1. I am very grateful to Nikolas Coupland for valuable comments and suggestions in respect of an earlier version of this study.
2. An interesting further example is the WI use of *keep* for *put away* as in *shall I keep the pots for you* — the Welsh *cadw* is the equivalent of both *keep* and *put away*. (A striking anecdote can be supplied here of an English teacher in a school in Wales who reacted incredulously to a pupil's offer of help which was worded *shall I keep the books, sir?*) There are instances of *keep* and *put away* in the corpus but it was not possible accurately to determine the use of *keep* as many instances could be interpreted in terms of 'retention' as well as 'putting away'. Welsh *rhoi* is the equivalent of *give* and *put* but, although *put* is generalised in the L2 English of young Welsh-speaking children (i.e. mainly incipient bilinguals), it does not seem to have had any lasting effect on WI.

References

APPLETON, G.V. 1982, *Document C10: Minitab Reference Manual*, Aberystwyth Computer Unit, UCW, Aberystwyth.

BAETENS-BEARDSMORE, H. 1982, *Bilingualism: Basic Principles*. Clevedon, Avon: Multilingual Matters.

BOWEN, E.G. 1969, *Daearyddiaeth Cymru fel cefndir i'w hanes*. Llundain: BBC (English translation in BOWEN, 1986).

——1986, The geography of Wales as a background to its history. In HUME & PRYCE (1986).

CHESHIRE, J. 1982, *Variation in an English Dialect*. Cambridge: Cambridge University Press.

COUPLAND, N. 1988, *Dialect in Use: Sociolinguistic Variation in Cardiff English*. Cardiff: University of Wales Press.

EDWARDS, J. 1985, *Talk Tidy*. Cowbridge: D. Brown & Sons Ltd.

——1986, *Talk Tidy* (sequel). Cowbridge: D. Brown & Sons Ltd.

HUME, I. and PRYCE, W.T.R. (eds) 1986, *The Welsh and Their Country*. Llandysul: Gomer Press.

JONES, M. and THOMAS, A.R. 1977, *The Welsh Language*. Cardiff: University of Wales Press for the Schools Council.

PALMER, F.R. 1974, *The English Verb*. London: Longman.

PARRY, D. 1972, Anglo-Welsh dialects in south-east Wales. In M.F. WAKELIN (ed.), *Patterns in the Folk Speech of the British Isles*. London: Athlone Press, 140–63.

PRYCE, W.T.R. 1986, Wales as a Cultural Region. In HUME & PRYCE (1986).

REID, E. 1976, Stylistic Variation in the Speech of some Edinburgh Schoolchildren. M. Litt. thesis, University of Edinburgh.

ROMAINE, S. 1984, *The Language of Children and Adolescents*. Oxford: Basil Blackwell.

THOMAS A.R. 1984, Welsh English. In P. TRUDGILL (ed.), *Language in the British Isles*. Cambridge: Cambridge University Press, 178–94.

TRUDGILL, P. 1974, *The Social Differentiation of English*. Cambridge: Cambridge University Press.

——1984, Standard English in England. In P. TRUDGILL (ed.), *Language in the British Isles*. Cambridge: Cambridge University Press, 32–44.

——1986, *Dialects in Contact*. Oxford: Basil Blackwell.

15 'Standard Welsh English': A Variable Semiotic[1]

NIKOLAS COUPLAND

The concept of standardness and the terms 'standard' and 'non-standard' are fundamental building blocks of theoretical and empirical sociolinguistics. The classical Labovian paradigm which maps patterns of accent and dialect variation in urban communities uses counting procedures that are, in turn, based on sociolinguistic variables with recognised standard and non-standard variants. The sociolinguistic structure of communities has therefore been charted in terms of variable patterns of scaled standard/non-standard usage (Labov, 1972). Using the same methods, stylistic variation has been analysed as the variable selection of more and less standard variants across social contexts, either within interviews or in more naturalistic environments (Coupland, 1980; 1988). Yet there are widely differing views on how the term 'standard' is best interpreted and about what criteria should be invoked to classify a variety as 'standard'. This chapter will argue that English in Wales offers particular challenges to any simple definition of standardness, but also that the complexities involved lie at the heart of the Welsh English sociolinguistic experience.

Recent years have seen a rapid growth of interest in regional standard varieties of English (Trudgill & Hannah, 1982), including the so-called 'New Englishes' (Pride, 1982; Platt et al., 1984). These works reflect the continuing expansion of English into communities around the world, unabated after the colonial era, to a point where there are estimated to be over 600 million users of English (native and second or foreign language) speakers. Welsh English clearly needs to be seen as one part of the 'inner circle' of English functional domains (Kachru, 1985: 12), contrasting with the 'expanding' and 'outer' (predominantly non-native) circles, where the extents and processes of English standardisation and codification are quite different. Nevertheless, Trudgill & Hannah list and describe Welsh English alongside accounts of other Standard Englishes, thereby making some explicit claims and encouraging certain other inferences that are the immediate focus of this

232

chapter. My aim is to challenge the claim that there exists *any single* variety that can appropriately be termed 'Standard Welsh English' (SWE), and in passing to critique Trudgill & Hannah's descriptive account. On the other hand, the chapter is an attempt to build on these authors' recognition that Welsh English (WE) cannot either be assumed to be simply 'non-standard' in relation to an English English model of standardness. I shall try to show that standardness is indeed important to our understanding of Welsh English as a symbolic system, but that the relationship between language and social identity in Wales is complex and multi-dimensional.

The chapter first attempts a theoretical reappraisal of the notion of 'standard dialect', then outlines some of the linguistic and socio-psychological processes at work in the use of apparently prestigious varieties of English in Wales. In its more theoretical first part, the chapter will find some valuable directions (though also some contradictions) in available literatures on English in Wales. A data-informed second part describes some Welsh politicians' speech styles, varieties which might be purported to represent SWE. The data are not presented simply in order to demonstrate the fallibility of existing claims as to what 'SWE' descriptively is; rather, they enable us to trace, in a brief series of case studies, some of the variable routes to prestige available to these varieties. As we shall see, Welsh English political dialects are very far from enshrining a 'standard' variety. On the contrary, they give us an insight into the symbolic functioning of English in Wales to mark political and ideological positions, a vehicle more for conflict than for consensus.

Descriptive Perspectives on 'Standard Welsh English'

Existing descriptive literatures are inconsistent in their recognition of SWE. Platt *et al.* (1984: 10) explicitly exclude Welsh (as well as Scottish and Cornish) English from what they consider the 'New Englishes', though their reference to Welsh simultaneously implies recognising it as a standard variety. (Welsh, Scottish and Cornish English simply do not fit the authors' precise criterion of 'New'-ness.) Consistent with Trudgill & Hannah (1982), Trudgill (1984: 32) refers to 'Standard English as used in . . . Wales'. Thomas (1984), on the other hand, makes no reference to *standard* regional syntactic or lexical forms among the catalogue of features he lists as Welsh English, although, referring to pronunciation, he notes that 'The relationship of accent and class status is much the same for the community of speakers of English in Wales as it is for those in England. Standardization of a local accent entails proximation to RP . . . '. At the same time, reference is made to 'regionally-modified RPs' (Thomas, 1984: 189). Again at the pronunciation level, Wells (1982: I, 117) does not see Wales as a special case; Montgomery's (1986) examples of Welsh English, overlapping in some respects with the list of Trudgill & Hannah (1982), is discussed in terms of its *non*-standardness.

It is not surprising that some sources seem to be drawn by the feasibility of there being a SWE, given that it is only relatively recently that English has become the majority language of Wales. Wells (1982: II, 377), for example, writes: 'one must remember that North America, for instance, has had a substantial body of native English speakers for longer than Wales has'. The values associated with variation in English English may plausibly not have come to be adopted by Welsh speakers of English. A contrary position might be built around the observation that some varieties of English in Wales are clearly stigmatised (cf. Coupland, 1988; Mees, this volume) and do bear the hallmarks of non-standard varieties. Does the issue of SWE therefore hinge on which varieties of Welsh English are to be considered standard and which are not?

Trudgill and Hannah (1982) give a detailed list of the linguistic characteristics they take to be SWE (a detailed critique is given in an Appendix to this chapter). Some of these are:

1. Lack of phonological contrast between /ʌ/ and /ə/; e.g. /'rəbə/ (*rubber*).
2. An additional /ei/ = [e:] versus /ɛi/ = [e] contrast: [me:d] (*made*), [meɪd] (*maid*).
3. *tune, music* have /tɪʊn/, /'mɪʊzɪk/.
4. Lengthening of intervocalic consonants; e.g. ['bətʰ:ə] (*butter*), ['mən:i](*money*).
5. Presence of Welsh-language-derived /ɬ/ and /x/; e.g. /ɬan'bɛrɪs/ (*Llanberis*), /ba:x/ (*bach*).
6. Use of the invariant tag-question *isn't it?*; e.g. *you're going now, isn't it?*.
7. *will* for *will be*; e.g. *is he ready? no, but he will in a minute.*
8. Predicate object inversion for emphasis; e.g. *coming home tomorrow he is.*
9. Negative *too*; e.g. *I can't do that too* (*too* = *either*).
10. Reduplication for emphasis; e.g. *it was high, high* (= *very high*).
11. Loan-words; e.g. *del* (a term of endearment), *eisteddfod* (the arts festival), *llymru* (porridge).
12. The different meanings attached to some words, such as *delight* (= interest), *rise* (= get, buy), *tidy* (= good, nice).

My own intuitions suggest that these features are in fact a diverse set, varying in distribution and prestige, including some heavily stigmatised stereotypes of Welsh English. Beyond the notes made in the Appendix, I shall not trade observations on the status of individual cases. The critical issue is to determine what criteria have been employed in listing features as SWE forms, and to judge the appropriateness of the general basis of classification. The overriding criterion invoked by Trudgill (1984: 32) in discussions of standard varieties is distributional: they are 'typically used in speech and writing by educated [or "highly educated" (1984: 43)] native speakers'. Beyond this, Trudgill (1984: 43) recognises that Standard English English itself 'is a somewhat fluid, dynamic and ill-defined entity' which is the inevitable consequence of the distributional claim. Who are the (highly) educated? Any criterion of performance will run up against well-established facts of intersecting group differences — for instance, predictable regional differences within Wales (cf. Part Two of this volume), and indeed social differences that the diffuse label 'educated' clearly permits.

Here, we can refer to well-known informal taxonomies of subcategories within the best-recognised high-prestige variety of English, Received Pronunciation (RP). Gimson (1970) and Wells (1982) offer age and attitudinal variables as correlates of 'affected' or 'conservative' versus 'advanced' RP. As well as these group-related differences, there is the whole gamut of intra-individual differences, the stylistic dimension (cf. Coupland & Bell, forthcoming) of dialect variation. These are significant challenges to the distributional approach to 'standard'. On the other hand, we might argue in support of Trudgill that heterogeneity should not be allowed to interfere with the framing of a generalisation, which may still hold at a more global level (as with definitions of most, if not all, sociolinguistic categories beyond the specific-instance idiolect — 'accent', 'style', 'dialect', 'language').

In fact, the inevitable impurity of sociolinguistic categories does *not* redeem a distributional definition of 'standard' English, particularly in relation to Wales. Even assuming there is a variety we could take to represent 'normal educated usage' of English in Wales which is not standard English English, it would then be entirely unclear how we should define 'non-standard'. What status would, say, RP have in relation to 'SWE'? Do we expect to find non-overlapping distributions of features as between 'educated' and 'non-educated' usage, and if not, are *any* WE features to be considered 'non-standard'? Later in the chapter, it will be suggested that the criterion of education is in any case particularly *in*appropriate as a predictor of dialect usage in Wales.

It is important to note that Trudgill & Hannah's description of standard varieties is made available principally for pedagogic purposes, and protects its readers from these theoretical concerns. It has probably broadened learners', teachers' and policy-makers' outlooks on Standard English; indeed, its first chapter explicitly preaches tolerance of regional standards. This ideological content is praiseworthy enough, though there is a corresponding danger that sociolinguistic accounts of regional standards in general might be debased if they are seen purely as exercises in legitimisation. It seems important to demonstrate that there is community endorsement of a standard, independently of a sociolinguistic description which assumes this.

Theoretical Perspectives on 'Standard'

More fundamentally, it is necessary to query the assumption that a standard *is* a variety, and it is to this *qualitative* dimension that we must turn. The composition of standard varieties has most often been discussed in terms of linguistic levels. Trudgill (1984: 32) argues that the term 'standard' is only really applicable to syntax and lexis (hence, 'writing' as well as 'speech' in the formulation below), which are more codifiable:

> Standard English can be characterised by saying that it is that set of grammatical and lexical forms which is typically used in speech and writing by educated native speakers . . . in Britain SE is spoken with a wide range of accents, although these normally include only Received Pronunciation (RP) and the 'milder' regional accents, the 'broader' regional accents most usually co-occurring with dialects that are non-standard to varying degrees. . .

The distinction between accent and dialect (if the latter is taken to exclude accent) is potentially significant. Accent and dialect are open to different degrees and kinds of institutional support or threat and public endorsement or censure; are possibly amenable to different degrees of speaker control; and are open to different rates and processes of change (cf. Trudgill, 1986; Price, 1984: 179ff.). On the other hand, standard/non-standard has become a conventional though not unproblematical dimension in sociolinguistic research addressing phonological/phonetic and syntactic variation *alike*, and both dimensions enter Trudgill & Hannah's account of SWE (and other standard varieties of English); again, it is probable that lay perceptions of spoken language do not systematically relate separately to dialect and accent. I will assume, for these reasons, that dialect and accent features are equally eligible for consideration as part of a putative standard variety, even though syntax and lexis may somehow be more 'natural' candidates.

But the qualitative definition of a standard hinges on considerations other than linguistic. Linguistic description and distributional information together can be suggestive of the social functioning of standards, but their *evaluative* essence cannot convincingly be overlooked. The need to taxonomise 'forms of a standard' (as Gimson does, cf. above), and the catalogue of intra-group differences that need to be acknowledged, do not merely reflect the fuzzy sets of social science. Variation in these respects should rather be open to interpretation as the consequence of individuals' stylistic selections, in context, from dialect repertoires that are to a considerable extent structured on a person-to-person basis through the recognition of 'standards'.

A distributional definition provides no sense of a standard variety or variant's place in a system of meaningful alternatives, though this is implied in any stylistic approach. Adopting or conforming to a standard necessarily implies an act of approbation at some level, rather than the automaticity assumed under the rubric of 'educated behaviour'. Pressing a point, there are ultimately ideological objections to the inductive reasoning from educated behaviour to social standard, and the denial of access to privilege that it appears to accept. By the evaluative account, on the other hand, standards are the sociolinguistic end-points of multi-dimensional value-systems; they are semiotic, not linguistic, entities.

This line of interpretation has been dominant in the discussion of standard languages at the macro level of analysis — in discussions of languages in communities, language typology and language maintenance or shift, but overlooked by micro-sociolinguists interested in dialect variation. Downes (1984: 34), for example, argues that 'Standardization is a complex of beliefs and behaviour towards language which evolves historically . . . A standard language is a social institution and part of the abstract, unifying identity of a large and internally differentiated society'. Milroy & Milroy (1985: 22–23) similarly conclude that 'it seems appropriate to speak . . . of standardisation as an *ideology*, and a standard language as an idea in the mind rather than a reality — a set of abstract norms to which actual usage may conform to a greater or lesser extent'. Standard languages may loosely be said to 'possess' or 'carry' prestige, but more appropriately they *embody* assessments of what is prestigious. There is therefore enormous potential variation, across individuals and across time, though the paradox is that standard languages tend above all else to embody evaluative consensus, a stable national identity through language loyalty. As Hudson (1980: 34) comments, standard languages are almost 'pathological in their lack of diversity', which is of course only true where there are uniform evaluations made throughout the community. We might even use 'extent of evaluative diversity' as a measure of the appropriateness of the label 'standard', and by that measure conclude that several presumed standards are at least somewhat fictional: they do not carry evaluative consensus.

The approach can be transferred directly from macro to micro concerns of standardness in the context of dialect use. Claims cannot be made lightly about the existence of regional standards without considering the attitudes and allegiances which underpin descriptions of dialect distribution. But perceptions of standardness contribute vitally to the semiotics of Welsh ethnicity and Welsh people's displays of cultural and political affiliations in speech. There are notoriously diverse conceptions of 'Welshness' in Wales, differing degrees of ethnic affiliation among the population and definitions of what is affiliated to. We should also expect variation across dimensions of social context of dialect use (such as interactional goals, topics, interlocutors and settings), and certainly diverse means of displaying ethnic identification. It is necessary to assume that 'standard' is an inherently unstable social attribution, perhaps most strikingly of all in Wales.

What clusters of speakers and sociolinguistic phenomena in contemporary Wales might enter a discussion of SWE? *At least* the following (selectively and informally observed) categories:

1. Members of the middle classes (including some professional people) in Wales who are not Welsh by birth, show little or no affiliation to Wales or Welsh language and culture, who speak Standard English English, employing some RP or near-RP variety (perhaps mildly modified in the direction of a *non*-Welsh-English, non-standard variety, probably reflecting their provenance).

2. Middle-class or lower middle-class Welsh-born people (again including some professionals) who speak Standard English English, either with RP accent or RP mildly modified towards Welsh English pronunciation (probably of the sort minimally or not at all influenced by the Welsh language, probably in the urban south-east — cf. Collins & Mees, Lewis, Thomas, all this volume) and who adopt highly ambivalent attitudes to Welsh ethnicity (cf. also Coupland, 1988).

3. Again the middle-classes, though perhaps typically teachers, lecturers, lawyers, doctors, etc., again Welsh-born, but predictably not in the conurbations, whose pronunciation of English is indeed (apparently) Welsh-language-influenced, to different degrees, and who construe themselves as focal retainers of 'Welsh' Welshness.

4. A particular but influential subgroup, traditionally associated with standard dialect usage: 'regional' (Wales) English-language television (BBC Wales or HTV) newsreaders, whose place of birth is often indeterminate from vocal characteristics, who employ Standard English English and a near-RP and often hypercorrect style but

who *assiduously preserve* Welsh (language) phonological rules and phonetic realisations in their pronunciation of Welsh loan-words and apparently Welsh proper names, wherever they occur.

5. Apparently first-language-Welsh speakers/equilinguals whose English is radically and comprehensively Welsh-influenced at all levels. As highly specific cases within this group, we might consider: the first-language-Welsh speaker who punctuates English discourse with overt markers that he/she is speaking in a second language: *as you [habitual English speakers] say . . . ; how is it you say this in English . . . ?*; and the first-language-Welsh speaker/writer who self-consciously misspells English academic written submissions, as a gesture of defiance.

Among these categories, there are those for whom using English can be a battleground for inter-group conflict (cf. Gallois *et al.*, 1988). In the terms of speech accommodation theory (cf. also Coupland *et al.*, 1988), they are among those who protect their in-group boundaries through linguistic divergence and 'counter-attuning'. The categories embody a vast range of attitudinal, political and ideological stances, which dialect is richly able to symbolise, among the population of Wales. While some seem to endorse the traditionally English sociolinguistic value-system, some will seemingly self-present as dismissive of the institutions and attitudes that sustain Standard English English and RP as high-prestige forms. There are degrees of long-term accommodation (cf. Trudgill, 1986) to English norms, though, as with many groups, there is the likelihood of short-term convergence or divergence from the RP model. The newsreader group demonstrates the availability of competing pronunciation norms of perceived correctness — RP, with its supposed associations of pan-UK acceptability and prestige, and 'authentic' Welsh in the limited domain of encoding Welsh proper-names (cf. Coupland, 1984). Some groups will presumably be untouched (e.g. group 1) or minimally influenced (e.g. group 2) by 'Welshness' in any clear sociolinguistic respect.

If this impressionistic taxonomy comes at all close to reflecting some of the attestable social groupings in contemporary Wales, then the idea of a fluctuating and internally complex standard is appealing and necessary. We need to recognise the existence of different routes to prestige and to the presentation of preferred identities, as processes underlying the diversity that we can expect any descriptive corpus to show. The same perspective is necessary to interpret findings in the sociolinguistic, social psychological and sociological literatures on Welsh English, which are revealing in the heterogeneity they point to.

Implications for SWE in Diverse Literatures[2]

As noted at the beginning of this chapter, quantitative *sociolinguistic* methods are premissed on there being recognisable, unitary planes of variation — from standard to non-standard — underpinning the pattern of variation each sociolinguistic variable shows. In some instances (cf. the discussion of Milroy, 1982, of the (a) system in Belfast), variants span more than one phonetic dimension, so that no simple scale can reflect the available range. The complementary problem is that, in communities where the identification of a standard is uncertain, individual variables may need to be established differently if they are to be able to capture *the same* social meaning (e.g. 'converging towards a prestige norm') of qualitatively *different* phonetic shifts, also plausibly the *different* social meanings, for different speakers, of *the same* phonetic shifts. In view of these considerations, quantitative research using paradigmatic Labovian procedures in some communities in Wales may be diagnostically unreliable.

Existing data seem to show that, phonologically/phonetically, there is little difference between Wales and England in patterns of sociolinguistic stratification. This is the conclusion reached by Thomas (1984: 189). Mees (1977; 1983; but cf. also Chapter 13 in this volume) found the general pattern of positive correlation between six phonological variables in the speech of Cardiff schoolchildren and their fathers' occupational prestige. My own work with 51 adults, tape-recorded in a Cardiff travel agency (Coupland, 1988), shows a similar pattern of association between more RP-type variants (assumed to be more standard) and both occupational prestige and educational attainment.

These studies are modest evidence for the relative prestige of variants approximating RP among the higher socio-economic groups in the capital city, though it is clearly impossible to generalise from these findings to other Welsh communities' use of English. There is an urgent need for such data. In this context, Morris Jones's quantitative findings, using syntactic and lexical Welsh English variants (Chapter 14, this volume), are particularly important, suggesting that socio-economic variables may not be the 'simple' predictors of dialect use that we have come to expect on the basis of non-Welsh studies.

Within *socio-psychological* investigations of Welsh English, quite imprecise designations of dialect varieties have been tolerated. Researchers have sought generalisations about the prestige-level (Giles, 1970), ethnicity value (Chapman *et al.*, 1977) and interpersonal signalling potential (e.g. Bourhis & Giles, 1976) of 'Welsh English', undifferentiated, except for some references to 'south Wales English' (for reviews, cf. Coupland, 1988: Chapter 4; and, in particular, Giles, Chapter 16 of this volume). Some striking conclusions have nevertheless been reached from this research, for example that 'south Welsh English' is a relatively high prestige variety in pan-UK terms (Giles & Powesland, 1975), but that its less 'broad' form is evaluated as more pleasant and more statusful than its more 'broad' form (Giles, 1972). This last finding does not conflict with the distributional sociolinguistic evidence from Cardiff referred to above. On the other hand, Bourhis *et al.* (1973) found evidence that 'the Welsh accent' can function to mark national identity, not altogether differently from the way in which the Welsh language itself does this. Their group of Welsh language-learners, enrolled for an evening class, considered themselves to be as 'Welsh' as Welsh language-speakers. In a controlled test, they downgraded more standard-accented speakers. Bourhis & Giles (1977) found they could elicit broader 'Welsh accents' from a group of Welsh language-learners by making national categorisation more salient. Chapman *et al.* (1977), though arguably on too limited evidence, claimed that 'the vast majority of Welsh people do not aspire to the English mode of speech'.

If we take this last assertion to refer to the high-prestige English English 'mode of speech', that is including RP, then it finds further support in a study by Bourhis & Giles (1976). They found more co-operative behaviour from an audience of Cardiff theatre-goers when an announcement was made to them in 'Welsh-accented English' than when it was made in RP. *But*, this was only the case when the audience comprised bilingual speakers (in fact when the audience had come to see a Welsh-language play). When the audience was Anglo-Welsh (at least when the play was in English), they responded more co-operatively to the mild-accented and the RP request than to the broad-accented one. The study hints at the probable diversity of social evaluations of dialect varieties in a single community (Cardiff) which clearly comprises some Welsh-speaking as well as non-Welsh-speaking individuals. There is some support in this literature as a whole for seeing *both* Welsh English and English English varieties as being prestige models in Wales.

Beyond these studies, some fundamental findings of socio-psychological linguistic research are worth highlighting here. The *multi-dimensionality* of social evaluations has been established in countless investigations of the social meanings of dialects (cf. Ryan & Giles, 1982, for a review). Consequently, we should be wary of any simple assessments of accents as being 'favourably responded to', since there are likely to be contextual constraints upon when and in what respects a favourable evaluation is made. A robust finding is that standard accents connote high status and competence, while non-standard regional accents tend to connote greater integrity and social attractiveness (Edwards, 1982). On the other hand, these findings relate primarily to majority groups, where there is a broadly accepted standard variety with predictable associated prestige.

Another strand of socio-psychological research has concentrated on minority groups, where it has been argued that some members — those who identify strongly with the minority in-group and feel their identity threatened by the dominant group — are predicted to emphasise strongly in-group solidarity by sociolinguistic means, at least in inter-group encounters (Gallois et al., 1988; Giles, this volume). We might expect, then, that the affiliation dimension does special work in the contexts of minority groups, perhaps overriding considerations of status as might be relevant in majority groups. The notion of 'high-status language variety' itself seems potentially problematical in some minority group settings, where 'high status' (probably associated with an out-group value system) might itself connote low affiliation (with the in-group). In terms of the in-group's natural repertoire, prestige may generally be a more appropriate dimension than status, and there might be no clearly orthogonal relationship between prestige and affiliation: the more in-group affiliative, the more prestigious.

These speculations do find some support in the *sociological* literature on the linguistic situation in Wales. Williams (1987: 85) for instance (referring, of course, to minority languages rather than to varieties of majority languages used by minority groups), argues that 'class varieties are nowhere as well developed within minority languages as they are in the dominant languages'. Williams characterises contemporary Wales as having a bourgeoisie that is predominantly English and in-migrant, and a local proletarian labour market. Managerial decisions are generally taken by non-Welsh people, and often (except possibly in the very largest urban centres) outside Wales. The Welsh language and its reproduction is increasingly being 'reinstitutionalised' in specific domains — notably education and the media (Williams, 1987: 90).

In terms of English dialect usage, this demographic diversity suggests that very different prestige models will again be available to groups for whom we can predict quite different identity profiles and aspirations. Social mobility in Wales is very differently construed and achieved by different sectors of Welsh society. In the limited domains and geographical or occupational communities where the Welsh language is highly influential and even normative, we might find prestige (which Williams, 1987: 97 in fact defines as 'the value of a variety for social mobility') attaching to strongly Welsh-marked English usage, and a positive antipathy to RP. At the other extreme, RP will have the appropriate ideological content for some people in Wales whose priorities or aspirations are locked into the class structure of the broader community. In between, there will be a fluid mix where Welsh ethnicity will predispose variable levels of Welsh and English marking in English speech.

It is clear, as Jones's results (in this volume) suggest, that class is unlikely to function throughout Wales as a reliable dialect predictor because the middle-classes are subdivisible into quite different ideological groups. It is here that the strongest empirical objections to Trudgill's distributional criterion of standardness lie. If in Wales it is high socio-economic status groups that are most prone to bringing up their children bilingually (Harrison *et al.*, 1981; Bellin, 1984) and who are leading the charge of 'the new ethnicity' (Khleif, 1978), but also the middle classes who are leading or supporting the influx of commerce and new industries into Wales, there will be variability in the allocation of prestige to dialect variants. Indeed, there is no single Welsh sociological base to sustain a regional standard, and groups and individuals will identify with and through competing models of speech.

Some Political Dialects in Wales

We now turn to a series of short case studies, to pin the debate down to particularities. Below, I sketch in broad terms the accent characteristics of 13 Welsh political figures — Members of Parliament or parliamentary candidates at the time of the 1987 general election campaign, based on audio-tape-recorded political speeches, interviews and election broadcasts in English that were available on radio and television (BBC Wales, HTV, Radio Wales and independent local radio). All four major political parties in Wales are represented, but not in any accurate proportion to their political weight (however calculated). Individuals were included simply on the basis of their voices featuring in the vocal media at the times of sampling during the two-week period before election day when the recordings were made. Notable absences are therefore either chance omissions or reflexes of political selectivity (e.g. there are, very noticeably, no women). I name the individuals[3] and list the political banners under which they operate, though biographical details are not relevant to this exploratory exercise.

The individuals sampled are of interest here simply because they inhabit a corner of public life in Wales where 'dialect standardness' might be an issue, and where vocal characteristics and their semiotic functioning might be particularly salient. I am not suggesting that dialect usage by

politicians is altogether a matter of self-monitored self-presentation and
conscious choice. But it would be naive to believe these processes are not
at all in question, and identity management and self-presentation will
certainly have been considerations (in the evaluations of significant others)
in the earlier careers of politicians, their nominations and accretion of
political status in their own parties, regions and classes.

As data, the characterisations I shall offer are limited in several ways
even beyond the absence of any rigorous sampling procedure. No systematic
attention is afforded to variability within the speech of individuals; no
quantitative data are offered. There is no exhaustive discussion of the same
set of phonological variables in each case, though all commonly documented
'Welsh English' segmental features (cf. Wells, 1982: II; Coupland, 1988; and
Chapters 4 to 12 of this volume) were scanned. Realisations are shown in
phonetic notation where there may be disputes as to their status as phonemic/
non-phonemic entities in the various idiolects. Almost no instances of lexical
or syntactic deviation from standard English English appear in the corpus.
Contemporary RP styles are not given descriptive space and some entries
are simply 'no Welsh English features'. Despite these limitations, the corpus
demonstrates the diversity of dialect varieties that surface in a public context
in Wales — in fact, broadly the same context in each case — where
'standard' pronunciation forms might be expected. The particular political
allegiances of the individuals sampled cross-reference with their dialect
characteristics in intriguing ways. The political context in general makes the
signalling power of dialect highly salient. In consequence, the case studies
are suggestive of the diverse psycho-social processes I have argued must
underlie the use of high-prestige English varieties in Wales.

Liberal-SDP Alliance

Tom Ellis

A style showing some North Walian features and Welsh-language influence,
occasionally tending to RP. RP /ʌ/ is pervasively [ə] (e.g. *country, nothing*),
and [a]-type realisations are the norm in *natural, back*, etc. *also* is [ɔlsoː],
but *force* and *forth* have [oː]. The *nurse* vowel is [œː]. *produce, news* have
the rising [ɪu] diphthong that is often associated with the Welsh phoneme
/ɪω/. *hear* is ['hiə] (i.e. RP-type, not the stereotypical [jøː]). RP /aː/ is
realised in the area of [aː] (*party, are*); *ask* has short [a]. The RP
diphthongs /eɪ/ and /əʊ/ are typically monophthongal [eː] (e.g. in
discriminating, training; though both syllables of *maintain* sometimes have

the diphthong), and [o:] (e.g. in *also, proposal, quotas*). Consonants are generally close to RP realisations, though some short trills are produced post-consonantally (e.g. in *agriculture, priority*).

Mike German

No Welsh English features.

Gwynoro Jones

Very recognisably and thoroughly Welsh-language influenced. Among the most prominent characteristics is the apparent contrast /o:/ (*force*) versus /ɔ:/ (*sort*). Interestingly, *support* is occasionally [sə'poʊt], presumably hypercorrect on the analogy of Welsh English [o:] often corresponding to RP /əʊ/. *absurd, work* are realised with [œ:]. [u:] occurs not only in *foolish* but also in the final unstressed syllable of *into*. The forms *unilateral, reduce* and sometimes even *you* have yod-less (ɪu]. RP /eɪ/ is not uniformly monophthongal; a glide occasionally appears (in *bases*, but not in *Nato, Labour, major*). RP /aʊ/ has a centralised first element [əʊ] in *now, how, out*, as does RP /aɪ/ — [əɪ] in *my* and *I*. Trills usually occur in all phonetic environment-classes of /r/, though a debating adversary is occasionally addressed as ['baɹi] (*Barry*).

Richard Livsey

No Welsh English features.

Conservative Party

Nicholas Bennett

No Welsh English features, a contemporary RP speaker.

Nicholas Edwards

Generally a conservative RP speaker. /ʌ/ in *umbrella, adjustment* is very retracted; /æ/ is typically closer than in contemporary RP (*massive, fact [of the] matter*). /ɜ:/ is unrounded and open [ɐ:]. Some unstressed syllables have [ä] where contemporary RP would have schwa, e.g. *figure, number*; also [ɪ] in *system*, where schwa is again more commonly found. /əʊ/ has the conservative centralised starting point in *process, hold* and *Jones*. The /aʊ/ phoneme is realised as a near steady-state vowel [ä:], in *profound, priority*. A slight 'lisping' quality is introduced with /s/ articulated with the tongue almost making contact with the teeth. One apparently inconsistent feature within this conservative RP catalogue is the absence of /j/ before /u:/, in *solution*, but also in *situation* which is [sɪtu:ˈeɪʃn̩]. Perceptually, this is reminiscent of the Welsh English pronunciation (cf. Wells, 1982: II, 386). /r/-flapping is very rare, even intervocalically.

Ian Grist

No Welsh English features; contemporary RP.

Wyn Roberts

This style is broadly an RP variety, occasionally tempered by Welsh English features. So, /ʌ/ (*adjust, but*) is indeed [ʌ], and /æ/ is quite close. But *more* has [o:] while *of course, support* have [ɔ:]. Words which have the long, open back vowel in RP (e.g. *mark, farmer*) vary between an RP-type [ɑ:] and [a̠:], but *ask* has short [a]. RP /eɪ/, /əʊ/ and /aʊ/ are realised as in RP, though /aɪ/ tends to have the centralised start-point. Unstressed syllables are reduced or syllabified according to RP conventions.

Labour Party

Denzil Davies

A very heavily and consistently Welsh-influenced variety. /ʌ/ is [ə] throughout (*once, nothing, Russians*). *forces, course* have [o:], while *always* is [ˈɔlweɪz]. RP /ɜ:/ is [œ:] in *German, world, concerned*. *sure* is [ˈʃu:ə] and *pure* is [ˈpɪuə]; indeed, most 'u' and 'w' words have the rising [ɪu] diphthong without yod, even in word-initial position. Hence *Euro-missile* is [ˈɪuro: ˈmɪs:əɪl]. RP /ɑ:/ is usually near to cardinal vowel 4, maximally open and front, in *jargon, hard, guard*. The /e:/ versus /eɪ/ opposition, common in south-west Welsh dialects, is generally but not consistently shown: *made* is [me:d] and *played* is [pleɪd], but *Reagan* is also [ˈreɪgən]. Equivalent to RP /əʊ/ we find consistent monophthongal usage, usually [o:] (*total, control, Nato*), but there can sometimes be a more open quality: *no* can be [nɔ:]. RP /aʊ/ and /aɪ/ always have central starting-points to their glides. Some post-vocalic /r/ appears where it does not in RP, and is trilled in *war*, and even medially in *warheads*. In environments where RP does have /r/, this idiolect has variable continuant, flapped and trilled realisations. Stress in continuous speech is very noticeably not the 'stress-timed' pattern of RP, but tends towards a more even, syllable-timed distribution. Correspondingly, there is little reduction of 'unstressed' syllables, so that *prevented, agreement* and *senate* all have [ε] as their final vowels (though *probably* is [ˈprobli]). Medial plosives and sibilants have long hold-phases.

Barry Jones

Perceptually, this style has a predominance of RP-type features, though with several minor and inconsistent regional variants. RP /ʌ/ is realised variably as [ʌ] (RP-type), [ə] (in the Welsh English mode), and [ʊ] (a north of England type). The RP /æ/ phoneme is realised variably as [æ] or [a]. RP /ɜ:/ (in *determined, nurses*) is a long, central vowel [ə:] and unlike RP; the open, back vowel has a uniform RP [ɑ:] quality. /əu/ is often [əʊ] as in RP, though·*only* is sometimes [o:nlɪ]. Since [o:] does occur for RP /əu/ and [a] does occur for RP /æ/, the pronunciation of *programme* as ['pɹəugɹæm] sounds hypercorrected relative to the Welsh English forms. Some post-vocalic /r/, realised with the continuant phone, occurs, in *barley* and *resources; says* is [seɪz].

Neil Kinnock

Several consistently Welsh English features are present, though not those best predicted by Welsh-language characteristics; there is some movement towards RP (most noticeably in the areas of RP /æ/ and /eɪ/). Generally a south Wales valleys accent. Schwa is highly prominent as a Welsh English feature in several variables. *country, government* have [ə] (the second of these in all three syllables); *utter* is ['ətə]. The RP diphthong /ɪə/ is a [i] + [ə] sequence in *fear, near*. The long RP vowel /ɜ:/ has a quality not unlike schwa, but rounded to [œ:] (e.g. in *years, work, service*). The *how* and *high* vowels, as we have seen in several other cases, have start-points in the area of schwa. *hours* is ['əuəz]; *higher* is ['həɪə]. The short vowel in *happy, actively* is generally [a], but can at times be slightly closer. *more, foresight* have long [o:]. *ruin, individual, pursue* are alike in incorporating the Welsh-type [ɪu] diphthong, and the last two examples do not have the /j/ glide found in RP. *heart, marching* have a very open, front vowel [a:]. [eɪ] is found in *ways* and *grain* as in RP, but the monophthong [e:] appears in some (not all) realisations of *capable, make, faced, Labour, age*, and *case*. This suggests the idiolect variably recognises the extra contrast in this area often noted as a south Walian characteristic. There seems to be little flapping and no trilling of /r/, though flaps very commonly appear for intervocalic /t/ (in *lot of, what is, out of [work]*).

Plaid Cymru

Dafydd Elis Thomas

An almost entirely consistent Welsh English style with very few RP features of the sort other styles have shown; Welsh-language influence is apparent, particularly in prosody and the related non-reduction of 'unstressed' syllables, also in the realisation of /r/. Equivalent to RP /ʌ/ we find consistent [ə] (*encourage, destruction, come*). *four* has [o:] and *short* has [ɔ:]. The long vowel in *work, universities* and *research* is best transcribed as [œ:]. Adverbial final 'y' is [i] not [ɪ], as in *happily* and *really* (which is ['ri:li:]/. *you* and *few* have the rising diphthong [ɪu], usually without /j/ (e.g. in *few, new*) but with it in initial position (*usually, unity*). RP /ɑ:/ is /a:/. RP /eɪ/ is generally monophthongal [e:] in *reflation, wages*, and always in *Wales*; but we also find [eɪ] in *maintain* (twice) and even in *danger*. The forms *coastline, social* have [o:], and even *own* has the monophthong. RP /aɪ/ has a central first element, as in *revitalise*. The most distinctive characteristic of this style is the extremely frequent trilling (more than flapping) of /r/, not only word-medially but also initially and post-consonantally. Orthographic 'e' is often pronounced with an [ɛ]-type phone in environments where RP would have /ɪ/: e.g. in the first syllable of *democracy* and *effective*; the last syllable of *heritage* has [e:].

Dafydd Wigley

Overall, another highly Welsh-influenced style, though not consistently in the /r/ area; also, there are some clear north Welsh English features and the odd feature associable with RP (i.e. again in variables which have Welsh English alternatives). *doubling, government* and *number* have [ə]. *sad, average*, typically have [a], though there are occasionally closer variants. The *horse* versus *course* opposition functions, though *always, also* and even *water* have short [ɔ]. *years* is not [jø:z] as in some Welsh English dialects, but ['iəz]. 'u' words (*constitutional, issue*) have the rising diphthong. RP /ɑ:/ is generally /a:/ (*party, Cardiff*). Both [e:] and [eɪ] are again available and not altogether predictably selected: *Wales, case* and the *-ation* morpheme seem to have a near-monophthong consistently, though *face* can have the long glide that *railway* has. *vote* and *manifesto* can have [o:], though *social* on some occasions has an RP-type diphthong [ɔu]. Central first elements of RP /aʊ/ and /aɪ/ occur, and when there is unstressed vowel reduction we find [ə'lɔɪəns] (*Alliance*). On the other hand, *package* can have [ɛ] in its final syllable and *language* and *Senate* always do. /l/ (particularly non-initially) can be heavily velarised, as part of north Wales velarisation/pharyngalisation setting. *Aberystwyth* has [ə] in its third and stressed syllable, where [ɪ] often occurs in 'anglicised' pronunciation.

A Semiotic Interpretation

Gross intercorrelation of dialect feature selection and political allegiance is to be resisted, at least in respect of the evidence available here. Not only are numbers small, but there are clear mediating variables. For example, the political map of Wales (after the 1987 election) shows very clear regional patterning within Wales. Plaid Cymru now hold an uninterrupted block of the north-west; the Alliance hold territory only in mid-Wales; Labour represent by far the greatest number of people in Wales through their seats in the north-east and in most of the south; the Conservatives hold small areas along the north coast, in the extreme south-west and south-east. Conceivably, there may be some appreciable positive correlation between the dialect varieties of candidates/MPs and the geographical areas they are seeking to represent, as well as their individual demographic histories. The aim of this discussion is, in any event, not to identify causal links[4] or to shed light on how the varieties attested came to be. Rather, it is an observer's account (in the spirit of Hopper, 1986) of the means by which plausibly standard varieties signify in their contexts of use. A review of the 13 cases presented indeed suggests how 'the variable semiotic' functions sociolinguistically.

First, there is clearly prestige to be derived from some patterns of selection, or more accurately avoidance, *within* the general remit of standard English English and RP. Although I have not commented on these features above, *all* the politicians observed here stay within the confines of standard English English syntax, and, with minimal exception, lexis. In their pronunciation, they all select RP-type variants of that range of phonological variables repeatedly shown to differentiate socio-economic classes and styles — the social dialect features (cf. Coupland, 1985) that have wide currency throughout the UK; for example, they select velar not alveolar nasals (avoiding so-called 'g-dropping'), preserve /h/ (avoiding 'h-dropping'), and generally resist the simplification of consonant clusters. Does it then follow that, to this extent, all varieties we have been observing are 'upper-class' dialects? In the terms of Coupland (1985), the issue is not only class here but also personality, not only group status but also the individual competence/expertise that social psychological studies have shown to be pervasively associated with very many 'standard' dialect-varieties. In support of Coupland (1985), the present data suggest that the few phonological variants that all speakers here have in common are precisely those that relate to speakers' individual and not community identities. The broad geographical currency of these features does not allow them to signify at the community level.

On the other hand, in their public performances, some of these politicians do employ supposedly 'non-standard' variants — at least, forms which have been shown to be used more by other-than-highest socio-economic groups or in 'informal' contexts (for example, Neil Kinnock's intervocalic /t/-flapping, and several speakers' centralised /ɑu/ and /aɪ/ onsets). Indeed all non-RP features that the case studies have focused on are 'non-standard' in this sense, though it would be ludicrous to claim that many or most Welsh politicians are not of high socio-economic status or tend to speak informally. Conversely, I have argued in this chapter that the assumption that they are regional standard forms (because apparently educated people in Wales use them) is too gross an inference. We need a model that allows for multiple evaluative processes to impinge even on a single dialect performance.

We can first consider what stands to be achieved through the use of RP variants. We cannot explain the use of those RP features which *do* have corresponding recognisably Welsh English alternates without seeing these selections as motivated. They have signalling potential because they are choices[5] between conflicting ideological systems: in the grossest terms, Welsh and English. Some politicians in the sample, of course, use no Welsh-associated or -associable features. Their phonology aparently aligns them with the pan-UK (but south-east England directed) system of values and rewards. Given the sociological commentaries reviewed earlier in the chapter, it seems that this semiotic association will be unexceptional or endorsed by specific sections of the Welsh community: commonly the managerial classes, perhaps particularly English in-migrants, whose occupational concerns in any case take them beyond Wales; perhaps a good deal of the Welsh urban middle classes in general, who often (I conjecture) orientate to RP and standard English English in their own speech; perhaps the upwardly mobile classes, too, who may see social advancement lying in communities or involvements beyond Wales. It is not surprising that avoidance of Welsh English varieties is most consistently a characteristic of Conservatives' dialects in the sample, since RP encodes the centralist and class ideologies of Conservative voters.

From a sociolinguistic point of view, the more interesting group are the remainder of the sample who shift to RP highly variably — in extents and in sociolinguistic dimensions. Four speakers employ WE features almost uniformly — Gwynoro Jones, Denzil Davies, Dafydd Elis Thomas and Dafydd Wigley — though it is interesting to note their limited shifts in the direction of RP. We find uneven application of some Welsh English distribution rules, particularly in the areas of diphthongal/ monophthongal /əu/ and /eɪ/ (as these are phonemicised in RP). The monophthongs do seem important indices of a Welsh identity, but (as far as the distributional rules influencing the pattern of alternation are understood, cf. Wells, 1982: II, 384) do not seem to need to be rigorously followed. We might speculate that the substantial presence of monophthongs serves the broad Welsh-identity-bearing function, and permits stylistic considerations to dictate at least some of the remaining variance. Even more speculatively, lexical and discursive considerations might be pertinent, as we seem to find monophthongs in passages of radical anti-Tory-establishment or anti-English discourse, particularly in the Plaid Cymru members' speech. The vowel in *Wales* in particular tends to be realised monophthongally by those speakers who shift between monophthongs and diphthongs in non-'i' or -'y' orthographic words. *Reagan* is subject to further particular considerations because of its unique referent; proper names do seem to establish their own pronunciation standards (cf. Coupland, 1984). These proto-explanations could at least be carried forward as hypotheses for future research.

There is a block of features which surface commonly, though again variably, in most of the sampled politicians' speech — those, that is, who do employ Welsh English variants. The use of /r/ flaps and trills in some or all environment categories is one of these. It is interesting that flapped /r/ is by no means unique to Welsh English, and has been noted as a feature of 'upper crust' RP (Wells, 1982: II, 282). It is clearly possible, then, for some features to attract positive evaluations from the 'English' prestige system and *at the same time* seem to symbolise Welsh in-groupness, or at least be ambiguous as to which value system is being appealed to. These might be glossed 'crypto-Welsh English' forms. We might hypothesise that flapped /r/ is one such, but that trilled /r/ is diagnostically Welsh-derived. Somewhat similarly, there may be a predictably favourable evaluation of the non-reduction feature (e.g., *agreement* having [ɛ] in its final syllable), along the lines that vowel reduction lessens the apparent correspondence between spoken and written forms. (Stubbs, 1980, emphasises the processes by which evaluations of written English are mapped onto spoken English.) The Welsh have been known to be proud of their 'phonetic spelling', and there is conceivably a body of dialect evaluators (including voters) outside Wales who would endorse such 'clarity' (as indeed with flapped /r/). This subset of features may therefore offer a compromise, and a means of resolving, in some particular respects, the dialect conflict situation assumed earlier.

The principal vocalic variables do indeed represent conflict between English and Welsh semiotic systems. It is very noticeable that some Alliance and many Labour and Plaid Cymru speakers in the sample regularly avoid the RP forms (certainly the RP pole of gradient variables). Hence, outside of the consistent RP speakers, the RP /ɑ:/ variable (e.g., in *party*) is very commonly in the area of /a:/. Even when it is diphthongised, /əu/ is usually [ɔu], not [əu]. Centralisation is very common in /au/ and /aɪ/. Certainly schwa is most commonly found where RP has /ʌ/. All the non-RP speakers in this sample have the centralised feature, which may then be said to be a valuable diagnostic cluster, of which the [ə:] or [œ:] quality of the RP /ɜ:/ phoneme may be a part. The rising diphthong [ɪu] with yod-avoidance is another area where a 'Welsh' formulation seems to be very commonly preferred. Another possible diagnostic is the cluster of features in the (RP) /æ/, /ɑ:/ areas, with [a] quality in both long and short phonemes (e.g., *Cardiff, back*) seeming to be a consistent 'Welsh' marker in this context.

But there are quite different degrees of attraction and resistance to RP here, and qualitatively different non-RP realisations in use. RP variants of the variables just discussed do not appear in the sampled speech of the two Plaid Cymru Dafydds, Gwynoro Jones and Denzil Davies. These four are all Welsh-language speakers, and their Welsh English displays this association clearly and reasonably consistently. For the two Plaid Cymru MPs, whose 1987 electoral campaign was consciously directed at English monolinguals as well as at bilingual speakers, the pervasive echoes of Welsh in their English usage are both appropriate and possibly strategic. For Jones and Davies, I assume, the symbolic Welsh association endorses their involvements in specifically Welsh political life as a focus for their involvements in their broader-based parties. Neil Kinnock's Welsh English allies him symbolically more with a south Welsh valleys community than with a Welsh-language culture, and generates images of working-class solidarity to which his party has traditionally appealed.

On the other hand, Tom Ellis (minimally), Wyn Roberts and Barry Jones (both of these considerably) do use some RP variants of potentially Welsh diagnostic variables. It is not clear, in fact, whether the variation apparent in these speakers' styles is best characterised as Welsh English shifting towards RP or the reverse process. Either way, these speakers seem to seek to draw prestige from multiple value systems, which other speakers we have been considering seem to view as *competing* systems.

Overview

When the communicative medium is English, speakers in Wales cannot avoid some involvement with the complex system of values that English dialect varieties have come to symbolise. Received Pronunciation is well known to have socio-historical associations with the empowered classes of south-east England, and is widely recognised to connote traditionalism and establishment values (Gimson, 1970). Welsh English has the potential to symbolise non-alignment with these values simply by competing for air-space with the English prestige model, and to mark a particular national, community or class allegiance. The politicians in this exploratory survey clearly differ in fundamental ideological respects among themselves, representing the full spectrum of right and left, centralist and decentralist positions. Pronunciation variation seems not to characterise political party affiliation uniquely in Wales, but is nevertheless an important dimension of ideological signalling. Social evaluations of politicians' and other public figures' spoken performances are inevitably made, and the social meaning of dialect varieties pervasively glosses the discourses they encode. Conversely too, the nature of particular individuals' and groups' styles will continuously refine their semiotic value. The politicians' use of Welsh English features can therefore also be seen as a *denial of non-standardness*, an incipient standardising and institutionalising process.

In the Welsh political context, we find heterogeneity on a scale that is often seen to differentiate the full spectrum of socio-economic classes within a speech community, but where 'social class' cannot itself explain the variability. Class is certainly an issue — not the class *of* speakers, but perhaps the classes they seek to align themselves with. RP avoidance would have some immediate symbolic relevance here in a political domain still generally dominated by the English middle classes. But cutting across class-considerations are ethnicity and the semiotics of Welshness. Since the political debate in Wales of course needs to be conducted in English as well as Welsh, varieties of English associable with the Welsh language and/or the Welsh community are an important marking resource to several MPs and aspirants.

But it is also apparent that the alternatives are not simply 'Welsh' and 'English', linguistically or ideologically. Major elements of the English prestige code *are* consistently employed by all politicians in Wales. This chapter has focused on segmental phonological/phonetic features only, and we have seen that it is only a subset of these that seems to carry contrastive symbolic value. Indeed, it is a commonplace of semiotic systems that they load intrinsically trivial behavioural features with cultural significance. The cases we have looked at show individuals seeming to represent quite different political ideologies and orientations to Wales in their habitual styles of pronunciation. The Welsh language seems to dominate some styles; others are just as clearly Welsh but not apparently

Welsh-language-derived; several are not Welsh-associated in any sense; several are compromises, mixing styles or fitfully echoing other varieties.

Among this fluidity of signifying, the notion of 'a standard variety' seems to find no natural place. Defined distributionally, there is no standard visible in the data we have considered, and there cannot be because of the complexities of class structuring and regional and ethnic affiliation in Wales. If a standard is defined evaluatively on the basis of attributed prestige, it still lacks the consensus the term 'standard' seems to demand. But at the same time, the very diversity that a consideration of 'standard' exposes is illuminating. The Welsh politicians in the sample adopt highly diverse positions *vis-à-vis* competing 'standards', certainly *vis-à-vis* competing sources of prestige and both ideological and popular appeal. Their styles are therefore best characterised in terms other than of standardness itself, perhaps best as variable acts of identity (Le Page & Tabouret-Keller, 1985), as constellations of meaningful sociolinguistic associations, or as 'semiotics'. This chapter has at least shown that interpretative sociolinguistic analyses can tap into the accounts of social processes given by the other social sciences, and can contribute to an integrative picture. In line with the broader interests of this volume, the chapter may also have confirmed that sociolinguistic ethnicity in Wales is as pertinent a dimension of English usage as it is of bilingual usage, and an issue in need of sustained future research.

Notes to Chapter 15

1. I am very grateful to Justine Coupland, Howard Giles and Penny Rowlands for detailed and helpful comments on an earlier version of this chapter.
2. The review that follows is very brief, and can be supplemented by the discussions of Giles, Mees, Morris Jones and Williams in this volume, and by their citations.
3. The broadcasting context and the public lives of the individuals I shall deal with seem to me to make this particularisation acceptable. I would see this study as an attempt to detail one small corner of the process by which politicians seek to represent us. The data are to that extent public property.
4. Certainly, there are interesting issues to be explored causally. What identities do Conservative, Labour, Alliance and Plaid candidates need to present in order to advance their political careers in (or in relation to) Wales? Do candidates' ethnic and regional affiliations that are vocally apparent influence patterns of electoral response, and differently across the regions and parties?
5. To talk of 'choice' is, of course, not to imply conscious choice. Also, there are clearly differences of repertoire here, and it could be objected that there is limited or no choice for, say, habitual RP speakers. But the perspective being adopted here is in any case that of the observer and evaluator, who in

Wales will of course perceive alternatives being available at some point — if not to that speaker at that time, certainly the speaker's historical judgement (cf. note 4) that he/she might appropriately be a Welsh political representative.

References

BELLIN, W. 1984, Welsh and English in Wales. In TRUDGILL (1984: 449–79).
BOURHIS, R.Y. and GILES, H. 1976, The language of cooperation in Wales: a field study. *Language Sciences*, 42: 3–16.
——1977, The language of intergroup distinctiveness. In H. GILES (ed.), *Language, Ethnicity and Intergroup Relations*. London: Academic Press, 119–36.
BOURHIS, R.Y., GILES, H. and TAJFEL, H. 1973, Language as a determinant of ethnic identity. *European Journal of Social Psychology*, 3: 447–60.
CHAPMAN, A.J., SMITH, J.R. and FOOT, H.C. 1977, Language, humour and intergroup relations. In H. GILES (ed.), *Language, Ethnicity and Intergroup Relations*. London: Academic Press, 137–70.
COUPLAND, N. 1980, Style-shifting in a Cardiff work-setting. *Language in Society*, 9: 1–12.
——1984, Sociolinguistic aspects of place-names: ethnic affiliation and the pronunciation of Welsh in the Welsh capital. In W. VIERECK (ed.), *Focus On: England and Wales. Varieties of English Around the World*, G5. Amsterdam: Benjamins, 29–43.
——1985, 'Hark, hark the lark': social motivations for phonological style-shifting. *Language and Communication* 5, 3: 153–72.
——1988, *Dialect in Use: Sociolinguistic Variation in Cardiff English*. Cardiff: University of Wales Press.
COUPLAND, N. and BELL, A. (forthcoming), *Sociolinguistics and Style*. Oxford: Basil Blackwell.
COUPLAND, N., COUPLAND, J., GILES, H. and HENWOOD, K. 1988, Accommodating the elderly: invoking and extending a theory. *Language in Society*, 17, 1.
DOWNES, W. 1984, *Language and Society*. London: Fontana.
EDWARDS, J.R. 1982, Language attitudes and their implications among English speakers. In RYAN and GILES (1982: 20–33).
GALLOIS, C., GILES, H., FRANKLYN-STOKES, A. and COUPLAND, N. 1988, Communication accommodation theory and intercultural encounters. In Y.Y. KIM and W. GUDYKUNST (eds), *Theorising Intercultural Communication*. Beverly Hills, CA: Sage.
GILES, H. 1970, Evaluative reactions to accents. *Educational Review*, 22: 211–27.
——1972, The effects of stimulus mildness–broadness on the evaluation of accents. *Language and Speech*, 15: 262–69.
GILES, H. and POWESLAND, P.F. 1975, *Speech Style and Social Evaluation*. London: Academic Press.
GIMSON, A.C. 1970, *An Introduction to the Pronunciation of English*. London: Edward Arnold.
HARRISON, G., BELLIN, W. and PIETTE, B. 1981, *Bilingual Mothers in Wales and the Language of their Children*. Cardiff: University of Wales Press.

HOPPER, R. 1986, Speech evaluation of intergroup dialect differences: the shibboleth schema. In W.B. GUDYKUNST (ed.), *Intergroup Communication*. London: Edward Arnold.

HUDSON, R.A. 1980, *Sociolinguistics*. Cambridge: Cambridge University Press.

KACHRU, B.B. 1985, Standards, codification and sociolinguistic realism: the English language in the outer circle. In R. QUIRK and H.G. WIDDOWSON (eds), *English in the World: Teaching and Learning the Language and Literatures*. Cambridge: Cambridge University Press, 11–30.

KHLEIF, B. 1978, Ethnic awakening in the First World: the case of Wales. In G. WILLIAMS (ed.), *Social and Cultural Change in Contemporary Wales*. London: Routledge and Kegan Paul, 102–19.

LABOV, W. 1972, *Sociolinguistic Patterns*. Philadelphia: Pennsylvania University Press.

LE PAGE, R.B. and TABOURET-KELLER, A. 1985, *Acts of Identity: Creole-based Approaches to Language and Ethnicity*. Cambridge: Cambridge University Press.

MEES, I. 1977, Language and social class in Cardiff: a survey of the speech habits of schoolchildren. Master's dissertation, University of Leiden.

——1983, The speech of Cardiff schoolchildren: a real time study. Doctoral dissertation, University of Leiden.

MILROY, J. 1982, Probing under the tip of the iceberg: phonological normalisation and the shape of speech communities. In S. ROMAINE (ed.), *Sociolinguistic Variation in Speech Communities*. London: Edward Arnold, 35–48.

MILROY, J. and MILROY, L. 1985, *Authority in Language: Investigating Language Prescription and Standardisation*. London: Routledge and Kegan Paul.

MONTGOMERY, M. 1986, *An Introduction to Language and Society*. London: Methuen.

PLATT, J., WEBER, H. and HO, M.L. 1984, *The New Englishes*. London: Routledge and Kegan Paul.

PRICE, G. 1984, *The Languages of Britain*. London: Edward Arnold.

PRIDE, J.B. (ed.) 1982, *New Englishes*. Rowley, MA: Newbury House.

RYAN, E.B. and GILES, H. 1982, *Attitudes Towards Language Variation*. London: Longman.

STUBBS, M. 1980, *Language and Literacy: The Sociolinguistics of Reading and Writing*. London: Routledge and Kegan Paul.

THOMAS, A.R. 1984, Welsh English. In TRUDGILL (1984: 178–94).

TRUDGILL, P. (ed.) 1984, *Language in the British Isles*. Cambridge: Cambridge University Press.

——1986, *Dialects in Contact*. Oxford: Basil Blackwell.

TRUDGILL, P. and HANNAH, J. 1982, *International English: A Guide to Varieties of Standard English*. London: Edward Arnold.

WELLS, J. 1982, *Accents of English* (3 vols). Cambridge: Cambridge University Press.

WILLIAMS, G. 1987, Bilingualism, class dialect and social reproduction. *International Journal of the Sociology of Language*, 66: 85–98.

Appendix

Trading informal observations on sociolinguistic descriptions is ultimately unsatisfactory. Still, there do appear (to my intuition) to be some important inaccuracies in the Trudgill & Hannah (1982: 27 ff.) characterisation of Welsh English features, even beyond their claims (discussed in the body of this chapter) about their status as standard forms. Below are notes on what I would consider the inaccuracies. Cross-references to Chapters 4–12 are sometimes also possible.

1. While unstressed orthographic 'a' is occasionally not reduced to schwa, this is not a general 'tendency', and probably very rare in the initial syllable of *above*.

2. It is true that *soar* can select [o:], equivalent to RP /ɔ:/; but *port* also selects [o:]. (Trudgill & Hannah suggest /ɔ:/ and the same assignation for *paw*.)

3. To claim that 'Educated Welsh English is, with a few exceptions in the east and far south-west of the country, not rhotic' is accurate only if Welsh-derived rhoticity is ignored. Many first-language-Welsh speakers and equilinguals have (often trilled) post-vocalic /r/ in *Cardigan, war*, etc. (Denzil Davies in the sample of politicians' dialects in this chapter shows this feature.)

4. To claim that '/l/ is clear [l] in all positions' is to ignore very heavy velarisation of /l/ in the north, and the usual clear–dark alternation in much of the south-east.

5. Absence of /g/ (e.g. from *language*) does occur, but is often heavily stigmatised. (Presumably /ɑ/ in the *longer* example (Trudgill & Hannah 1982:29) is a misprint.)

6. I have never attested /kʊm/ for *comb*; /ku:m/ certainly appears, but is decidedly stigmatised when it does.

7. *Most* of the syntactic and lexical examples cited (see the chapter text) are dubiously considered standard forms; they certainly do not form a natural set. Some are plausibly standard forms (e.g. use of Welsh lexis such as *eisteddfod*, but hardly *llymru*). Some are forms with restricted currency (*I can't do that too* in the sense of 'I can't do that either'). Some are heavily stigmatised forms (*it was high, high* = 'it was very high') or stereotypes of Welsh English (*you're going now, isn't it?, tidy* = 'nice') which of course are attested but increasingly highly stigmatised.

Generally, the listing does not take into account the highly variable degrees of prestige and stigmatisation the features attract or (in line with Trudgill's criteria for 'standard') their geographical and social distribution. In consequence, it seriously overrepresents 'standard Welsh English' and underrepresents the complexities inherent in the designation.

16 Social Meanings of Welsh English[1]

HOWARD GILES

It is now widely accepted that a full account of a speech community's activities must include some statements about the social meanings associated with the language varieties used by it. The present volume is no exception and many of the foregoing chapters have, with varying degrees of explicitness, referred to attitudes towards Welsh-English (WE) language varieties. The present chapter overviews the actual empirical research that has emerged over the last 20 years on attitudes to WE speech styles and which itself represents a substantive contribution to the literature on the social evaluation of speech styles world-wide (Giles, Hewstone, Ryan & Johnson, 1988). I shall overview the social attributions accorded (and the behavioural outcomes contingent upon) WE varieties both inside multicultural Wales and outside it, and consider the role of message content in relation to WE usage. Finally, I shall propose a research agenda for future work in this field.

Before commencing this overview, a few preliminary remarks on methods and varieties studied are in order. The research methodology used in this area — unlike the direct questionnaire method (see Agheyisi & Fishman, 1970) utilised in studies concerning attitudes towards the Welsh *language* (Lewis, 1975; Sharp *et al.*, 1973; Williams, 1979) — is that of the 'matched-guise' technique (MGT) (see Lambert, 1967). This involves bidialectal speakers tape-recording the various guises at their command on tape for social appraisal. They do this by reading the same neutral passage of prose, in their different guises (e.g. in WE and Received Pronunciation); these are usually separated on a stimulus tape by so-called 'filler' voices. Listeners are instructed to listen to these supposedly different speakers and make social judgements about them on a series of rating scales. This is felt to be analogous to attending surreptitiously to someone behind you whom you have not yet seen or listening to the radio or talking to a stranger on the telephone. Very often, the traits employed in these studies are those determined by means of pilot studies to be of special concern to the raters themselves.

The strength of the MGT is in its ability to hold many variables in dimensions other than dialectal features (e.g. speech rate, projected personality) constant across recordings. Listeners never detect that the same person is talking and in the more rigorous (later) studies care is taken to ensure that no mimicry is involved. Rather, only speakers who shift between varieties naturally and frequently are used and their products are subjected to the scrutiny of dialectologists and independent samples of 'naive' listeners before the study proper begins. The technique has not been without criticism and such criticism has been answered by us on a number of occasions (e.g. Giles & Bourhis, 1976a).

All of the studies to be reported involve WE varieties in evaluative contrast to Received Pronunciation (RP). These are supplemented on occasion by comparisons with Welsh language varieties and other regional English accents. It should be stressed that, as Coupland has pointed out in Chapter 15, the exact phonological specifications of these WE (and other) varieties are unavailable. South-east Welsh varieties of English predominate (unless otherwise specified) and naturally enough there is a dire need for new contrastive studies to assess the diverse social meanings of other WE varieties.

Welsh-English Language Attitudes

In 1970, Giles (1970) investigated the perceived status of various accents heard in Britain. Using the MGT, 13 different accents including a WE variety were presented to 177 high-school pupils in south Wales and in south-west England. The results suggested that the accents portrayed could be considered as occupying positions along a value continuum of social prestige. At the top was ranked RP (mean rating of 2.1 on a seven-point scale), and the bottom position (mean rating of 5 2/3) was occupied by certain English urban accents (Cockney and Birmingham). WE was the highest-rated British accent (with a mean of 4.3 accorded it by the south-west English pupils) and can be posited as having intermediate status given that it was followed by 'Irish', 'northern', 'Somerset' to name a few.

There was evidence of accent loyalty in that Welsh raters reacted more favourably to WE than did the English judges; nevertheless, even the youngest (12-year-old) Welsh listeners conceded that their local variety was less prestigious than RP. Amongst the older judges (17-year-olds), it was those who scored more highly on an ethnocentric questionnaire that differentiated between RP and WE the most (Giles, 1971a); more specifically, they polarised the evaluative difference between the varieties in RP's favour. Moreover, it was generally the case that respondents rated the aesthetic value and the comfort they felt while listening to WE lower than RP. It should also be stated that these informants were also asked for their opinion about the same accents by the use of name labels (e.g. 'south Welsh accented speaker') and another sample of subjects heard different representative speakers of the accents concerned (rather than using the MGT). All in all, the results were clear and consistent: the prestige appeal of WE was lower than RP.

In another study, south Welsh listeners were confronted by milder and broader WE varieties (produced by the same speaker) than used above. It was found in accord with the above pattern that the more accented the WE guise the lower prestige it was awarded. Interestingly, 17-year-olds discriminated perceptually more between the mild and broad variants than their 12-year-old counterparts yet at the same time were evaluatively much more tolerant of any differences.

The relative accent prestige of WE has also a pertinent impact on how people form impressions of you. Giles (1971b) had matched groups of south Welsh and Somerset adolescents listen to RP, WE, and Somerset guises. This time there were two sets of matched-guise stimulus speakers and these were judged by respondents on a series of *personality* traits. It was found that the RP speakers were upgraded significantly compared to the non-standard guises as more ambitious, intelligent, self-confident, determined and industrious. Indeed, the WE speakers were accorded intermediate positions along these traits between the RP and Somerset speakers. However, when it came to the less socio-economically-related traits (Tajfel, 1959), then a converse pattern emerged wherein the regional voices were upgraded in terms of integrity and social attractiveness. More specifically, the WE speakers (and the Somerset ones) were rated as less serious and more talkative, good-natured and humorous than the RP speakers; there were also tendencies in the same direction for the traits of reliability and entertainingness.

Language varieties are, of course, not as *static* as they are represented in the above extracts. As sociolinguistic studies attest (e.g. Coupland, 1988), we shift our WE accents in terms of standardness–non-standardness from situation to situation. Bourhis, Giles & Lambert (1975) therefore attempted to see if the same pattern of findings could be gleaned when WE speakers were heard to move nearer to and further away from RP. Using speech accommodation terminology (Giles, 1984), it was predicted that as WE speakers converged towards an RP interlocutor they would gain in terms of perceived competence and when they diverged away from said individual to a broader WE benefit would accrue in terms of judged sociability, and so forth. South Welsh respondents in this study were randomly divided into six groups. They were all told that a Welsh athlete had recently been placed seventh in a Commonwealth diving competition and that they were to hear him in two consecutive radio interviews, purportedly taped after the competition. In one interview, the athlete's interviewer was an RP speaker while in the other the interviewer possessed a mild WE accent. In this latter interview, the athlete always employed a mild WE accent also — the baseline condition — but with the RP interviewer his speech style (via the MGT) varied from condition to condition. Thus, in one condition he maintained his mild WE accent in conversation with the RP interviewer (the no-shift condition), in another he modified his accent towards that of the interviewer (more RP-/less WE-like), and in yet another condition he broadened his WE accent (away from the interviewer). The interview order was balanced and yielded six experimental conditions. Since the two consecutive interviews were to be presented to each separate group of six respondents, the dialogue had to differ slightly in order to make the interviews interesting and plausible. The texts were, however, matched for duration, information content, vocabulary and grammar.

The results showed that the athlete was perceived as more intelligent when he shifted to RP than when he did not shift at all, and more intelligent in the latter case than when he broadened his WE accent. However, this accommodation to the RP interviewer also involved a decrease in perceived trustworthiness and kindheartedness relative to the no-shift condition. The shift to more WE-sounding with the RP interviewer (although associated with diminished estimates of intelligence) resulted in the athlete's being rated as more trustworthy and kindhearted than in any other stimulus condition.

Hence, it is very likely that maintaining or emphasising one's perceived nationality by means of accent in the kind of intergroup situation outlined above is a valued tactic asserting cultural identity. This interpretation is, of course, inferential, yet we are fairly confident that national (rather than, say, regional or class-based) affiliations were at issue here on the basis of post-experimental discussions with the informants involved. A follow-up study by Bourhis (1977) also points to social benefits which can accrue for the accentuation of WE usage — at least in the minds of third-party in-group observers.

In this study, Anglo-Welsh listeners rated a dialogue sequence involving two south Welsh accented 'suspects' who were supposedly being interrogated by an RP-accented English 'policeman' in an enactment of the so-called Prisoner's Dilemma simulation (or game, see Eiser, 1978). The same two Welsh-accented actors played the role of two suspects in different guises by either converging to the RP accent of the English policeman or by diverging from their interrogator by significantly accentuating their Welsh accent in English. Though the content of the interviews was kept the same across the different experimental conditions, Anglo-Welsh listeners' evaluations of the suspects differed depending on which accent strategy was adopted. Results showed that the suspects were rated more favourably on social attractiveness traits, and as more 'nationalistic' when they diverged away from rather than converged towards the policeman. However, as in the previously cited study, the converse was the case on competence-related scales. That notwithstanding, the suspects were rated as less guilty and worthy of a milder sentence when they diverged than when they converged during the interrogation. Taken in the intergroup setting of the day, these findings suggest that listeners were ready to 'punish' the suspect for having betrayed 'in-group solidarity' (by converging) and would have rewarded him for upholding his Welsh identity and integrity (by diverging) even in this threatening encounter.

Bourhis & Giles (1977a) devised an experiment to determine whether WE accent divergence would occur 'naturally' in an interactive setting. It was conducted in a language laboratory where there were two groups of people learning the Welsh language for the first time. One group — the so-called 'instrumental learners' — were taking this course during their work hours, it was being paid for by their employers, and allowed them better promotional prospects within Wales if they achieved a certain level of proficiency. On the basis of post-experimental data, it was ascertained that they did not value their Welshness nor the language very highly. The other group — our so-called 'integrative' learners (Gardner & Lambert, 1972) — were taking essentially the same course but in the evening on their own time, paying the fees themselves, and decidedly valued their Welshness and the language as an expression of this; by taking this course they were aiming to get closer to their cultural roots.

What we considered their 'baseline' speech was obtained from both groups in the language laboratory setting, representing the Welsh accents they had in their English 'normally' in these sessions. More specifically, the course director asked them to tell him via their microphones in their individual cubicles what they had done the previous weekend. This (baseline elicitation procedure) was accomplished ostensibly so as to see whether all the equipment was operative. Then learners were asked to help in a survey concerned with second language acquisition. The questions were presented to each of them over their headphones and their replies tape-recorded. The researcher, they were told, unfortunately could not be present but had sent ahead an audio-tape of his questions to which they could respond. This researcher possessed an RP accent and first of all asked them ('neutral') questions about their second language learning experiences. After they had responded, he introduced some questions in what can be termed a 'threat' condition, wherein he arrogantly challenged their reasons for what he called a 'dying language with a dismal future'. At the same time, he talked in terms of group divides ('us' versus 'them') as well as admitting that he was from an English university.

It was expected that in the neutral condition, the less ethnically-involved instrumental learners would converge towards RP as is typical in much previous research (see Giles, Mulac, Bradac & Johnson, 1987). This they did significantly and they converged even more under the threat condition. After all, this was not too much of a threat *to them* as they virtually agreed with the English person's sentiments. This was not the case with the integrative learners, who maintained their Welsh accents in what to them was probably an intergroup encounter even under the neutral condition (cf. Tajfel *et al.*, 1971). In the final phase, this group diverged their Welsh accents significantly in reply. The shifts were measured by two independent and reliable raters who rated extracts from respondents' answers under the three conditions 'blind'; the judgemental dimension of relevance here is the global Welsh-English accented one. Some informants introduced Welsh words and phrases into their answers, while one woman did not reply for a while; silence could be construed as a strong form of communicative dissociation. Then she gently conjugated a quite obscene verb in Welsh into the microphone. To our knowledge this was the first reported empirical demonstration of accent divergence.

The role of accent as a marker of ethnicity was also underscored in an MGT study conducted by Bourhis, Giles & Tajfel (1973). They had three groups of south Welsh persons (from Pontypridd) listen to a series of speakers from Wales who were either using RP, a WE accent or speaking Welsh. The listener groups were: bilingual Welsh; Welsh-learners; and monolingual (English) Welsh-born people. They also differed predictably along other relevant dimensions, not least their sentiments regarding Welsh political autonomy and their views concerning the need for their children to learn Welsh. Interestingly, of these groups, it was the *learners* who self-reported having the most 'Welsh' in their accents when using English. In other words, it could be suggested from these data that a Welsh person is able to assert his/her Welsh identity by making an effort to learn the national tongue and uses the accent to emphasise this identity until such time as it can be replaced by the language itself.

Given the heterogeneity apparent between these three groups, it was ultimately surprising to find no evaluative divergences. Whether respondents could speak Welsh or not, or how Welsh they felt themselves to be, all groups upgraded the Welsh language speaker on most traits. Indeed, on many traits such as trustworthiness, friendliness and sociability, the mere possession of a Welsh accent appeared sufficient to secure for the speakers ratings as favourable as those accorded the Welsh-language speakers.[2] RP speakers were rated most highly on self-confidence as well as on traits of conservatism, snobbishness and arrogance. Note that the RP speaker was categorised as 'Welsh' and therefore we do not know whether he would have received more or less favourable ratings had he been deemed English.

The lack of between-group differences on the part of the raters is worthy of a brief further comment. Using multi-dimensional scaling procedures, Giles, Taylor & Bourhis (1977) examined the ethnic identity profiles of bilingual Welsh persons and their English-only-speaking (Anglo-Welsh) counterparts. Both groups considered themselves to be psychologically distant from each other. Indeed, the bilinguals felt closer to Welsh-speaking *English* persons than they did to (labels reflecting) the Anglo-Welsh subjects, while the English-only-speaking sample identified most closely with speakers of English and not with other Welsh persons. In another study, when ethnic identity was made contextually salient for Anglo-Welsh respondents (that is, by writing an essay about how Welsh identity had suffered through English domination), they still felt distant from Welsh bilinguals even though there was evidence of closer identification with Welsh political and cultural issues (Christian *et al.*, 1976). However, in a study which confrontively examined the values of Welsh bilingual and Anglo-Welsh informants, no differences whatsoever emerged (Johnson & Giles, 1982), a finding somewhat in line with the MGT results here. Perhaps, then, there is more of a need to establish psychological boundaries (and probably for quite different reasons for the different groups) than actually exist given the vast communalities (e.g. shared parliamentary, judicial, media, and educational systems) under which all Welsh persons have to operate.

Recently and relatedly, Louw-Potgieter & Giles (1987) have produced an analysis of intra-group relations where a two-dimensional space is located within which individuals can construe whether they want to be a member of the in-group or not, and whether they feel the elite/governing body of the group defines them in or out. The various psychological strategies that folk who are in the so-called 'incongruent' cells utilise to withstand the 'pulling-in' pressures when they want 'out' and the various 'pushing-in' tactics adopted to combat in-group disqualification may be usefully applied in the present WE context. For instance, it might be predicted that those English-only-speaking Welsh who felt they were not regarded as 'proper Welsh' by certain visible organisations might be more prone to accentuate their own WE in certain situations, and upgrade those who were heard also to do so on stimulus tape, far more than those who self-defined themselves more in 'British' than in 'Welsh' terms (cf. Mercer *et al.*, 1979). Furthermore, it could be hypothesised that those among the latter who felt nevertheless that they were vigorously other-defined as 'Welsh' would be most prone to accommodating RP habits and devaluing WE taped representatives. The original Louw-Potgieter & Giles (1987) framework derived from an analysis of Afrikaner identity in South Africa. The present WE context is arguably more complex to the extent that a WE accent can also define one into a socio-economic category as well as an ethnic one (Taylor & Giles, 1979). Balancing perceptions of ethnic identity and socio-economic status so as to attain appropriate social rewards in particular situations can be a sociolinguistically risky business and one that is worthy of far more empirical research. Furthermore, stressing one's WE accent in public can be an ambiguous cue (cf. Coupland, this volume) variously interpreted as signalling not only ethnicity and class location, but also, it is proposed here, sympathy and empathy, humour, informality, intimacy, surprise, pleasure or anger, and so on (see Brown & Fraser, 1979). Because we are given to shifting constantly along standardness continua with WE usage even within a single speaking situation (Coupland, 1984; 1985), we doubtless use WE in diverse manners so as to instil in others particular social images from moment to moment in ways that are hitherto underexplored.

Interestingly, an MGT study by Price *et al.* (1983) is in rather stark contrast with the Bourhis, Giles & Tajfel (1973) findings. This was conducted in Carmarthenshire, where there is a greater evidence of Welsh-speakers, not to mention Plaid Cymru representation, than in south-east Wales. Bilingual pre-adolescents were confronted with an RP, a (west Wales) WE and a Welsh-language speaker. It was found that the bilingual west Walian judges did not evaluatively discriminate between RP and the Welsh-language speaker but did denigrate the WE individual in terms of 'badness' and 'snobbishness'. The authors argued that perhaps WE, in the perception of the same bilinguals, is a 'linguistic no man's land' and that given the pre-eminence of English nationally and internationally it is best to be able to use (and value) the out-group prestige form as 'proficiently' as possible. As one bilingual informant from west Wales in another investigation put it

(Giles & Johnson, 1986: 107), 'it isn't necessary to speak in a Welsh accent to prove that you are Welsh. The ability to speak the language is more important.' While recognising that the methodological circumstances are grossly different, this finding is somewhat in contrast to the results of Bourhis, Giles & Tajfel (1973) where WE was judged on certain dimensions *as favourably* as the Welsh language. Future research must be sensitive to the different, and doubtless complex, set of conditions under which accent and language become relatively more and less valued as markers of cultural identity.

An innovative feature of the Price *et al.* study was the manipulation of the language of testing; half the respondents were provided their instructions and questionnaire in English, the other half in Welsh (see also, Gibbons, 1983). This variable had a profound effect on the dimensions along which the WE speaker was downgraded. When provided with an English-language set, WE was rated unfavourably on 'intelligence' relative to the other guises, but when the instructional set was the Welsh language, it was on the trait of 'selfishness' that WE suffered. The authors argued on the basis of a previously-cited study which elicited Welsh bilinguals' understanding of English peer values in addition to their own (Johnson & Giles, 1982), that '*intelligent*–unintelligent' was more salient in and associated with a materialistic, English value system whereas *hunanol* (Welsh for '*unselfish*-selfish') was more pertinent to a Welsh value system stressing solidarity and support. It would be interesting in future MGT studies to vary the *dialect* of testing to determine whether a WE instructional set had any appreciable effects on how you viewed different-accented speakers compared to an RP set. Recent work by Wiemann *et al.* (1986) has been examining different cultural groups' 'beliefs about talk'. People seem to differ in these regards to the extent that, for example, they tolerate silence, enjoy small talk, value talk for its affiliative advantages, and so on. It could well be that WE involves not only perhaps different discourse structures (cf., for example, Tannen, 1982) from, say, RP but also relates to a different belief structure about the value of talk which might be triggered by a WE instructional set.

It should be mentioned that, although ethnicity is commonly associated with Welsh-English relations within Wales, there is a substantial number of Black and Asian people in Wales, concentrated largely in certain urban areas. In other words, we must conceive of WE in a multicultural context. One particular community studied was the Cardiff West Indian community in the mid-1970s. In a series of investigations involving the audio-taped voices of 11-, 21- and 40-year-old second- and third-generation Cardiff immigrants, 75–80% were miscategorised as 'white' by Caucasian residents

(Bourhis & Giles, 1977b; Giles & Bourhis, 1975; 1976b). More particularly, they had accommodated local sociolinguistic habits by adopting a 'Cardiff' (WE) accent.

Our question, then, was how would white Cardiffians evaluate West Indians who had linguistically assimilated towards them, as well as others who manifest an RP accent? The study (Giles & Bourhis, 1976c) involved two male representatives of each of the following ethnic-accent categories: Cardiff-accented (working-class) whites; Cardiff-accented (working-class) West Indians; RP-accented (middle-class) West Indians; RP-accented (middle-class) whites; and West Indian-accented blacks. It is important to emphasise that the RP- and Cardiff-accented blacks were unanimously identified as 'whites' by an independent white sample. These ten speakers, who were reading a passage about American drug use, were randomly assigned a position on a stimulus tape. Lower-middle-class white 17-year-olds, who had moderate contact with blacks, were told that the study was concerned with forming impressions of folk from Cardiff. They were presented with minimal, neutral information about each of the speakers (together with their racial origins) in the form of a small booklet and asked to evaluate each of them on a series of 22 rating scales.

The first set of analyses examined listeners' reactions to the three categories of West Indian speakers. On some scales, the RP blacks were perceived more positively than the other two speaker categories: for instance, as more trustworthy, sociable, and likeable as colleagues. However, on 13 scales, a definite hierarchy emerged from whites' reactions. Once again, the RP speakers were rated more favourably (e.g. educated, intelligent, confident) but also (again) more conservative, snobbish, and arrogant. Yet on all the scales, it was the West Indian speakers who were rated more favourably than the Cardiff black speakers. Hence, those who had maintained or acquired their own ethnic styles were rated more favourably than those who had assimilated linguistically. Either Cardiff whites value authenticity in others or they lend the Cardiff accent a particularly low prestige. In this latter sense, Coupland (1988) has data which well attests to the low esteem in which this form of WE accent is held; indeed, for many it hardly even *sounds* 'Welsh-like'. The social problem for immigrants, who usually only have the opportunity linguistically to assimilate to local, lower-working-class speech, is that accommodation in some urban contexts for them may actually mean a *lowering* of their perceived status. In the terminology of accommodation theory, then, while West Indian accommodation could be described objectively as 'downward convergence', in terms of white listeners' definitions of the situation, such shifts *may* not be perceived as 'convergence' by them at all but rather, psychologically, as *downward divergence* towards a speech style from which local white Cardiffians strongly wish to dissociate themselves.

Another set of statistical analyses examined evaluations of target speakers who varied in terms of ethnicity (black versus white) and accent (Cardiff versus RP). It was found that, irrespective of ethnicity, RP speakers were rated higher on 18 scales. For example, such speakers were seen as more intelligent, proud, understanding and likeable as superiors, snobbish, etc. In addition, Cardiff accents were perceived as less fluent, unpleasant, and less appropriate for use at work and in commercial contexts (Bates, 1983). Significant interactions emerged on four scales such that RP blacks were evaluated as more sociable, friendly, understanding, and less likeable as subordinates than white RP speakers.

All of the above studies relate to individuals' *cognitions*. The question then arises as to whether the social connotations associated with WE usage are transferred from 'mere' mental judgements to actual behaviour when meeting representative speakers. Bourhis & Giles (1976) had a request put out over a tannoy system during the interval in theatre performances in Cardiff. In one case, the show was a film in English, and in the other a dramatic performance was on stage in the Welsh language. On different nights in each context, the request to help in an audience survey was voiced in either RP, mild WE, or broad WE; in the second context it was also voiced in Welsh. In fact, the guises were repeated on different nights to control for audience effects. It should be emphasised that the request was quite a demanding one as the questionnaires were known to be placed beyond the bar in the foyer. Hence, in order to comply audience members would probably have to forgo the opportunity for having a proper break and a drink. Interestingly, in the first study there was no difference between compliance with a mild WE accent and RP. However, the broad Welsh accent was three times less likely to gain co-operation than the other language varieties. A completely different profile emerged, in contrast, in the context of the Welsh-language dramas. Here, it was the Welsh-language request that was by far the most successful of the four guises. Indeed, it was ten times more so than the RP plea. The two WE varieties were quantitatively more successful than the RP; the mild variant did not quite attain a statistically significant superiority over it. In this context, then, and for these bilingual theatre-goers, any appearance of English (whether RP or WE) is not socially influential. Another apparent contradiction then emerges here when we compare these findings with those of Price *et al.* (1983). Yet the totally different regional and situational contexts as well as testing parameters may well account for such disparities in these sociolinguistic meanings.

The actual predictability of communicative behaviour on the basis of language attitudes must come by working with attitudes and behaviours defined at an equivalent level of specificity (Giles, Hewstone, Ryan & Johnson, 1988). Put another way, general attitudes towards WE can only really be expected to predict the amount of time spent speaking WE over, say, a week. It can have little predictive power when aligned with particular social situations, such as whether you will emphasise WE with your aunt. Hence, Ajzen & Fishbein (1980) put forward their theory of reasoned action which seems important for any consideration of when WE will be accentuated or attenuated, and why. Although it may not be useful to pursue the mathematical formulation in this context, suffice it to say that attitude-behaviour predictions are made partly on the basis of *expectancy-value* conceptualisations. More specifically, a speaker's attitude towards a communicative behaviour is a function of the beliefs about the consequences of performing a particular behaviour and the speaker's evaluations of these consequences. Hence, if our target speaker believes that there is a very strong likelihood that use of WE with her family is likely to engender familial warmth (and probably not irritation) and this is an outcome (together with related others) she welcomes, the intention to produce this speech style is high. Moreover, if she believes that the family actually expect her to speak in this manner and there are strong grounds for complying (e.g. she will be thought of as 'hoity-toity' and growing away from them by using, say, RP) then the behavioural intention will be in favour of using WE.

These are beliefs which are not normally tapped by traditional language attitude studies but we suggest that they should be afforded some consideration as we need to move away from generalised attitudes to specified situations. Indeed, how different people view the same social situations quite differently along a finite set of cognitive dimensions (Giles & Hewstone, 1982) and construe the norms variously operating in them (McKirnan & Hamayan, 1984) has recently been the fruit of some theoretical concern in ways that should be considered in our studies. Finally in this regard, we have not sought data regarding how speakers view their accent repertoires and their feelings about the flexible or inflexible command they have over their development. An RP-only speaking Welsh person who strongly regrets his inability to sound anything but non-WE is likely to find some communicative difficulties in certain situations if he does not attune his language and discourse (Coupland et al., 1988) to compensate for the sociolinguistic distance apparent (cf. Peng, 1974). Indeed, how we attribute motives for accent repertoires and their development may be an important constituent in language attitude (and thereby attribution) study.

A number of studies have utilised WE accents *outside* the principality not for their own sake, but, as originally envisaged, for their theoretical relevance in representing non-standard English regional speech generally (see, for example, Creber & Giles, 1983); that said, this begs the question of whether national versus regional versus class (etc.) identities were evoked when English listeners judged WE varieties (cf. Coupland, this volume). Most of these studies have been conducted in Bristol (some 20 miles from the English–Welsh border). Such studies are important for our purposes as they also allow us access to how outsiders construe WE speech patterns — an important socio-psychological force presumably in WE maintenance and change (cf. Trudgill, 1986) and probably even standardisation.

The Giles (1971b) study discussed earlier demonstrated that south-west English and south Welsh listeners had essentially the same views of RP versus WE. More recent studies, however, not only extend the traditional language attitudes paradigm in useful ways but also question the robustness of specific findings over a historical period of time.

The first of these, by Giles, Wilson & Conway (1981), examined the perceived job suitability of speakers with RP and WE accents. Different groups of Bristolian undergraduate listeners (from heterogeneous, regional English backgrounds) were provided with an audio extract from a supposed job interview. The candidate, by means of the MGT, spoke in either one of these accents and was rated for his suitability for seven different jobs rated independently as varying in perceived social prestige (e.g. from production control manager down to industrial plant cleaner). Even though the candidate said exactly the same thing in both conditions, he was rated as significantly more suitable for each of the top three positions when he spoke in RP than when he spoke WE, just as suitable for the middle-range job (foreman) when he used either, and far more suitable when he spoke WE than when he spoke RP when considered for each of the three lower positions. Again, then, outside Wales, the social power of WE is occupationally inferior (Kalin, 1982). Whether these findings would generalise to other kinds of job (e.g. in education) is contentious.

Two other traditional MGT studies are also of note as neither has been able to replicate the positive social attractiveness connotations of WE. Giles & Marsh (1979) had south-west English students rate male and female speakers of RP and WE on tape and a couple of sex-by-accent interactive findings emerged of note. On the scales of 'intelligence' and 'professional employability', being male or female with a WE accent had no evaluative significance. Both were rated less positively than a female RP speaker on these dimensions who in turn was judged less favourably than a male RP speaker. However, across the board the WE accent received no positive ratings relative to RP and hence no differences between them emerged on the more *humane* scales. Interestingly, the RP speakers were rated as more egalitarian and pro-feminist than the WE-accented speakers perhaps because such ideological parameters are associated with higher educational involvements.

Another study by Brown *et al.* (1985) also told the same story, although this time it was even more evaluatively dismal for WE. In this factorial study, accent (RP versus WE) was varied along with speech rate (slow, medium and fast) and context (either a read monologue or an extract from a more interactive setting). It was found that the WE speaker was rated as *less* intelligent, ambitious, active, happy, just and good-looking than the RP one. Only on one trait was the former upgraded, namely on the trait of 'religiousness', which was negatively associated with perceived competence. For the Welsh-accented voices in the dialogue context, there was some decrease in perceived competence as one moved from a fast to a medium speech rate, but very little further decrease emerged as one went on to a slow rate. Indeed, there were greater differences overall between RP and WE under the dialogue than under the monologue conditions. In this vein, another study has found that the opportunity to discuss the taped speaker with other listeners present will induce the individual rater to polarise his/ her ratings between RP and WE as compared with a (control) condition where informants are asked to contemplate further their impressions for an equivalent time period (Giles, Harrison, Creber, Smith & Freeman, 1983).

Although, sadly, there are almost no media analyses of WE accent usage inside or outside Wales (though see Coupland, 1988), it would seem that the variety has not only low social status but low institutional support (Giles, Bourhis & Taylor, 1977). Although there are some WE-accented national and international sportspersons, politicians, and entertainers on our airwaves, they are arguably cumulatively of less prominence and influence than other English regional varieties certainly in the pan-UK media. In sum, WE, despite its doubtless high demographic profile (yet probably high perceived heterogeneity), likely has overall low *perceived* 'vitality' (cf. Young *et al.*, 1986). According to aspects of ethnolinguistic identity theory (Giles & Johnson, 1987), this probably does little to maintain the variety's survival when other Welsh people decry its identity value in a period of rapid technological and communications change. That said, the variety of evaluative profiles emerging for WE from the studies overviewed above suggests that any speculation about the perceived vitality of WE must be tempered with extreme caution; necessarily, vitality will be a function of time, place and elicitation procedure.

Yet, it may well be that Welsh people outside Wales *do* accentuate their WE features in ways that have functional value for them and have not been alluded to in the above investigations. A myriad of interrelated and

complex motives may arise in such situations including the desire to dissociate
from upper-class and 'yuppie' images; the wish to underscore an assertive,
macho image with Welsh connotations of rugby and beer or alternatively a
more gentle musical propensity in choral situations, trading off diverse
national stereotypes; a sense of solidarity with trade union or socialistic
principles; a unique sense of personal and cultural differentiation in the
midst of a homogeneously-perceived, alien backdrop; and the desire to
remove oneself psychologically from occasions of guilt by association when
matters of British imperialism, oppression, or economic vitality are
conversationally rife. Whether the linguistic and discourse markers in these
differential cases will be identical is a moot point. My guess is that they will
vary in significant yet subtle ways if they are to be effective in fulfilling the
encoder's self-presentational needs (Baumeister, 1982). In this vein, it is
worth pointing out that the processing of speech styles is likely on occasion
to bring to light complex social images involving causal networks, account
systems, and interrelated belief systems in a manner not at all touched by
traditional MGT studies. The social psychological literature on 'social
representations' (Moscovici & Farr, 1983) is likely to yield an important
reservoir of theoretical ideas relevant to our understanding of the complex
social meanings associated with decoding WE. Indeed, the other side of the
coin, namely the discernible option of a non-RP stance having been taken
in certain situations wherein RP should have been normative, may also be
an important element in forming impressions of others (cf. Jaccard, 1981).
However, it is important to point out that the social meanings of WE not
only influence listeners' evaluations of speakers of it but also mediate the
latter's options in constantly monitored self-presentation as well (Giles &
Street, 1985).

Another instructive feature of the Brown *et al.* study is that speech
rate is evaluatively more important than accent under these experimental
conditions for these listener-judges. Hence, while the focus of this volume
is obviously on WE, we must be wary of exaggerating its importance relative
to other vocal cues. Indeed, one obvious characteristic in this regard is the
actual content of the message, and it is to this we now turn.

It is important to point out that the judged quality of a message is,
partly at least, a socio-psychological process. Giles (1973) tested over 500
south Welsh high-school pupils for their attitudes towards capital punishment
(they were rather in favour, as it happened) and found them to be stable
over a period of a week. On the basis of their scores, six groups of 50
subjects each matched for sex and attitude were obtained. These individuals
were told at a subsequent session that various views about capital punishment
had been recorded by the investigator and that he would value their opinions

about some of these views. Each group was provided with such views, one of them being in the form of typescript. The other five had the same content (anti-capital punishment) but were provided to the different groups via the MGT in RP, WE, Somerset and Birmingham (that is, accented speech varying in perceived prestige). The respondents were asked for two things: their assessment of the quality of the argument propounded, and their own views regarding capital punishment at that moment. It was found that there was a direct and negative linear relationship between accent prestige and the rated quality of the argument. Interestingly, the typescript message was rated as superior to the RP version. In contrast, however, and having examined their pre- and post-tape views about capital punishment, these were the only conditions *not* to produce an opinion change; there were no differences in the persuasive appeal of the non-standard guises. In other words, the WE version was rated significantly poorer in quality than the RP version, yet nevertheless *more persuasive*. The finding that WE was just as effective as the English regional guises accords well with the findings of Giles (1971b) where no evaluative difference emerged between WE and Somerset on the integrity and social attractiveness scales. That said, it is intriguing that on such dimensions there appears no evidence yet of a judgemental hierarchy for different language varieties; future research sensitive to this possibility across a wider range of affective measures may, however, uncover such a pattern.

The dramatic differences which emerged in mean responses between conditions serve to underscore the old adage 'it's not what you say but how you say it'. This is also illustrated in a study on ethnic humour by Gadfield, Giles, Bourhis & Tajfel (1979). They had south-west Welsh informants listen to a joke told by a person (using the MGT) in RP or in a WE accent. The joke was of such a nature that its butt could be changed so that the humour was anti-Welsh or anti-English. A third factor introduced into the study was whether Welsh–English relations were salient or not at the time of testing. Hence, before hearing the tape-recorded joke incident, half the subjects (older adolescents) had to write an essay describing 'the ways in which the Welsh way of life has suffered through English domination over the last 100 years or so', while the other half wrote on 'the ways in which the environmental balance has suffered through industrial intervention over the last 100 years or so'. Akin to the findings of Chapman et al. (1977) with young bilingual children, the Anglo-Welsh were not appreciative of anti-in-group humour under any circumstances. However, the rated funniness of the anti-out-group joke depended on the accent used and salience of ethnic relations. When the latter was low (that is, the subjects had written the environmental essay), then the anti-English joke was rated funnier when told in WE, yet when ethnic salience was high, that same joke was judged funnier when it was delivered in an RP accent. As the authors remarked, it could have been that when conflictual relations between groups are made apparent, a derisory attack on the out-group is obvious and ineffectual. But when that group attacks itself verbally it may be particularly pleasing as it gives an indication of its being in disarray.

Content, like accent itself (Spencer, 1958), can often be more in the mind of the hearer than the speaker. Nevertheless, a couple of studies conducted in west Wales by Giles & Johnson (1986) suggest that objective content is of fundamental importance in ways that the entire language attitudes literature has thus far neglected. Their first study required bilingual adolescents to be involved with a study on language planning policy. First of all, they were to listen to an audio-taped speaker on the subject of bilingualism, form an impression of him on the usual rating scales, and anticipate what kinds of language behaviour they would use were they to discuss these matters with him further. The anticipated linguistic strategy scales consisted of three 10 cm lines labelled bipolarly as 'Welsh accented – BBC English accented'; 'Welsh language 100% – English language 100%'; 'Many Welsh words and sayings – few Welsh words and sayings'. This speaker was known to be either English or Welsh (as also evident from his WE and RP accents respectively produced by the MGT) and he was known to be either sympathetic or antithetic to bilingual education in Wales. The actual content of the taped message, however, related to bilingualism in Quebec as a preparatory introductory for his consideration of the Welsh case.

Overall, the anticipated linguistic strategies were more a function of the speaker's accentedness and perceived status than his known attitudes. Informants would be prepared to attenuate their distinctive ethnic markers by using less of a Welsh accent and fewer Welsh words and phrases with the RP than with the WE speaker. Nevertheless, there was an apparent awareness of his attitudes from a number of the interactive effects; for example, they found the supportive WE speaker most ingratiating and the supportive RP most co-operative.

The study was replicated with a view to it being less contextually status-stressing (Day, 1982) and more ethnically threatening (cf. Gallois et al., 1984). Older bilingual adolescents who were highly committed to Welsh ethnolinguistic ideals were used and this time the views of the speaker (for or against bilingual education in Wales) were made very explicit indeed and the taped message this time discussed the pros and cons of these Welsh issues in a balanced manner. In this study, as with the previous one, respondents made their ratings twice; once after hearing the tape and a second time after discussing the issues with other peers present. Mention of it is included on this particular occasion as it had a more significant effect on ratings.

It was found that after an initial (individual) listening to the stimulus speaker, the ethnically-threatening target would be the recipient of more anticipated Welsh language (particularly by males) than the more supportive target, irrespective of cultural group membership. After group discussion, however, the accent of this target did have an important effect. The threatening RP speaker was to then receive the most Welsh, followed next by the WE of both persuasions, followed last by the supportive RP speaker. This time the Welsh accent, words and phrases were rated as inconsequential as from comments made by participants it was the language that was required to mark their displeasure and strong sense of cultural identity. Regarding personality attributions levied at the targets, it was again the content of what he said that determined attitudinal reactions rather than his ethnic group membership as evident from his WE or RP accent. In this case, supportive speakers, for example, were seen as more intelligent, sincere, kind and less hostile than threatening speakers. This study then reminds us — like Brown *et al.* (1985) before it — that vocal and verbal dimensions other than accent affect our impressions of others. An external criterion such as accent is only one of an array of cues that are processed to attribute ethnic loyalty and identification to Welsh people. As such, we should not overestimate its theoretical importance.

Epilogue

A complex picture emerges wherein WE varieties are downgraded on competence traits generally but upgraded on those of social attractiveness within Wales. While the accentuation of a WE brogue may be appreciated in some contexts for its identity-stressing values, in others it has little compliance value for the English-only-speaking Welsh or for bilinguals. Indeed, this is particularly so when the message content is ethnically involving and threatening. That said, for Welsh-language learners in particular, a WE accent can have significant promise for reflecting in-group cultural solidarity. Yet, a WE accent can also be a cue to socio-economic status as implied above (as well as reflecting other emotional states, situational and relational definitions) and inferences of job suitability and ideology ensue as a consequence.

An important task ahead of us is to build on the above, admittedly rather piecemeal, beginnings in a more programmatic fashion than hitherto. We need to elucidate more precisely the roles of the myriad variables that impinge upon the social meanings of WE and a key issue here must be the delimitation of perceptual varieties; this variation alone may account for much of the complexity of the findings. Indeed, as I have noted many times before, the language attitudes literature as a whole is replete with one-off studies. Elsewhere and with colleagues I have proposed methodological (Giles & Ryan, 1982), empirical (Giles, Hewstone & Ball, 1983), and conceptual and theoretical (Ryan, Hewstone & Giles, 1984; Ryan, Giles & Sebastian, 1982) refinements not only for this research domain but also with respect to the way language attitudes mediate interpersonal and intercultural communication (Giles & Johnson, 1987; Giles & Street, 1985; Giles & Wiemann, 1987). Moreover, and especially in the latter concerns, there are other important models available to sharpen our approach (e.g., Coupland, 1988; Graumann & Hermann, 1987; Kraut & Higgins, 1984; Street & Cappella, 1985; Young & Gudykunst, 1988). Indeed, there may be some mileage and allure in outlining the implications of these proposals for the further study of WE. However, I have resisted this, believing there may be a distinct danger in sprinting before we can toddle. Certainly, we would wish to encourage more researchers to delve into our sociolinguistic context for the betterment of scholarship. On the other hand, we have adequate cognisance of relevant socio-psychological variables and processes not to pursue basic descriptive work in a blinkered fashion.

It seems to me that the next significant volume on Welsh English ought, within its wide interdisciplinary purview, focally to address a number of socio-psychological issues. First, using perhaps the descriptive data derived from other chapters herein and elsewhere, we should understand what WE varieties from around Wales are perceptually discriminable to whom (inside and outside Wales). Are, for instance, south Walians sensitive to different north Welsh varieties and what kinds of social inference derive from such categorisations? By judicious and imaginative use of multi-dimensional scaling procedures with taped extracts we can provide cognitive maps of what is perceived where and how, maps that are potentially as useful as those that geolinguists such as Williams (1979; this volume) and Cartwright (1987) have produced with demographic data on Welsh-language usage. Individuals' maps charting the complexity and diversity of these perceptions can then be related to cognitive and more social variables as well as ascertaining which, if any, WE varieties are considered more 'standard' than others, and by whom (cf. Coupland, this volume).

The second issue which could be addressed is under what social circumstances we ascribe particular WE uses to ethnic, class, and regional identity, on the one hand, and to anxious and emotional states under other conditions, on the other. This would require a sensitive series of case studies following through speakers' own feelings and cognitions post-speaking under playback conditions as well as others' views of their states and intentions as observers. Furthermore, the use of more interpretative work and more interview-based approaches would be a very useful complement. Such an enterprise would also allow us access to when other features of voice and content assume more salience than say, accent.

Third, what forms of discourse structure, topic selections, and non-verbal behaviours are, if at all, peculiar to intragroup WE conversations? What are people's beliefs about the value of talk and the modes in which it can be most profitably followed? What values appear to emerge as central when WE forms are utilised? In this sense, social network analyses (of the type recently described innovatively by Bourhis (1987) in the work-place) would allow us insight into when and with whom WE varieties are used and valued.

Fourth, how do Welsh speakers and different kinds of non-Welsh speakers (cf. Jones, this volume) value WE and for what purposes? How are RP and various approximations to it valued in what contexts? Various measures of ethnic *and class* identification, vitality, and ethnic boundary (Giles & Johnson, 1987) and views about cultural maintenance and socio-political relationships (Berry, 1984) with other Britons might be usefully explored in this direction as might the contextual (social and discourse) conditions under which different forms of WE are attenuated and accentuated. As above, speakers' value expectancies might be profitably pursued in support of these goals.

Finally and relatedly, Welsh people's knowledge and views about their cultural history and contemporary events may form an important backdrop to the foregoing. For instance, the studies reviewed in this chapter were conducted at different times and against fluctuating socio-political conditions that may have had a distinct impact on the findings emerging (Bourhis, Giles and Tajfel, 1973; Giles & Marsh, 1979). Hence, following through language attitudes longitudinally and cross-sectionally with different age groups while monitoring in tandem media events, WE media personalities, media use of WE for different realms of discourse, and people's appraisals of these, would be essential in any assessment of future trends in standardisation and the evolution of WE varieties.

The foregoing is obviously a biased selection of empirical questions and others might be just as important and suit other theoretical and ideological tastes. Moreover, it does involve some costs in terms of casting aside disciplinary loyalties and questioning older assumptions. Interdisciplinary research for the future is essential if we are to give the study of WE the academic status it deserves. Indeed, the mere appearance of this volume and the attention it might attract scholastically in Wales and elsewhere is also likely to infuse it with added vitality and interest.

Notes to Chapter 16

1. I am most grateful to Nik Coupland for his thorough and critical reading of previous drafts of this chapter.
2. Similar findings have recently been found in a matched-guise study in progress with modest samples in *north* Wales (Elena McCretton & Peter Garrett, personal comunication). Preliminary analyses suggest that bilingual sixth-formers from the Bangor area attending a Welsh-medium school rated 'North Welsh-accented' English on a series of mostly solidarity-like traits as favourably as the north Welsh-Welsh translated guise, both of which were rated evaluatively superior to the RP guise; the standard English speaker, however, was judged most favourably in terms of perceived intelligence. Interestingly, English-only-speaking sixth-formers from Anglesey attending an English-medium school also conceded 'intelligence' to this RP speaker, but they, too, downgraded the guise on the remaining eight scales in relation to the north Welsh-accented English guise; on these latter scales, no evaluative differences emerged between the RP speaker and the north Welsh language speakers.

References

AGHEYISI, R. and FISHMAN, J.A. 1970, Language attitude studies: A brief survey of methodological approaches. *Anthropological Linguistics*, 12: 131–57.

AJZEN, I. and FISHBEIN, M. 1980, *Understanding Attitudes and Predicting Social Behaviour*. Englewood Cliffs, NJ: Prentice Hall.

BATES, S. 1983, Attitudes towards Cardiff-accented speech: Some social and educational implications. Unpublished Master's dissertation: University of Wales.

BAUMEISTER, R.F. 1982, A self-presentation view of social phenomena. *Psychological Bulletin*, 91: 3–26.

BERRY, J.W. 1984, Multicultural policy in Canada: A social psychological analysis. *Canadian Journal of Behavioural Science*, 16: 353–70.

BOURHIS, R.Y. 1977, Language and social evaluation in Wales. Unpublished PhD thesis, University of Bristol.

——1987, Linguistic work environments and language use in bilingual settings. Paper delivered at the Second World Basque Congress, San Sebastián, August.

BOURHIS, R.Y. and GILES, H. 1976, The language of cooperation in Wales: A field study. *Language Sciences*, 42: 13–16.

——1977a, The language of intergroup distinctiveness. In H. GILES (ed.), *Language, Ethnicity and Intergroup Relations*. London: Academic Press.

——1977b, Children's voices and ethnic categorization in Britain. *La Monda Linguo-Problemo*, 6: 85–94.

BOURHIS, R.Y., GILES, H. and LAMBERT, W.E. 1975, Social consequences of accommodating one's style of speech: A cross-national investigation. *International Journal of the Sociology of Language*, 6: 55–72.

BOURHIS, R.Y., GILES, H. and TAJFEL, H. 1973, Language as a determinant of Welsh identity. *European Journal of Social Psychology*, 3: 447–60.

BROWN, B.L., GILES, H. and THAKERAR, J.N. 1985, Speaker evaluations as a function of speech rate, accent and context. *Language and Communication*, 5: 207–22.

BROWN, P. and FRASER, C. 1979, Speech as a marker of situation. In K.R. SCHERER and H. GILES (eds), *Social Markers in Speech*. Cambridge: Cambridge University Press.

CARTWRIGHT, D. 1987, Geolinguistics in the context of status language planning. Paper delivered at the Second World Basque Congress, San Sebastián, August.

CHAPMAN, A.J., FOOT, H.C. and SMITH, J.R. 1977, Language and humour in intergroup relations. In H. GILES (ed.), *Language, Ethnicity and Intergroup Relations*. London: Academic Press.

CHRISTIAN, J., GADFIELD, N., GILES, H. and TAYLOR, D.M. 1976, The multidimensional and dynamic nature of ethnic identity. *International Journal of Psychology*, 11: 281–91.

COUPLAND, N. 1984, Accommodation at work: Some phonological data and their implications. *International Journal of the Sociology of Language*, 46: 49–70.

——1985, Hark, hark the lark: Social motivations for phonological style-shifting. *Language and Communication*, 5, 3: 153–71.

——1988, *Dialect in Use: Sociolinguistic Variation in Cardiff English*. Cardiff: University of Wales Press.

COUPLAND, N., COUPLAND, J., GILES, H. and HENWOOD, J. 1988, Accommodating the elderly: Invoking and extending a theory. *Language in Society*, 17: 1–41.

CREBER, C. and GILES, H. 1983, Social context and language attitudes: The role of formality–informality of the setting. *Language Sciences*, 5: 155–62.

DAY, R. 1982, Children's attitude toward language. In E.B. RYAN and H. GILES (eds), *Attitudes toward Language Variation: Social and Applied Contexts*. London: Edward Arnold.

EISER, J.R. 1978, Interpersonal cooperation and competition. In H. TAJFEL and C. FRASER (eds), *Introducing Social Psychology*. Harmondsworth: Penguin.

GADFIELD, N., GILES, H., BOURHIS, R.Y. and TAJFEL, H. 1979, Dynamics of humour in ethnic group relations. *Ethnicity*, 6: 373–82.

GALLOIS, C., CALLAN, V.J. and JOHNSTONE, M. 1984, Personality judgements of Australian aborigine and white speakers: Ethnicity, sex and context. *Journal of Language and Social Psychology*, 3: 39–58.

GARDNER, R.C. and LAMBERT, W.E. 1972, *Attitudes and Motivation in Second-Language Learning*. Rowley, MA: Newbury House.

GIBBONS, J. 1983, Attitudes towards languages and code-mixing in Hong Kong. *Journal of Multilingual and Multicultural Development*, 4: 129–48.

GILES, H. 1970, Evaluative reactions to accents. *Educational Review*, 22: 211–27.

——1971a, Ethnocentrism and the evaluation of accented speech. *British Journal of Social and Clinical Psychology*, 10: 187–88.

——1971b, Patterns of evaluation in reactions to R.P., South Welsh and Somerset accented speech. *British Journal of Social and Clinical Psychology*, 10: 280–81.

——1972, The effect of stimulus mildness–broadness in the evaluation of accents. *Language and Speech*, 15: 262–69.

——1973, Communicative effectiveness as a function of accented speech. *Speech Monographs*, 40: 330–31.

——(ed.) 1984, The dynamics of speech accommodation. *International Journal of the Sociology of Language*, 46.

GILES, H. and BOURHIS, R.Y. 1975, Linguistic assimilation: West Indians in Cardiff. *Language Sciences*, 38: 9–12.

——1976a, Methodological issues in dialect perception. *Anthropological Linguistics*, 19: 294–304.

——1976b, Voice and racial categorization in Britain. *Communication Monographs*, 43: 108–14.

——1976c, Black speakers with white speech — a real problem? In G. NICKEL (ed.), *Proceedings of the 4th International Congress on Applied Linguistics, Vol. 1*. Stuttgart: Hochschul-Verlag.

GILES, H., BOURHIS, R.Y. and TAYLOR, D.M. 1977, Towards a theory of language in ethnic group relations. In H. GILES (ed.), *Language, Ethnicity and Intergroup Relations*. London: Academic Press.

GILES, H., HARRISON, C., CREBER, C., SMITH, P.M. and FREEMAN, N.H. 1983, Developmental and contextual aspects of British children's language attitudes. *Language and Communication*, 3: 1–6.

GILES, H. and HEWSTONE, M. 1982, Cognitive structures, speech and social situations: Two integrative models. *Language Sciences*, 4: 187–219.

GILES, H., HEWSTONE, M. and BALL, P. 1983, Language attitudes in multilingual settings: Prologue and priorities. *Journal of Multilingual and Multicultural Development*, 4: 81–100.

GILES, H., HEWSTONE, M., RYAN, E.B. and JOHNSON, P. 1988, Research in language attitudes. In U. AMMON, N. DITTMAR and K.J. MATTHEIER (eds), *Sociolinguistics: An Interdisciplinary Handbook of the Science of Language*, Vol. 1. Berlin: de Gruyter.

GILES, H. and JOHNSON, P. 1986, Perceived threat, ethnic commitment, and inter-ethnic language behaviour. In Y. KIM (ed.), *Interethnic Communication: Recent Research*. Newbury Park, CA: Sage.

——1987, Ethnolinguistic identity theory: A social psychological approach to language maintenance. *International Journal of the Sociology of Language*, 68: 69–99.

GILES, H. and MARSH, P. 1979, Perceived masculinity and accented speech. *Language Sciences*, 1: 301–05.

GILES, H., MULAC, A., BRADAC, J.J. and JOHNSON, P. 1987, Speech accommodation theory: The next decade and beyond. In M. McLAUGHLIN (ed.), *Communication Yearbook 10*. Newbury Park, CA: Sage.

GILES, H. and RYAN, E.B. 1982, Prolegomena for developing a social psychological theory for language attitudes. In E.B. RYAN and H. GILES (eds), *Attitudes toward Language Variation: Social and Applied Contexts*. London: Edward Arnold.

GILES, H. and STREET, R.L. JR. 1985, Communicator characteristics and behaviour: A review, generalisations, and model. In M. KNAPP and G. MILLER (eds), *The Handbook of Interpersonal Communication*. Beverly Hills, CA: Sage.

GILES, H., TAYLOR, D.M. and BOURHIS, R.Y. 1977, Dimensions of Welsh identity. *European Journal of Social Psychology*, 7: 29–39.

GILES, H. and WIEMANN, J. 1987, Language, social comparison and power. In S. CHAFFEE and C.R. BERGER (eds), *The Handbook of Communication*. Newbury Park, CA: Sage.

GILES, H., WILSON, P. and CONWAY, A. 1981, Accent and lexical diversity as determinants of impression formation and employment selection. *Language Sciences*, 3: 92–103.

GRAUMANN, C.F. and HERMANN, T. (eds) 1988, Other relatedness in language processing. *Journal of Language and Social Psychology*, 6 (3–4).

JACCARD, J. 1981, Attitudes and behaviour: Implications of attitudes toward behavioural alternatives. *Journal of Experimental Social Psychology*, 17, 286–307.

JOHNSON, P. and GILES, H. 1982, Values, language and intercultural differentiation: The Welsh-English context. *Journal of Multilingual and Multicultural Development*, 3: 103–16.

KALIN, R. 1982, The social significance of speech in medical, legal and occupational settings. In E.B. RYAN and H. GILES (eds), *Attitudes toward Language Variation: Social and Applied Contexts*. London: Edward Arnold.

KRAUT, R.C. and HIGGINS, E.T. 1984, Communication and social cognition. In R.S. WYER and T.K. SRULL (eds), *Handbook of Social Cognition, Vol. 3*. Hillsdale, NJ: Lawrence Erlbaum.

LAMBERT, W.E. 1967, The social psychology of bilingualism. *Journal of Social Issues*, 23: 91–109.

LEWIS, E.G. 1975, Attitude toward language among bilingual children and adults in Wales. *International Journal of the Sociology of Language*, 4: 103–21.

LOUW-POTGIETER, J. and GILES, H. 1987, Imposed identity and linguistic strategies. *Journal of Language and Social Psychology*, 6, 261–86.

McKIRNAN, D.J. and HAMAYAN, E.V. 1984, Speech norms and attitudes toward outgroup members: A test of a model in a bicultural context. *Journal of Language and Social Psychology*, 3: 21–38.

MERCER, N., MERCER, E. and MEARS, R. 1979, Linguistic and cultural affiliation among young Asian people in Leicester. In H. GILES and B. SAINT-JACQUES (eds), *Language and Ethnic Relations*. Oxford: Pergamon.

MOSCOVICI, S. and FARR, R. (eds) 1983, *Social Representations*. Cambridge: Cambridge University Press.

PENG, F.C.C. 1974, Communicative distance. *Language Sciences*, 31: 32–38.

PRICE, S., FLUCK, M. and GILES, H. 1983, The effects of language of testing on bilingual preadolescents' attitudes towards Welsh and varieties of English. *Journal of Multilingual and Multicultural Development*, 4: 149–61.

RYAN, E.B., GILES, H. and SEBASTIAN, R.J. 1982, An integrative perspective for the study of attitudes towards language variation. In E.B. RYAN and H. GILES (eds), *Attitudes toward Language Variation: Social and Applied Contexts*. London: Edward Arnold.

RYAN, E.B., HEWSTONE, M. and GILES, H. 1984, Language and intergroup attitudes. In J.R. EISER (ed.), *Attitudinal Judgement*. New York: Springer Verlag.

SHARP, D., THOMAS, B., PRICE, E., FRANCIS, G. and DAVIES, I. 1973, *Attitudes to Welsh and English in the Schools of Wales*. London: Macmillan Educational.

SPENCER, J. 1958, R.P. — some problems of interpretation. *Lingua*, 7: 7–29.

STREET, R.L. JR, and CAPELLA, J.N. (eds) 1985, *Sequence and Pattern in Communicative Behaviour*. London: Edward Arnold.

TAJFEL, H. 1959, A Note on Lambert's 'Evaluational reactions to spoken language'. *Canadian Journal of Psychology*, 13: 86–92.

TAJFEL, H., FLAMENT, C., BILLIG, M.G. and BUNDY, R.F. 1971, Social categorization and intergroup behaviour. *European Journal of Social Psychology*, 1, 149–77.

TANNEN, D. 1982, Ethnic style in male–female conversation. In J.J. GUMPERZ (ed.), *Language and Social Identity*. Cambridge: Cambridge University Press.

TAYLOR, D.M. and GILES, H. 1979, At the crossroads of research into language and ethnic relations. In H. GILES and B. SAINT-JACQUES (eds), *Language and Ethnic Relations*. Oxford: Pergamon.

TRUDGILL, P. 1986, *Dialects in Contact*. Oxford: Blackwell.

WIEMANN, J., CHEN, V. and GILES, H. 1986, Beliefs about talk in cultural context. Top 3 Paper in the Intercultural Division of the Annual Speech Communication Association Convention, Chicago, November.

WILLIAMS, C.H. 1979, An ecological and behavioural analysis of ethnolinguistic change in Wales. In H. GILES and B. SAINT-JACQUES (eds), *Language and Ethnic Relations*. Oxford: Pergamon.

YOUNG, L., GILES, H. and PIERSON, H. 1986, Sociopolitical change and perceived vitality. *International Journal of Intercultural Relations*, 10: 459–69.

YOUNG, Y. and GUDYKUNST, W.B. (eds) 1988, *Theories in Intercultural Communication*. Newbury Park, CA: Sage.

List of Contributors

Beverley Collins was born in Cardiff and educated at University College Cardiff and University College London. Formerly lecturer in phonetics at Lancaster University, he has, since 1975, been a lecturer in English at the University of Leiden in Holland. He has published (with Inger Mees) *The Sounds of English and Dutch* and books on English pronunciation for Dutch and Danish students. His main interests are contrastive phonetics, sociophonetic dialectology and historiography of phonetics. He has just completed part of a biography of the British phonetician, Daniel Jones.

John Connolly holds the post of lecturer in the Department of Computer Studies at Loughborough University of Technology. He has a broad range of interests in the study of human speech and language, and in the application of linguistics and phonetics to the design of computer-based technology. He has previously written on the subjects of south Wales English, functional grammar, diachronic syntax, computational linguistics, automatic speech recognition, and language disability.

Nikolas Coupland was born in 1950 in Carmarthen, Dyfed, where he lived until 1969. He is founding director of the Centre for Applied English Language Studies at the University of Wales College of Cardiff (and formerly UWIST), where he has lectured since 1979. His other book-publications are *Dialect in Use: Sociolinguistic Variation in Cardiff English*, and the edited collection *Styles of Discourse*. Forthcoming (co-authored or co-edited) books include *Sociolinguistics and Style*, *Problem Talk in Context: A Handbook of Miscommunication*, *Contexts of Accommodation*, and *Communication, Health and Ageing*, reflecting current interests in applied sociolinguistics, dialectology, discourse analysis and gerontology. From 1989 to 1990, he is Visiting Professor and Fulbright Scholar at the University of California, Santa Barbara.

Howard Giles is Professor of Social Psychology and Director of the Centre for Communication and Social Relations at the University of Bristol, England. He is an Editor of both the *Journal of Language and Social*

Psychology and *Journal of Asian Pacific Communication* as well as General Editor of two Multilingual Matters book series. His research interests include language attitudes, intergroup communication (particularly between ethnic and age groupings), and second language acquisition.

Bob Morris Jones is Senior Research Associate within the Faculty of Education, University College of Wales, Aberystwyth. He is concerned with the presentation of language studies which are relevant to education in relation to second/foreign language teaching, mother tongue teaching and teaching across the curriculum. His main recent research interest has been the language of primary school children, both from the point of sentence-grammar and discourse analysis. He has published several articles and papers, including: *The Welsh Language* (with A.R. Thomas), *Agweddau ar Ystyron a Phatrymau Iaith Plant Pump Oed* (Aspects of the Meanings and Patterns of the Language of Five Year Olds) and *The Present Condition of the Welsh Language.*

Jack Windsor Lewis is Lecturer in the Department of Linguistics and Phonetics at the University of Leeds. His principal interests are forms of spoken English (worldwide), notably prosodic features and EFL. Major publications include: *A Guide to English Pronunciation, Oxford Advanced Learner's Dictionary of Current English* (with A.S. Hornby, etc.), *Concise Pronouncing Dictionary of British & American English* and *People Speaking: Phonetic Readings in Current English.* He is a life member of the International Phonetic Association and was elected to their governing Council in 1985.

Inger M. Mees was born in France in 1953. She read English at the University of Leiden, Holland, where she became a lecturer in 1977 and obtained her doctorate in 1983. At present, she teaches in the Department of English in the Copenhagen Business School, Denmark. Together with Beverley Collins she has published several textbooks and articles on the pronunciation of English for Dutch and Danish students, including *The Sounds of English and Dutch* and *Sound English.* Her main research interest is in the field of English phonetics, language variation and sociolinguistics.

David Parry is Lecturer in English at University College, Swansea. He is Director of the seminal *Survey of Anglo-Welsh Dialects* (Phase I Rural, 1968–85; Phase II Urban, in progress). Currently, he is preparing for publication *A Grammar and Glossary of the Conservative Anglo-Welsh Dialects*, and working as co-editor (in charge of Grammar section) with Professor John Widdowson and Dr. Clive Upton on the projected *Dialect Dictionary* based on the *Survey of English Dialects.*

W.T.R. Pryce is Senior Lecturer and Staff Tutor in the Social Sciences for the Open University in Wales and a founder member of the University. He was born in old Montgomeryshire (now north Powys) and was brought up at Llanfair Caereinion. His main research activities are in cultural and historical geography. Publications include the section of the definitive *National Atlas of Wales* dealing with the historical geography of the Welsh and English languages in Wales c. 1750–1961, numerous papers and reviews. He is the major author (with T. Alun Davies) of *Samuel Roberts Clock Maker: an Eighteenth-century Craftsman in a Welsh Rural Community*. In addition he has edited and contributed (with Ian Hume) to *The Welsh and their Country: Selected Readings in the Social Sciences*. At the Open University he has devised and contributes to the fourth-level honours course *Wales: a Study of Cultural and National Identity*. His studies include a number of regional surveys of language change within Wales — north-east Wales and Glamorgan as well as Gwent.

Paul Tench is a Lecturer in English phonetics in the School of English Studies, Journalism and Philosophy in the University of Wales College of Cardiff. He is also Director of Studies of the M.Ed programme in TEFL. His main area of research has been the description of English intonation, but he is also involved in studies of the form that English pronunciation takes in other parts of the world. He is married, with four children brought up in a bilingual English–Welsh setting.

Alan Thomas is Professor in the Linguistics Department, University College of North Wales, Bangor. He graduated with a BA and MA from the University of Wales and is now a leading authority on contemporary Welsh. He is author of three major books on the Welsh language and its dialects — *The Linguistic Geography of Wales*, *The Welsh Language*, and *Areal Analysis of Dialect Data by Computer: a Welsh Example* — and of numerous articles in the same field. He is currently Director of three major Welsh language research projects. His research interests include language variation and shift; language maintenance and language planning policy; linguistic interference and change in multilingual contexts; areal dialectology, particularly that of Welsh in Wales, and English in Britain and America.

J.C. Wells is Professor of Phonetics at University College London, where he has been a member of the academic staff since 1962. He is best known for his highly influential three-volume work *Accents of English*, but has also published, among other things, a two-way dictionary *Geiriadur Esperanto/ Kimra Vortaro*. He was Pronunciation Editor of the new 1988 edition of the *Hutchinson Encyclopedia*, as well as of the Reader's Digest *Universal Dictionary*.

Colin H. Williams was born in Barry in 1950 and obtained his PhD from the University of Wales in 1978. A former Visiting Professor and Fulbright

Scholar in Residence at the Pennsylvania State University, he is currently Professor in the Department of Geography and Recreation Studies at North Staffordshire Polytechnic, Stoke-on-Trent. His principal research interests are bilingualism, geolinguistics and ethnic relations in Wales, Europe and Canada.

Index

Note: Numbers in italics refer to tables and diagrams

294 INDEX